Medieval attitudes toward dreaming encompassed both deep fascination and strong suspicion. In *Dreaming in the Middle Ages*, Steven Kruger explores the ambivalence of the medieval dream through a close examination of philosophical, legal, and theological writings, as well as literary and autobiographical works. To place the medieval dream in its historical and cultural context, Kruger studies the development of theories of dreaming from late-antique Neoplatonic and patristic writers to the dream theorists of the late Middle Ages, and situates these erudite and complex theories in relation to more popular treatments of dreaming like the *Somniale Danielis*. He considers previously neglected material, including an important dream vision by Nicole Oresme, and arrives at a new understanding of the literary genre of the dream vision. Finally, he asks how much we can discover about the medieval dreamer's "real-life" experience of dreaming, and looks to autobiographical accounts, particularly the dreams of conversion in Hermann of Cologne's *Opusculum de conversione sua*, to provide a partial answer. *Dreaming in the Middle Ages* presents a wide-ranging and challenging reinterpretation of the medieval dream, exploring an experience of crucial importance for our broader understanding of medieval culture.

CAMBRIDGE STUDIES IN MEDIEVAL LITERATURE 14

Dreaming in the Middle Ages

CAMBRIDGE STUDIES IN MEDIEVAL LITERATURE 14

General Editor: Professor Alastair Minnis, Professor of Medieval Literature,
University of York

Editorial Board
Professor Piero Boitani (Professor of English, Rome)
Professor Patrick Boyde, FBA (Serena Professor of Italian, Cambridge)
Professor John Burrow, FBA (Winterstoke Professor of English, Bristol)
Professor Alan Deyermond, FBA (Professor of Hispanic Studies, London)
Professor Peter Dronke, FBA (Professor of Medieval Latin Literature,
Cambridge)
Tony Hunt (St Peter's College, Oxford)
Dr Nigel Palmer (Lecturer in Medieval German, Oxford)
Professor Winthrop Wetherbee (Professor of English, Cornell)

This series of critical books seeks to cover the whole area of literature written in the major medieval languages – the main European vernaculars, and medieval Latin and Greek – during the period *c.* 1100–*c.* 1500. Its chief aim is to publish and stimulate fresh scholarship and criticism on medieval literature, special emphasis being placed on understanding major works of poetry, prose and drama in relation to the contemporary culture and learning which fostered them.

Dreaming in the Middle Ages

STEVEN F. KRUGER

Queens College, City University of New York

CAMBRIDGE
UNIVERSITY PRESS

Published by the Press Syndicate of the University of Cambridge
The Pitt Building, Trumpington Street, Cambridge CB2 1RP
40 West 20th Street, New York, NY 10011-4211, USA
10 Stamford Road, Oakleigh, Victoria 3166, Australia

First published 1992

Printed in Great Britain at the University Press, Cambridge

*A catalogue record for this book
is available from the British Library*

Library of Congress cataloguing in publication data

Kruger, Steven F.
Dreaming in the Middle Ages / Steven F. Kruger.
p.   cm. – (Cambridge studies in medieval literature; 14)
Includes bibliographical references and index.
ISBN 0 521 41069 X
1. Literature, Medieval – History and criticism.   2. Dreams in
literature.   3. Visions in literature.   4. Dreams – History.
5. Civilization, Medieval – Psychological aspects.   1. Title.
II. Series.
PN671.K7   1992
809'.93353'0902 – dc20   91-26934 CIP

ISBN 0 521 41069 X hardback

For my parents

Contents

Acknowledgments

Many people have contributed, wittingly or not, to the completion of this book. Sherron E. Knopp helped me begin my research into medieval dream literature and has been an interested guide ever since. Morton W. Bloomfield provided important support in the earliest stages of this project, and carefully critiqued an earlier version of my first three chapters. Donald R. Howard also read much early material, and his perceptive and provocative comments helped, more than any other factor, to determine the final shape of this work. I deeply regret that neither Professor Howard nor Professor Bloomfield lived to see this project, to which each gave so much energy, in its finished state. Theodore M. Andersson, Sara Blair, Nancy L. Coiner, J. Allan Hobson, and John Kleiner read portions of the book, and their suggestions have greatly enriched the final product. George H. Brown, Mary F. Wack, and David J. Wallace read, with much generosity, several versions of the entire project. Professor Wallace has, as teacher and colleague, pointed me always in new and exciting directions. Professor Brown has freely offered his keen literary insight and understanding ear. Professor Wack has been, at one and the same time, my most sympathetic and most critical reader; without her energetic, demanding, and pragmatic advice, this book would be the poorer. For less tangible, but no less important, contributions, I also thank Diane Bassett, Barbara Bowen, Rita Connolly-Tilton, Rita Copeland, Jonathan Dull, Mary Favret, Lydia Fillingham, Susan Frye, Deborah Geis, Catherine McKenna, Thomas C. Moser, Jr., Sara Myers, Anthony O'Brien, Robert Postawko, Judith Raiskin, Loren Rusk, Michael Sargent, Ron Scapp, Roger Smith, Robert Tilton, W. Marc Tognotti, and E. Gordon Whatley. Finally, I must acknowledge, with gratitude and love, the support and encouragement of my family: my brother, Joshua D. Kruger, my sister, Susan D. Kruger, my father, Stanley I. Kruger, and my mother, Alice S. Kruger. They have been infinitely understanding.

This project was completed with the financial support of Stanford University, the Charlotte W. Newcombe Foundation, and the Professional Staff Congress of the City University of New York. The resources of the

Acknowledgments

Queens College Library and the Stanford University Libraries, and the bibliographic aid of John Rawlings, William McPheron, and Richard Wall, have been indispensable to my work.

Abbreviations

AHDLMA	*Archives d'Histoire Doctrinale et Littéraire du Moyen Age*
EETS	Early English Text Society
ES	Extra Series
NS	New Series
OS	Original Series
PG	J.-P. Migne (ed.). *Patrologiae cursus completus, Series graeca.* 161 vols. (Paris, 1857–66)
PL	J.-P. Migne (ed.). *Patrologiae cursus completus, Series latina.* 221 vols. (Paris, 1841–79)
QDV	*Quaestiones disputatae de veritate*
RSV	Revised Standard Version
RTAM	*Recherches de Théologie Ancienne et Médiévale*

Introduction: modern and medieval dreams

Ours is the century of the private dream. In the wake of Sigmund Freud's *Die Traumdeutung* (1900), we have learned to read our night-time experiences psychologically, as expressions of our intimate thoughts and desires.[1] Even though Freud's theories have been extensively modified and deeply challenged, and various post-Freudian schools now argue vehemently over the "proper" way to read dreams,[2] we have largely followed Freud in his suggestion that the dream is the "royal road to ... the unconscious."[3]

Recently, researchers working on the physiology of sleep and dreams have challenged the dominant psychological, and particularly psychoanalytic, theories of dreaming – but in such a way as to confine the dream even more strictly to a realm governed by internal human process. In 1977, in an influential and controversial paper, J. Allan Hobson and Robert W. McCarley proposed that "*the primary motivating force for dreaming* is not psychological but physiological," and that "the dream process" has "its origin in sensorimotor systems, with little or no primary ideational, volitional, or emotional content."[4] While careful not to deny dreams meaning,[5] Hobson and McCarley *do* seriously delimit the scope of the dream's significance. Dreaming becomes for them not Freud's "royal road," but a much reduced "royal road to the mind and brain in a behavioral state, with different rules and principles than during waking."[6]

Following on from such physiological work as Hobson and McCarley's, other researchers have denied that dreams can, or should, be interpreted. Perhaps most radically, Francis Crick and Graeme Mitchison have suggested that dreaming serves as a kind of "'reverse learning' or 'unlearning,'" by which "unwanted or 'parasitic' modes of behaviour" in "the cortical system" can be erased:[7]

In this model, attempting to remember one's dreams should perhaps not be encouraged, because such remembering may help to retain patterns of thought which are better forgotten. These are the very patterns the organism was attempting to damp down.[8]

The dream's neurobiological function becomes paramount, and its content not worthy of consideration.

Dreaming in the Middle Ages

The confinement of dreaming to a psychological or physiological realm is, of course, relatively recent. For most of its long history, the dream has been treated not merely as an internally-motivated phenomenon (although, as we shall see, such explanations of dreaming have their own ancient roots),[9] but as an experience strongly linked to the realm of divinity: dreams were often thought to foretell the future because they allowed the human soul access to a transcendent, spiritual reality.

In our own century, Freud and the physiologists have worked vigorously to remove such a "superstitious" view from official dream theory. Indeed, the most visible manifestation of this belief in transcendent, revelatory dreams is provided by books to which we give (or claim to give) only amused attention: dream-guides for games of chance, often sold in drugstores alongside lottery tickets;[10] and popular keys to the interpretation of dreams, relegated, along with other "pseudo-science," to the "Occult" section of the bookstore.[11] Such handbooks often recognize, and even proclaim, their own exotic and marginal status:

This is a unique dream dictionary. It represents the very ancient and mysterious Far Eastern interpretations for the very first time in book form. Long-lost secrets on the value of the psychic warnings in various dreams are given. They are carefully gleaned from a variety of ancient manuscripts found at a secluded monastery located deep in the mountains of Tibet.[12]

At the same time, however, that these books are made marginal, they continue to be popular, and can be found in almost any bookstore. And the dreambooks claim authority not only from the "mysterious" East, but also from the mainstream of Western thought: they quote the Bible, Aristotle, and Cicero; report the creative dreams of Goethe, Bunyan, and Coleridge; and even take upon themselves the authority of psychoanalytic dream theorists such as Karen Horney, Alfred Adler, Erich Fromm, and even Freud himself.[13] Often the dreambooks' authenticating claims are exaggerated or invented. Aristotle's deep skepticism about the meaning of dreams is ignored, his thinking on dream divination represented only by his least skeptical statement: "There is a divination concerning some things in dreams not incredible."[14] But despite the distortions, the dreambooks are legitimate heirs to Western tradition. Not only are they often actual descendants of ancient and medieval works (see chapter 1 below, esp. n. 12), but their assertion of the dream's predictive status and of its access to a transcendent realm binds them to major philosophical, theological, and scientific traditions.

The continued popularity of the dreambooks thus points to a conclusion that the "scientific" student of dreaming may find disturbing: despite all

2

attempts at its suppression, the tradition of the transcendent dream still grasps our imagination. Indeed, at least at moments, it escapes from its marginal realm to influence (or invade) mainstream treatments of the dream.

Thus Freud, in the last paragraph of his *Interpretation of Dreams*, cannot resist raising an ancient question that his own relentlessly. psychological explanations of dream phenomena would already seem to have put to rest: "And the value of dreams for giving us knowledge of the future?"[15] His answer, predictably enough, is that dreams have no such value; but in that answer, and thus in the last words of his *Interpretation*, Freud surprisingly moves to accept, if only partially, "the ancient belief that dreams foretell the future":

There is of course no question of that [Daran ist natürlich nicht zu denken]. It would be truer to say instead that they give us knowledge of the past. For dreams are derived from the past in every sense. Nevertheless the ancient belief that dreams foretell the future is not wholly devoid of truth. By picturing our wishes as fulfilled, dreams are after all leading us into the future. But this future, which the dreamer pictures as the present, has been moulded by his indestructible wish into a perfect likeness of the past.[16]

Freud's move, in this final passage, to merge past, present, and future calls to mind – though weakly – mystical modes of thought, and mysticism shows its face even more boldly elsewhere in twentieth-century dream theory. Carl Jung, in his attempts to revivify "the mythic side of man,"[17] writes:

In the majority of cases the question of immortality is so urgent, so immediate, and also so ineradicable that we must make an effort to form some sort of view about it. But how?
My hypothesis is that we can do so with the aid of hints sent to us from the unconscious – in dreams, for example.[18]

Since the unconscious, as the result of its spatio-temporal relativity, possesses better sources of information than the conscious mind – which has only sense perceptions available to it – we are dependent for our myth of life after death upon the meager hints of dreams and similar spontaneous revelations from the unconscious.[19]

For Jung, the unconscious and the dreams it manifests may provide revelatory access to a reality beyond mere "sense perceptions." And even in work that has followed on directly from physiological research into the dream-state, where we might expect to find only the most fully sense-bound theories, we again discover associations between dreaming and the transcendent. Stephen LaBerge of the Stanford University Sleep Research Center, in describing dream experiences (lucid dreams) in which we "learn to recognize that we are dreaming while the dream is still happening,"[20] suggests:

The fully lucid dreams we have been describing are instances of transcendental experiences, experiences in which you go beyond your current level of consciousness. Lucid dreamers (at least during the dream) have gone beyond their former views of themselves and have entered a higher state of consciousness. They have left behind their former way of being in dreams, no longer identifying with the dream characters they play or thinking that the dream world is reality. In this way, fully lucid dreams are transcendental experiences.[21]

If we were to undertake a study of our own culture's largest treatment of dreaming, we would be faced with a massive, perhaps an impossible, project. Freudian and post-Freudian dream theory in all its complexity; the sometimes controversial findings of physiological research; popular, "superstitious" attitudes toward dreaming; popular skepticism about oneiric significance; the treatment of dreams in literature, film, and television – all inform our "view" of the dream. To complicate matters further, these different realms of dream thought are, as I have begun to suggest, by no means distinct: they interpenetrate and interact in sometimes surprising ways.

Given the complexity and difficulty of treating twentieth-century attitudes toward the dream, it may seem foolhardy to undertake a similar project with respect to *medieval* dreaming. After all, we have easy and essentially complete access to texts for a study of contemporary dreams, and, perhaps more importantly, we are surrounded by living people and their dreams. We can survey populations to determine prevalent beliefs about dreaming; and we can compile accounts of actual dreams and ask questions of actual dreamers.

None of this is true for the Middle Ages. Important texts have undoubtedly been lost, and others remain unedited. Most disturbingly, we have irremediably lost touch with the everyday fabric of medieval dream life. We do not know if "average" people dreamt differently than we do now, whether they discussed their dreams over breakfast, or how they responded to particularly portentous dream images.

Yet we can, however tentatively, begin to draw a picture of the medieval dream. A vast assortment of dream texts *does* survive. They include erudite works of theory, usually in Latin; vernacular popularizations of the theoretical material; and keys to various systems of dream interpretation. In the medieval poetic corpus dreams are set within longer narratives, and we find a separate, extremely popular, literary genre, the dream vision. Also available are accounts of "real-life" dreams in historical works, biographies, and autobiographies. From this last kind of material especially, we can begin to understand everyday attitudes toward dreaming and the sorts of roles dreams played in people's lives.[22]

We must be cautious, though, in interpreting the material that has come down to us. Dream theory and practical responses to dreams are not necessarily commensurate. Literary depictions of dreams, even when directly invoking theoretical material, also depend upon literary traditions and "real-life" experience. Historical and (auto)biographical accounts may be distorted in a variety of ways, their form shaped by literary *topoi*, their content determined by political, didactic, and religious motives.[23] Furthermore, the surviving accounts of "real-life" dreams are undoubtedly atypical: we would expect dreams perceived as especially significant to be preserved with greater care than those judged vain or misleading. Indeed, the accounts we have of actual dreams are most often contained within religious and mystical texts.

Our distance from the Middle Ages magnifies the difficulties we encounter in considering medieval dreaming. In studying contemporary dreams we can, with some ease, identify a dream that is extraordinarily striking, a dream theory that is particularly eccentric, a literary dream that is highly stylized or, on the other hand, essentially "life-like." Looking six or seven centuries into the past, however, it becomes extremely difficult to make such judgments; the material that survives often points not to definitive answers, but to intriguing and ultimately unanswerable questions. How common were dreams and visions like those reported by Margery Kempe? Our answer can only be based on the internal evidence of Kempe's *Book* (the sometimes outraged responses Kempe receives), and on the existence of accounts of dreams like Kempe's in other works. Were popular keys to dream divination used on a day-to-day basis? Some of them come complete with instructions for use, and writers sometimes forbid consulting them as if this were a common practice; still, any answer we arrive at finally remains speculative.

In the work that follows I try to define, as closely and clearly as possible, a late-medieval "view" of dreaming. I examine at greatest length the rich and complex literature of medieval dream theory. Doing so requires looking at the late-antique and early Christian writings of Macrobius, Calcidius, Augustine, and Gregory the Great, since these remained strong influences throughout the Middle Ages. Having defined, in chapters 2 and 3, what might be called the late-antique Christian Neoplatonic construction of the dream, I go on to suggest, in chapters 4 and 5, the ways in which theorists of the twelfth, thirteenth, and fourteenth centuries – encyclopedists like

Vincent of Beauvais, philosophers and theologians like Hildegard of Bingen and Albertus Magnus, "psychologists" like Jean de la Rochelle, exegetes like Richard of St. Victor and Robert Holkot – used and modified that construction.

In my consideration of dream theory, I try not to become enmeshed in minutiae, but instead to excavate the larger structures inherent in the material – the most general and characteristic ways in which authors attempt to encompass the dream. In so doing, I wish to point toward the attitudes that underlie explanations and categorizations of dream experience, to define a common ground linking theories that are in many ways disparate. As a result, my treatment at times de-emphasizes the peculiarities of individual dream theories – and there are many such peculiarities. There is also, however, a remarkable unity of opinion about the essential, fundamentally complex and ambiguous, nature of the dream. It is that unity that I am most concerned to explore.

In defining the assumptions and beliefs that underpin medieval dream theory I hope to begin delineating the larger cultural "view" of the dream, and to flesh out that "view" I have also examined various non-theoretical materials. In autobiographical accounts like Hermann of Cologne's *Opusculum de conversione sua* (see chapter 7), and in the medieval treatment of handbooks of dream divination like the *Somniale Danielis* (see chapter 1), we find ambivalent attitudes toward dreaming strikingly similar to those that underlie dream theory. "Real-life" dreams are treated as both precious and dangerous; handbooks of dream divination are enormously popular, and yet their use is often expressly forbidden.

The habit of mind that allows for such double treatments of the dream expresses itself quite generally in the Middle Ages, and in chapter 6 I consider briefly how such an attitude is reflected in, and affects, the shape of literary dreams. I focus attention especially on one fascinating but rarely studied dream vision, the conclusion of Nicole Oresme's *Tractatus de commensurabilitate vel incommensurabilitate motuum celi*. Dream visions like Oresme's provide the late Middle Ages with its most flexible and complex instrument for exploring the ambiguous possibilities of dreaming, and they provide us with an extraordinarily rich ground for examining medieval attitudes toward a complicated and perpetually interesting human experience.

Dreambooks and their audiences

DREAM DIVINATION

Writers of the high and late Middle Ages treated the experience of dreaming with simultaneous anxiety and fascination. On the one hand, they saw dreams as dangerous, associated with pagan practices and demonic seduction. On the other, they claimed that dreams could be divinely inspired and foretell the future. After all, saints' lives were filled with revelatory dreams, and the Fathers of the church recounted veridical dreams that they themselves experienced.[1] The Bible itself – in the Old Testament stories of Joseph and Daniel (Genesis, chapters 37, 40, 41; Daniel, chapters 2, 4, 7–8, 10–12) and in the appearances of God's angel to the New Testament Joseph (Matthew 1:20–24, 2:13, 2:19–22) – validates the use of dreams as predictive tools.[2] But the Bible also lends its authority to a distrust of the dream, at certain points strongly condemning the practice of dream divination:

Quando ingressus fueris terram quam Dominus Deus tuus dabit tibi cave ne imitari velis abominationes illarum gentium / nec inveniatur in te ... qui arioles sciscitetur *et observet somnia* atque auguria ne sit maleficus / ne incantator ne pythones consulat ne divinos et quaerat a mortuis veritatem / omnia enim haec abominatur Dominus.[3]   (Deuteronomy 18:9–12; my emphasis)

When thou art come into the land which the Lord thy God shall give thee, beware lest thou have a mind to imitate the abominations of those nations. Neither let there be found among you any one ... that consulteth soothsayers, *or observeth dreams* and omens, neither let there be any wizard, Nor charmer, nor any one that consulteth pythonic spirits, or fortune-tellers, or that seeketh the truth from the dead. For the Lord abhorreth all these things.

The tension thus implicit in biblical treatments of dreaming survived and was intensified in the Middle Ages as the idea that dreams might be used to divine future events came to be treated with both approbation and suspicion.

Medieval approval of dream divination was expressed in the existence and popularity of manuals designed to reveal the future significance of dreams. Three distinct kinds of medieval dreambook survive.[4] The first of these, the "dream alphabet" or "chancebook," consists of a list of potential dream significations keyed to the letters of the alphabet. The future is divined by means of a random process, unconnected to the dream's specific content:

Si quis aliquid sompniauerit, querat librum quemcunque uoluerit et dicat "in nomine patris et filii et spiritus sancti. amen," et per primam literam quam scriptam inueniet in prima pagina quando liber aperitur significationem sompni inueniet. *A* significat prosperum iter et uiam felicem. *B* dominacionem in plebe.[5]

If someone has dreamed something, let him seek out whatever book he wants and say, "In the name of the Father and the Son and the Holy Spirit. Amen." And he will find the meaning of his dream by means of the first letter that he finds written on the first page when the book is opened.
A signifies a fortunate journey and a successful way. *B* [signifies] lordship among the people.[6]

The second kind of dreambook, the "dreamlunar," similarly disregards content in disclosing the meaning of dreams. Here, the only key to a dream's significance is the phase of the moon during which it occurs; thus on any given night, all dreams predict the same outcome:

Luna prima quicquid uideris, in gaudium erit; *et* si uideris te uinci, tu tamen uinces omnes inimicos tuos annuente deo. Luna .ii.^{da} si uideris somnium, nullum effectum hab*et*; nec in animo ponas siue bonum siue malum.[7]

Whatever you may have seen on the first moon [of the month], will [have its outcome] in joy; even if you have seen yourself conquered, nevertheless you will conquer all your enemies, with God willing. If you have seen a dream on the second moon, it will have no effect; nor should you reckon in [your] mind on either a good or bad [effect].

Each of these two manuals is closely related to a wider range of prognostic material – the dream alphabet to other divinatory practices involving the random opening of books,[8] the dreamlunar to works (the *lunaris de nativitate, lunaris de aegris, lunaris ad sanguinem minuendam*) using the phase of the moon to predict the outcome of events.[9] Dreamlunars were, in fact, often combined with these other specialized *lunaria* to make up *lunaria collectiva*, handbooks concerned simultaneously with a variety of mantic practices, including dream interpretation;[10] and both the dreamlunar and dream alphabet are frequently associated, in manuscripts, with other "superstitious" works such as horoscopes, lists of lucky and unlucky days, and predictions based on the day of the week on which New Year falls.[11]

From a Christian perspective, the two kinds of dreambook must be viewed with suspicion. Both are closely affiliated to prognostic works that have no official sanction; and both claim to give access to hidden knowledge about the world through an essentially random process, the randomness of their operation implying a certain randomness in the way the world works. Indeed, these dreambooks implicitly deny the importance of any human influence on the future, and fail to make clear God's controlling role in the ordering of events.

Like the dream alphabet and lunar, the third kind of medieval divinatory manual, the "dreambook proper," is often found associated with other "superstitious" prognostic texts. Although this kind of dream manual differs from the others in basing its interpretations on the dream's content, its method of arriving at a knowledge of the future is as rigid and mechanical as theirs. Like modern popular dreambooks – some of which are descended more or less directly from medieval models[12] – the dreambook proper simply provides a list of the consequences that will follow from a variety of possible dream contents:

Aves in somnis qui viderit et cum ipsis pugnaverit: lite[m] aliquam significat... Cum sorore concumbere: damnum significat. Cum matre: securitatem significat... Dentes sibi cadere viderit: de parentibus suis aliquis morietur.[13]

For one who may have seen birds in [his] sleep and may have fought with them, [the dream] signifies a certain strife... To sleep with [one's] sister [in a dream] signifies loss; with [one's] mother, it signifies security... [For one who] may have seen his teeth fall out: some one of his kinsmen will die.

Such a method of dream interpretation again leaves itself open to the charge of arbitrariness. Can the dream of losing one's teeth, under all circumstances, for all dreamers, predict the same event? The dreambook claims that in fact it can, and in so doing, ascribes to a fatalism that leaves little room for efficacious human action or the just and merciful governance of God.

But medieval dreambooks do not leave themselves wholly vulnerable to such criticisms: they attempt to avoid disapprobation by affiliating themselves in a variety of ways with orthodox Christianity. In some *lunaria collectiva*, each stage of the moon is associated with a biblical event: "Luna prima. Adam natus fuit... Luna secunda. facta fuit Eua" [On the first moon, Adam was born... On the second moon, Eve was made].[14] The dream alphabet includes Christian prayer ("in nomine patris et filii et spiritus sancti") as part of its divinatory ritual. Furthermore, in some versions, the instructions for using the dream alphabet specify that the "librum quemcunque" consulted should be a book of Holy Scripture, usually the psalter.[15] And in an even more direct way, both the dream alphabet and the dreambook proper claim for themselves biblical authority. The dream alphabet calls itself, in some manuscripts, the *Sompnile*

9

Joseph, claiming one of the two most famous Old Testament dream interpreters as its author. One version begins: "Sompnile Joseph, quod composuit, quando captus fuit a Pharaone" [The dreambook of Joseph, which he composed while he was held captive by Pharaoh].[16] In a similar way the dreambook proper claims Daniel as its author, calling itself the *Somniale Danielis.* In an elaborate introductory passage found in one of the two main manuscript groups, it invents for itself a direct connection with Nebuchadnezzar's divinely-inspired dreams and Daniel's divinely-inspired interpretation of them:

Incipit Somniale Danielis prophetae, quod vidit in Babilonia in diebus Nabuchodonosor regis. Quando petebatur a principibus civitatis et ab omni populo ut eis somnia quae videbant judicaret, tunc Daniel propheta haec omnia scripsit, et eis ad legendum tradidit, dicens: "Ego sum Daniel propheta, unus de filiis Israel, qui captivi ducti sumus de Hierusalem, civitate sancta. Haec omnia a Deo facta sunt; nihil tamen per memetipsum dixi vel sustuli, sed ea a Domino accepi." Quicumque legerint, Danielem intellegant.[17]

Here begins the dreambook of Daniel the prophet, which he saw in Babylon in the days of Nebuchadnezzar the king. When he was sought out by the nobles of the city and by all the people so that he might judge for them the dreams that they saw, then Daniel the prophet wrote down all these things and handed them over to them to be read, saying: "I am Daniel the prophet, one of the sons of Israel who were led captive from Jerusalem, the holy city. All the things [written here] were brought about by God; I have indeed said or affirmed nothing by myself, but have received these things from the Lord." All those who may have read [this], may understand Daniel.

The medieval dreambooks thus call to their aid the most striking of biblical sanctions for the prognostic use of dreams, attempting to bolster their credibility by strong appeals to divinely-approved precedent.[18]

Indeed, the three types of dream interpretation manual were successful in gaining widespread credibility, to judge by the number of surviving manuscripts. At least thirteen manuscript copies and three early printed editions of the dream alphabet exist, and the Latin text was widely translated – into Old and Middle English, as well as into Middle High German, Old French, Italian, Old Romanian, and Welsh.[19] The dream-lunar similarly survives in many Latin and vernacular versions. Max Förster, and Lynn Thorndike and Pearl Kibre list a total of over twenty Latin manuscripts of the specialized dreamlunar, the earliest dating from the ninth and tenth centuries.[20] This work was translated into the vernacular as early as the eleventh century: Förster has edited three distinct Old English versions existing in five separate copies.[21] In the later Middle Ages, specialized dreamlunars and *lunaria collectiva* containing dream prognostications were translated into Middle English, Middle High German, Netherlandish, French, Provençal, Italian, and Middle Welsh, and were published several times in the early years of printing.[22] Even more popular was the *Somniale Danielis*. Lawrence T. Martin lists seventy-three Latin manuscripts, the earliest from the ninth century;[23] André Paradis suggests that there are "in all between 150 and 200 variants";[24] and Förster testifies to the existence of "hundreds" of texts.[25] The *Somniale* was translated into Old and Middle English, Old French, Italian, Middle High German, Old Norse, Welsh, and Irish, and was put into verse in England, France, and Germany.[26] Its popularity did not wane with the waning of the Middle Ages: Maurice Hélin cites twenty-eight Latin, three German, two French, and four Italian incunabular editions.[27]

THE DREAMBOOKS AND CANON LAW

Despite the apparently tremendous popularity of dreambooks, and despite all attempts to affiliate them with orthodox Christianity, the ecclesiastical establishment, or at least part of it, met the handbooks of dream divination with strong resistance. The biblical association of dreams, in a passage like Deuteronomy 18:9–12, with pagan rites and a wide range of illicit mantic practices, helped provide the basis for a long tradition of legal objection to dream divination. The law collections of Charlemagne already condemned the consultation of dreams for predictive or magical purposes, in one passage clearly echoing Deuteronomy 18:10–11:

Ut nemo sit *qui ariolos sciscitetur* vel *somnia observet*, vel ad *auguria* intendat: nec sint *malefici, nec incantatores, ne phitones* [i.e., *pythones*] cauculatores, nec tempestarii, vel obligatores. Et ubicumque sunt, emendentur vel damnentur.[28]

Let there be no one *that consults soothsayers, or observes dreams*, or pays attention to *omens*; neither let there be *wizards or charmers* or those calculating according to *pythonic spirits* or weather-makers or magic healers. And wherever they are, let them be corrected or condemned.

Elsewhere, "somniatorum conjectores" [dream interpreters] are included among those perpetrating "perniciosissima mala, quae ex ritu Gentilium remansisse non dubium est" [the most pernicious evils, which without doubt have remained from pagan ritual].[29] The reference here to pagan rite again calls to mind Deuteronomy ("ne imitari velis abominationes illarum gentium"), and the law goes on to quote further biblical precedent: Leviticus 20:6–8 and Exodus 22:18, both passages concerned with setting the Israelites apart from their heathen neighbors.

Later medieval law continued along these same lines, vigorously attacking dream prognostication. The most influential medieval collection of canon law, Gratian's *Decretum*,[30] condemns more or less explicitly each of the three kinds of dreambook. Thus, at several points, it calls into question astrological and calendrical methods of predicting the future:

Non liceat Christianis tenere traditiones gentilium, et obseruare uel colere elementa, *aut lunae aut stellarum cursus*.[31]

> (Part 2, case 26, question 5, chapter 3; my emphasis)

Let it not be permitted to Christians to keep pagan traditions and observe or worship the elements *or the courses of the moon or stars*.

Non obseruetis ... aliquos menses, aut tempora, aut dies, et annos, *aut lunae et mensis solisque cursum*, quia qui et has, et quascumque diuinationes, aut fata, aut auguria obseruat, aut adtendit, aut consentit obseruantibus inutiliter et sine causa, et magis ad sui dampnationem quam ad salutem tendit.

> (Part 2, case 26, question 7, chapter 16; my emphasis)

Do not observe ... any months or times or days or years, *or the course of the moon and the month and the sun*, since one who observes or attends to these things and to any divinations or fates or omens, or consents to those who observe [these things] uselessly and without cause, is also inclined more to his own damnation than to [his] salvation.

The proscriptions here against divinatory observation of the moon would include the dreamlunar and related *lunaria*.

Elsewhere, Gratian also condemns the "inspection" of "scriptures" for prognostic purposes, a condemnation applicable to the dream alphabet:

Aliquanti clerici siue laici student auguriis, et sub nomine fictae religionis per eas, quas sanctorum Patrum sortes uocant,[32] diuinationis scientiam profitentur, aut quarumcumque scripturarum inspectione futura promittunt. Hoc quicumque clericus aut laicus detectus fuerit uel consulere uel docere, ab ecclesia habeatur extraneus.[33]

> (Part 2, case 26, question 5, chapter 6)

A certain number of clerics or laymen cultivate omens, and under the name of a made-up religion, claim a knowledge of divination through what they call the "lots of the blessed Fathers," or predict future things by the inspection of certain scriptures. Let any cleric or layman who will have been found either to consult or to teach such [practices] be considered as not belonging to the church.

Interestingly, the law here seems to take notice of attempts made by the *Sompnile Joseph* and related works to associate themselves with "true" religion, and it explicitly denies the validity of any such association: chancebooks are part of an invented religion ("fictae religionis") beyond the pale of Christianity.

In the *Decretum*, Gratian similarly moves to negate the claims of authority attached to the extremely popular *Somniale Danielis*, which, in one passage, he even cites by name:

Qui ... per Pitagoricam nigromantiam egrotantium uitam uel mortem, uel prospera uel aduersa futura inquirunt, siue qui adtendunt *somnialia scripta, et falso in Danielis nomine intitulata*, et sortes, que dicuntur sanctorum Apostolorum, et auguria auium ... sciant, se fidem Christianam et baptismum prevaricasse, et paganum, et apostatam, id est retro abeuntem et Dei inimicum, iram Dei grauiter in eternum incurrisse, nisi ecclesiastica penitencia emendatus Deo reconcilietur.[34]

(Part 2, case 26, question 7, chapter 16; my emphasis)

Those who ... through Pythagorean necromancy search for the life or death of people who are sick, or for prosperous or adverse future things, or who pay attention to *dreambooks written down and entitled with the false name of Daniel*, and to [those] lots which are called [the lots] of the blessed Apostles, and to the omens of birds ... let them know that they have committed a crime against the Christian faith and against baptism, and that, pagan and apostate (that is, going backward and hostile to God), [they have] gravely incurred the ire of God for eternity – unless, corrected by ecclesiastical penitence, [they] will be reconciled to God.

The *Decretum* here continues the work of earlier legal collections, and of the Bible's condemnation of dream augury, by associating Daniel's dreambook unambiguously with a wide range of forbidden practices, including necromancy. And by directly challenging the ascription of the *Somniale* to Daniel ("falso in Danielis nomine intitulata"), Gratian moves to deny it all religious authority.[35]

In the late Middle Ages, dream divination continued to come under attack alongside astrological and other divinatory practices. Thus, in the early fourteenth century, Agostino de Ancona (Augustinus Triumphus) composed a *Tractatus contra divinatores et sompniatores* in which he challenged dream divination as well as other "superstitious" practices earlier condemned by canon law.[36] And later in the same century, the scientist Nicole Oresme cited Aristotle in challenging the idea that dreams might provide a reliable knowledge of the future.[37]

A resistance to divination, and specifically to the dreambooks, was still in force well into the fifteenth century, as found, for instance, in a German manuscript containing both the *Sompnile Joseph* and *Somniale Danielis*. As Wolfram Schmitt reports, each of these two dream texts is vigorously crossed out, and part of the *Somniale* is excised from the manuscript. Marginal comments in two different hands make clear the censors' sentiments:

Ist erlogen vnd abgoterey glaben.

[This is untrue and idolatrous belief.]

Ist als erstuncken vnd erlogen vnd wider das erst gepot gotz.

[This is as though putrid and untrue and against God's first commandment.]

Jst erlogen ding vnd wider got vnd vesten glawben.

[This is an untrue thing and against God and firm belief.][38]

Dreaming in the Middle Ages

It might be argued that the split in medieval attitudes toward predictive dreams – the immense popularity of works forbidden by at least some important authorities – resulted from a corresponding split in medieval culture between a largely uneducated populace only imperfectly comprehending orthodox Christian doctrine and fascinated by the potential power of forbidden lore, and an educated ecclesiastical hierarchy responsible for making laws and concerned about the possibly disruptive (and heretical) beliefs of the "folk." To adopt such a position would essentially be to accept the suggestion of the medieval legal establishment that augury and divination were survivals of native pagan ("folk") religion; and there may, in fact, be some truth in such a view. A study, like Jonathan Sumption's, of medieval pilgrimage makes it clear that "superstitious" beliefs not fully sanctioned by the Church were an important part of popular Christianity in the Middle Ages.[39] And, as Carlo Ginzburg has so convincingly argued, remnants from the rites and ideologies of agrarian cults, complex enough to form the basis for an essentially complete non-Christian cosmology, survived into the Renaissance in Italy and provided the basis for some of the heretical activity attacked by the Inquisition.[40]

But while such remnants may indeed have contributed to the popularity of a belief in dream divination, it must be remembered as well, as Förster never tires of emphasizing in his work, that, though the medieval dreambooks may be called works of folklore, they are written texts with long *literary* traditions behind them.[41] Indeed, Förster argues that the dreambooks come ultimately from Greek models, and that they were probably translated into Latin in the seventh century.[42] In any case, the transmission of these texts, and their translation into the vernacular, of course depended upon literacy in the language of the Church. While oral traditions and folk beliefs probably contributed to the alteration and growth of the dreambooks,[43] and while a lively folk interest in dreams and dream divination would certainly have helped fuel the dreambooks' proliferation, the number of manuscripts testifies to popularity among a literate population.[44]

In fact, some of the manuscripts containing the *Somniale Danielis* and related texts are clearly intended for learned audiences. Thus, the dreambook proper is sometimes closely associated with abstruse and erudite medical writings. In one manuscript, the oneiric teachings of the famous Arabic physician, Rasis, immediately precede a version of the *Somniale*,[45] while the preface to a German verse redaction of "Daniels Traumdeutungen" consists of other medical material.[46]

The dreambooks also had their aristocratic readers. Some *Somniale* manuscripts are elaborately and opulently produced; Martin has suggested, in fact, that two of them may have been intended for presentation to Richard II. These two contain, alongside the *Somniale*, historical works and a treatise on the duties of kings clearly directed at the nobility.[47]

Still other manuscripts were apparently intended for a clerical audience: codices that belonged to Reading Abbey and Bury St. Edmunds Abbey contain dreambooks alongside strictly religious works.[48] A fourteenth-century English manuscript includes the *Somniale* along with "religious tracts, prayers and hymns (some of them in the same hand as the *Somniale*)."[49] The very ecclesiastical structure that produced Gratian's interdictions also included interested readers of the dreambooks.

In sum, those who were part of the medieval "establishment" did not view dream divination with simple and unambiguous disapproval. Albertus Magnus, in his *Summa de creaturis*, cites the "liber somniorum Danielis" as an authority on the way in which dreams should be interpreted ("de modo interpretandi somnia").[50] And Abbot Guibert of Nogent, famed for his rational skepticism toward the cult of relics, wholeheartedly embraced the idea that the future can be revealed through dreams – though he was careful, in a way the dreambooks were not always, to emphasize that the source of revelatory dreams is God:

O Lord, thou knowest with what inward sight she [Guibert's mother] used to speak of the good and ill that would befall me . . . I now experience these things, and they are hidden neither from me nor from others. By many visions [we discover elsewhere in Guibert's memoirs that these visions include both sleeping and waking experience] in which I and others figured, she foresaw things that would happen long afterward, some of which I see are surely coming to pass or have already come, and the rest I as certainly expect to befall.[51]

Such strong belief in the prognostic power of the dream was not uncommon among rich or poor, educated or uneducated alike.

On the other hand, distrust of dream experience was not confined to the ecclesiastical hierarchy or to educated skeptics. Margery Kempe's mystical experiences – which include both dreams and waking visions – received the repeated approbation of important religious authorities.[52] Still, Kempe was met most often with great hostility – not only by priests and preachers whom she criticized, nor only by civic officials who felt her freedom threatened social order, but also by her peers. For the most part, simple folk were not ready to believe her claims of revelatory experience, even when she had the testimony of ecclesiastical experts to back her up.[53]

Ultimately, then, the doubleness of attitudes toward dreams cannot simply be attributed to a split between popular and elite culture; it expresses itself instead as *simultaneous* caution and enthusiasm. The same social groups, even the same individuals, were drawn toward and, at the same time, backed away from a belief in the predictive significance of dreams. The twelfth-century humanist, John of Salisbury, struggled to reconcile his distrust of the *Somniale Danielis* with a belief in the biblically-attested dream divination of Daniel and Joseph;[54] in this struggle he expressed such strongly conflicting views that a modern reader may wonder, as Francis X. Newman wonders, whether part of what John affirms is, after all, meant ironically.[55] Pascalis Romanus, though he compiled a dreambook of his own, admits, in his introduction to it, that not all dreams are to be trusted; in doing so, he echoes the biblical and legal language condemning divination: "sed demonice incantationes, maleficia, sortilegia, insompnia ac vana fantasmata ne facile hiis credas, condempnantur" [but demonic enchantments, wizardry, sortilege, unreliable dreams, and vain phantasms are condemned so that you should not believe in them (too) easily].[56] There is also a thirteenth-century Middle English dreambook in verse that begins with the usual claims of authenticity, but ends by calling its own validity into question:

> Of alle sweuenes, þat men meteþt
> day oþer nyþt, when hue slepeþt,
> nomon ne con þat soþe þyng
> telle, bote þe heuene-kyng.[57]

Should we leave our dreams to God or actively search out their meanings? Should we distrust dreams or believe in their significance? Writers of the Middle Ages often tried to have it both ways. As Giraldus Cambrensis argued (rather unhelpfully for anyone who wants a firm answer about the nature of dreams): "quicquid ceteri de somniis somnient, mihi quidem sicut rumoribus sic et somniis credi oportere et non oportere visum est" [whatever vain imaginings other men may have on the subject of dreams, I think we should sometimes believe and sometimes disbelieve them, just as we do rumours].[58]

Such double statements are the norm rather than the exception in medieval writings about the dream; the ambivalent attitude toward dream experience seen played out in the tension between legal sanctions against the dreambooks and their continued popularity asserts itself repeatedly and pervasively in the culture of the Middle Ages.

2

The doubleness and middleness of dreams

GOD-SENT OR AGITATED DREAMS

Toward the beginning of his satiric "Dream, or Lucian's Career," the second-century Greek author Lucian confidently announces that the dream he is about to relate was divinely-inspired:

What you shall hear next, gentlemen, is not to be made light of; it deserves a very receptive audience. The fact is that, to use the words of Homer, "a god-sent vision appeared unto me in my slumber Out of immortal night" [*Iliad* 2.56–57], so vivid as not to fall short of reality in any way.[1]

After Lucian has recounted his dream, however, he abandons the notion that its source is divine, invoking instead a different kind of oneiric causation: "it was due, I suppose, to my agitation" (p. 231). In one description of the dream, it is a psychological phenomenon; in the other, it comes from an external, and elevated, source. The divine dream "deserves a very receptive audience," but the psychologically-motivated dream it becomes only inspires the audience's derision:

Even as I was speaking . . . someone said, "what a long and tiresome dream!" Then someone else broke in: "A winter dream, when the nights are longest[2] . . . What got into him to tell us this idle tale and to speak of a night of his childhood and dreams that are ancient and superannuated? It is flat to spin pointless yarns. Surely he doesn't take us for interpreters of dreams?"   (p. 231)

Lucian calls the status of his dream into question by framing it with these conflicting explanations of origin. Is the dream to be trusted as "god-sent," or disregarded as the meaningless product of psychological disturbance? Lucian thus disorients us. The doubleness of the dream – its association with both the divine and the mundane, with both meaningful revelation and individual agitation – helps impart to the satire a thoroughgoing ambiguity: even as Lucian claims to be telling a divinely-sanctioned story with "a certain usefulness," we cannot be sure that we are not hearing merely an "idle tale" (p. 231).

Lucian's ambivalent treatment of dream experience provides a neat illustration of the complicated position that dreams occupied in classical and late-antique thought. In Western tradition, discussions of the dream's significance most often involved, as Lucian's "Dream" does implicitly, a consideration of the relations between divinity and humanity. Dreams may be insignificant, arising purely from internal human process; if, however, they are meaningful and revelatory, they provide evidence of gods who meddle in mundane affairs.

This tension between divine and mundane explanations of dream experience appears repeatedly in the writings of antiquity. As Lucian's contemporary, Artemidorus, recognized, the controversy has its roots in much earlier writers:

I do not, like Aristotle, inquire as to whether the cause of our dreaming is outside of us and comes from the gods or whether it is motivated by something within, which disposes the soul in a certain way and causes a natural event to happen to it.[3]

Not only Aristotle but such major figures as Plato, Cicero, and Lucretius also participated in the debate over the origin and significance of dreams.[4] As early as Plato we find an ambivalence similar to that in Lucian. Asserting, at one point, that dreams can provide "true and inspired divination,"[5] Plato also suggests that dreams release "the wild beast in us," allowing the expression of desires that "the reasoning and human and ruling power" represses when awake.[6] Certain questions about the origin and significance of dreams remained current and important throughout the classical period and into Late Antiquity: Can dreams give access to divine knowledge? Are dreams "god-sent," or rather stirred up by the "agitation" of passionate psychological process?

Some dream theorists advanced one of these two extreme possibilities as the explanation of at least most dream phenomena. Aristotle may not completely rule out prophetic dreams, conceding that it is "not incredible" that "divination in dreams should, as regards some subjects, be genuine" (462b), and granting that some dreams may be "daemonic" in origin (463b);[7] but his argument does work largely to deny dreams their divinatory power: "Most [so-called prophetic] dreams are . . . to be classed as mere coincidences" (463a). Aristotle elaborates a theory in which dreams are essentially internal phenomena, caused by the interaction of psychology (sense perception, imagination) and physiology (the movement and purification of blood attendant upon the processes of eating and digestion). In such a view, god(s) have nothing to do with the dream: transcendent knowledge is unlikely to inhere in an experience caused by indigestion or by the remnants of mundane sense process.

At an opposite extreme, Synesius of Cyrene (c. 370–414) treated dreams as essentially revelatory:

The doubleness and middleness of dreams

The Penelope of Homer assumes that there are two gates of dreams and makes half of them deceptive dreams, only because she was not instructed in the matter. For if she had been versed in their science, she would have made them all pass out through the gate of horn [the gate of reliable dreams].[8]

Although the internal state of the individual is important in determining the clarity with which a particular dream will reveal the truth – the purer the soul, the clearer the revelation[9] – in Synesius, dreams do not arise primarily from within the human being. Rather, they come from an elevated, divine realm, and reveal truths normally inaccessible to waking consciousness: "In the waking state man is the teacher, whereas it is God who makes the dreamer fruitful with His own courage."[10]

Neither the extreme theory of a Synesius nor the opposite extreme of an Aristotle gained victory in the debate over the nature of dreaming. In the period foundational for medieval ideas about the dream – the fourth and early fifth centuries of the Christian era – discussions of dreams in fact tended to occupy a middle ground between such extreme views. The balance that Lucian displays in presenting two opposed explanations of oneiric causation without choosing between them also commonly characterizes the theoretical discussion of dreaming in Late Antiquity. Thus the Neoplatonist Iamblichus (died *c.* 330) considered both "human" and "divine" dreams possible.[11] Human dreams arise from within an individual, "excited by the soul, or by some of our conceptions, or by reason, or by imaginations, or certain diurnal cares."[12] They are, therefore, fallible: "sometimes true and sometimes false ... in some things they apprehend reality, but in many deviate from it."[13] Divine dreams, on the other hand, come from beyond the self (Iamblichus calls them *theopemptoi*, "sent from God"),[14] and allow the soul to transcend its usual condition, uniting it to divinity: "it then receives the most true plenitudes of intellections ... and derives the most genuine principles of knowledge."[15]

Other late-antique authorities – most notably Macrobius in his *Commentary on the Dream of Scipio*, and Calcidius in his *Commentary on Plato's Timaeus* – similarly chose a middle road in treating the dream.[16] Macrobius and Calcidius, Neoplatonists like Iamblichus, both admit the possibility of dreams that "are of no assistance in foretelling the future" as well as those by whose means "we are gifted with the powers of divination" (Macrobius, I.iii.8). Rather than asserting that all dream experience was either divine or mundane, such authors took a more inclusive approach, accepting the possibility that, under different sets of circumstances, both divine (externally-inspired) and mundane (internally-stimulated) dreams can occur.

Newman has suggested that the inclusiveness of such writers as Macrobius and Calcidius results from a kind of intellectual timidity: "We find them ... attempting, as is the habit of less daring minds, to work out a synthesis of traditional theories of dreaming that will solve the problem arising from conflicts between ... inherited theories."[17] Certainly these writers treated dreams in derivative ways.[18] Calcidius openly reviews the work of Aristotle, the Stoics, and Plato before coming to his own, conclusive treatment – itself highly derivative, as the work of J. H. Waszink and others has shown. Indeed, Calcidius explicitly presents his classification of dream experience as an attempt to reconcile distinct traditions: "Consentit huic Platonico dogmati Hebraica philosophia" [Hebrew philosophy agrees with this Platonic doctrine] (256). Macrobius's fivefold division of dreams is likewise not original: Artemidorus, two centuries earlier, proposed essentially the same scheme. Although Macrobius apparently did not use Artemidorus directly, the two depended at least on a common source.[19]

Nevertheless, the project of these Neoplatonic writers was less passive than their reliance on earlier work might imply. The inclusiveness of their treatment of dreams does not finally reflect an inability to make the kind of distinctions that "more daring minds" do. Rather, these writers consciously refused to depict dream experience as unvarious. Calcidius strongly emphasizes the diversity of dreams: "Plato ... uidit atque assecutus est non unam somniorum esse genituram" [Plato ... saw and understood that there is not just one way that dreams are engendered] (253); "Multiformis ergo est ratio somniorum" [Therefore, the explanation of dreams is multiform] (256). He explicitly presents his own position as a reaction against theories like Aristotle's that define dream experience too narrowly:

Aristoteles, ut qui ... tollat omnem diuinationem negetque praenosci futura, unum genus somniorum admittit atque approbat, quod ex his quae uigilantes agimus aut cogitamus residens in memoria mouet ... Nec errat; est enim etiam haec progenies somniorum, sed non sola.   (250)

Aristotle, as one who ... would dismiss all divination and deny that future things may be known, admits and approves one kind of dream: that which, persisting in [our] memory, proceeds from those things that we do or think while awake ... Nor does he err. Indeed, this is also an origin of dreams, but not the only one.

Calcidius firmly rejected Aristotle's unitary approach as overly simple. In response, he and his fellow Neoplatonists proposed complex, inclusive systems to describe the dream. Both Macrobius and Calcidius collected previous authoritative opinions, but not simply "to work out a synthesis of traditional theories." Rather, they selected and synthesized earlier ideas in order to advance a particular view of the complex experience of dreaming and of how that experience fits into a coherent universe. Considered in the larger context of late-antique Neoplatonism, the dream theories of Macrobius and Calcidius promote a consistent set of ideas about human experience and its place in the cosmos.

MACROBIUS AND CALCIDIUS

Both Macrobius and Calcidius organized their discussions of dreaming around the commonplace idea that the dream can be of two opposed kinds. Neither writer, however, treated his subject in a purely dualistic way. Even as Calcidius and Macrobius set up strictly opposed categories – true and false, divine and mundane – they refused to characterize dreams only in terms of opposition.

Still, an important part of Macrobius's discussion serves to establish the claim that all dreams are either true or false, opaque or revealing. Dreams with "no prophetic significance" (I.iii.3) come from "the gate of ivory," "the composition of which is so dense that no matter how thin a layer of it may be, it remains opaque" (I.iii.20). "Reliable" dreams (I.iii.12), on the other hand, belong to "the gate of horn," "the nature of which is such that, when thinned, it becomes transparent" (I.iii.20). The ancient *topos* of the two opposed gates provides a simple structure into which all dream experience fits. But Macrobius complicates this structure by identifying, within the broad categories of true and false, five distinct kinds of dream: three true (*oraculum*, *visio*, and *somnium*), and two false (*insomnium* and *visum*). Distinguishing a variety of dream-types works against any scheme of strictly maintained opposition. In fact, Macrobius moves beyond dualistic description to range dreams on a continuum stretching between and connecting the mundane and the transcendent.

Thus, while Macrobius places both the *insomnium* and the *visum* at the ivory gate, at the false and mundane pole of dream experience, he also takes pains to differentiate these two kinds of dream from each other. The *insomnium* is "caused by mental or physical distress, or anxiety about the future" (I.iii.4). It arises "from some condition or circumstance that irritates a man during the day and consequently disturbs him when he falls asleep" (I.iii.5).[20] In other words, the *insomnium* is a completely mundane experience: everyday events affect an individual's internal mental and physical condition, and that condition, with no interference from higher forces, expresses itself in deceptive dreams. *Insomnia* are generated out of the self's recollection of its waking life, and they consequently have no significance beyond the self. Such dreams "flee when [the dreamer] awakes and vanish into thin air"; they remain "noteworthy only during their course and afterwards have no importance or meaning" (I.iii.5).

Like the *insomnium*, the *visum* deceives, but it does so in a less solipsistic –
and therefore potentially "higher" – way. Occurring "in the moment
between wakefulness and slumber" (I.iii.7), it does not, like the *insomnium*,
originate solely from an immersion in individual physical and psychological process; instead it also involves a movement (however slight) beyond
the confines of the self:

> In this drowsy condition the dreamer thinks he is still fully asleep and imagines he
> sees spectres rushing at him or wandering vaguely about, differing from natural
> creatures in size and shape, and hosts of diverse things, either delightful or
> disturbing. To this class belongs the *incubus*, which according to popular belief
> rushes upon people in sleep and presses them with a weight which they can feel.
> (I.iii.7)

In the *visum*, the dreamer perceives "spectres" and *incubi* that at least seem
to exist externally. Yet, of course, this dream arises from "imagination,"
from a misconstruction of reality; it remains self-delusive. Still, the *visum*
begins to move beyond the self, suggesting, if only faintly, the transcendence of the purely mundane – the contact with a spiritual (spectral) realm –
that will characterize higher, revelatory dreams.[21]

Those higher dreams, typified by Macrobius's *oraculum* and *visio*, directly
reveal a truth otherwise unavailable to the dreamer. They bring human
beings authoritative knowledge from beyond the realm of mundane
experience. But while both the *oraculum* and *visio* stand in opposition to
lower, unreliable dreams, Macrobius also distinguishes the two from each
other. The oracular dream is more impressive than the *visio*. In it, truth is
revealed by an austere figure of authority: "A parent, or a pious or revered
man, or a priest, or even a god clearly reveals what will or will not transpire,
and what action to take or to avoid" (I.iii.8). Through the authoritative
speaker ("even a god") who gives instruction to the dreamer, the *oraculum*
announces itself as a revelation from the other world.

In the *visio*, however, the dreamer receives no direct instruction and no
clear indication of the dream's divine origin. He or she simply sees some
event that is to occur in day-to-day life:

> For example, a man dreams of the return of a friend who has been staying in a
> foreign land, thoughts of whom never enter his mind. He goes out and presently
> meets his friend and embraces him. Or in his dream he agrees to accept a deposit,
> and early the next day a man runs anxiously to him, charging him with the
> safekeeping of his money and committing secrets to his trust.   (I.iii.9)

The *visio* "actually comes true" (I.iii.9), and the truth it reveals is one that
the dreamer could not otherwise know. Still, the dream's truth is mundane.

The doubleness and middleness of dreams

The *visio* remains rooted in the events of the everyday world in a way that the *oraculum* does not.

At either pole of his dream classification, Macrobius thus moves away from a scheme of strict opposition. At the mundane end of things, the *visum* begins hesitantly to approach the spiritual; and from its transcendent realm, the *visio* gazes down toward earthly things. With his descriptions of *visum* and *visio*, Macrobius suggests that the gap between divine and mundane dreams might be bridgeable; with his introduction of the *somnium*, he fulfills that suggestion.

The *somnium* stands between the *oraculum* and *visio* on the one hand, and the *insomnium* and *visum* on the other. This dream, which "conceals with strange shapes and veils with ambiguity the true meaning of the information being offered" (I.iii.10), is in fact the perfect middle term between revelation and deception. It reliably exposes a truth like the two higher kinds of dream, but it presents that truth in fictional form. Like the *insomnium* and *visum*, the *somnium*, at least at first, appears to be deceptive. Its false appearance, its "strange shapes and veils" of "ambiguity," make no immediately apprehensible sense; the *somnium* "requires an interpretation for its understanding" (I.iii.10). Ultimately, proper interpretation yields truth, but never a truth as clear and unambiguous as that of the *oraculum* or *visio*. As one medieval reader of Macrobius, John of Salisbury, suggests, the *somnium* is an "intermediate class," neither "absolutely without significance" nor "present[ing] truth to the understanding ... in visible form," but "stretch[ing] before the body of truth a curtain ... of allegory."[22]

Thus, while Macrobius depicts the realm of dreams as split between the true and the false, the predictive and the deceptive, he simultaneously describes that realm as a hierarchy, a graded system that proceeds steadily from one extreme term to another:

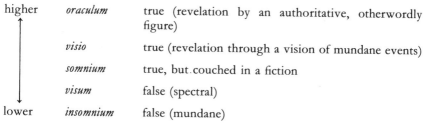

higher	*oraculum*	true (revelation by an authoritative, otherwordly figure)
	visio	true (revelation through a vision of mundane events)
	somnium	true, but couched in a fiction
	visum	false (spectral)
lower	*insomnium*	false (mundane)

We find the *somnium* in a place where we might expect (given Macrobius's general marshalling of dreams into opposed camps) to find simply an empty space separating two mutually-exclusive realms. This "enigmatic dream" (I.iii.10) stands between, and in some sense unites, the opposed realms of truth and falsehood.

The course thus pursued by Macrobius closely resembles that taken by Calcidius in his *Commentary on the Timaeus* (249–56). Like Macrobius, Calcidius begins by opposing two extreme, seemingly unbridgeable, realms, and then proceeds to bridge them.

Aware of the controversy that traditionally surrounded the subject of dreams ("uarie senserunt ueteres" [the ancients have felt variously]), Calcidius begins his "tractatu[s] somniorum" (250) by contrasting two of the most controversial of ancient dream theories; he thus establishes the extreme limits of his own ensuing discussion. At one extreme of his debate stands Aristotle, who strictly confines the dream to a sublunary realm.[23] Calcidius presents Aristotle as denying that the divine ever becomes immanent in human affairs, even through intermediaries ("angeli," "daemones") or by means of experiences such as dreaming:

Aristoteles [est] ut qui dei prouidentiam usque ad lunae regionem progredi censeat, infra uero neque prouidentiae scitis regi nec angelorum ope consultisque sustentari nec uero daemonum prospicientiam putet interuenire proptereaque tollat omnem diuinationem negetque praenosci futura. (250)

Aristotle [is] as one who would consider that the providence of God advances [only] to the region of the moon, and indeed would judge that [the region] below is not ruled by the decrees of providence nor sustained by the might and plans of angels; nor indeed would he judge that the foresight of demons intervenes. And therefore he would dismiss all divination and deny that future things may be known.

Dreaming is a wholly mundane phenomenon, determined only by what we do or think while awake:

Unum genus somniorum admittit atque approbat, quod ex his quae uigilantes agimus aut cogitamus residens in memoria mouet interpellatque per quietem gestarum deliberatarumque rerum conscias animas. (250)

He admits and approves one kind of dream: that which, persisting in [our] memory, proceeds from those things that we do or think while awake and disturbs in [their] rest souls conscious of things done and deliberated.

In such a view, all dreams are of the same kind as Macrobius's *insomnium*.

At the opposite extreme from Calcidius's Aristotle stands "Heraclitus . . . consentientibus Stoicis" [Heraclitus . . . with the Stoics agreeing] (251).[24] Not content with simply denying a strict segregation of trans- and sublunary realms, "Heraclitus" asserts a radical union of human and divine reason: "rationem nostram cum diuina ratione conectit regente ac moderante mundana" [he connects our reason with the divine reason that rules and controls the things of the universe] (251). Because of this "inseparabilem comitatum" [inseparable association] between the human and divine, when human souls are at rest they gain entry to truths not normally accessible: "futura" [future things], "imagines ignotorum locorum simulacraque hominum tam uiuentium quam mortuorum" [images of unknown places and likenesses of men both living and dead] (251).

In presenting the opposed theories of Aristotle and "Heraclitus," Calcidius makes it clear that he himself gives full assent to neither. He can admit Aristotle's mundane dream as possible, but he cannot accept a philosophy of universal fissure that would make such a dream the *only* possibility. In fact, Calcidius argues that there is experiential evidence of divinity communicating through dreams; many dreams have nothing to do with everyday thoughts and actions:

Multa quippe incognita inopinataque neque umquam temptata animis somniamus, quotiens prouenisse uspiam significantur quae nondum scientiae fama conciliauerit uel futura portenduntur quae nondum prouenerint. (250)

Indeed, we dream many unknown and unexpected things, and things never experienced in our souls, whenever at any point things that rumor has not yet made known are shown [by a dream] to have come about, or [whenever] future things that have not yet come about are portended.

Calcidius thus claims that dreams provide a kind of knowledge that human beings, left to their own devices, can never discover; like "Heraclitus" and the Stoics, he asserts that dreams allow access to "futura" and to the unknown.

But, despite his contradiction of Aristotle, Calcidius does not fully embrace the extreme Heraclitean–Stoic position. Asserting belief in revelatory dreams, he nonetheless denies the possibility of a radical union between the human and divine:

Hi quoque parte abutentes sententiae pro solida perfectaque scientia sunt, qui nostrum intellectum et peruolitare conuexa mundi putent miscereque se diuinae intellegentiae, quam Graeci *noyn* uocant.[25] (252)

They also are wrongly using the function of opinion in place of solid and perfect knowledge, who would consider that our intellect both flies around the vault of the universe and mixes itself with divine intelligence, which the Greeks call *nous.*

While some dreams eventually emanate from the divine, Calcidius cannot admit that they result from an *immediate* linkage of human and divine *ratio*. In any case, the Heraclitean assertion that all dreams derive from a transcendent realm is clearly wrong:

Sed cum pleraque non inreligiosa modo, uerum etiam impia somniemus, quae imaginari summam eximiamque intellegentiam siue mentem seu prouidentiam fas non sit putare, falsam esse hanc opinionem hominum liquet. (252)

But since we may dream many things [that are] not just irreligious but also impious, [and since] it cannot be right to consider that the highest and [most] distinguished intelligence or mind or providence conceives such things, it is clear that this human opinion is false.

Some dreams really do owe their existence, as Aristotle claims, to impulses divorced from the divine.

In the first several sections of his dream discussion, Calcidius thus balances extreme positions against each other. Each of the opposed theories explains some, but not all, dream phenomena; each expresses a partial truth, but simultaneously excludes important aspects of dream experience. By invoking the existence of divine ("Heraclitean") dreams against Aristotle, and the reality of mundane (Aristotelian) dreams against "Heraclitus," Calcidius begins to force each of these extreme theories toward a more central ground, where divinely-inspired and internally-stimulated dreams coexist. In so doing, he rejects models that assert either an irreparable split or an immediate unity of divine and human realms, and he affirms in their place a structure (like Macrobius's) in which the divine and the mundane are simultaneously divided from and connected to each other.

In fact, Calcidius uses the remainder of his discussion to demonstrate that the dream is not confined to either earth or heaven. Taking Plato as his authority, he first explicitly affirms the variousness of dreams:

Sed Plato magna diligentia summaque cura discussis penitus latibulis quaestionis uidit atque assecutus est non unam somniorum esse genituram.   (253)

But when the obscurities of the question had been thoroughly dispersed through great diligence and supreme care, Plato saw and understood that there is not just one way that dreams are engendered.

Considering Plato's scattered comments on dreaming, Calcidius moves to depict Platonic theory as accepting both the mundane and the divine associations of dreams. At one extreme, Plato confirms the Aristotelian view that dreams result "ex reliquiis cogitationum et accidentis alicuius rei stimulo" [from the remnants of thoughts and (from) the stimulus of something happening] (253).[26] As Plato describes it, however, such mundane dream experience is not unitary, but will be more or less rational and reliable depending upon the dreamer's internal condition before going to sleep:

Sunt porro reliquiae commotionum uel ex modestis uel ex intemperantibus interdumque sapientibus, interdum stolidis cogitationibus sedatae uel ad iracundiam incitatae, proque locis ut in capite, ubi est sedes domiciliumque rationis, uel in corde, in quo dominatur uirilis ille indignationis uigor, uel in iecore subterque; dimensa porro haec omnis regio libidini[s].   (249)

Further, the remnants of motions [that cause dreams] derive either from moderate [thoughts] or from intemperate [ones], and sometimes from wise thoughts, sometimes from dull ones; [these remnants are] either calm or excited to irascibility, and [they differ] according to [their] locations, that is to say [whether they are] in the head, where the seat and domicile of reason is, or in the heart, in which the virile vigor of indignation rules, or in the liver and below; further, all this [last part] is measured out as a region of appetite [libido].

On the one hand, those who make no attempt to curb passion in their waking lives experience an uncontrolled, even violent release of passion in their dreams:

Tunc quippe nihil est quod non audeat uelut soluta et libera honestatis uerecundiaeque praeceptis; namque maternos, ut putat, amplexus concubitusque non expauescit nec quemquam dubitat lacessere uel hominum uel deorum nec ab ulla sibi uidetur caede aut flagitio temperare.[27]   (253)

Then, indeed, there is nothing that it [the non-rational part of the soul] may not dare to do, as though [it has been] released and freed from the precepts of virtue and modesty; for indeed, as it judges, it does not fear to embrace and lie with [the dreamer's] mother, nor does it hesitate to provoke any man or god, nor does it seem to itself to refrain from any slaughter or shameful act.

On the other hand, those who are temperate and rationally govern their waking lives dream controlled, even truthful dreams:

Contra cum erit in salubri statu posita casteque cubitum ibit, rationabili quidem mentis industria uigiliis imperatis eaque pasta sapienti uirtutis indagine ... tunc certe rationabilis animae pars nullis sibi obstrepentibus libidinis aut iracundiae uitiis perueniet ad indaginem ueri, quae est sincera prudentia, nec ulla existet species nefaria somniorum.[28]   (253)

On the contrary, when it [the soul] is put in a healthy state and goes chastely to bed, when waking life has indeed been governed by the rational diligence of the mind, and [when] it [the soul] [has been] nurtured in its wise search for virtue ... then surely the rational part of the soul, with no faults of desire [libido] or irascibility molesting it, attains to that search for truth which is genuine prudence, nor will any impious kind of dream [then] arise.

A waking "indago uirtutis" makes possible an oneiric "indago ueri."

Thus, in considering dreams that arise from waking thoughts and actions, Calcidius already distinguishes between a higher and a lower type. Only a short distance separates the higher of these two from the dream that Calcidius next identifies in his survey of Platonic theory.[29] Like higher "internal" dream experience, the third kind of Platonic dream comes to

27

those who have dedicated themselves to a pure life: "Socratem uero haec euidenter solitum somniare arbitror ex eo, quod tam corporis quam animae puritate totum eius animal uigeret" [Truly, I judge that Socrates was accustomed to dream such things clearly because his whole being flourished in a purity as much of the body as of the soul] (254). But unlike even the purest dreams that arise from mundane or internal causes, these dreams – "quae diuina prouidentia uel caelestium potestatum amore iuxta homines oboriuntur" [which arise from divine providence or from the love of the celestial powers for men] (254) – clearly come from beyond the human realm:

Ait enim diuinas potestates consulere nobis, quotiens per quietem ea quae grata sunt deo intimant ueris minimeque fallacibus uisis.   (254)

He [Plato] truly says that the divine powers look out for us, by however much during our sleep, in true and by no means misleading visions, they intimate those things that are pleasing to God.

Such dreams reveal truths that no person, unaided, could hope to attain.

The revelation of divine truth occurs not just in dreams, and Calcidius ends his consideration of Platonic dream theory by examining the waking vision:

Denique etiam uigilanti non deerat propitia diuinitas, quae eiusdem moderaretur actus, ut Plato demonstrat in Euthydemo[30] dicens ita: "Est ab ineunte aetate numen mihi comes quoddam idque uox[31] est quae, cum ad animum sensumque meum commeat, significat ab eo quod agere proposui temperandum, hortatur uero ad nullum actum; atque etiam si quis familiaris uti meo consilio uolet aliquid acturus, hoc quoque agi prohibet."   (255)

Finally, the gracious divinity that governed his [Socrates's] acts was not absent from him even while he was awake, as Plato shows in the Euthydemus, saying thus: "There has been from [my] youth a certain divine power [that is] my companion, and this is that voice which, when it comes to my soul and sense, indicates [that I should] refrain from that which I intended to do and truly enjoins [me] to no action; and also, if any one of my friends wishes to obtain my advice when he is about to do something, it also prohibits this [planned action] from being done."

Calcidius probably intends us to see the waking revelation as a more exalted experience than the revelatory dream.[32] In a later summary discussion of visionary phenomena (256), Calcidius places the waking *spectaculum* one step up from the *admonitio*, the dream of divine counsel. He emphasizes that waking visions occur "forma et uoce mirabili" [in a wondrous form and voice] (*ibid.*), and that they seem, on the whole, more impressive than even divinely-inspired dreams. But clearly, Calcidius closely associates waking visions with revelatory dreams. Both are sent to provide help to a weak humankind: "eget enim imbecilla hominum natura praesidio melioris praestantiorisque naturae, ut idem asseruit supra" [the feeble nature of humans truly needs the protection of a better and more excellent nature, as the same one (Plato) asserted above] (255). Both belong to a larger group of phenomena by which the divine becomes immanent:

Nec uero dubitare fas est intellegibilem deum pro bonitate naturae suae rebus omnibus consulentem opem generi hominum, quod nulla esset sibi cum corpore conciliatio, diuinarum potestatum[33] interpositione ferre uoluisse; quarum quidem beneficia satis clara sunt ex prodigiis et diuinatione uel nocturna somniorum uel diurna.   (255)

Nor truly is it proper to doubt that the intelligible God, because of the goodness of his nature, wanted to bring forth a force [that would] look out for the human race in all things – [which he did] through the interposition of divine powers, since there could be for him no direct union with body. Truly the benefits of these [divine powers] are evident enough from portents and from both the nocturnal divination of dreams and diurnal [divination].

In his review of Platonic doctrine, Calcidius here comes closest to validating the "Heraclitean" theory of dreaming. Dreams sometimes come from God ("intellegibilis deus"). But Calcidius stops short of allowing, even in the most clearly revelatory of dreams and waking visions, a full union of God and man. "Diuinae potestates" are always interposed between earth and heaven; God acts not directly, but through intermediaries. Calcidius never lets the opposition of divine and human collapse, though he does allow it to be bridged.

The structure by which Calcidius describes the whole of dream experience involves, as in Macrobius, both opposition and hierarchy:

higher	["Heraclitus"	transcendent dream experience]
	waking visions	from the divine
	revelatory dreams	from the divine
	"rational" dreams	from internal process
	"passional" dreams	from internal process
lower	[Aristotle	mundane dream experience]

Actual dream experience stretches between the ideal limits set by Aristotle and "Heraclitus."

In the last section of his "tractatu[s] somniorum," Calcidius strongly reasserts the structure thus presented in his consideration of the Platonic dream. Claiming once more the dream's diversity – "Multiformis ergo est ratio somniorum" [Therefore, the explanation of dreams is multiform] (256) – Calcidius goes on to summarize in two distinct ways the range of dream experience.[34] These summaries do not completely correspond to his earlier review of Platonic dream theory, though Calcidius refers to the first of the two as "Platonicum dogma" [Platonic doctrine] (256); nor do they wholly match up with each other, though Calcidius asserts that they should: "Consentit huic Platonico dogmati Hebraica philosophia" [Hebrew philosophy (i.e., Calcidius's second summary) agrees with this Platonic doctrine] (256).[35] Nonetheless, in each of the classifications, Calcidius presents essentially the same larger structure.

The first of the two summaries takes the following form:

1   Sunt [somnia] quae uelut percussa grauius uerberataque mente uestigiis doloris penitus insignitis per quietem refouent imagines praeteritae consternationis,
2   sunt item quae iuxta cogitationes rationabilis animae partis (a) uel purae atque immunis a perturbatione (b) uel in passionibus positae oboriuntur,
3   nihiloque minus (a) quae diuinis potestatibus consulentibus praemonstrantur (b) uel etiam poenae loco ob delictum aliquod formata in atrocem et horridam faciem.   (256)

1   There are [dreams] that, as though the mind has been gravely struck and beaten by the deeply imprinted vestiges of pain, revive in sleep images of a past consternation,
2   there are likewise those that arise in consequence of the thoughts of the rational part of the soul (a) [when it is] either pure and free from perturbation (b) or situated among passions,
3   and not at all less (a) those that are shown as predictions by divine powers looking out [for us], (b) or even those fashioned in a dreadful and horrid shape in place of a punishment [for us] because of some transgression.

Here, three different kinds of dream (1, 2a, 2b) arise from internal process – instead of the two Calcidius identifies in his review of Plato – and Calcidius does not mention the waking vision of his earlier discussion. However, this summary generally presents the same progression from lower to higher terms that characterizes Calcidius's survey of Platonic dreaming. Those dreams (1) are lowest that arise from the remnants of diurnal sense process and emotional disturbance ("dolor" and "consternatio"). The events that stimulate such dreams act on the mind ("mente"), yet are involved not with reason but with lower mental functions, those that feel pain and consternation. Other internally-motivated dreams (2), however, do occur in the rational part of the soul and consequently are of a higher sort. This second class includes two subtypes, which correspond closely to the two kinds of mundane dream distinguished in Calcidius's discussion of Plato (253): such dreams are either disturbed by passion (2b), or are "immune" from perturbation (2a). Of internally-stimulated dreams, those that arise from pure and undisturbed rational process approach most closely to Calcidius's last, and highest, version of the dream (3). Sent by "diuinae potestates" – that is, arising from a transcendent realm – these revelatory dreams bring the supernatural to the dreamer. They give counsel about things that are to occur in the future (3a), or serve as an appropriately fearful punishment for the erring dreamer (3b).[36]

Immediately following this first summary of dream experience comes a second scheme, in which five kinds of visionary phenomenon are named and briefly described:

1 *somnium* quidem, quod ex reliquiis commotionum animae diximus oboriri
2 *uisum* uero, quod ex diuina uirtute legatur
3 *admonitionem*, cum angelicae bonitatis consiliis regimur atque admonemur
4 *spectaculum*, ut cum uigilantibus offert se uidendam caelestis potestas clare iubens aliquid aut prohibens forma et uoce mirabili
5 *reuelationem*, quotiens ignorantibus sortem futuram imminentis exitus secreta panduntur. (256)

1 indeed, the *somnium*, which we have said arises from the remnants of the motions of the soul
2 truly, the *uisum*, which is appointed by a divine power
3 the *admonitio*, when we are ruled or admonished by the counsels of angelic goodness
4 the *spectaculum*, as when a celestial power presents itself to be seen by those who are awake, ordering or prohibiting something clearly, in a wondrous form and voice
5 the *reuelatio*, whenever secret things of imminent issue are revealed to those ignorant of future fate.

This second summation ranges over the same territory, mundane and divine, that Calcidius has already twice traversed. Lowest in this last scale of dreams is the *somnium*, not to be confused with Macrobius's dream of the same name. *Somnium* here refers to a mundane dream experience (like Macrobius's *insomnium*) arising from the remnants of waking sensory and cognitive process. Next comes the *uisum*, which Calcidius clearly intends to be a step up from the *somnium* since he explicitly associates it with divinity ("quod ex diuina uirtute legatur"). The brevity of Calcidius's description, however, makes it difficult to understand fully this dream's characteristics. J. H. Waszink plausibly suggests that the "diuina uirtus," through which this dream is said to function, belongs to the individual soul; the *uisum* would then correspond to Plato's "higher" mundane dream, in which the rational part of the soul, freed from passion, is able to search out truth. As

Waszink proposes, the *uisum* would include those dreams "die dem höheren Teil der Seele verdankt werden, und die Zukunft, wenn auch in dunkler Form, vorhersagen" [that are indebted to the higher portion of the soul, and that foretell the future, if only in a darker form].[37] Higher still stand the *admonitio* and *spectaculum*, clearly corresponding to Plato's revelatory dreams and visions. These arise in sleep and waking respectively, through the agency of celestial (angelic) powers. Finally comes the *reuelatio*, which has no clear counterpart elsewhere in Calcidius's treatment of dreams. As its name makes explicit, this dream is revelatory, and can be associated generally with the *admonitio* and *spectaculum* as a "higher" dream. But *reuelatio* seems to be more immediate than either *admonitio* or *spectaculum*: these two give counsel ("angelicae bonitatis consiliis regimur atque admonemur"; "iubens ... aut prohibens"), while *reuelatio* directly reveals imminent future events and secret things. In its immediacy, the *reuelatio* is perhaps to be considered Calcidius's highest dream-type, approaching divinity more closely than any other.[38]

Like Macrobius, Calcidius thus finally depicts the realm of dreams as a hierarchy that stretches from the wholly mundane to the clearly revelatory, from dreams arising out of the "uestigia doloris" to those sent by "diuinae potestates." Two opposed terms – displayed at their most extreme in the theories of Aristotle and "Heraclitus" – are shown, in the course of Calcidius's discussion, to be mediated by a series of intervening entities.

NEOPLATONIC HIERARCHIES

The simultaneously dual and hierarchical structure central to the classification of dreams in both Macrobius and Calcidius characterizes Neoplatonic treatments of a wide range of phenomena, not just dreams.[39] Built into the Neoplatonic universe is a pattern of opposition and mediation. An incorporeal Creator, stable and unitary, stands opposed to corporeal creation, a realm of multiplicity and change; still, these two extremes are ultimately linked:

God ... in a bounteous outpouring of his greatness, created from himself Mind. This Mind [*nous*] ... so long as it fixes its gaze upon the Father retains a complete likeness of its Creator, but when it looks away at things below creates from itself Soul. Soul, in turn, as long as it contemplates the Father, assumes his part, but by diverting its attention more and more, though itself incorporeal, degenerates into the fabric of bodies ... Since Mind emanates from the Supreme God and Soul from Mind, and [Soul],[40] indeed, forms and suffuses all below with life, and since this is the one splendor lighting up everything and visible in all, like a countenance reflected in many mirrors arranged in a row, and since all follow on in continuous succession, degenerating step by step in their downward course, the close observer will find that from the Supreme God even to the bottommost dregs of the universe there is one tie, binding at every link and never broken.[41]

(Macrobius, I.xiv.6–7, 15)

A perfect and distant God communicates with "degenerate" creation, but only through a system of intermediaries.

Similarly, in Calcidius, intermediate terms allow a universe radically divided to be at the same time a unified whole:

As the divine and immortal race of beings is dwelling in the region of heaven and the stars, and the temporal and perishable race, which is liable to passion, inhabits the earth, between these two must be some intermediate connecting the outermost limits . . . As there is an immortal animal which is impassible and at the same time rational, which is said to be heavenly, and as likewise there exists another, mortal, being liable to passions, our human race, it must needs be that there is some intermediate race, which partakes both of the heavenly and of the terrestrial nature, and that this race is immortal and liable to passion. Now such is the nature of the demons, in my opinion, living in communion with the gods because of their immortality, but also in a relationship with perishable things, because the race of demons is passive and not exempt from passions, and its sympathy takes care of us, too.[42]　　　　　　　　　　　　　　　　　　　　　　　　　　　　(131)

The mediative processes that work to unify the Neoplatonic universe also operate, on a smaller scale, within the individual human being. According to the philosophical tradition arising from the *Timaeus*, the human species and the universe were created in similar ways; as a consequence, the cosmos and the human individual resemble each other as macrocosm and microcosm.[43] The human being results from the bringing together of exalted and base entities, just as the universe arises from the imposition of an intellectual form, conceived in the Mind of the First Cause, on base, chaotic matter. Simultaneously intellectual and physical, both the microcosm and macrocosm combine opposed, apparently irreconcilable extremes. And in each case, the interposition of Soul makes possible a unified being.

The individual soul, joining itself to a particular body, moves gradually from the single to the multiple, from the pure to the corrupted, in much the same way that the "World-Soul" does in proceeding from *Nous* to the realm of generation:

It [the soul] does not suddenly assume a defiled body out of a state of complete incorporeality, but, gradually sustaining imperceptible losses and departing farther from its simple and absolutely pure state, it swells out with certain increases of a planetary body: in each of the spheres that lie below the sky it puts on another ethereal envelopment, so that by these steps it is gradually prepared for assuming this earthy dress.[44]　　　　　　　　　　　　　　　　　(Macrobius, I.xi.12)

Having joined itself to body, the soul still contains, in its rationality, a recollection of its original divine state, and consequently it keeps divinity alive in the human being. But, endowed with passions, it can also turn to the sensual and attend to the bodily:

Souls, whether of the world or of the individual, will be found to be now unacquainted with division if they are reflecting on the singleness of their divine state, and again susceptible to it when that singleness is being dispersed through the parts of the world or of man. (Macrobius, I.xii.6)

So just as to the pure World-Soul is granted the sovereignty in the perpetual movement of the world, the souls inspiring men needed reason mixed with irascibility and cupidity, in order that, whenever the whole living being had turned itself to reason, it would concern itself about celestial things and contemplate these; whenever, however, it would look down to earthly things, this looking down might equally not be useless, but from the same inclination care for the earthly affairs might result.[45] (Calcidius, 187)

Just as the "World-Soul" acts to mediate between the divine idea and the sensible world, the individual soul links the highest and lowest portions of the human being.

For Neoplatonism, the great universe and the little human cosmos are thus constructed in similar ways, each stretching from the corporeal and corruptible to the divine and indivisible. In each, opposed terms communicate through a series of intermediate entities "distinguished by a difference and associated by a similarity" (Macrobius, II.xv.25). And as we have seen, the same Neoplatonic bent of mind is at work in shaping late-antique descriptions of dream experience. Dreams, arising in the activity of the soul, partake fully of the range of qualities of the soul (and the universe). Dream, soul, and universe are all, in some sense, coextensive.

By depicting dreams in this way, the Neoplatonists assigned to them an important position. Potentially both divine and mundane, dreams mirror a world that is itself double. Neither wholly of this earth nor of the heavens, dreams, like soul, are able to navigate that middle realm where connections between the corporeal and incorporeal are forged, where the relationship between the ideal and the physical is defined. Dreams can thus explore a wide range of human and universal experience, from the most exalted to the most debased. The purely mundane dream is locked into the realm of earth, while the dream of divine revelation soars to the heavens; and a dream like Macrobius's *somnium* is capable of examining that middle area where body and idea meet to work out their mutual roles.[46]

3

The patristic dream

In their consideration of dream experience, late-antique and medieval writers often concentrated attention on intermediate kinds of dream and on the middle realm that those dreams especially explore. Higher and lower dreams are relatively unambiguous in their ability or inability to reveal truth; but dreams like Macrobius's *somnium* raise a host of tricky questions about the relationship between the divine and the mundane, truth and fiction, abstract ideas and the figural means by which those ideas may be expressed. While not always addressing such questions directly, authors tended to treat the "middle" dream, with its difficulties, more completely and complexly than less problematic dream-types.

Macrobius and Calcidius themselves repeatedly focus attention on intermediate entities. Calcidius moves away from the extreme views of Aristotle and "Heraclitus" toward a middle ground where dreams are neither wholly mundane nor fully divine. Macrobius also emphasizes middle dreams: dividing the *somnium* into a hierarchy of sub-species ("personal, alien, social, public, and universal," I.iii.10), he stresses the intermediate dream's ability to address a wide range of experience, from the self-concerned to the cosmic.[1] In his reading of Cicero's *Somnium Scipionis*, too, Macrobius displays a particular concern with the middle dream: while he classifies Scipio's dream as simultaneously *oraculum*, *visio*, and *somnium* (I.iii.12), he treats it almost exclusively as *somnium*. After all, *oraculum* and *visio* reveal truth directly and thus do not demand interpretation.[2] As dream *interpreter*, Macrobius concerned himself largely with elucidating the unclear truths of the *somnium*, examining how hidden meaning and the fiction in which it is dressed interact.

The writings of St. Augustine take up and intensify the late-antique emphasis on the middleness of dreams. Influenced, like Macrobius and Calcidius, by Neoplatonism,[3] Augustine expressed a complicated theory of dreaming in many ways akin to theirs. On the one hand, dreams can be miraculous, effecting cures and revealing sacred secrets.[4] Divinely-inspired dreams played a central role in Augustine's own life: Monica's vision of the rule – framed by assertions of its heavenly source – predicted Augustine's conversion.[5] Some dreams, however, arise from purely mundane motives; like Macrobius's *insomnium* or Calcidius's *somnium*, these reflect only hunger or thirst, only worldly troubles.[6] Dreams in Augustine, as generally in Neoplatonic thought, are double, either heavenly or earthly.

But while his treatment of the dream recalls Macrobius and Calcidius, Augustine's approach differs radically from theirs. Calcidius and Macrobius worked mainly to classify the varieties of dream experience; Augustine also includes, in his most extensive discussion of dreams (*De Genesi ad litteram* XII), a schematization of dream-types (XII.18.39, pp. 203–04), but his essential concern is not with classification. Instead, he spends most of his energy locating the dream in its relation to other kinds of human "vision." While Macrobius and Calcidius for the most part leave us to infer the relations between dreaming and other experiences, Augustine explicitly asks how the dream fits into the whole of human perception, and how it allows us to confront phenomena not otherwise encountered. He thus addresses complex problems of epistemology – and as he begins to look at the ways in which human beings *use*, for good or ill, the knowledge they gain through dreams, he also broaches questions of morality.

Augustine's treatment of human perception comes as a coda to his long literal commentary on Genesis. Having discussed the Old Testament Paradise, he turns, in conclusion, to the New Testament:

> In this twelfth book I shall deal with the question of Paradise with greater liberty and at greater length. Otherwise I might seem to have dodged the difficulty in the passage where St. Paul apparently hints that Paradise is in the third heaven, when he says, *I know a man in Christ who fourteen years ago – whether in the body I do not know, or out of the body I do not know, God knows – such a one was caught up to the third heaven. And I know such a man – whether in the body or out of the body I do not know, God knows – that he was caught up into Paradise and heard secret words that man may not repeat* [2 Corinthians 12:2–4].   (*De Genesi* XII.1.1, p. 178)

In choosing this Pauline passage as his text, Augustine does not just undertake a more complete consideration of "the question of Paradise"; he also effectively sets up a discussion of epistemology.[7] The biblical passage's almost obsessive emphasis on knowledge, and particularly on the gap between human and divine knowledge, allows Augustine to raise that crucial Christian (and Neoplatonic) question: how can a human being, bound to the prison of body, come to know the divine?

In proposing an answer, Augustine elaborates a model to account for the full range of human perception, from day-to-day sense process to the transcendent vision of a "third heaven." To encompass such disparate sorts of experience, Augustine posits three distinct kinds of "vision":

When we read this one commandment, *You shall love your neighbor as yourself*, we experience three kinds of vision: one through the eyes, by which we see the letters; a second through the spirit,[8] by which we think of our neighbor even when he is absent; and a third through an intuition of the mind, by which we see and understand love itself. (XII.6.15, p. 185)

Let us call the first kind of vision corporeal, because it is perceived through the body and presented to the senses of the body. The second will be spiritual, for whatever is not a body, and yet is something, is rightly called spirit; and certainly the image of an absent body, though it resembles a body, is not itself a body any more than is the act of vision by which it is perceived. The third kind will be intellectual, from the word "intellect."[9] (XII.7.16, p. 186)

The three visions thus defined are distinct yet intimately interconnected. Corporeal vision, the lowest of the three, depends upon spiritual vision, the power by which the likenesses of bodies are imagined. An external object impinging upon a sense organ is not really "seen" unless the imaginative faculty, or "spirit," forms an image of it. The image, itself not a body but the likeness of a body, has a status between corporeality and incorporeality, and thus allows the corporeal object to be made present to the incorporeal soul. Corporeal vision "cannot take place unless there is a concomitant spiritual vision"; however, "there can be spiritual vision without corporeal vision" (XII.24.51, p. 214). In the absence of an actual body, its image can be recalled from memory, and such remembered images can be combined to create composite pictures – conjectural likenesses of bodies that exist but that have never been seen, or even likenesses of non-existent bodies.[10] Furthermore, the soul can receive spiritual images directly from other spiritual beings: angels can present images through a commingling of their spiritual nature with ours (see, for instance, XII.22.45–48). While spiritual sight may thus function independently of sense process, it itself depends on intellectual vision "if a judgment is to be made" (XII.24.51, p. 214); "images and likenesses of things ... demand an intuition of the mind to be understood; and when they are not understood ... they are in the spirit, not in the mind" (XII.8.19, p. 188). If we are truly to comprehend images, we must employ an intellectual understanding abstracted from body, and even from the likenesses of body. Only then can the process of perception be complete; only then can perception lead to knowledge "in the mind."

The essential structure thus articulated is familiar to us from Macrobius and Calcidius. As Augustine himself makes clear, "there is ... a hierarchy [*ordinem*] in these visions" (XII.24.51, p. 213) stretching between the extremes of body and intellect. The human psyche is so constructed as to allow thought to progress "from our own plane to that of the gods" (Macrobius, I.v.4), and as in the Neoplatonists, there is a correspondence between a hierarchically-ordered soul and a similarly hierarchical universe, between a microcosm that perceives and a macrocosm that is perceived. This correspondence makes the full range of vision possible.[11] Corporeal vision perceives corporeal objects from the basest "earthly bodies" to that "heaven which we see above the earth and from which shine forth the luminous bodies and stars" (*De Genesi* XII.30.58, p. 221). Spiritual vision sees images that arise "in the ordinary course of our daily life," as well as those "more excellent and truly divine, which angels reveal in wondrous ways" (XII.30.58, p. 221). And intellectual vision addresses itself to abstractions: ideas "seen in the soul itself" ("for example, the virtues"), or even, in rarer moments, the object of perception *par excellence*, "the Light by which the soul is illumined ... God Himself" (XII.31.59, p. 222).

Integral to a continuous universe and allowing movement, within the soul, from a sensual involvement in corporeality to an intellectual consideration of idea, is the intermediate realm of spirit. It stands unambiguously above the corporeal – "every spirit is unquestionably superior to every body" (XII.16.32, pp. 199–200) – but it can never quite attain the pure abstraction of intellect, "enjoy[ing] visions of a kind inferior to those which the mind or intelligence with its light beholds" (XII.24.50, p. 213). As Augustine makes explicit, spirit mediates between two extreme entities:

> Spiritual vision can be reasonably and naturally said to occupy a kind of middle ground between intellectual and corporeal vision. For I suppose that a thing which is not really a body, but like a body, can be appropriately said to be in the middle between that which is truly a body and that which is neither a body nor like a body.[12]   (XII.24.51, p. 214)

It is to this intermediate kind of vision that all dream experience – significant and insignificant – belongs: "It is the spiritual nature of the soul ... that is affected when dreams come in sleep, either with or without a meaning" (XII.23.49, p. 212). Like spiritual vision itself, dreams may address themselves to a wide range of objects.[13] At one end of things, they encounter mundane images: as "men in their waking hours think of their troubles, turning over in their minds the likenesses of bodily things ... so in their sleep, too, they frequently dream of something they need" (XII.30.58, p. 221). At the opposite extreme, "a man in sleep" can have visions "inspired by a spirit that reveals something" (XII.22.45, p. 209):

> Aliquando et haec falsa, aliquando autem uera sunt, aliquando perturbata, aliquando tranquilla, ipsa autem uera aliquando futuris omnino similia uel aperte

dicta, aliquando obscuris significationibus et quasi figuratis locutionibus praenuntiata. (*De Genesi*, Zycha [ed.], p. 406)

Dreams are sometimes false and sometimes true, sometimes troubled and sometimes calm;[14] and true dreams are sometimes quite similar to future events or even clear forecasts, while at other times they are predictions given with dark meanings, and, as it were, in figurative expressions. (XII.18.39, pp. 203–04)

With such a statement, Augustine moves toward the kind of double and hierarchical system of dream classification found in Calcidius and Macrobius:

	Augustine	Macrobius	Calcidius
uera	1 futuris omnino similia	*visio*	*reuelatio*
	2 aperte dicta	*oraculum*	*admonitio*
	3 obscuris significationibus et quasi figuratis locutionibus praenuntiata	*somnium*	[*uisum?*]
falsa		*insomnium/visum*	*somnium*

Dreams can be true or false, and true dreams are more or less unambiguous. The dream that presents its meaning dressed in obscure figures, like Macrobius's *somnium*, serves as a middle term linking truth and fiction.[15]

But although Augustine thus differentiates higher and lower dreams, he is careful, throughout the corpus of his writings, to emphasize the essentially unitary nature of dream experience. He consistently insists on the spiritual character of *all* dreams: whether they appear to be God-sent or somatically-inspired, all dreams are alike "imaginations in sleep."[16] Dreams always operate through images, showing not bodies nor abstract ideas, but the intermediate, incorporeal likenesses of bodies.

Augustine devotes much of his *De cura pro mortuis gerenda* to the development of such an argument, proposing that even seemingly miraculous dreams – the oracular apparitions of the dead – are spiritual phenomena, in many ways no different from the most commonplace of dreams.[17] When we dream of mundane bodies, we do not see the bodies themselves, but rather likenesses of them, and when we dream of living people, we see not those people but their images: those who appear to us during sleep are unconscious of any role they play in our dream life. Similarly, when the dead appear to us, we do not see them *in propriis personis*:

It chanced at Carthage that the rhetorician Eulogius[18] ... dreamed [that] I expounded to him that which he did not understand; nay, not I, but my likeness, while I was unconscious of the thing, and far away beyond the sea, it might be, doing, or it might be dreaming some other thing, and not in the least caring for his cares. In what way these things come about, I know not: but in what way soever they come, why do we not believe it comes in the same way for a person in a dream to see a dead man, as it comes that he sees a living man? both, no doubt, neither knowing nor caring who, or where, or when, dreams of their images.[19]

Dreams all work through the imagination, and sometimes those that seem other-worldly and revelatory, showing us the venerable dead, are not divinely-inspired at all, but are merely called up out of our memories, like dreams with a clearly mundane etiology.

By insisting on the imaginative quality even of dreams that seem to involve visitations from the other world, Augustine does not, however, rule out the possibility of supernaturally-inspired dreams. On the contrary, he repeatedly affirms that knowledge transcending this corporeal world can come to us in dreams: "angelic operations" sometimes work on our imaginations.[20] But he stresses that even the highest dreams operate within the intermediate sphere of spirit. All dreams function through images neither unambiguously intellectual or corporeal.

In the De cura, Augustine aims to prevent a credulous attitude from ruling our interpretation of dream phenomena. By refusing to concede a special supernatural status to our dreams of the dead, Augustine pulls us back from overconfidence in the imperfect images of spiritual vision, allowing that these can be the means of transcendent revelation, but simultaneously warning that they are capable of deception and illusion, tied up not only with the world of angels, but also with the bodies of which they are likenesses and with our own fallible imaginations: "fallacious visions" can "cast [us] into great errors."[21]

While Augustine's treatment of dreams in the De cura thus works to prevent an overly high valuation of dream experience, his emphasis elsewhere on the imaginative nature of dreams serves a symmetrically opposite purpose, directing our attention to dreams we might otherwise dismiss. As Augustine makes clear in the De Genesi, revelation may come even from dreams caused by corporeal process:

We must not suppose that when the cause is in the body, the soul always ponders over images of bodies by its own power, without any prophetic insight.

(XII.21.44, p. 209)

Corporeal forces can act in concert with higher, angelic ones, and when this occurs, meaningful dreams result:

When the body causes the human spirit to direct its gaze intently upon them [images], it must not be thought that they always have a meaning. However, they have a meaning when they are inspired by a spirit that reveals something, whether it is to a man in sleep or to one who is afflicted with some bodily ailment that takes him out of his senses. (XII.22.45, p. 209)

Augustine thus allows that dreams like Macrobius's *insomnium* may in reality be more exalted than they appear, just as he argues in the *De cura* that dreams formally similar to Macrobius's *oraculum* may in fact be "fallacious."[22] While Augustine *does* set up a hierarchy of dreams much like that of Macrobius, he also undercuts that hierarchy, throwing all dreams – "either with or without a meaning" (*De Genesi* XII.23.49, p. 212) – together as spiritual experience. Whether divinely-inspired or corporeally-generated, impressively portentous or seemingly nonsensical, all dreams work through images and the imagination. All are caught between the embodied and the bodiless.

Strictly consigning dreams to the middle realm of "spirit," Augustine emphasizes even more strongly than Macrobius or Calcidius the essential middleness of the dream. Dreams can, like spiritual vision more generally, provide a route to knowledge, but they must do so ambiguously. Poised between corporeal and intellectual vision, dreams occupy a space between the mundanely real objects of sense perception and the transcendently real objects of abstract thought.

But while Augustine firmly places dreams in this middle position, he does not present them as static, immovably fixed in place. The power of middle experience comes from its potential to turn in either of two directions. Ideally, in Augustine's view, fallible spiritual vision would direct its gaze upward, placing itself wholly under the control of the intellect. Only if intellectual vision functions can dreams provide reliable knowledge;[23] in order to attain the status of prophecy, a dream must be seen not only spiritually, but also intellectually:

Those to whom signs were manifested in the spirit by means of certain likenesses of corporeal objects had not yet the gift of prophecy, unless the mind had performed its function, in order that the signs might be understood; and the man who interpreted what another had seen was more a prophet than the man who had seen. (XII.9.20, p. 189)

Left alone, spiritual vision cannot interpret the images it forms, or even decide which images are worthy of interpretation.

Full intellectual enlightenment of spiritual (and corporeal) vision occurs in the life of the angels:

They behold the immutable essence of the Creator with such clarity that because of this vision and the love it inspires they prefer the divine essence to all else, according to it judge everything, are directed towards it in all their impulses, and by it direct all the actions they perform. (XII.36.69, p. 230)

Such an ideal, in which all aspiration is properly directed toward ultimate Good, will also characterize the lives of the blessed after resurrection:

There will be joy in the things of the intellect, and they will be far more luminously present to the soul than the corporeal forms that now surround us ... Everything will be clear without any error and without any ignorance, all things occupying their proper place, the corporeal, the spiritual, and the intellectual, in untainted nature and perfect beatitude. (XII.36.69, pp. 229–30)

In our present life, however, the three visions are necessarily imperfect and often imperfectly ordered in relation to each other. Even the most complete revelatory experience – a divinely-inspired intellectual vision like that of St. Paul – falls short of the full vision of the angels:

Although St. Paul was carried out of the senses of the body into the third heaven and Paradise, he was wanting in one point the full and perfect knowledge of things that the angels have: he did not know whether he was in the body or out of the body. (XII.36.69, p. 230)

Corporeal and spiritual vision are even more imperfect, subject to outright mistakes in a way intellectual vision is not: we often see bodies distortedly and may erringly identify spiritual objects with corporeal ones (see XII.14.28–30, pp. 196–98; XII.25.52, pp. 215–16). Such imperfections are, to a certain extent, beyond our control. But they result in part from a common human refusal to give intellectual vision its rightful precedence. Far too often we live improperly, dwelling with the earthly, placing the corporeal before the intellectual and spiritual: "many are now so absorbed in these material forms that they judge them to be the only ones" (XII.36.69, p. 229). In contrast, "wise men" strive to attain as full an intellectual vision as possible, living in the corporeal world, but "clinging with greater surety to the world beyond bodily forms and beyond the likenesses of bodies, the world which they see with the intellect according to their measure, although they are not able to behold it in the mind so vividly as they do these other objects with the sense of the body" (XII.36.69, p. 230). Our goal should be to put the corporeal and spiritual in their proper places, to "use" and not "enjoy" them on our journey toward God, the ultimate (intellectual) object of striving.[24]

The "many" and the "wise" play out two opposed human impulses – toward the pleasure of the body, and toward the satisfaction of the mind. In the tug of war between the two, spiritual vision and the dream play a crucial (middle) role. On the one hand, the spiritual is threatened by the corporeal realm beneath it. We can insistently interpret images – even those that are meaningful and angelically-inspired – as merely corporeal; we can fail to read the spiritual in the light of the intellect, and refuse to move toward a realm beyond body. On the other hand, we can turn our spiritual gaze upward, striving to distinguish the meaningful dream from the meaningless, reading images in an intellectual light, imperfect though it may be.

By stressing the middleness of spiritual vision and of dreams as strongly as he does, Augustine moves in essence to remind us of the middle nature of the human being. Made up of both body and soul, humans experience a reality neither wholly corporeal nor fully intellectual. To perceive even the simplest of bodies, our spiritual vision must function along with our senses, forming an image in the mind, abstracting an incorporeal picture from corporeality. Similarly, it is only rarely that we glimpse the intellectual stripped of the products of imagination: we may receive an inkling of the divine, but usually through a veil of images.[25]

Sometimes spiritual vision allows us to perceive a higher truth, but it also pulls us back to bodies and their false delights. Depending on how they are used, spiritual vision and the dream take on different *moral* valences. Properly employed, spiritual vision furthers our journey toward God; but abused, it leaves us mired in the vanities of earth. The human relation to dreams and the spiritual expresses, in embryo, the problematic position of human beings who must attend to the demands of both an immortal soul and a corruptible body.

ANGELS AND DEMONS: AUGUSTINE, TERTULLIAN, GREGORY

The theorists so far examined strongly emphasize the connection between dreaming and knowledge. For Augustine, the dream is a kind of "vision" by which we sometimes approach truth. For Calcidius – who discusses dream experience alongside direct physical vision (236–48) and the reflected vision made possible by mirrors (257–67) – the dream may provide access to unaccustomed knowledge. And for Macrobius, a dream like Scipio's – simultaneously *oraculum*, *visio*, and *somnium* – acts as the key to a vast store of information.

These writers, however, were not always content to consider the dream *only* in its relation to knowledge: moral concerns become entwined with epistemological ones. The state of purity of a dreamer's soul may be crucial in determining the clarity of a given visionary experience,[26] and the dream can have profound moral consequences: vision, when properly used, leads not just to knowledge, but to a knowledge of the Good and of God.[27] A writer like Augustine, even while addressing epistemological concerns, keeps moral implications constantly in view.[28] Indeed, especially in early Christian writers, there begins to be a strong emphasis on "good" and "bad," as well as true and false, dreams.

The late-antique "moralization" of the dream did not, however, proceed in a wholly straightforward way. We might expect the moralist to connect the dream *content* directly to a dreamer's moral state. But for writers like Augustine, Tertullian (*c.* 160–230), and Gregory the Great (*c.* 540–604), dreaming about sin did not necessarily implicate the dreamer. Because the rational, estimative powers of the soul are inactive during sleep, the dreamer cannot be held accountable for the subject matter of the dream, or for the judgments made while dreaming. Even "chaste people" sometimes "dream ... of having carnal intercourse contrary to their previous good resolutions, as well as against what is lawful," "because [in their sleep] they cannot control the appearance of those corporeal images"; sometimes "when the image ... becomes so vivid in the dream of the sleeper that it is indistinguishable from actual intercourse, it immediately moves the flesh and the natural result follows" (*De Genesi* XII.15.31, pp. 198–99). "Yet," according to Augustine, "this happens without sin" (XII.15.31, p. 199).[29] As Tertullian suggests in more general terms:

In our dreams, any good actions we perform are without merit and our crimes are blameless. We will no more be condemned for a rape committed in a dream than we will be crowned for dreaming we were martyrs.[30]

Rather than investing the subject matter of the dream with moral significance, patristic authors tended to locate such significance outside the dream itself, in its etiology and after-effects, in the way it is generated and in the way individual dreamers respond to its suggestions. To explain the origin of certain dreams, Christian writers invoked a spirit world split between good and evil, angelic and demonic, forces. And in ascribing dreams to such agents, these writers came to see dream experience as affecting, in important ways, the health of the soul.

We can thus begin to set patristic dream theory off from Neoplatonism, but we must remember that Neoplatonic and early Christian theories of dreaming share a great deal. The old question of where the dream originates, inside or outside the dreamer, plays a central role in Christian as well as Neoplatonic treatments. Implicit in Tertullian's classification of dreams is a general distinction between external and internal motivation:[31] two kinds of dream come from outside the human psyche, but a "tertia species" includes dreams arising from the soul's own action – "somnia

quae sibimet ipsa anima uidetur inducere ex intentione circumstantiarum"
[dreams ... which the soul somehow seems to induce of itself by the
attentive contemplation of the things surrounding it].[32]

Gregory the Great also divides dreams according to their origin,
whether inside or outside the dreamer:

> Sciendum ... est quia sex modis tangunt animam imagines somniorum. Aliquando
> namque somnia (1) uentris plenitudine (2) uel inanitate, (3) aliquando uero
> inlusione, (4) aliquando cogitatione simul et inlusione, (5) aliquando reuelatione,
> (6) aliquando autem cogitatione simul et reuelatione generantur.[33]

> It is important to realize ... that dreams come to the soul in six ways. They are
> generated (1) either by a full stomach, (2) or by an empty one, (3) or by illusions, (4)
> or by our thoughts combined with illusions, (5) or by revelations, (6) or by our
> thoughts combined with revelations.

The first two kinds of dream, dependent entirely on the individual's
physical state, are akin to Macrobius's *insomnium*. At the opposite extreme
stand dreams of pure revelation and illusion, generated outside the
individual dreamer from the activity of autonomous spiritual agents (see
below). Such purely external dreams can, however, be moderated by
internally-generated material: "our thoughts" may work in concert with
either illusion or revelation. Dreams thus stimulated stand between the
wholly external and the fully internal, and complete a hierarchical
description of dreaming:

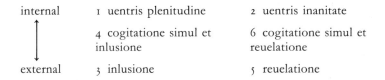

Such a hierarchy would certainly be familiar to Neoplatonic dream
theorists.[34]

Yet patristic dream theories also diverge from their Neoplatonic
counterparts. In defining the external sources of dreams, early Christian
writers balanced demonically- and angelically-stimulated dreams symmetrically against each other. As Augustine suggests in the *De Genesi*, the agent
responsible for spiritual vision can be either good or evil, an angel or a
devil:

> By means of corporeal vision as well as by means of the images of corporeal objects
> revealed in the spirit, good spirits instruct men and evil spirits deceive them.
>
> (XII.14.29, p. 197)

When an evil spirit transports men ... he either possesses them or makes them frenzied or false prophets. When, on the contrary, a good spirit transports them, he inspires them to give a reliable account of mysteries.   (XII.19.41, p. 206)

The bifurcated spirit world of Christian dream theory itself owes something to Neoplatonism: Neoplatonic writers sometimes distinguished "good" and "bad" *daemones*, usually on the basis of their proximity to heaven.[35] But the Christian appeal to angels and devils involves a more radical split than does the Neoplatonic distinction. At some point in the Neoplatonic scheme, "good" and "bad" demons meet each other on a ground between pure good and evil; there is no such common ground shared by Christian demons and angels. It is not surprising, then, that a distinction between benevolently- and malevolently-inspired dreams, based on the action of radically-opposed spiritual beings, does not figure in writers like Macrobius and Calcidius. In Calcidius, all those dreams arising from outside the dreamer are essentially stimulated by *benevolent* "daemones," "diuinae potestates" acting to protect and better humankind. And while it might be tempting to ascribe Macrobius's *visum* to the action of mischievous or even maleficent spirits (the *incubi* Macrobius attributes to popular belief), Macrobius himself emphasizes the role the imagination plays in producing this particular kind of untrustworthy dream. In Macrobius, as in Calcidius, all those dreams that *clearly* transcend the individual's human powers – *oraculum, visio,* and *somnium* – act to the dreamer's benefit, revealing otherwise inaccessible truths; although Macrobius never says so explicitly, they all seem to come from a beneficent spiritual realm.[36]

Early Christian writers did not *always* divide external dream experience into angelic and demonic camps. As we have seen, Augustine's description of dreams often closely resembles that of a writer like Calcidius. Indeed, in contrasting internal and external visionary experience, Augustine sometimes seems to claim that the latter arises solely from the action of angels or "good spirits" (see, for instance, *De Genesi* XII.22.45–48, pp. 209–11, and XII.30.58, p. 221). But, while the ascription of externally-motivated dreams to either angels or devils is not the *only* way patristic writers treated dreams, it was a common and important way.

Thus, Tertullian highlights the opposition between the divine and the demonic, suggesting that external dreams come either from demons or directly from God:

(1) The first type of dreams we have declared to emanate from [demons][37] ... (2) The second class of dreams must be considered to come from God, since He has promised to pour out the grace of the Holy Spirit upon all flesh and has ordained

that His sons and handmaidens shall utter prophecies and dream dreams [Joel 2: 28–29].[38]

Similarly, Gregory the Great balances the *inlusio*, caused by demonic action ("ab occulto hoste"),[39] against the *reuelatio*, arising "ex mysterio reuelationis" [from the mystery of a revelation], as when "Mariae sponsum, ut ablato puero in Aegyptum fugeret, per somnium angelus admoneret" [through a dream, the angel . . . warned the spouse of Mary to take the child and flee into Egypt].[40]

Gregory's definition of these two kinds of dream parallels Tertullian rather closely; but Gregory also allows for hybrid dreams: the addition of "our thoughts" to primarily angelic or demonic dreams must moderate or dilute the purely good or evil motives underlying them. Such dreams, the product of an individual's internal processes as well as of external forces, are not unambiguously associable with either pure malevolence or benevolence.[41] If, finally, we take the dreams of the stomach to be morally neutral – since presumably they arise out of neither benevolent nor malevolent intentions – we can see Gregory establishing a hierarchy of dreams based on the relative "goodness" or "badness" of the motives underlying them:

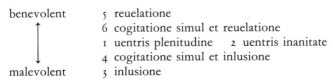

benevolent   5 reuelatione

                    6 cogitatione simul et reuelatione

                    1 uentris plenitudine   2 uentris inanitate

                    4 cogitatione simul et inlusione

malevolent   3 inlusione

The patristic distinction between malevolent and benevolent dreams, which plays an important role in Christian attempts to order dream experience, is not wholly separable from questions of truth and falsehood. Such questions – so central to Neoplatonic treatments – remain important in Tertullian, Augustine, and Gregory, even as these authors began to shift their attention to problems of morality. In Gregory, demonic dreams of "illusion" are, as their name indicates, not just demonic, but deceptive; revelatory dreams clearly tell the truth. Dreams that arise from excessive eating or from inanition, on the other hand, occupy a more or less neutral position. They are clearly not revelatory, but though they may be *meaningless*, they are not, like *inlusio*, downright deceptive. Finally, dreams of revelation or illusion, to which *cogitatio* has been added, occupy mediate positions. Such dreams, unlike the dreams of the stomach, remain essentially true or false, but the complicating presence of individual thought may partially obscure their meaning, making them less unambiguous in their truth or falsehood. Indeed, Gregory's dream categories can be arranged in one last hierarchy – this time of increasing truth value – to obtain much the same arrangement found when the categories are ordered between the poles of malevolence and benevolence:

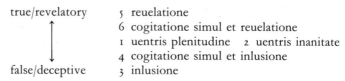

The *general* correspondence in Gregory between the truth value of dreams and the malevolence or benevolence of their source also holds in Tertullian and Augustine. Divine or angelic dreams never lie. For Tertullian, they are "honest, holy, prophetic, inspired, edifying, and inducing to virtue": "the majority of mankind get their knowledge of God from dreams."[42] And as Augustine suggests, "when a good spirit seizes or ravishes the spirit of a man to direct it to an extraordinary vision, there can be no doubt the images are signs of things which it is useful to know, for this is a gift of God" (*De Genesi* XII.13.18, p. 196). On the other hand, demons often send "false" prophecies (XII.19.41, p. 206) through dreams that Tertullian characterizes as "vain, deceitful, vague, licentious, and impure."[43] As Augustine concludes, "good spirits instruct men and evil spirits deceive them" (XII.14.29, p. 197).

Issues of truth thus remain involved in patristic discussions of the dream, but the consideration of angelic and demonic motivations in these discussions does not serve simply to provide another means of separating revelatory and non-revelatory dreams. In fact, the distinction between demonic and divine dream experience is not based primarily on the differentiation of truth and falsehood. Demonic dreams are, in fact, not *always* false and delusive; they can sometimes reveal reliable information. Tertullian claims that dreams inspired by devils may "sometimes" be "uera et gratiosa" [true and favorable to us].[44] Gregory similarly qualifies the suggestion – made implicitly in naming demonic dreams *inlusiones* – that all such dreams are untruthful. In his view, demonic dreams are always intended *ultimately* to deceive the dreamer, but *proximately* they can present reliable information:

If the mind is not on its guard against these, it will be entangled in countless vanities by the master of deceit, who is clever enough to foretell many things that are true in order finally to capture the soul by but one falsehood.[45]

Similarly, Augustine is careful to stress that demonically-inspired visions are not uniformly false. The devil's plan of "deception" sometimes operates through the presentation of what is objectively true and "useful":

There is, of course, no cause for wonder if even those possessed by a devil occasionally speak the truth about objects beyond the reach of their senses at the time... [Sometimes] the evil spirit acts in a seemingly peaceful manner and, without tormenting the body, possesses a man's spirit and says what he is able, sometimes even speaking the truth and disclosing useful knowledge of the future.

(*De Genesi* XII.13.28, p. 196)

The essential difference between demonic and angelic visions lies not so much in the reliability of the information they impart, as in the motives for good or evil that underlie them: when Tertullian draws a direct comparison between demonic and divine dreams, he emphasizes not their truth or lack of truth, but their moral position *vis-à-vis* humanity:

Therefore, just as the mercy of God abounds for the pagans, so the temptations of the Devil attack the saints; he never relaxes his vigor, trying to trap them while they are asleep, if he is unsuccessful while they are awake.[46]

God sends dreams out of "mercy" or "grace":

Such dreams may be compared to the grace of God... Their bountiful nature causes them to overflow even to the infidels since God with divine impartiality causes the rain to fall and the sun to shine upon just and unjust alike.[47]

The angelic revelation of "quas nosse utile est" [things which it is useful to know] is "a gift of God" (Augustine, *De Genesi* XII.13.28, p. 196). Demons, on the other hand, when they disclose "uera" [the truth] and "utilia" [useful information], do so only to prepare the way for ultimate deception:

In this case he [the evil spirit] transforms himself, according to Scripture, as if into an angel of light [2 Corinthians 11:14], in order that, once having gained his victim's confidence in matters that are manifestly good, he may then lure his victim into his snares.   (*De Genesi* XII.13.28, p. 196)

Demonic action may parody the angelic, but no matter how "true" or "useful," the demonic dream plays an essentially different role for its recipient than does one angelically-inspired. It is always a temptation, "affectantia atque captantia" [attempting to capture and enticing];[48] it always arises from a motive opposed to God's benignity:

Our designing foe, in proportion as he is utterly unable to get the better of them when awake, makes the deadlier assault upon them asleep. Whom yet the dispensation of the Highest in loving-kindness [*benigne*] alone allows to do so in his malevolence [*maligne*], lest in the souls of the Elect their mere sleep, though nothing else, should go without the meed of suffering.[49]

God may allow demons to tempt humankind and those demons may imitate angelic action, but divine and demonic influences remain sharply divided: when dreaming, the human being becomes the object of actions either malign or benign.

THE DISCERNMENT OF DREAMS

None of the Christian writers we have examined bases his classification of dream experience solely on the distinction between angelic and demonic activity. Although Augustine introduced such a distinction into the *De Genesi*, he remains primarily concerned in that work with epistemology. Tertullian's differentiation between the divine and the demonic, while central to his presentation, remains only part of a broader discussion that includes a defense of the revelatory dream (chapter 46), a consideration of the physiology of sleep and dreams (chapter 43), and a treatment of how circumstances – diet, the time of the dream's occurrence, the body's position in sleep – affect the dream (chapter 48). Gregory's six-tiered classification also brings together various late-antique beliefs; it distinguishes dreams not only on the basis of their origin in malevolent or benevolent motives, but also according to their truth or falsehood, their origin inside or outside the dreamer, and – a criterion we have not yet mentioned – the frequency or rarity of their occurrence.[50]

However, even when the distinction between angelic and demonic dreams forms a relatively small portion of a particular dream discussion, its presence necessarily shifts the tenor of that discussion. Putting the theoretical concerns of a Macrobius or a Calcidius into action involves searching out the answer to one especially thorny question: how can any given dream be determined as true or false, worthy or unworthy of attention and interpretation? But when Gregory's disciple asks him "si hoc quod per nocturnas uisiones ostenditur debeat obseruari" [whether we need to take these nightly visions seriously],[51] Gregory makes clear that it is not only the dream's truth or falsehood which must be determined before the dream can safely be "observed." Although the question of truth remains, another has been added: the source underlying the dream, the motives – in a world divided between angels and demons – that have given it birth. Gregory's use of the word "obseruari," echoing as it does biblical and legal injunctions against dream divination, immediately suggests the moral implications embedded in his treatment.[52] For patristic writers, the "observation" of dreams entailed a moral choice. Any given dream might harm or profit the soul, and before believing in it, the dreamer must ask whether it has been sent to help or to tempt.

Addressing this morally-charged question becomes, in Christian discussions, a crucial concern. Human beings can err in judging questions of truth without being held morally culpable: "men in general do not suffer any harm from the fact that in their dreams they mistake the likenesses of bodies for real bodies" (Augustine, *De Genesi* XII.14.30, p. 197). Even when the source of deception is demonic, the deception *per se* is not damaging:

If the Devil should cozen the soul with a spiritual vision by means of the images of bodies, leading it to think there is a body where there is none, no harm is done the soul if it does not consent to an evil suggestion. (*De Genesi* XII.14.30, p. 198)

But demonically-inspired dreams remain dangerous, and the differentiation of demonic and angelic dreams remains important, and difficult. As we have seen, the truth value of a dream is no sure test of its nature, since demonic dreams sometimes reveal the truth, and dreams may seem angelic even when they are not. The devil can "transform himself . . . as if into an angel of light," and "the discernment of these experiences is certainly a most difficult task when the evil spirit acts in a seemingly peaceful manner" (*De Genesi* XII.13.28, p. 196). Believing ourselves to be following angelic instructions, we may end by "consenting to an evil suggestion": "once having gained his victim's confidence in matters that are manifestly good, he [the evil spirit] may then lure his victim into his snares" (*De Genesi* XII.13.28, p. 196).

In fact, it seems, most people can identify a dream as demonic only after it has had its intended pernicious effect:

When the evil spirit has achieved his purpose and led someone on to what is contrary to good morals or the rule of faith, it is [no great] achievement to discern his presence – for in that case there are many who discern him.

(*De Genesi* XII.13.28, p. 196)

A few people are granted a special gift that allows them easily to differentiate angelic visions from demonic ones:

This spirit [transformed as if into an angel of light], so far as I know, cannot be recognized except by that gift mentioned by St. Paul, where he speaks of the different gifts of God: . . . *to another the distinguishing of spirits* [1 Corinthians 12: 10] . . . The gift of discernment enables one in the very beginning (when the spirit appears as a good spirit to the majority) to judge immediately whether he is evil.

(*De Genesi* XII.14.28, pp. 196–97)

But as Gregory suggests, this gift is exceedingly rare – in his opinion, granted only to saints:

The saints, however, can distinguish true revelations from the voices and images of illusions through an inner sensitivity. They can always recognize when they receive communications from the good Spirit and when they are face to face with illusions.[53]

"The majority" of people have no easy task in deciding what to do about their dreams (*De Genesi* XII.14.28, p. 197). They certainly cannot accept all dream experience uncritically. As Gregory demonstrates, "the mind" that "is not on its guard"[54] against illusion is at great risk:

One of our men who believed strongly in dreams ... was promised [in a dream] a long life. After collecting a large sum of money to last him for many years, he died very suddenly, leaving all of his wealth behind untouched, without having so much as a single good work to take with him.[55]

One must always be "very reluctant to put one's faith in" dreams, "since it is hard to tell from what source they come."[56]

But while it is dangerous to treat dreams uncritically, neither can they be ignored, or dismissed out of hand. Some dreams, after all, are divine or angelic, and *should* be believed: a work like Gregory's *Dialogues*, despite its clearly avowed skepticism toward dreams, is filled with accounts of miraculous dreams and visions, dreams surely worthy of our attention. The dreamer who believes in the possibility of both divinely-inspired and demonic dreams thus finds him- or herself in a difficult position, both attracted to and repelled from dreams. The only possible response is one of extreme caution, taking care neither to believe nor to distrust dreams too easily.[57]

As I have argued above, the doubleness of dreams as regards the question of truth pushes them into a middle position where they are involved in both the true and the false, exploring relations between divinity and the mundane, between mind and body. Similarly, we may argue that the doubleness of dreams in relation to their motivating force places them in an undecided, middle realm. As dreamers forced to respond to a dream of either angelic or demonic origin, we are in some sense paralyzed. Wanting neither to accept hastily nor reject carelessly the "suggestions" of our dreams, we are left in a state of moral suspension. Perhaps we should read a particular dream as an encouragement or injunction from God; perhaps following its advice will help us along the way to salvation. But at least some dreams that seem to lead us in the proper direction, offering "useful knowledge" "in matters that are manifestly good" (Augustine, *De Genesi* XII.13.28, p. 196), are demonic and hence to be shunned. The dreamer stands in a precarious position, between a potential good and a potential evil that are (without that rare gift, the "distinguishing of spirits") essentially indistinguishable. The realm of dreams, poised between truth and fiction, is also torn between good and evil; it provides a ground on which both benevolent and malevolent forces work, and in relation to which human beings must make complicated decisions – decisions with crucial implications for their moral lives.

The precarious stance of the early Christian dreamer *vis-à-vis* the complicated realm of dreams is perhaps best dramatized by Prudentius (348-after 404) in his "Hymnus ante somnum" (*Cathemerinon* 6).[58] Beginning his poem calmly, with a confident invocation of God's presence (lines 1–8), Prudentius at first treats sleep as an unambiguously peaceful release from the troubles of waking life (13–24). But as the poem progresses, it becomes less and less calm; the "blandus sopor" (11) [caressing slumber] with which it opens is deeply disturbed.

In his first description of dreaming, however, Prudentius gives no hint of the complications later introduced. He describes a dream, like the higher dreams of both Neoplatonic and Christian theory, that is clearly revelatory. As the body sleeps, the ever-active soul, divine in origin and acting in harmony with the universe that surrounds it, gains access to "hidden" truths:

> Liber vagat per auras
> rapido vigore sensus,
> variasque per figuras
> quae sunt operta cernit;
>   quia mens soluta curis,
> cui est origo caelum
> purusque fons ab aethra,
> iners iacere nescit.   (29–36)

The spirit roams free through the air, quick and lively, and in diverse figures sees things that are hidden; for the mind, whose source is heaven and whose pure fount is from the skies, cannot lie idle when it is freed from care.

Prudentius here describes dreaming as an educative experience pursued vigorously, even joyously, by the soul. But the specter of another kind of dream suddenly breaks in upon the vision of restful sleep and quiet, productive dreams: "sed sensa somniantum / dispar fatigat horror" (41–42) [But by contrast terror troubles our thoughts in dreams]. "Horror" here enters the seemingly secure world of sleep, and its presence makes necessary a reevaluation of the nature of dream experience. How can dreams bring both useful revelation and disturbing terror? The answer must be that dreaming is more complicated than Prudentius's poem initially allows, that it can be played out in a variety of ways.

Dreaming in the Middle Ages

As Prudentius makes explicit in what follows, the dream is double. Both informative, useful dreams, and false, disturbing nightmares are possible:

> Nunc splendor intererrat,
> qui dat futura nosse;
>   plerumque dissipatis
> mendax imago veris
> animos pavore maestos
> ambage fallit atra.   (43–48)

At times a brilliant light comes in upon them and gives knowledge of things to be; often reality is scattered and a lying image makes our minds unhappy and afraid and deceives them with a dark obscurity.

Prudentius's redefinition of dreaming follows the pattern set out by the theorists: dreams can be both true and false, both revelatory and misleading. But Prudentius does not rest content with this formulation; as the "Hymnus" proceeds, he, like other patristic writers, begins to emphasize the dream's involvement in a moral realm. At first he does so in a way not foreign to the Neoplatonic tradition, drawing a connection, like that found in Calcidius, between the purity of human action and the clarity of dreams:

> Quem rara culpa morum
> non polluit frequenter,
> hunc lux serena vibrans
> res edocet latentes;
>   at qui coinquinatum
> vitiis cor inpiavit,
> lusus pavore multo
> species videt tremendas.   (49–56)

If a man's stains of guilty conduct are few and far between, him the clear flashing light teaches secret things; but he who has polluted and befouled his heart with sins is the sport of many a fear and sees frightful visions.

But Prudentius goes on, in the remainder of the poem, to connect dreaming to more specifically Christian traditions. He reiterates at length the connection between a good life and lucid dreams, and as proof of that connection, he invokes religious texts, citing both Old and New Testament *exempla* of prophetic visionary experience (57–72 and 77–112).[59] This long passage (comprising almost a third of the "Hymnus") moves us back toward the poem's beginning: it emphasizes veridical, divinely-inspired dreams, and in doing so, returns, at least momentarily, to a confident belief in oneiric revelation. Twice Prudentius makes explicit the point that the biblical *exempla* help drive home:

> O quam profunda iustis
> arcana per soporem
> aperit tuenda Christus,
> quam clara, quam tacenda!   (73–76)

How deep the mysteries Christ lays open to the sight of the righteous in their sleep! How clear, and not to be uttered!

> Tali sopore iustus
> mentem relaxat heros,
> ut spiritu sagaci
> caelum peragret omne.   (113–16)

Such is the sleep with which the righteous hero rests his mind, that with prophetic spirit it traverses the whole heaven.

But even as Prudentius thus stirs up admiration for revelatory dreams, he subtly reminds us of certain limitations. Revelation comes only to the "iustus" [righteous] dreamer (73 and 113), and revelation depends upon the grace of God: Christ must "lay open" "mysteries" for us. Indeed, Prudentius ultimately makes it clear that, just as truly righteous people are rare, miraculous dreams are the exception rather than the rule:

> Nos nil meremur horum,
> quos creber inplet error,
> concreta quos malarum
> vitiat cupido rerum.   (117–20)

As for us, we merit none of these things, for many an error fills our heart, and a hardened desire for evil things corrupts us.

We – the majority of humankind – in our depravity, do not deserve God-sent dreams; instead, while we sleep, we are often tormented by the deceptive attacks of the devil (137–48). As theorists like Tertullian, Augustine, and Gregory propose, the dream, while it can be used by God to aid us, is also potentially destructive.

Having begun by describing "kindly repose" and useful dreams, the "Hymnus" draws to its end in a much altered fashion, with the recognition of threatening demonic dreams and with a prayer for protection from them:

> Procul, o procul vagantum
> portenta somniorum,[60]
> procul esto pervicaci
> praestigiator astu.

> O tortuose serpens,
> qui mille per meandros
> fraudesque flexuosas
> agitas quieta corda,
>   discede, Christus hic est,
> hic Christus est, liquesce.
> Signum quod ipse nosti
> damnat tuam catervam.   (137–48)

Away, away with the monstrosities of rambling dreams! Away with the deceiver and his persistent guile! O twining serpent that by a thousand winding ways and twisting deceptions dost disturb hearts at rest, depart, for Christ is here! Christ is here: vanish away! The sign thou thyself knowest condemns thy company.

In the poem, the appeal to Christ is ultimately effective in blocking the worst dangers of demonic seduction. The last stanza of the "Hymnus" evokes once more a sleep protected against disturbance:

> Corpus licet fatiscens
> iaceat recline paulum,
> Christum tamen sub ipso
> meditabimur sopore.   (149–52)

Though the weary body lie down for a little, yet even in sleep our thoughts shall be of Christ.

But sleep here, unlike the sleep of the poem's beginning, depends upon a certain vigilance – a constant awareness, and warding off, of danger. Even in sleep one must remain wakefully on guard against temptation, alertly concentrated on Christ.

The possibility of a relaxed and innocent sleep, which the poem raises at its outset, has disappeared by its end. Dreams can, after all, be true or false, calm or disturbed, God-sent or demonic. If it were possible in dreams to differentiate the educative from the deceptive and the divine from the demonic, oneiric experience could be used to help guide the way we live. But Prudentius gives no indication that we can accurately assess the nature of our own dreams. Ultimately, in the "Hymnus," the dreamer cannot react to dreams with any certainty, and must "be very reluctant to put . . . faith in them."[61] Faced with the vicissitudes of dreaming, one can do nothing other than attend vigilantly to God; the final response to the confusing realm of dreams can only be a prayer for divine protection.

From the fourth to the twelfth century

Geoffrey Chaucer's *House of Fame* begins with a comic discussion of dreams that raises many of the questions addressed by late-antique authorities.[1] The poem's narrator presents dreams as sometimes reliable, sometimes not: "th'effect folweth of somme, / And of somme hit shal never come" (lines 5–6). And asking repeatedly what might cause dreams, he lists a variety of familiar possibilities: dreams can arise from the physical and psychological condition of the dreamer (like Macrobius's *insomnium*) (21–40), from the action of external "spirites" (like Gregory's *reuelationes* and *inlusiones*) (41–42), or from the natural motion of the "parfit" soul (like Calcidius's *uisum*) (43–51).[2]

But while Chaucer's narrator demonstrates a wide knowledge of dream theory, he consistently refuses to acknowledge his own learnedness, asserting instead a confused ignorance (12, 14–15, and 52) and deferring to the superior knowledge of others ("grete clerkys," 53). He refuses to organize dream lore into any coherent system, refuses to become a theorist. While echoing authoritative treatments of the dream, Chaucer points up – in his narrator's repeated confusions – the problems that such complex treatments pose for the particular dreamer attempting to deal practically with his own "wonderful" (62) dreams.

The response here to the complex potential of dreams strongly recalls Prudentius's "Hymnus ante somnum." The speaker of that poem, reacting to the dream's variousness and possible hidden dangers, does not try to codify or contain dreaming within a systematic theory. Instead, he expresses his fear and retreats into prayer, into the protective custody of faith. Chaucer's narrator similarly retreats from theory, framing his discussion of dreaming with statements – prayers, in fact – that effectively remove the ability to comprehend dreams from the human realm. "God turne us every drem to goode!" (1), the narrator begins, and he ends the discussion of dreams by returning, apparently no wiser, to the poem's hopeful, but confused, opening:

Dreaming in the Middle Ages

> ...I of noon opinion
> Nyl as now make mensyon,
> But oonly that the holy roode
> Turne us every drem to goode![3]   (55–58)

Chaucer's speaker asserts his inability to sort out the dream's complications and turns that problem over to God. The narrators of both the *House* and the "Hymnus" respond to a complexity they cannot fully fathom by referring it to a higher, divine, perspective.

This parallel between Chaucer and Prudentius does not imply a direct connection between the two, but instead begins to suggest the ways in which late-antique and late-medieval treatments of dreaming may be significantly interrelated. In comparing the fourteenth century and Late Antiquity, we see that specific bits of dream lore, and even whole theories, have been transmitted across the centuries. More surprisingly, not only ideas, but also attitudes – complex ways of approaching the dream – link the worlds of Prudentius and Chaucer. In comparing the *House of Fame* to the "Hymnus ante somnum," we see poets using dream theory for similar literary ends. In choosing to consider the vexed relation between individual dreamers and their dreams, Chaucer and Prudentius confront a common question: in practice, how can one kind of dream be distinguished from another? And both poets, despite their differences in tone, end up responding to that question in remarkably similar ways.

THE MEDIEVAL RECEPTION OF LATE-ANTIQUE DREAM THEORY

I can here only begin to suggest the avenues by which late-antique thought influenced medieval treatments of dreaming – the reasons why, after a millennium, the ideas and attitudes of a Calcidius or an Augustine still had the power to shape responses to the dream. The most important factor in maintaining such an influence was the simple preservation of texts. The works of major dream theorists survived and were, in fact, used and reproduced well into the Renaissance.

Thus, the commentaries of Calcidius and Macrobius became standard medieval reference works, playing a central role (along with the Hermetic *Asclepius* and the writings of Boethius, Martianus Capella, pseudo-Dionysius, and Augustine) in the diffusion of Platonic and Neoplatonic ideas in the Latin West.[4] Macrobius's work "seem[s] to have reached England in s. x or xi,"[5] and it was known in Wales in the eleventh century.[6] The *Commentary* occupied a prominent place in medieval library catalogues and lists of textbooks;[7] Max Manitius lists about ninety manuscripts.[8] Indeed, many copies have survived into modern times. Thorndike characterizes the *Commentary* as "one of the treatises most frequently encountered in early medieval Latin manuscripts,"[9] and Ludwig von Jan, in his edition of Macrobius, describes forty-eight manuscript versions.[10] Alison Peden has identified, from the ninth, tenth, and eleventh centuries alone (that is, from a period before the height of the *Commentary*'s popularity), "thirty surviving full copies of the text" as well as "five other MSS [that] contain the passage on dreams as an excerpt or gloss."[11] And collating the available evidence, Stahl estimates that a full list of manuscripts "would quickly run into the hundreds."[12]

Calcidius's *Commentary on the Timaeus* enjoyed a similar popularity. Manitius cites well over 100 manuscripts from medieval library catalogues,[13] and Waszink, in his edition, lists 137 manuscripts containing either Calcidius's translation of Plato, or his commentary, or both.[14] Like Macrobius's work, the Calcidian *Commentary* was used as a textbook,[15] and again like Macrobius, it probably available in the British Isles at an early date.[16]

For their part, Augustine and Gregory were two of the most influential "doctors" of the Church, and the *De Genesi ad litteram*, *Moralia in Job*, and *Dialogi* circulated widely, exerting a constant pressure upon medieval thought. The compilers of "Die handschriftliche Überlieferung der Werke des heiligen Augustinus" [The Manuscript Tradition of the Works of St. Augustine], still incomplete, have already listed 122 manuscripts of the *De Genesi*.[17] At the University of Paris in the late thirteenth century, the "Super Genesim ad litteram" was sold as a textbook.[18] And Augustine's exegetical treatise has a long history in England: already used as a source by Bede in the eighth century, and preserved in at least one eleventh-century English manuscript,[19] the *De Genesi* later occupied a prominent place in the theological library catalogue of Merton College, Oxford (*c.* 1360).[20]

Gregory's works, like those of Augustine, entered English intellectual life at an early date – in J. D. A. Ogilvy's view, as early as the late seventh century.[21] And like the *De Genesi*, these works remained important in the later Middle Ages: they too are found in thirteenth-century lists of textbooks at Paris, and in the fourteenth-century Merton College catalogue.[22] Codicological evidence leaves no doubt as to the popularity of the *Moralia*: Marc Adriaen cites almost 550 copies of the *Moralia* in a tabulation which he calls "haud exaustiua" [by no means exhaustive].[23] Gregory's *Dialogi* also enjoyed widespread diffusion. In the later Middle Ages, according to Kibre, "in most libraries there were copies of the *Dialogues* and *Homelies* of Gregory the Great."[24] Georg Dufner concurs, suggesting that "es müsste bedeutend leichter sein, jene Bibliotheken aufzuzählen, welche die *Dialoge* nicht besassen, als jene, die eine oder mehrere Handschriften derselben im Besitze hatten" [it would have to be considerably easier to count up those libraries that did not possess the *Dialogues* than those that had one or more manuscripts of it in their possession].[25] The *Dialogues* circulated not only in a "très grand nombre" of Latin manuscripts,[26] but also in a remarkable variety of translated versions:[27]

eighth century:	Greek
ninth century:	Old English
	Slavic
tenth century:	Arabic
eleventh century:	Slavic
twelfth century:	French
	Icelandic
thirteenth century:	Anglo-Norman verse
	Catalan
	Bulgarian
fourteenth century:	French
	Portuguese (2 versions)
	Castilian
	Dutch (3 versions)
	Italian (5 versions)
fifteenth century:	German (2 versions)
	Italian

As one might expect, works so popular did not fail to shape medieval thought in important ways;[28] most crucial for our purposes, we find the dream lore of each of our authors cited, and often reproduced more or less *verbatim*, by many medieval writers. In gaining the attention of later dream theorists, Gregory's six-part classification of dreams had a certain advantage. Not only was it contained in two of Gregory's most popular treatises, but it was also incorporated (sometimes in slightly altered form) into several influential early works: Isidore of Seville's *Sententiarum libri tres* (early seventh century); a pseudo-Isidorian "Liber quartus," sometimes appended to the *Sentences*; Tajo of Saragossa's *Sententiarum libri quinque* (seventh century); and Rabanus Maurus's *Commentariorum in Ecclesiasticum libri decem* (ninth century).[29] Isidore's work, "the first collection of sentences or systematic body of doctrine and pastoral practice," was itself extremely popular, and when we encounter Gregory's six-fold division of dream-types in later authors, it is often by way of Isidore.[30] In addition, as Richard Hazelton shows, Gregory's scheme, "in one form or another, appears in all the *glossulae*" on the *Disticha Catonis*, a common medieval school text; it may have been by means of such a gloss – "what every schoolboy learned," as Hazelton has it – that an author like Chaucer gained access to Gregorian dream theory.[31] Whether directly or indirectly,

Gregory became known as a great authority on the dream, and the "ideas and very phrases" of his discussion "utterly commonplace."[32] In the eleventh century, Otloh of St. Emmeram, in the prologue to his *Liber visionum*, presented Gregory as an expert on all kinds of dreams and visions with authority rivalling that of the Bible.[33] Pascalis Romanus incorporates parts of the Gregorian system for classifying dreams into his compendium of Eastern dream lore, the *Liber thesauri occulti*, with an ease that suggests great familiarity.[34] And though a discussion like St. Bonaventure's of the five causes of dreaming does not strictly follow Gregory's scheme, it is clearly indebted to it.[35] Elsewhere, Gregory's dream categories were reproduced more directly: by Onulf (*Vita Popponis*) in the eleventh century; Alain de Lille (*Liber sententiarum*) and Thomas of Froidmont (*Liber de modo bene vivendi*; sometimes ascribed to Bernard of Clairvaux) in the twelfth; Caesarius of Heisterbach (*Dialogus miraculorum*), Thomas de Chobham (*Summa confessorum*), Albertus Magnus (*Commentarius in Danielem* and *Summa de creaturis*), Jean de la Rochelle (*Summa de anima*), Vincent of Beauvais (*Speculum naturale*), Johannis Michaelis (*In Danielem*; falsely attributed to Thomas Aquinas), and Albert of Orlamunde (*Philosophia pauperum* [= *Isagoge in libros Aristotelis*]; often ascribed to Albertus Magnus) in the thirteenth; and William of Vaurouillon (*Liber de anima*) in the early fifteenth.[36] Gregory's scheme even appeared in popular vernacular works of the thirteenth, fourteenth, and fifteenth centuries: William of Wadington's *Manuel des péchés*; Robert Mannyng of Brunne's *Handlyng Synne* (the dream lore here comes from William's Anglo-Norman *Manuel*); Richard Rolle's *Form of Living*; and Peter Idley's *Instructions to His Son*.[37]

An educated person of the late Middle Ages had a good chance of knowing Gregory's system for classifying dreams, and was even more likely to have been familiar with Augustine's three-fold definition of vision, and with his concomitant identification of dreaming as a function of spiritual sight. Augustine's tripartite view, while most fully expressed in the *De Genesi ad litteram*, functions as well in Augustine's other works (most notably in the *De Trinitate*);[38] and as Augustinian thought spread, so did the tendency to differentiate corporeal, spiritual, and intellectual vision.[39] Sometimes Augustine's three-fold scheme was distorted, and was often used for purposes different from those of its author. Alain de Lille, for instance, transforms Augustine's hierarchy of *vision* into a hierarchical description of *dream*-types (contemplative, imaginative, and slothful);[40] similarly, the Augustinian system was adapted in the triple division of dreams (*somnium naturale*, *somnium animale*, *somnium coeleste*) discovered by Walter Clyde Curry in such writers as Petrus de Abano.[41] Still, even if reinterpreted and altered, Augustine's tripartite view became central to medieval discussions of perception and of dreaming. Isidore of Seville reproduced Augustine's scheme in his *Etymologies*, the most influential of early medieval encyclopedic works.[42] In the Carolingian period, Augustine's discussion was quoted in such works as the *Libri Carolini*, and Alcuin's *Commentarii in Apocalypsin*.[43] The Augustinian system remained popular in the later Middle Ages, and is found in a variety of twelfth- and thirteenth-century works:

Twelfth century
    Clarenbaldus of Arras, *Tractatulus* on Genesis
    Pseudo-Augustine, *De spiritu et anima*
    Richard of St. Victor, *In Joelem* and *In Apocalypsim*
    Gilbert of Poitiers, *De discretione animae, spiritus et mentis*[44]

Thirteenth century
    Albertus Magnus, *Summa de creaturis*, *Enarrationes in Evangelium Lucae*, and
        Enarrationes in Apocalypsim sancti Joannis
    Thomas of Cantimpré, *De natura rerum*
    Caesarius of Heisterbach, *Dialogus miraculorum*
    Thomas Aquinas, *Summa theologiae*
    Pseudo-Aquinas, *Super Apocalypsim* and *De humanitate Jesu Christi Domini Nostri*
    Hugh of St. Cher (?), *Super Apocalypsim*
    Jean de la Rochelle, *Tractatus de divisione multiplici potentiarum animae* and *Summa*
        de anima
    Vincent of Beauvais, *Speculum naturale*
    Nicolaus de Gorran, *In septem epistolas canonicas*
    Johannis Michaelis, *In Danielem*
    Petrus Johannis Olivi, *Postilla in librum Geneseos*[45]

Augustine's scheme was also widespread in the fourteenth and fifteenth centuries, appearing in such Latin works as William of Vaurouillon's *Liber de anima*, as well as the vernacular *Chastising of God's Children*: again, late-antique dream theory had made its way into fourteenth-century English.[46] Nor did medieval writers limit themselves to replicating Augustine's tripartite treatment of vision. Guillaume de Conches is indebted more specifically to Augustine's classification of veridical dream-types.[47] Thomas Aquinas, in discussing dreams, takes into consideration not only Book XII of the *De Genesi*, but also Augustine's *De cura pro mortuis gerenda*.[48] Ailred of Rievaulx also uses the *De cura* extensively in a discussion that emphasizes, as does Augustine's short treatise, the firmly imaginative character of the dream.[49]

While Macrobius's five-fold dream classification was probably less widely known than either of the two patristic schemes, it nonetheless also enjoyed significant medieval popularity. Macrobius's fame in the Middle

Ages depended, at least in part, on his dream theory. As Stahl notes, Macrobius is distinguished in "many manuscripts" of the *Commentary* by epithets derived from the Greek *oneirokrites* [dream interpreter]; these garbled forms ("Oriniocensis," etc.) are often correctly glossed in the manuscripts as *somniorum iudex* or *interpres*.[50] Although, as Peden points out, Macrobius's fame as a dream interpreter had its vicissitudes – strongest in the twelfth century, it seems to have weakened considerably by the fourteenth[51] – his discussion of dreams finds its way into a great variety of works, some obscure, but some themselves important in shaping late-medieval ideas and attitudes. In the eleventh century, Onulf, in his *Vita Popponis*, referred to Macrobius's five-fold classification.[52] In the twelfth century, several important authors quoted Macrobius's discussion at length: John of Salisbury, in the *Policraticus*; Pascalis Romanus, in the *Liber thesauri occulti*; and pseudo-Augustine, in the *De spiritu et anima*. All three list Macrobius's five kinds of dreams, giving definitions of each clearly drawn from the *Commentary*.[53] In the thirteenth century, Macrobius's scheme continued to exert a strong influence. Raoul de Longchamps, in his commentary on Alain de Lille's *Anticlaudianus*, used the five-part system to structure his own discussion of dreams.[54] Albertus Magnus, in his commentaries on Daniel and Matthew, followed Macrobius in distinguishing between *somnium*, *visio*, and *oraculum*, referring also to Macrobian dream lore in the *De fato*.[55] In his *Philosophia pauperum*, Albert of Orlamunde cites Macrobius at length, as do Thomas de Chobham in the *Summa confessorum*, Vincent of Beauvais in the *Speculum naturale*, Thomas of Cantimpré in the *De natura rerum*, Jean de la Rochelle in the *Summa de anima*, and Johannis Michaelis in the *In Danielem*.[56] Some of these thirteenth-century authors only knew Macrobius at second- or third-hand.[57] While both Raoul and Albertus Magnus (in the commentary on Matthew) cite Macrobius by name, Albert of Orlamunde clearly refers the five-tiered division of dreams to "Augustine," that is, to the Augustinian *De spiritu et anima*. Jean de la Rochelle, Thomas of Cantimpré, and Johannis Michaelis also cite Macrobius by way of the *De spiritu*. And Vincent of Beauvais quotes most directly from Jean de la Rochelle, while attributing Macrobius's ideas to "Hugonem vel Augustinum."[58] Still, Macrobian dream theory was handed down relatively intact, and at least some of the later writers who quote Macrobius were aware that he was the ultimate source of the five-part division of dreaming. Boccaccio, reproducing Macrobius's schema in his *Genealogiae deorum gentilium*, attributes it to its genuine author, as does Guido da Pisa in his *Expositiones et glose super Comediam Dantis*.[59] And William of Vaurouillon, when quoting Macrobius's scheme, refers to both Macrobius and Augustine as authorities.[60]

Calcidius's discussion of dreams seems to have been less frequently cited than Macrobius's. Surely, Calcidius's fame was not linked to his treatment of dreaming in the same way that Macrobius's was. After all, Macrobius presents his whole work as the interpretation of a dream, and his discussion of dreaming is prominently placed near the beginning of the *Commentary*. In contrast, the dream is less central to Calcidius's project, and the dream discussion is tucked away in the middle of his work. And yet, Calcidius's ideas about dreaming did influence medieval writers. In the early twelfth century, Adelard of Bath cited the authority of "Plato" in a brief discussion of the sleeping soul's liberation from the body and its consequent access to truth.[61] Not surprisingly, Guillaume de Conches made use of Calcidian dream lore in his twelfth-century commentary on Plato/Calcidius, as well as in the *De philosophia mundi* and *Dragmaticon*.[62] And Calcidius's discussion influenced Pascalis Romanus, a writer who, though he worked at some remove from the twelfth-century "School of Chartres," apparently had Chartrian connections.[63] Nor is Calcidius's popularity limited to writers of the twelfth-century renaissance. Petrarch, in a letter to Giovanni Andrea, cites Calcidius alongside Macrobius, Aristotle, and Cicero, as an important authority on dreams,[64] and Chaucer's discussion of dreams in the *House of Fame* may be partially indebted to Calcidius.[65] We might expect to discover further citations of Calcidius's dream lore in other, as yet unpublished, works, for example, in twelfth-century (and later) commentaries and glosses on the *Timaeus*. And Guillaume de Conches's unedited commentary on Macrobius might be expected to merge Calcidian and Macrobian dream lore.

Medieval authors, especially from the twelfth century onwards, thus often resorted to late-antique material in composing their own explanations of dream phenomena. Detailed elements from late-antique theory were transmitted to the Middle Ages, and late-antique ways of organizing dream experience – ways of defining the complex relations between the everyday, the divine, and the oneiric – found their way into medieval writings. As suggested in my brief comparison of Chaucer and Prudentius above, the spirit, as well as the letter, of late-antique dream thought influenced the Middle Ages: often, even without identifying particular borrowings from Macrobius, Calcidius, Augustine, or Gregory, we can trace an indebtedness to the late-antique construction of the dream.

It would be wrong to suggest that late-antique dream theory itself was in any way monolithic, that it presented a wholly unified way of looking at dreams. Each theorist had his own distinctive approach. Even the systems of Calcidius and Macrobius cannot be fully correlated, and differences between Christian and Neoplatonic treatments are especially striking. But the various theories also shared a common ground that allowed them, in certain ways, to present a coherent position. Most simply, all these theories depicted dreaming as a complex experience arising from a range of possible causes, and capable of addressing a variety of divergent concerns. The late-antique dream was both potentially transcendent and potentially mundane; it could arise from within the human microcosm or from the macrocosm outside, reflecting present anxieties or predicting future events. And, at least for Christian writers, the dream could play a role in either divine revelation or demonic seduction. Late-antique authorities described dreams in terms of dualities; yet, they did not reduce the dream to a set of black and white oppositions. Certain types of dream, like Macrobius's *somnium* or Gregory's "cogitative" revelation, combine opposed qualities: the dream can be simultaneously fictional and true, or can arise from both internal and external causes. Indeed, in practice, dreaming most often expresses itself as an experience of middleness. In the dilemma of the Christian dreamer, as defined by Gregory and dramatized by Prudentius, we see uncertainty and disorientation: individuals – caught between the different categories elaborated by theory, suspended between equally plausible interpretations of their experience – remain finally unsure of how to pin down the nature of any given dream. Because it leaves the dreamer in a position between clearly defined entities, the dream becomes an important way of exploring "betweenness." Poised between opposed categories of transcendent and immanent, divine and demonic, the dream becomes an instrument for examining the gray areas that bridge the terms of polar opposition.

Doubleness and middleness are central to the dream discussions of Late Antiquity, and they again become essential in medieval treatments. The revival of late-antique approaches resulted most directly from the renewed interest in Neoplatonic texts during the renaissance of the twelfth century.[66] That revival of classical learning was marked by "a renewed and increasingly sophisticated interest in Plato's cosmology": the *Timaeus*, in Calcidius's Latin translation, became "the single most authoritative model of the cosmic order," and works like the commentaries of Calcidius and Macrobius became increasingly important as explanations and elaborations of Platonic thought.[67] Copies and citations of these works proliferated: over one-third of the Calcidius codices listed by Waszink date from the twelfth century, and the greatest interest in Macrobius's dream discussion occurred during this same period.[68]

Along with this revival of classical and late-antique texts came a serious reconsideration of the ideas they expressed. Neoplatonism was the subject of renewed scrutiny, and though such scrutiny entailed no blind acceptance – indeed, it often provoked profound and bitter debate[69] – there was a widespread adoption of certain important Neoplatonic ways of organizing experience.

The depiction of the universe as a hierarchical continuum of "means" connecting opposed extremes gained new vitality in the twelfth century. In Bernardus Silvestris's *Cosmographia*, for instance, the personified hypostases of Timaean cosmology provide an explanation of the mediative process by which the eternal One comes to communicate with the generated, regenerating many:

As Noys [Mind] is forever pregnant of the divine will, she in turn informs Endelechia [the World-Soul] with the images she conceives of the eternal patterns. Endelechia impresses them upon Nature, and Nature imparts to Imarmene [who stands for temporal continuity] what the well being of the universe demands.[70]

The basis of creation is the yoking together of opposed terms by means of intermediaries: "a sacred embrace brought together forces previously in conflict, and ... a new born mean rendered equal forces formerly imbalanced."[71]

The tendency to view universal phenomena thus through a Neoplatonic lens is strongest in the works of "Chartrian" writers like Bernardus, but others also organized experience in terms of oppositions and their mediation. Thus, the Cistercian author of the *De spiritu et anima* presents a hierarchical view of the universe similar to that of Bernardus.[72] And Hugh of St. Victor, while much less enthusiastic about Platonic doctrine than his Chartrian contemporary Guillaume de Conches, nonetheless adopted certain Neoplatonic concepts and structures.[73] Hugh evolved a cosmology more firmly orthodox than Bernardus's, but one still dependent on the Neoplatonic (and Augustinian) idea of a gradual decline from perfect, unitary Being into the fragmented, multiple, and mutable: bridging the gap between the "eternal" and stable, on the one hand, and the "temporal" and mobile, on the other, is an intermediate realm of "perpetual" beings that are now stable ("immutable") but once moved (because created).[74]

Writers of the twelfth century were thus, like their late-antique counterparts, liable to describe the world in terms of a hierarchical continuum made whole by the interposition of proportional "means." And like Macrobius or Calcidius, these writers tended to emphasize the exploration of *middle* regions. They discussed especially those terms, like "Nature," that stand between divine Idea and the material.[75]

Along with this twelfth-century interest in universal "connection" came a deep concern with the articulation of human psychology – with the processes by which the abstractions of an individual's intellect communicate, through an often elaborate hierarchy of internal *potentiae*, with the corporeality of the body and the outside world. Paralleling the twelfth-century multiplication of works about Nature and the universal hierarchy, we find a proliferation of *summae de anima*, works anatomizing psychological function, and thus seeking to explain the interactions between sensuality and intellect.[76] The concept of microcosm and macrocosm became central to such important works as Bernardus's *Cosmographia* and Godefroy of St. Victor's *Microcosmus*.[77] As in Late Antiquity, this concept provided writers with a rationale for drawing parallels between the construction of the human being (from soul and body) and that of the universe (from the informing thought of the Creator and primordial, chaotic matter): "Physis knew that she would not go astray in creating the lesser universe of man if she took as her example the pattern of the greater universe."[78] Twelfth-century authors commonly described the human being as, like the larger cosmos, torn between upper and lower parts; as in descriptions of natural phenomena, however, the opposition of divine and earthly creates no unbridgeable schism. Opposed terms are again connected through intermediaries:

The highest part of the body and the lowest part of the spirit have much in common, which makes it possible for them to be easily joined in a personal union without a confusion of natures... Thus the soul, which is truly a spirit, and the flesh, which is truly a body, easily and fittingly meet at their extremes. The extremes are the imaginative faculty – which is not a body, but similar to a body[79] – and the faculty of sensation in the flesh – which is almost a spirit since it cannot exist without the soul.[80]

The body and soul, of contrary natures... agree and are able to exist together. For through two very apt intermediaries two diverse extremes can be easily and firmly joined; something that is easily seen in the structure of the great animal, as some call it, that is, of this world.[81]

Given the intellectual atmosphere in which they worked, it is not surprising to find twelfth-century writers defining oneiric experience in ways that call to mind the strategies of late-antique dream theory. But these writers did not simply imitate their Neoplatonic and patristic predecessors; rather, they moved to reinterpret them.

The twelfth-century renaissance brought with it a desire to reconcile pagan thought and Christian doctrine. Classical myth was read as allegorically expressive of Christian truths, and classical writers as prefiguring, if darkly, Christian revelation. Augustine himself had recognized the partial truth of Neoplatonism and incorporated aspects of pagan philosophy into his thought.[82] Bolstered by the Christian Neoplatonism of an Augustine or a pseudo-Dionysius, medieval authors often worked to harmonize Christian and classical ideas, in dream theory as elsewhere. Thus, in his eleventh-century *Vita Popponis*, Onulf draws an explicit comparison between Gregory's six-part and Macrobius's five-part classification of dreams, suggesting that the two may properly be viewed as supporting each other:

Sciendumque est, secundum plerosque sex, et secundum plerosque quinque sompniorum modos tantum inveniri. Et sex quidem, ut in divinis paginis legimus, non ab re hic interserimus, quae ventris plenitudine, inanitate, illusione, cogitatione simul et illusione, revelatione, cogitatione simul et revelatione, eveniunt... Qui vero praefatorum distinctiones sompniorum in quinque tantum modos nosse desiderat, Macrobium in sompnium Scipionis legat, dum nichil diversum inter utrumque reperiatur, si intime eorum significatio inspiciatur.[83]

And it should be known that, according to many, there are six kinds of dream, but according to many [others], only five. And truly, we here insert the six as we find [them] in divine pages, [since this is] not impertinent to the matter at hand: those that come about from the fullness of the stomach, from [its] emptiness, from illusion, from thought together with illusion, from revelation, from thought together with revelation... Anyone who truly wishes to investigate the division of the aforesaid dreams into just five types, should read Macrobius on the dream of Scipio, provided that nothing contrary between the two [systems] may be found, if their meaning is closely examined.

In the twelfth century, Pascalis Romanus also emphasized the bringing together of secular and Christian teachings: "Collectus autem est liber iste ex divina et humana scriptura" [This book moreover has been gathered together from divine and human writings]; "secundum divine et humane pagine assertionem" [according to the claim of divine and human pages].[84] John of Salisbury, whose dream theory is most strikingly indebted to Macrobius, in addition includes material drawn from such patristic writers as Augustine and Jerome.[85] The author of the *De spiritu et anima* similarly marries patristic and Macrobian dream lore: he cites Augustine and Macrobius without clearly differentiating the two, and thus gives the impression that Augustine's three kinds of vision, his classification of dream-types, and Macrobius's five kinds of dream all form one integrated system.[86] Somewhat later (*c.* 1215), Thomas de Chobham cites Macrobius, with the comment that "huic ... philosophice opinioni non multum discrepat catholicorum doctorum traditio" [the tradition of the catholic doctors does not differ greatly from this philosophical opinion]; he then quotes Gregory as representing the "traditio ... et opinio catholicorum virorum" [tradition and opinion of catholic men].[87] Just as late-antique authors had been concerned to reevaluate and synthesize previously-existing dream theories, so these medieval writers elaborated synthetic models of dreaming.

Such models take into account not just late-antique Neoplatonic and patristic authorities – though these remain dominant – but also a body of Greek and Arabic texts made newly accessible to the Latin West through translation.[88] Leo Tuscus translated pseudo-Achmet's Byzantine dreambook in the 1170s, thus bringing into the Latin tradition an extensive stock of specific dream interpretations.[89] Gerard of Cremona's Latin version (c. 1167–87) of al-Kindi's Arabic *Liber de somno et visione* brought a new theoretical discussion of dreams – made up of Neoplatonic, Aristotelian, and Galenic material – to the attention of Western Europe.[90] And a dream theorist like Pascalis Romanus was himself an important translator: the *Liber thesauri occulti* (c. 1165) presents material drawn from Artemidorus's *Oneirocritica*, pseudo-Achmet's dreambook, and Greek and Arabic medical works.[91]

Also newly available were more general treatments of body and soul that themselves played an important part in shaping twelfth-century attitudes toward the dream. Translation of Arabic medical writings began in the late eleventh century with the activity of Constantine the African, and during the twelfth century, both Aristotle's *De anima* and Avicenna's Aristotelian psychology became available in Latin.[92] Such works often displayed a very different psychology from that found in Plato and his followers; Aristotle's work, treating the soul as closely allied to body,[93] presented a strong challenge to Plato, as a Neoplatonic writer like Macrobius recognized.[94] And the new medical treatises emphasized somatic process in a way foreign to Neoplatonism.

Still, both Aristotelian psychology and the medical texts were susceptible to a synthesis with Neoplatonic material. They themselves usually presented hierarchical schemes of classification. Aristotle distinguishes "vegetative, sensitive, intellective, and motive powers" of the soul, and moves, in his consideration of the first three, from the more to the less corporeal.[95] Medical writers, too, distinguish a *virtus* or *spiritus* concerned with the most basic of physical processes (*naturalis*); one concerned with higher, mental functions (*animalis*); and an intermediate one involved with both mind and body (*spiritualis*).[96] In their general structure, such models line up with, and reinforce, the Neoplatonic–Augustinian conception of human internal activity as divided between intellectual, spiritual, and corporeal functions.

Dreaming in the Middle Ages

In twelfth-century dream theory, the new medicine and Aristotelian philosophy were indeed often invoked along with Neoplatonic material to explain the bodily involvement in the processes of sleep and dreaming. We perceive, during the twelfth century, a clear "somaticization" of certain aspects of dream theory.[97] Writers who used Macrobius's five-part scheme tended to emphasize more strongly than did Macrobius the lower sorts of dream (*insomnium* and *visum*), and to expand on the relations of such dreams to bodily disorder. Macrobius himself recognized the body's role in generating *insomnia*:

Nightmare may be caused by mental or physical distress, or anxiety about the future ... The physical variety might be illustrated by one who has overindulged in eating or drinking and dreams that he is either choking with food or unburdening himself, or by one who has been suffering from hunger or thirst and dreams that he is craving and searching for food or drink or has found it. (I.iii.4)

But Macrobius presented the *visum* (or *phantasma*) as resulting simply from the "imagination" of spectral forms, without any reference to bodily disturbance. In contrast, Macrobius's twelfth-century followers concentrated attention on the physiology of both *visum* and *insomnium*, particularizing and elaborating the suggestion that dreaming has a somatic component.

Especially reliant on medical authority was Pascalis Romanus, a writer familiar with the medical translations of Constantine and perhaps with certain untranslated works of Galen and Hippocrates.[98] He explained the *visum* as arising "ex capitis infirmitate" [from an infirmity of the head], and suggested that the "ymagines" of such dreams disappeared when the head was purged ("capite purgato").[99] The *ephialtes*, or *incubus*, which Macrobius includes in his discussion of *visum*, provided Pascalis with the occasion for an especially detailed medical discussion:

De incubo autem habet vulgaris opinio quod sit animal parvum ad similitudinem satiri, et sic comprimit dormientes noctu et pene suffocando extingit. Sed secundum rei veritatem, quidam sanguis est in corpore humano, qui non discurrit per venas neque per aliquos certos meatus, sed est in corde vel circa cor. Hic itaque sanguis quando aliquis dormit, jacens super latus sinistrum vel etiam resupinus, quedam habunda[n]tia humorum ad eandem partem decurrit corque suffocat; itaque est proximum sinistro lateri quod non potest aperiri vel claudi. Nam cor, quia sedes est semper spiritus, est in motu naturaliter nec vult impediri. Cum autem cor ita suffocatum est a sanguine et humoribus, quod non potest se libere aperire et claudere nec esse in suo motu naturali, gravantur humores in dormiente, ut putet se totam domum vel aliquam molem sustinere ... Aliquando vero fiunt fantasmata ex cerebri pertubatione [*sic*]. Cum enim jacet resupinus, memorialis pars cerebri opprimitur ab intellectuali et intellectualis a fantastica ... Fit preterea fantasma et accidentaliter nichil predictorum significans, quando cuilibet jacenti stragula, vel aliquod cooperimentum vel etiam sua ipsius vel alterius manus sive bracchium gulam lento modo compresserit et viam spiritus vel sanguinis impedierit. Quod qui aliquociens patitur per noctes, si mox evigilaverit inveneritque pannum vel aliquid super gutur suum, hoc sciat fuisse causam illius fantasmatis, sin autem, in fundamentis nature sanguinis sui, vel cerebri sede patitur, ut predictum est.[100]

But common opinion about the incubus considers that it is a small being in the likeness of a satyr and that it presses sleepers at night in such a way that it almost kills them by suffocation. But according to the truth of the matter, there is a certain blood in the human body that does not run about through the veins nor through any other fixed routes, but is in the heart or around the heart. And when one sleeps lying on the left side or even supine, this blood is so disposed [that] a certain abundance of humors runs down to that same part and chokes the heart; and it [the heart] is so close to the left side that it cannot [then] be opened or closed [i.e., beat]. For the heart, since it is always the seat of the spirit, is naturally in motion nor does it wish to be obstructed. When, however, the heart is so choked by blood and humors that it cannot freely open and close itself nor be in its natural motion, the humors become heavy in the sleeper, so that he thinks that he is holding up a whole house or some other mass ... Sometimes, truly, phantasms occur from a perturbation of the brain. Indeed, when one lies supine, the memorial part of the brain is pressed on by the intellectual [part] and the intellectual by the fantastic ... Further, a phantasm also may occur accidentally, signifying none of the aforesaid things, when the bedclothes or some other covering, or even one's own or another's hand or arm, has pressed lightly on the throat of whoever is lying down and has obstructed the course of the spirit or blood. For whoever suffers [this kind of dream] at different times during the night, if he awakens then and finds a piece of cloth or something else over his throat, should know that this has been the cause of that phantasm; if not, however, he suffers in the fundamental nature of his blood or in the seat of the brain, as has been said above.

Pascalis's treatment of the *insomnium* is similarly indebted to medical material. He argues that this kind of dream can originate in the liver ("ab epate") and reflect a variety of constitutional disturbances: "Nam insompnia fiunt et ab interioribus, scilicet ab humoribus et ab imminentibus infirmitatibus, et a cibariis incongruis vel desideratis et necessariis nature, ut sapienti phisico non est occultum" [For *insomnia* also come from interior things, namely from the humors and from impending infirmities and from incompatible foods or from things desired and the necessities of nature – as is not hidden from the wise physician].[101]

Pascalis displays unusual medical erudition, but other twelfth-century dream theorists also appealed to the physicians, if in more limited ways. The author of the *De spiritu et anima* suggests that the *ephialtes* results from "a certain gaseousness which rises to the brain from the stomach or the heart and there oppresses the animal powers."[102] In discussing the genesis of the *insomnium*, he expands the causative role granted by Macrobius to somatic process:

According to one's different infirmities, different dreams can take shape. Dreams also vary according to the diversity of one's customs and humors. For example, the sanguine have certain dreams which differ from those of the choleric; phlegmatics and melancholics have still other dreams. The sanguine and the choleric see red and mottled dreams, while phlegmatics and melancholics dream in shades of black and white.[103]

The association of unreliable dreams with the humors has a long history in Greek and Arabic works. Introduced into Latin in the twelfth century in such texts as Algazel's *Metaphysics* and Gerard of Cremona's translations of Avicenna (*Liber canonis*) and Rasis (*Liber ad Almansorem*), it quickly became a commonplace of European dream theory.[104]

In the twelfth century, even reliable dreams came to be associated in certain ways with physiological process. Dreams experienced in the morning were often depicted as those most likely to be true, since they occurred after the completion of digestive processes thought to distort the clarity of dream images. As Adelard of Bath suggests:

In somnis anima, quia quodammodo tunc liberior est a uexatione sensuum, aciem stringit et de futuris etiam aut uerum aut uerisimile quandoque deprehendit et sub aurora minus fallitur, utpote iam digestis cibis expeditior. Adeo hi ibi dominantur, uerum suffocant.

The soul, in sleep, since it is then in a certain way freer from the harassment of the senses, draws together its insight and sometimes seizes upon truth or probability even concerning future things. And it is less deceived at dawn, inasmuch as [it is] then more unimpeded, since [any] food has been digested. For so long as food remains in control there, it chokes the truth.[105]

This association of dreams and digestion, like that of dreaming and the humors, had sources in newly available scientific works like those of Avicenna,[106] and it became extremely widespread in later dream theory, making its way even into such a vernacular work as Dante's *Divine Comedy*.[107]

The twelfth-century emphasis on the somatic component of dreaming appears in writers as diverse as Guillaume de Conches and Hildegard of Bingen.[108] In the fourth century, Macrobius had summed up the value of lower dreams disparagingly: "The two types just described are of no assistance in foretelling the future" (I.iii.8). In the twelfth century, the disparagement of such dreams took on a peculiarly medical ring: "All these types are in need of the doctor rather than of our verbal treatment, especially as the only reality that is apparent in them is the fact that they are very real but very disagreeable forms of mental ill health."[109]

While medieval dream theorists thus focused attention on the somatic, they did not upset the essential balance between divine and mundane, corporeal and incorporeal, inherited from Late Antiquity. Even a medically-sophisticated writer like Pascalis Romanus did not emphasize the body's role in the etiology of dreaming to the exclusion of other factors. In Pascalis's adoption of Macrobian lore, we must recognize not only the strong emphasis on lower, somatic dreams, but also a firm belief in higher revelation. A major portion of Pascalis's treatise is, after all, a dreambook, claiming to show how specific dreams reliably predict future events. When he discusses *somnium*, *visio*, and *oraculum*, Pascalis adheres closely to the letter of Macrobius's exposition, and when he does elaborate on Macrobius, as in the following treatment of the *oraculum*, he shows himself quite willing to attribute dreams to higher causes:

Cum enim divinus spiritus conjungit se humano spiritui, quia anima in se spiritus est, impellit et impingit ad hoc ut ymaginentur tales personas apparentes eis et dicentes aliquid esse cavendum vel non.[110]

Truly, when a divine spirit joins itself to a human spirit (since the soul in itself is a spirit), [that divine spirit] impels and drives [dreamers] to a point where they may imagine such [oracular] persons appearing to them and announcing that something either should or should not be guarded against.

Like his late-antique predecessors, Pascalis balances the mundane and the transcendent. He perhaps expresses this balance most strongly simply by adhering to Macrobius's scheme, but he expresses it in other ways as well. Throughout the *Liber*, Pascalis emphasizes the dream's connections to soul as well as body. Sleep quiets bodily process and allows the soul a freedom of movement that may result in reliable, predictive dreams:

Est enim ratio nostra radius quidam divine mentis; sed per molem corporis occupata, vim suam excercere non potest; per dormitionem vero, sopitis sensibus etiam curis omnibus exterioribus exerciciisque depositis, libere veritatem rei contemplatur.[111]

Truly, our reason is a certain ray of the divine Mind; however, when it is occupied with the mass of the body, it cannot exercise its own power. But indeed, in sleep, when the senses have been lulled and all external cares and occupations put aside, it freely contemplates the truth of a matter.

Though Pascalis's "prohemium" (I.1–2, pp. 141–47) begins with Aristotelian and medical lore (pp. 141–44), it ends by asserting the reality of divinely-inspired dreams:

Sompniorum usus et cognitio maxime oraculorum vehemens ac aperta demonstratio est contra eos qui dubitant de angelis, de animabus sanctis utrum sint vel non. Si enim non essent, quomodo eorum oracula vera essent? Nam cuicumque anima sancta vel angelus aliquid in sompn[i]o dixerit absque omni interpretatione et scrupulo, ita fiet ut predixit angelus vel anima.[112]

The experience of dreams and most of all the knowledge of *oracula* provide a powerful and clear demonstration against those who have doubts concerning the existence of angels and blessed souls. Truly, if these did not exist, in what way could oracular visions of them be true? For if a blessed soul or angel has made a statement to one in a dream that does not need interpretation and that contains no doubt, things will turn out for that one just as the angel or soul has forecast.

Furthermore, just prior to presenting Macrobius's classification of dream-types, Pascalis, following "Plato" (i.e., Calcidius), suggests that "ymaginatio ... sompniorum" [the imagination of dreams] "tribus de causis evenit" [comes about from three causes]:

1. aut ... per recordationem quandam exterorum circa que sensus vigilantis exercebantur
2. aut per angelicam revelationem
3. aut quoniam ratio nostra avida futurorum, sopitis sensibus, libera, divine memor originis, tu[n]c melius futura recognoscit.[113]

1. either through a certain recollection of those external things concerning which one's senses were exercised when awake
2. or through angelic revelation
3. or, since our reason longs for future things, when the senses are sleep-lulled, it [reason], free and mindful of its divine origin, then better recognizes future things.

The first kind of dream, arising out of the remnants of sensory process, is confined to a human realm; the second derives from the divine; and the third falls somewhere in between, at a point where humanity and divinity interact. In following both Macrobius and Calcidius, Pascalis chooses, like them, to depict the realm of dreams as a hierarchy composed of extreme and mediate terms.

Over and over in twelfth-century dream theory, we encounter descriptions of dreaming based on oppositions and their mediation. The

"Chartrian" writer Guillaume de Conches, in his commentary on Plato, divides dreams into two clearly opposed camps based on their place of origin: "Somniorum igitur quedam cause sunt interiores, quedam exteriores" [Therefore, certain causes of dreams are interior and certain exterior].[114] Correlated with this first division is a further opposition between the meaningful and the meaningless: "hec somnia (ea quorum causa est interior) nichil significant. Sed ea quorum causa est exterior aliquid significant" [these (interior) dreams signify nothing. But those of which the cause is exterior signify something].[115] Similar oppositions characterize the presentation of dreaming in the Cistercian *De spiritu et anima*: "the soul ... proceeds on its own either to produce likenesses of corporeal things ... or to consider the objects which are offered to it by some spirit or other"; "sleeping persons often see things which may have much meaning or none at all."[116] And John of Salisbury likewise emphasizes the dream's doubleness:

This matter of truth and error did not escape the notice of him [Virgil] who, depicting the gates of sleep, imagined one to be of ivory and the other of horn, since horn is penetrable for vision, which rarely errs, while ivory is of an opaque nature and even when worked down to a thin veneer is not transparent. Ivory is more like the teeth, horn more like the eyes. By the one gate true, by the other false "Dreams the Manes send to heaven."[117]

Twelfth-century theorists thus admitted both internal and external, meaningless and meaningful dreams. Furthermore, they recognized that dreams may arise from either malevolent or benevolent causes, transmitted, as in Gregory, Augustine, and Tertullian, by both devils and angels. Even writers chiefly indebted to Macrobius incorporate into their discussions the morally-charged opposition of the demonic and angelic. Thus, both John of Salisbury and the author of the *De spiritu* recognize "good" and "evil spirits" as causative agents.[118] For writers more explicitly concerned with religious questions and more fully dependent on patristic sources, the dream's positioning on a scale of good and evil was even more crucial. Those authors who reproduced Gregory's six-part classification necessarily depicted dreams as torn between demonic *illusio* and divine *revelatio*. And Honorius of Autun, in the immensely popular *Elucidarium*, presents a tripartite division of dream-types reminiscent of Tertullian:

D[iscipulus] – Unde veniunt somnia?
M[agister] – Aliquando a Deo, cum aliquid futuri revelatur, sicut Joseph per stellas et manipulos quod fratribus suis praeferretur, aut aliquid necessarium admonetur, ut alius Joseph, ut fugeret in Aegyptum. Aliquando a diabolo, cum aliquid turpe videtur aut bonum impedire nititur, ut in passione Domini de uxore Pilati

legitur.[119] Aliquando ab ipso homine, cum, quod viderit vel audierit vel cogitaverit, hoc in somnis imaginatur et in timore positus per tristia, in spe per laeta ludificatur.[120]

Student: Where do dreams come from?
Teacher: Sometimes from God: when something of the future is revealed, just as [it was revealed to] Joseph through the stars and sheaves that he would be preferred to his brothers; or [when] something necessary is urged, as that other Joseph [was urged to] flee to Egypt. Sometimes from the devil: when something seems shameful or strives to impede the good, as we read concerning the wife of Pilate in [the account of] the Lord's passion. Sometimes from the man himself: when he imagines in his sleep that which he may have seen or heard or thought [when awake] and [thus] deludes [himself], made fearful by sad things and hopeful by happy ones.

Hildegard of Bingen similarly assigns both the devil and the grace of God important roles in the formation of dreams; indeed, she structures her whole dream discussion around the opposition of the divine and demonic.[121]

Hildegard, however, goes further than most of her late-antique predecessors in assigning moral significance to dreams. In what might be read as an extended explanation of Gregory's suggestion that dreams arise "cogitatione simul et reuelatione" [by our thoughts combined with revelations] and "cogitatione simul et inlusione" [by our thoughts combined with illusions], she correlates the individual dreamer's internal, moral state quite directly with the quality of her or his dreams. God and the devil evaluate the moral fitness of prospective dreamers' *cogitationes* in the process of deciding who will receive dreams:

Nam multotiens cogitationibus et opinionibus atque voluntatibus, quibus homo vigilans occupatur, his etiam et in somnis gravatur, et in eis interdum ita elevatur ut fermentum, quod massam farinae elevat, sive cogitationes illae bonae sive malae sint. Quod si bonae et sanctae sunt, gratia dei illi saepe vera in eis ostendit; si autem vanae sunt, diabolus hoc videns animam hominis illius multotiens tunc terret et mendacia sua cogitationibus illis intermiscet.[122]

For often a man is also oppressed in [his] sleep by those thoughts and opinions and desires by which he, when awake, is occupied, and sometimes in [sleep] he is lifted up as yeast, which lifts up a lump of flour, [depending on] whether those thoughts are good or bad [i.e., he is "lifted up" by good thoughts and "oppressed" by bad ones]. Now, if they are good and holy, the grace of God often shows true things to that man in [his sleep]; if, however, they are idle, the devil, seeing this, then [during sleep] often terrifies that man's soul and mixes in with those thoughts his own lies.

In Hildegard, the correlation between the morality of thoughts and the demonic or divine quality of the resulting dreams is very strong:

76

Cum enim homo aut inepta laetitia aut tristitia aut ira aut angustiis aut ambitione dominandi aut aliis huiusmodi causis in animo occupatus obdormit, hoc ei diabolus illusione sua multotiens in somnis proponit, quoniam cum vigilaret, ea in ipso vidit. Sed et cum in delectatione carnis interdum obdormit, hanc ei etiam et diabolica illusio interdum obicit, ita quod viventium corpora ei ostendit et etiam aliquando corpora mortuorum, cum quibus aliquando familiaritatem habuit vel quos etiam numquam corporalibus oculis vidit, ita quod sibi videtur, quod cum eis hoc modo in peccatis et in pollutionibus delectatur, quasi vigilet vel quasi illi etiam, qui defuncti sunt, vivunt; ita quod etiam turpia in semine suo sibi accidunt.[123]

Truly, when a man falls asleep, occupied in his soul by either an unsuitable happiness or sadness or anger or by hardships or an ambition to rule or other motives of this sort, the devil, through his illusion, often displays this [preoccupation] to [the man] in his sleep, since, when he was awake, he saw those things in himself. Also, when sometimes he falls asleep in delight of the flesh, diabolic illusion will also sometimes produce this [delight] in him [when he sleeps], in such a way that it shows to him the bodies of the living and even sometimes the bodies of the dead, with whom [the dreamer] has sometimes had familiarity or whom he truly never saw with corporeal eyes. [This happens] in such a way that it seems to him that he takes delight with them [the imagined bodies] in sins and pollutions, as though he were awake and as though even those who are dead are alive; [and this happens] in such a way that foul things also occur to him in [regard to] his semen.

Isti terrores facile omnibus hominibus accidunt, cum dormiunt, exceptis illis, qui valde securae et valde laetae naturae [sunt]. Et his dormientibus terrores isti raro eveniunt, quia magna et honesta laetitia, quam habent naturaliter in se, non potest esse absque gustu boni spiritus, et ipsi etiam ex natura sua mansueti sunt et non fallaces nec dolosi in moribus suis.[124]

Those terrors occur easily to all men when they sleep, except to those who [are] of a very tranquil and happy nature. And to them these terrors rarely happen when they sleep because the great and proper happiness that they naturally have in themselves cannot exist without [their having] tasted [i.e., come into contact with] a good spirit, and in addition they themselves are, of their own nature, mild and not deceitful nor crafty in their conduct.

Though writers like Augustine were careful not to identify individual morality too closely with the nature of dreams, such an association is at least implied in certain late-antique works, including Calcidius's *Commentary* and Synesius's *De insomniis* (see chapter 2, above). In addition, works newly available in the twelfth century, and perhaps known to Hildegard, emphasized that temperate living and well-ordered physiology lead to undistorted and reliable dreams.[125] Indeed, various twelfth-century writers, like Hildegard, connected the moral quality of one's life to the truth or falsehood of one's dreams. Richard of St. Victor correlated the reliability of dreams to the soul's cleanliness,[126] and Alain de Lille linked untrustworthy dreams to foolish behavior: "dum rationis circumspectio minus provide mentis januam servat, diabolus callide ad interficiendam animam per hoc ostium intrat" [when the circumspection of reason less prudently guards the entrance of the mind, the devil shrewdly comes in through this door to slay the soul].[127] As John of Salisbury suggests: "The light of truth shines out more frequently in the case of certain personalities inasmuch as they possess well-ordered minds; others are more prone to be led astray."[128]

Twelfth-century writers, like their late-antique forerunners, thus associated dreams with a variety of opposed terms: truth and falsehood, internality and externality, demonic and divine agents, moral probity and perversity. But, as also in late-antique thought, none of these oppositions was allowed to stand without qualification, without the suggestion that there existed mediate kinds of dream. Guillaume de Conches, in his *Glosae super Platonem*, differentiates two kinds of interior, insignificant dream – "Interiorum alia ex anima, alia ex corpore" [Of interior (dreams), some (are) from the soul, some from the body] – intending dreams of the soul to be seen as the higher of the two.[129] He also subdivides exterior, significant dreams: "aliquando Deus aliquid ita ut futurum est manifestat, aliquando introducit personam in somnis alloquentem, aliquando per simile vel per contrarium quod futurum est insinuat" [sometimes God manifests something just as it is to be, sometimes He introduces a person speaking in (one's) sleep, sometimes he insinuates, either by simile or by contrary, what is to be].[130] Guillaume's distinction here comes from Augustine's differentiation of the kinds of revelatory dream,[131] and as in Augustine, the three sub-types correspond closely to Macrobius's *visio*, *oraculum*, and *somnium*. Guillaume describes the three in terms of their degree of clarity and transcendence: moving from one to the next, revelation becomes progressively more indirect. God acts in less and less immediate ways – at first "manifesting" the future directly, then "introducing" an intermediary to do His talking for Him, and finally only "insinuating" the truth "per simile" or, even less directly, "per contrarium." Ultimately, then, Guillaume elaborates a fully-fledged hierarchical description of dreaming:

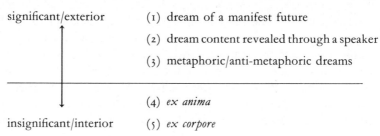

significant/exterior (1) dream of a manifest future

(2) dream content revealed through a speaker

(3) metaphoric/anti-metaphoric dreams

(4) *ex anima*

insignificant/interior (5) *ex corpore*

Similarly, John of Salisbury and the author of the *De spiritu*, in adopting Macrobius's classification, commit themselves to dream hierarchies, and each emphasizes, in his own way, the middle quality of dreaming. John makes explicit the intermediate character of Macrobius's *somnium*, which he suggests is, due to its mixed character, the most common kind of dream: "As the first two classes of dreams are absolutely without significance and the last two present truth to the understanding as it were in visible form, He [God] generally employs the intermediate class, which stretches before the body of truth a curtain, as it were, of allegory."[132] In the *De spiritu*, the author follows Augustine to establish firmly the dream's position between the bodiless and the embodied: he insists on the imaginative nature of dreaming[133] and on the intermediate nature of imagination – "At its highest point the imagination is a corporeal spirit, and at its lowest something rational which informs bodily nature and is in contact with rational nature."[134]

Even when not dependent on a previously proposed system of dream classification like that of Macrobius, twelfth-century writers tended to describe dreams in terms of hierarchy, emphasizing their middleness. Ailred of Rievaulx, in his *De anima*, sets up a dream hierarchy whose members, one mediate and two extreme, correspond roughly to the eschatological realms of heaven, hell, and purgatory: "Diximus, adverte, visionibus alios erudiri, alios etiam falli et erroribus implicari, alios purgari" [Take note: we say that some are instructed by visions, but that others are deceived and entangled in errors (by them), (and that still) others are purged (by them)].[135] In a discussion indebted to Augustine's *De cura pro mortuis gerenda*, Ailred consistently stresses the dream's imaginative status – its position between body and mind, true and false.[136]

Richard of St. Victor, in his commentary on Joel, and Alain de Lille, in his *Summa de arte praedicatoria*, recognize a similar range of dream-types. Having first presented Augustine's "tria genera visionum" [three kinds of vision], Richard proceeds, in a series of triplets, to define "tria genera somniorum" [three kinds of dream]:

Tria sunt quoque genera somniorum: unum faeculenti animi, alterum sobrii, tertium defaecati. Primum genus falsitati servit; secundum alterutri aut veritati aut falsitati famulatur; tertium veritatem contemplatur. Et ut aliquid de secretis physicae interseram, primum genus est ante digestionem realium phantasmatum, secundum in digestione eorum, tertium post digestionem ipsorum. In primo genere anima obruitur phantasmatum mole: inde falsitatis error. In secundo, quia anima incipit defaecari, aliquid lucis incipit contemplari; quia tamen ex parte maxima manet faeculenta, cito cedit decepta falsitati. In tertio eliquatur ad purum onus faeculentorum phantasmatum: inde veritatis splendor. Est igitur primum genus somnii deceptorium, secundum revelatorium, tertium contemplatorium.[137]

There also are three kinds of dream: one of the impure soul, a second of the moderate [soul], a third of the cleansed [soul]. The first kind [of dream] is subject to falsity; the second serves either truth or falsity; the third contemplates truth. And that I may [here] insert something from the secrets of natural science: the first kind [of dream] occurs before the digestion of real apparitions, the second during their digestion, the third after the digestion of those same things. In the first kind, the soul is buried under a mass of apparitions: thence the error of falsity. In the second, since the soul begins to be cleansed, it begins to contemplate something of the light; nevertheless, since it remains impure in its greatest part, it quickly submits, deceived, to falsity. In the third, the burden of polluting apparitions is melted away to purity: thence the splendor of truth. Therefore, the first kind of dream pertains to those who deceive, the second to those who reveal, the third to those who contemplate.

The discussion here simultaneously emphasizes the gaps in the realm of dreaming – between true and false, pure and impure – and the terms that bridge those gaps. Richard's middle dream, glimpsing some light in the midst of darkness, stands decidedly as a "mean" between two extremes.

Alain, also partly dependent on Augustine, likewise presents the dream in a tripartite pattern:

Sunt autem tres species somnii. Primum et praecipuum est contemplationis, per quod rapitur homo ad videndum coelestia. Secundum est, imaginationis, per quod imaginatur visibilia. Tertium autem est, pigritiae, per quod somniat stulta ... Per primum somnum fit homo deus, per secundum fit homo spiritus, per tertium fit pecus. In primo apparet Deus, in secundo spiritus, in tertio diabolus.[138]

There are, moreover, three kinds of dream. The first and [most] excellent is [the dream] of contemplation, through which a man is ravished to the sight of celestial things. The second is [that] of imagination, through which he imagines visible things. The third, moreover, is [that] of sloth, through which he dreams foolish things ... Through the first [kind of] sleep, a man becomes a god; through the second, a man becomes a spirit; through the third, he becomes a beast. In the first, God appears; in the second, a spirit; in the third, a devil.

Here, Alain defines the dream in its relation to epistemological modes (*contemplatio, imaginatio, pigritia*), ontology (*deus, spiritus, pecus*), and the moral forces operative in the universe (*Deus, spiritus, diabolus*). In each case, the range of dreams corresponds to the whole gamut of possibilities – to higher, lower, and middle moral agents, beings, and ways of knowing. Alain suggests, moreover, that the *middle* dream, in its middleness, is the quintessentially *human* dream: "Primus somnus fit supra hominem; secundus secundum hominem; tertius infra hominem" [The first (kind of) sleep comes into existence above man, the second in accordance with man, the third below man].[139] Both higher and lower dreams arise anomalously.

The higher dream is "miraculosus," resulting from a rapturous contemplative state in which the dreamer rises above the self: "Est somnus, quando quis rapitur ad contemplationem coelestium, et tunc quiescunt naturales vires; de quo dicitur: *Misit Dominus soporem in Adam* (*Gen.* ii)" [There is a (kind of) sleep during which one is ravished to the contemplation of celestial things, and then the natural forces (of the body) are at rest, concerning which it is said: *The Lord God cast a deep sleep upon Adam* (Genesis 2:21)].[140] Inversely, the lower dream is "monstruosus," a descent below rational humanness: "Tertius somnus est quando dormit ratio, et sensualitas exorbitat" [The third (kind of) sleep is when reason sleeps and sensuality runs rampant].[141] But the middle dream results from normal human process. It occurs in sleep "quando quiescunt animales virtutes, et operantur naturales" [when the animal powers are at rest and the natural (powers) at work];[142] here, Alain reproduces the most common medieval definition of normal sleep. The middle dream, neither "monstruosus" nor "miraculosus," is instead "imaginarius";[143] it arises within a common, and intermediate, faculty of the human soul.

The human being – for the twelfth century, as for Late Antiquity – was the microcosm of a universe that stretched from a perfect God to fragmented matter. Like that universe, humanity was torn between its upper and lower nature, but simultaneously joined those two natures in a single, middle being.

Twelfth-century psychology highlighted the conflict of oppositions and the moderation of that conflict within the human being. As a writer like Gilbert of Poitiers makes strikingly clear, the human psyche contains both the means and extremes of a hierarchical order. Gilbert, in his *De discretione animae, spiritus et mentis*, distinguishes three, interrelated psychic powers – *anima*, *spiritus*, *mens* – the presence or absence of which defines a living being's status in the overall hierarchy of Being. The lowest "brute animals" possess only *anima*, while God, the highest being, is pure mind: "In Deo . . . mens sola est absque omni animae et spiritus admixtione" [In God . . . there is mind alone without any admixture of soul or spirit] (p. 187).[144] Intermediate creatures find their place between these two extremes. Some lower animals are gifted with both *anima* and *spiritus*, though they lack mind; and angels combine spirit and mind, but lack *anima*. At the very center of this ontological scheme stands the human being, the only creature composed of *mens*, *spiritus*, and *anima* all together: "In solo . . . homine talis occurrit conexio" [In man alone does such a joining occur] (p. 188). The extreme terms, *mens* and *anima*, are connected only in human beings, their connection made possible by the mediative action of *spiritus*:

Non etiam, ut anima et spiritus alicubi absque mente, et mens et spiritus alicubi forsitan absque anima reperiuntur, sic anima et mens alicubi absque spiritu reperiri possunt. Spiritus enim, utpote utrique illarum affinis, utrique potest uniri per se.

Illae vero, a se distantes longius, sibi ad unionem nisi spiritu mediante non consentiunt. Proinde spiritus eas conectens et in confoederationem unam compagemque adducens non incongrue quasi quoddam ipsarum dici potest vinculum. (p. 188)

In addition, soul and mind cannot be found anywhere without spirit, as soul and spirit in some places [are found] without mind, and mind and spirit in some places are perhaps found without soul. Truly, spirit, seeing that [it is] contiguous to each of the others, can in itself be united to each.

But those others [soul and mind], standing further apart from each other, do not agree to a union with each other unless spirit mediates. Consequently, the spirit that connects them and draws them into one confederation and connection can, not inappropriately, be called as it were a certain bond between them.

For Gilbert, humanness itself consists of doubleness and middleness, opposed terms held together by a kind of "spiritual" glue.

It is such a double and middle human being who dreams; consequently, the dream itself is most often characterized by both opposition and mediation. In Gilbert (as in Augustine), the middle realm of *spiritus* is also the realm of dreams:

Ad spiritum itaque pertinent quaecumque in somniis sic agimus vel patimur quasi corporaliter ea ageremus aut pateremur et quaecumque nobis ibi ita occurrunt velut ab exteriori carnis occurrerent sensui. (p. 185)

Thus, [all these things] pertain to the spirit: whatever we do or experience in dreams as though we were doing or experiencing them corporeally, and whatever things occur to us there [in dreams] as though they were occurring to our senses from the exterior of the flesh.

The dream stands, for Gilbert and for most of his contemporaries, in a quintessentially human position: between brute animals on the one hand, and God and the angels on the other; between the mundane and divine, body and idea, deception and truth.

5

Aristotle and the late-medieval dream

In the late twelfth century, Thomas of Froidmont warned strongly against a belief in dreams:

Somnia similia sunt auguriis, et qui ea observant, augurari noscuntur.[1] Ergo somniis fides non est adhibenda, quamvis videantur esse vera. Qui in somniis vel auguriis spem suam ponit, non confidit in Deo; et talis est qualis ille qui ventum sequitur, aut umbram apprehendere nititur.[2] Auguria mendacia, et somnia deceptoria, utraque vana sunt.[3] Non debemus credere somniis, ne forte decipiamur in illis. Spes nostra in Deo semper sit firma, et de somniis nulla nobis sit cura. Dignum valde est ut in Deo ponamus spem nostram, et in somniis nullam habeamus fiduciam. Ideo, soror charissima, te moneo, ut mens tua non sit in somniis vel auguriis intenta, sed in Deo omnipotenti sit firma. Si enim auguria vel somnia observaveris, cito decipieris. In omni vita tua contemne auguria et somnia, et pone spem tuam perfecte in Dei providentia; et in hac vita et in futura venient tibi prospera.[4]

Dreams are similar to auguries, and those who observe them are known as participating in augury. Therefore, faith is not to be had in dreams, however much they may seem to be true. The one who places his hope in dreams or auguries, does not have complete faith in God, and such a person is like one who follows after the wind, or tries to catch a shadow. Lying auguries and deceitful dreams are both vain. We ought not to believe in dreams, lest perchance we be deceived in them. Let our hope always be firm in God, and let us care not at all about dreams. It is most proper that we place our hope in God and have no confidence in dreams. I admonish you, most dear sister, to this end: that your mind be not intent on dreams or auguries, but rather firm in almighty God. Truly, if you observe auguries or dreams, you will quickly be deceived. In all your life, disdain auguries and dreams, and place your hope perfectly in the providence of God; and in both this and the future life favorable things will come to you.

Echoing biblical injunctions against divination, Thomas here drives home, with his insistent repetitions, the dangers of dreaming. The dream may promise truth, but it is nonetheless like wind and shadow, "deceptorium" and "vanum"; it threatens to lead us away from God, the rightful object of our attention.

However, while Thomas stresses oneiric deception, he also presents the whole of Gregory the Great's six-part classification of dreams, including *revelatio*,[5] and explicitly concedes that "quaedam vera somnia sunt" [there are certain true dreams].[6] As in Gregory, doubts about the dream do not arise out of a conviction of its complete worthlessness. Certain dreams are true and useful; still, because of the variety of possible dream-types and the difficulty of differentiating them from each other, the individual dreamer must be wary.

Other followers of Gregory writing in the twelfth, thirteenth, and fourteenth centuries cautioned against an unexamined belief in dreams; recognizing the difficulty of distinguishing divine and demonic visions, they emphasized the dream's danger.[7] But no one in the Gregorian tradition denied that some dreams were valuable, reliable, and divine; none of these writers called into question the basic balance between true and false, good and bad, dreams.

Certain intellectual changes in the thirteenth and fourteenth centuries did, however, begin to challenge traditional views of the dream's double and middle nature. By the beginning of the thirteenth century, Aristotle's *De somno et vigilia*, *De somniis*, and *De divinatione per somnum* had been (anonymously) translated into Latin.[8] During the thirteenth century, William of Moerbeke revised that translation (*c.* 1260–70),[9] and a Latin version of Averroes's epitome of the *Parva naturalia*, perhaps by Michael Scot, appeared (*c.* 1220–35).[10] Aristotle's treatises quickly became important authorities: in the two centuries after their Latin recension they received extensive formal commentary,[11] and provided late-medieval encyclopedists with a most important source of dream lore.

These Aristotelian works reinforced the growing tendency to associate dreams with somatic and psychological process. More radically, they reintroduced into European discourse the possibility that dreams are never divine in origin. To Aristotle "it is absurd to combine the idea that the sender of such [divinatory] dreams should be God with the fact that those to whom he sends them are not the best and wisest, but merely commonplace persons" (462b),[12] and he suggests that "most [so-called prophetic] dreams are ... to be classed as mere coincidences" (463a). While admitting that some dreams are "tokens" or "causes" of future events, he claims that such dreams "signify" or "cause" by means of natural physiological or psychological process. Thus, dreams may signal an incipient disease because the "beginnings" of bodily illness, too "small" to be observed "in waking moments," become "evident in sleeping," when "even trifling movements seem considerable" (463a). And just as waking thoughts and actions influence dreams, so dreams affect human psychology and can cause the dreamer, when awake, to behave in certain predictable ways: "it must happen that the movements set up first in sleep should also prove to be starting-points of actions to be performed in the daytime, since the recurrence by day of the thought of these actions also has had its way paved for it in the images before the mind at night" (463a). For Aristotle, physical process explains even the most extraordinary dreams – those in which "the persons who see the dream hold not in their own hands the beginnings [of the event to which it points]" (464a):

As, when something has caused motion in water or air, this [the portion moved] moves another [portion of water or air], and, though the cause has ceased to operate, such motion propagates itself to a certain point, though there the prime movent is not present; just so it may well be that a movement and a consequent sense-perception should reach sleeping souls... [These movements] shall be perceived within the body owing to sleep, since persons are more sensitive even to slight sensory movements when asleep than when awake. It is these movements then that cause 'presentations', as a result of which sleepers foresee the future.

(464a)

Aristotle's emphasis on the physics and physiology of dreaming, his tenacity in presenting natural explanations of divinatory phenomena, his confinement of the dream to a mundane realm – all influenced in important ways late-medieval treatments of dreaming. Indeed, recent scholars have suggested that thirteenth-century considerations of the dream, as they became increasingly involved in Aristotelian thought, departed significantly from late-antique and earlier medieval dream theory. Thus, while Peden proposes that the new learning of the *twelfth* century stimulated interest in already familiar theories of the dream like that of Macrobius, she suggests that the continued elaboration of that learning led ultimately to a reassessment and rejection of such older theories:

By the xiii century, Macrobius' *Commentary* was not ... the familiar source it had once been: the prevailing dream theory in the Schools was Aristotelian, and tended to emphasize the physiological origin and consequent non-significance of dreams.[13]

C. H. L. Bodenham similarly sees a decline in Macrobius's importance as a dream authority. He suggests that "for most audiences in mid-xiii-century France, Macrobius was little more than a name," and he proposes that, in order to understand the dream theory underlying a work like the *Roman de la rose*, we need to take into account "the new learning derived from Aristotle and more particularly from the medical teaching of an Avicenna schooled in the Aristotelian view of things."[14]

Dreaming in the Middle Ages

Peden and Bodenham rightly focus attention on the importance of Aristotelian dream theory. Others have too often overemphasized the influence of Macrobius,[15] and consequently have not adequately attended to the ways in which medieval dream theory *changed*. Still, one must challenge the implication in Bodenham and Peden that Aristotelian approaches to the dream *drove out* theories like that of Macrobius.

Some medieval authors do present a relatively pure Aristotelian dream theory, defining the dream almost wholly as a physical and psychological phenomenon. The Danish philosopher Boethius of Dacia (active *c.* 1270) pays almost no attention to divine dreams, though he is careful not "to deny that by divine will an angel or a devil can in truth appear to a person who is sleeping or to one who is ill."[16] Following Aristotle closely in recognizing three kinds of predictive dream – those that are true "signs" of future events; those that help "cause" them; and those that are related merely coincidentally to the future – Boethius expends most of his energy exploring the natural processes by which dreams may "signify" or "cause." As Gianfranco Fioravanti suggests, Boethius argues "that the knowledge of the future that one has by means of dreams ... is based on the natural order of causes and effects" [che la conoscenza del futuro che si ha mediante i sogni ... si fonda sull'ordine naturale delle cause e degli effetti]: Boethius displays a "rigorous ... loyalty to the methods of 'natural science'" [rigorosa ... fedeltà ai metodi nella 'scientia naturalis'].[17]

A writer like Adam of Buckfield, in his commentary on the *De somno, De somniis*, and *De divinatione per somnum*,[18] also follows Aristotle closely. He elaborates Aristotelian ideas largely without challenging them, not hesitating even when it comes to the denial of divine dreams:

Hujusmodi somnia fiunt in aliis animalibus, ergo non sunt missa a deo, nec fiunt per gratiam divinam ... homines mali et infimi somniant et praevident futura per somnia: sed talibus non immittit deus aliquam gratiam sive cognitionem: ergo solum a casu, et non per immissionem divinam, sic somniant ... infert conclusionem, quod, quia hujusmodi somnia sic fiunt per influxiones idolorum et non per immissionem divinam, ideo eveniunt indifferenter etiam fatuis et imprudentibus.[19]

Dreams of this sort occur in other animals [than man]; therefore, they are not sent by God nor do they occur through divine grace ... Evil men and the most inferior dream and foresee future things through dreams. But to such [men] God does not send any grace or knowledge. Therefore, they dream thus only by chance, and not through a divine sending ... He [Aristotle] infers this conclusion: that, since dreams of this sort thus occur through influxes of images and not through a divine sending, they come about indifferently, even to the foolish and imprudent.

Such a full acceptance of Aristotelian positions, however, was the exception rather than the rule. The denial of divine dreams clashed with biblical and patristic authorities and thus presented difficulties for Christian writers. Roger Bacon notes that Aristotle's "librum de divinacione sompniorum, qui est tertius de sompno et vigilia" [book about the divination of dreams, which is the third (book) on sleep and waking] provided one reason for the "excommunication" of Aristotle's natural philosophy and metaphysics before the year 1237.[20] The Parisian Condemnation of 1277 included the proposition: "That raptures and visions do not take place except through nature." The attack on this particular statement may respond most directly to Boethius of Dacia; in any case, it reflects anxiety about the new, "natural" explanations of visionary phenomena.[21]

The rejection of a strict Aristotelian dream theory was not confined to conservative religious milieux. Petrarch, in his *Rerum memorandarum libri*, follows Aristotle and Cicero (*De divinatione*) quite closely in expressing skepticism about the dream:

Non decere philosophum aut prudentem hominem ineptis atque anilibus superstitionibus aurem inclinare, sed ridiculum opinari qui vigilantes nec presentia intelligere nec preteritorum meminisse queant, eos cum obdormierint etiam ventura prenoscere, quasi amicior familiariorque sopitis ac stertentibus, quam vigili animo apertisque oculis meditantibús sit Deus.[22]

[It is] not proper that a philosophical or prudent man incline his ear to the silly superstitions of old wives, and [it is] ridiculous to suppose that those who, when awake, may be able neither to understand present things nor remember past ones should, when they have fallen asleep, foresee even those things that are to come, as though God were more friendly and familiar to those lulled to sleep and snoring than to those meditating with a wide-awake soul and open eyes.

But Petrarch hesitates to take too strong a position, ultimately leaving the question of the trustworthiness and divinity of dreams unanswered:

Scio quidem de hac re alios aliter sentire; nec sum nescius quantum glorie puer olim hebreus ex sompniorum interpretatione perceperit: sed illic non ars humana, verum celestis revelatio. Hec tandem de sompniis, utcunque meis verbis explicita, non tam mea quam Ciceronis intentio est.[23]

Indeed, I know that others feel differently concerning this matter; nor am I ignorant of how much glory the Hebrew boy [i.e., Joseph] once upon a time garnered from the interpretation of dreams: in that case, however, not human art but celestial revelation [was involved]. But finally, this opinion concerning dreams, though explicated in my words, is not so much mine as Cicero's.

The biblical example of the "puer ... hebreus" and the general disagreement of authorities ("others feel differently") prevent any easy rejection of the divine dream.

Similarly, Albertus Magnus, commenting on Aristotle's theory of sleep and dreams, struggles, when he comes to the *De divinatione per somnum*, to reconcile the Aristotelian treatment of dream divination with orthodox Christian views of *prophetia*. As he begins to discuss the *De divinatione*, Albert claims that Aristotle, more than any other philosopher, approaches a reliable view of dream divination: "quod dicit Aristoteles plus accedit veritati, quam aliquid quod ante vel post scripsit aliquis Philosophorum, cujus scripta ad nos devenerunt" [that which Aristotle says approaches more to the truth than anything written before or after by any one of the philosophers whose writings have come down to us].[24] But even this best of philosophers falls short of perfection:

Quod de divinatione dicit Aristoteles, breve quidem est et imperfectum, et habens plurimas dubitationes. Dico autem *breve*, quia carens probatione, sed simplex, et parum philosophiae habens videtur esse narratio, nec species somniorum neque probationem somnii aliquid significandi in se continens. *Imperfectum* autem est, quoniam licet sine magicis et astronomicis non possit ars interpretandi somnia adipisci, tamen solis physicis sufficienter scitur ex quibus et qualibus simulacris consistit somnium de quo debet esse divinatio: et hoc neque ab Aristotele, neque a Philosophis quidquam determinatum est. *Plurimas autem dubitationes habet*, quia in incerto relinquitur causa talium somniorum.[25]

That which Aristotle says about divination is indeed brief and imperfect and has many doubtful points. Now, I say "brief," because the account seems to be lacking in proof and simple, having too little philosophy and containing in itself neither [an account of] the species of dreams nor proof of a dream that signifies something. Moreover, it is "imperfect," since, though the art of interpreting dreams cannot be obtained without magical and astrological [knowledge], nevertheless [the following] may be adequately known by natural science on its own: which and what kind of images make up that dream from which divination is bound to arise. And [yet] nothing of this has been determined either by Aristotle or by the [other] philosophers. Moreover, "it has many doubtful points," since the cause of such [divinatory] dreams is left in uncertainty.

Ultimately, Albert accepts much of what Aristotle argues about dream divination. But he can do so only by narrowly delimiting the implications of Aristotle's discussion, making Aristotle's treatment valid only from the perspective of natural philosophy:

Est ... et aliud genus visionis et prophetiae secundum altissimos theologos qui de divinis loquuntur inspirationibus, de quibus ad praesens nihil dicimus ... eo quod hoc ex physicis rationibus nullo modo potest cognosci: physica enim tantum suscepimus dicenda.[26]

There is ... also another kind of vision and prophecy according to the greatest theologians who speak about divine inspirations, about which at present we say nothing ... because this [kind of vision] can in no way be understood from the reasoning of natural philosophy, and truly we have [here] undertaken only the discussion of physical things [i.e., natural philosophy].

Most often, late-medieval dream theorists did not accept Aristotle uncritically; neither did they reject "older" dream authorities out of hand. Thirteenth- and fourteenth-century writers – even those strongly influenced by the "new learning" – continued to cite and expound late-antique theory. Albertus Magnus, Jean de la Rochelle, Vincent of Beauvais, all "Aristotelians," each refer at some length to the ideas about dreaming expressed by Macrobius, Augustine, and Gregory. Petrarch's response to the question, "quanta sit somniis habenda fides" [how much faith one should have in dreams],[27] makes clear the continuing late-medieval heterogeneity of opinion:

Not only do the people disagree, but learned men also... You know the commentary of Chalcidius on the *Timaeus* and the commentary of Macrobius on the sixth book of the *Republic* where he presents a clear and brief distinction between types of dreams. You have Aristotle's book on these and related matters. Finally you have Cicero's book on prophesy [*De divinatione*], in which you will find how he himself, as well as others, viewed the matter.[28]

Cicero, Aristotle, Macrobius, and Calcidius were all available to, and all used by, the dream theorists of the late Middle Ages.

THE NEW DREAM THEORY: BARTHOLOMAEUS ANGLICUS, PIERRE BERSUIRE, ROBERT HOLKOT, RAMON LULL, THOMAS OF CANTIMPRÉ, GIOVANNI BOCCACCIO

The dissemination of Aristotelian material led to a greater and greater emphasis on the somatic and psychological causes of dreaming. The balance in dream theory between the mundane and the transcendent, already affected by twelfth-century intellectual movements, shifted even further toward the mundane. Nevertheless, the balance survived in most thirteenth- and fourteenth-century discussions of dreaming: writers continued to argue that dreams come from internal and external, divine, mundane, and demonic sources, and the dream remained strongly associated with the intermediate psychic realm of imagination, bridging body and mind, the physical and the abstract.

Thus, Bartholomaeus Anglicus, in the treatment of sleep, waking, and dreams that appears in his *De proprietatibus rerum* (VI.24–27),[29] combines new Aristotelian and medical material with late-antique and Christian dream theory. Bartholomaeus depends on such authors as Aristotle (pp. 331–34, 336, and 338), Avicenna (pp. 332 and 334–35), and Constantine the African (pp. 332–35 and 337), but he also refers explicitly to Gregory and Macrobius (p. 336), draws on biblical material (pp. 333 and 337), and cites Augustine's *De quantitate animae* (pp. 331–32) and *De Genesi ad litteram* (pp. 336–37). Aristotelian and medical lore predominates in his discussion of sleep and waking (chapters 24–26), but Bartholomaeus takes a more eclectic approach in treating the dream itself (chapter 27).

On the one hand, the *De proprietatibus* emphasizes dreams whose cause is naturally explicable, arising from internal physiological or psychological process and from the action of external physical forces. In characterizing such "lower" dreams, however, Bartholomaeus draws not only on the "new" authorities; in his discussion, the various influences of Aristotle, Macrobius, and Gregory also intermingle:

> Sweuenynge is a certeyn disposicioun of sleping men and p[re]ntiþ in here inwit by imaginacioun schap and liknes of diuers þinges, as Gregori seiþ and also Macrobius *de sompno Cipionis*. Sweuen comeþ and falleþ in many maner wise. For bicause of bindinge and onynge þat þe soule haþ wiþ þe body disposiciouns and passiouns þat springeþ of þe body reboundiþ in þe soule by a maner applicacioun of þe fleisch. þerfore ofte in slepinge þe soule seþ such ymages and liknes of þinges as he assaied somtyme wakinge, as vnresonabil beestis metiþ sweuenes also, as Aristotel seiþ *libro 3°*, For an hound haþ sweuenes as it semeþ by his berkinge, and an hors as it semeþ by his neyhinge.[30] And somtyme such sweuenes comeþ of to moche replecioun oþir of to grete fastinge, and somtyme of grete ymaginacioun and þouȝt þat is toforehonde in wakynge.[31]
> (p. 336)

Similarly, when Bartholomaeus later lists seven kinds of lower dream, he blends information from various sources, including Constantine, Macrobius, and Aristotle:

> Also diuers sweuenes comeþ of diuers causes, somtyme of complexioun, as he þat is *sanguineus* haþ glad and likinge sweuenes, *malancolius* metiþ of sorwe, *colericus* of fire and of firy þinges, and *flewmaticus* of reyne and snowe, and of watres and of watery þinges and of oþire such. And so eueriche man metiþ sweuenes acordinge to his complexioun, witt, and age.[32] So seiþ Constantinus. And somtyme sweuenes comeþ of appetite, affeccioun, and desire, as he þat is anhongred metiþ of mete, and a dronken man þat is aþurst metiþ of drinke, and of þe contrarie þerof lacke and defaute of mete and drinke.[33] þe more sich on metiþ þat [he] etiþ oþir drinkeþ, þe worse he is anhongred oþir aþurst whanne he is waked. Somtyme of gret study and þouȝt iset on a þing, as a coueitous man alwey metiþ of golde, and þat he acountiþ and telliþ his moneye, and makeþ it lasse oþir more.[34] Somtyme of yuel disposicioun of þe brayn, as it fareþ in ham þat beþ disposid to frenesie and to madnes, þey haueþ wondirful sweuenes þat neuer man herde speke of toforehonde, for as vapour infectiþ and varieþ þe celle of fantasie so þe sweuenes varieþ and beþ diuers. Somtyme of corrupt blood, for þay [þat] hauen infecte and corrupt blood

metiþ þat he gooþ in corrupt, stinkinge, and vnclene place. Somtyme of liknes and changing of aier, for aier disposid to liknes and to chaunginge chaungiþ and likneþ þe body to his owen liknes, and so þe smoke þat is þanne resolued and departid makeþ newe impressioun and prentinges in þe brayne and þerof comeþ vnliche and diuers sweuenes. Somtyme of dyuers ages and chaunginge of age; smale children metiþ nouʒt.[35]   (pp. 337–38)

Bartholomaeus thus strongly emphasizes the dream's involvement in corporeality, while also recognizing, with Augustine, that dreams may have a supernatural origin:

Inpressioun and prenting is imaad in his inwit þat slepiþ by inspiracioun of God, and somtyme by seruyse of aungelis, as it ferde of Iacob, þat siʒ in his slepe poplere ʒerdes and [an] angel þat seide to hym: Take ʒerdis, *et cetera*, *Genesis 30°*;[36] and somtyme by scorn and gile [o]f iuel spiritis, as it fareþ in fantastik and fals prophetis. Hereof Austin spekeþ þere and seiþ þat whanne a good spirit takeþ and rauischeþ mannes spirit into þese siʒtes, wiþoute [doute] þilke ymages þat beþ iseye beþ ymages of som þinges, and it is good to knowe þilke þinges for þat knowinge is Goddes ʒifte. Somtyme Satanas his aungel desgisiþ him as þeyʒ he were an angel of liʒt and makeþ siche images to bigile and deceyue men to his purpos, whanne me trowiþ him in doinges þat beþ opunlich goode. Whanne sweuenes comeþ by reuelacioun sober inwitt demeþ redilich wiþ help of goddis grace. Noʒt alle sweuenes beþ trewe noþir alle false, for somtyme by sweuenes God sendiþ serteyn warnynge and bodinge of þinges þat schal bifalle.[37]   (p. 337)

Bartholomaeus chooses not to ignore biblical evidence of angelic dreams; he recognizes, citing Augustine, the possibility of both divine and demonic dream experience, and follows patristic authorities in expressing a concern with the problem of distinguishing the demonic from the divine.

The dream in the *De proprietatibus rerum* is thus involved both with the body and with higher, spiritual forces. It occurs in the intermediate faculty of "imaginacioun" (p. 336), presenting likenesses of bodies, but not bodies themselves – "ymages and liknes of þinges and of bodyes and nouʒt þe same þynges" (p. 337).[38] Even dreams arising from corporeal stimuli depend upon the positioning of oneiric experience *between* body and soul: "bicause of bindinge and onynge þat þe soule haþ wiþ þe body disposiciouns and passiouns þat springeþ of þe body reboundiþ in þe soule by a maner applicacioun of þe fleisch" (p. 336). Because of its intermediate position, Bartholomaeus's dream, like late-antique and twelfth-century dreams, can be of many different kinds:

Somtyme sweuenes beþ trewe and somtyme fals, somtyme clere and playne and somtyme troubly. Sweuenes þat beþ trewe buþ somtyme opun and playne and somtyme iwrappid in figuratif, mistik, and dim and derke tokenynges and bodinges, as it ferde in Pharaoes sweuene.[39]   (p. 337)

Subject to psychological and somatic influences, and even to the quality of the surrounding air, dreams nonetheless are also connected to higher forces: they may be meaningless or even demonically deceptive, but they can also be revelations of divine truth.

Thirteenth- and fourteenth-century encyclopedic treatments of dreaming generally followed the course taken by Bartholomaeus.[40] As Peden suggests, late-medieval encyclopedists quickly assimilated the "new learning," using "greater or lesser proportions of Aristotle, Galen, and Avicenna,"[41] but they also continued to promulgate a variety of other, "older" approaches.

Pierre Bersuire, in his fourteenth-century *Reductorium morale, De proprietatibus rerum* and in his *Dictionarium morale*, presents much the same mixture of dream lore as Bartholomaeus, indeed often quoting his predecessor directly.[42] Bersuire, however, was concerned with moralizing knowledge rather than merely expounding it: "intentio nostra non est tractare de aliquo, nisi proprie possit ad aliquid moraliter applicari" [our intention is not to treat anything unless it can be properly applied to something else in a moral sense] (6.112). As a result, he tends to concentrate his attention on lower dreams, which – involved as they are with body and with the things of the world – provide striking metaphors for moral error:

Somnium nihil aliud est, quàm amplexatio umbrae, pro re, signi pro signato, imaginis pro veritate, falsi pro vero.[43] Et ideò somnians, dum somniat, multa imaginatur, quia aliquando videtur sibi, quòd est rex vel episcopus, & quòd videt & facit mirabilia & stupenda, sed cum evigilaverit, invenit omnia esse falsa. Sic verè opinio malorum de mundo & mundi foelicitate, non est nisi quoddam somnium, quia sc. ipsi amplexantur umbram pro re, signum pro signato, imaginem pro veritate, & falsum pro vero, hoc est dictum, amplexantur bona mundi, quae non sunt nisi quaedam umbra, quoddam signum, quaedam imago futurorum bonorum, quae reputant esse vera, fixa, solida atque certa. (2.77)

The dream is nothing other than an embracing of the shadow for the thing, the sign for the signified, the image for the truth, the false for the true. And for this reason the dreamer, while he is dreaming, imagines many things, since sometimes it seems to him that he is a king or bishop and that he sees and does miraculous and amazing things, but when he has awakened, he finds all these things to be false. Thus, truly, the opinion of evil people concerning the world and the felicity of the world is nothing other than a kind of dream: namely because they themselves embrace the shadow for the thing, the sign for the signified, the image for the truth, and the false for the true; that is to say, they embrace the good things of the world, which are nothing other than a kind of shadow, a kind of sign, a kind of image of future good things, which they consider to be true, fixed, solid, and certain.

However, despite the seeming absoluteness here of "somnium nihil aliud est," Bersuire also recognizes the possibility of true and divine dreams.

Summarizing the full range of dream experience, he includes both the mundane and transcendent, the true and the false:

Somnia quandoque proveniant à Deo per inspirationem, quandoque à libertate animae per suiipsius à dormiente corpore expeditionem, quandoque à diabolo per fallacem deceptionem, & machinationem, quandoque à mente per nimiam solicitudinem seu circa aliquam rem intentionem, quandoque ab humore in corpore abundante per fumorum, & phantasiarum cerebri elevationem ... quandoque à complexione corporis secundùm suam naturalem dispositionem.

(6.112)

Dreams may sometimes arise from God through inspiration, sometimes from the freedom of the soul in its own expedition from the sleeping body, sometimes from the devil through treacherous deception and contrivance, sometimes from the mind through excessive solicitude or concentration on some matter, sometimes from a humor abounding in the body [operating] through the elevation of vapors and phantasies to the brain ... sometimes from the complexion of the body according to its natural disposition.

Psychosomatic, divine, and diabolic dreams are all possible. While the adoption of Aristotelian lore and the attachment of dreaming to moral concerns result in an increased emphasis on lower, somatic dreams, for Bersuire the realm of dreaming remains complex.

Another fourteenth-century moralizing treatment of the dream, found in Robert Holkot's *In librum Sapientiae*, also makes use of the new Aristotelianism while preserving the balance and complexity of earlier dream theory.[44] (Holkot's treatment is especially interesting to the student of English literature since it seems to have been a major source of Chaucerian dream lore.)[45] Holkot presents standard Aristotelian definitions of sleep and of the dream:

Causatur enim somnus ab euaporatione ascendente ad cerebrum.[46]

Truly, sleep is caused by an evaporation ascending to the brain.

Somnium secundum Arist. 2. de somno & uigilia, est phantasma factum a motu simulachrorum in ... dormiente.[47]

According to Aristotle in the second [book] of *De somno et vigilia* [i.e., *De somniis*], the dream is an apparition caused by the movement of images in one who is asleep.

Thus focusing attention on bodily process, Holkot tends, like Bersuire, to find in sleep and dreams suggestions of moral turpitude and excessive involvement in physicality.[48] Moreover, Holkot voices a strong skepticism about the dream's reliability, warning strongly and repeatedly against believing too easily in dreams:

Patet, quòd in quibusdam somniis est aliqua certitudo, sed in paucis, & ideò *Somnia ne cures, nam fallunt somnia plures.*[49]

It is clear that in certain dreams there is some certainty, but in few of them [is this true], and therefore, "Do not pay attention to dreams, for dreams deceive many."

Periculosum est ergo per somnia nimis communiter diuinare: quia poetice dicitur:
   Somnia ne cures, nam fallunt somnia plures.[50]

It is therefore perilous to practice divination through dreams too commonly, since it is stated poetically: "Do not pay attention to dreams, for dreams deceive many."

Interestingly, Holkot's skepticism relies both on the Aristotelian tradition and on biblical and patristic sources. Concluding, in *lectio* 202, "quòd somniorum diuinationi indulgere est multum periculosum" [that to indulge in dream divination is very perilous],[51] Holkot cites Aristotle:

Sicut dicit Arist. licet somnia sunt significatiua futurorum aliquando, tamen non est necesse euentum somniorum accidere: quia possunt superiores causae impedire.[52]

As Aristotle says, though dreams sometimes signify future things, nevertheless it is not inevitable that the [predicted] outcome of dreams occur, since higher causes can impede [its fulfilment].

In support of the same conclusion, Holkot also cites the skepticism found in patristic writers like Gregory:

Haec conclusio patet ... propter deceptionem malorum spirituum, qui per somnia nituntur decipere illos, uel seducere, qui somniis fidem praestant: & ideo faciliter posset homo nimis credens somniis labi in desperationem, ad suggestionem Diaboli.[53]

This conclusion is evident ... on account of the deception of evil spirits, who try, through dreams, to deceive or seduce those who show faith in dreams; and therefore the man who believes too much in dreams can easily fall into despair, as a result of the devil's suggestion.

Thus relying on both Christian and Aristotelian authority, Holkot must eventually confront the biggest barrier to a reconciliation of the two traditions: Aristotle's denial of divinely-inspired dreams. Holkot notes the Aristotelian claim that "inconueniens est dicere, quod diuinatio somniorum fit a DEO: cùm uidemus quòd talis diuinatio conueniat fatuis, idiotis & melancholicis, & non sapientibus" [it is unsuitable to say that dream divination comes from God, since we see that such divination may suit foolish, ignorant, and melancholic people and not the wise].[54] And in response, he turns to biblical material (for instance, the story of Balaam) to show that the denial of divine dreams is based on faulty reasoning:

Quia potest contingere quòd unus malus homo est aliquando aptior ad quoddam certum mysterium, quàm alius, qui tamen est simpliciter magis bonus, & similiter quia est ad honorem DEI, de suis hostibus habere testimonium, ideò donum prophetiae dat etiam inimicis, aptis tamen ad tale mysterium perficiendum.[55]

Because it can happen that an evil man is sometimes more suited to some particular mystery than another man who is nonetheless in and of himself more good, and likewise, because it is to God's honor that He have testimony from His enemies, therefore, He gives the gift of prophecy even to His foes, [when they are] nevertheless suited to accomplish such a mystery.

When, in *lectio* 103, Holkot comes to define the range of possible dreams, he presents a hierarchy dependent on both Aristotelian and Christian authority, a hierarchy stretching from the more corporeal to the more celestial:

Somnia signatiua aliquando in nobis causantur ex corporibus coelestibus, aliquando ex nobismetipsis. Et illa sunt in duplici genere: quia quaedam habent originem ex parte corporis, quaedam autem ex parte animae. Ex parte corporis quidem, sicut quando aliquis humor dominatur in homine... Ex parte animae habentes originem propter uehementem sollicitudinem animae circa aliquid in uigilia. Ecclesiast. 5. Multas curas sequuntur somnia. Et ideò dicit Aristoteles: Amici procul existentes maximè sunt solliciti de se inuicem. Contingit quòd anima format sibi idolum de dilecto[56]... Tertio modo habent somnia in nobis originem ex corporibus coelestibus, quae alterant organa uirtutum sensitiuarum secundum quasdam qualitates.[57]

Significant dreams are caused in us sometimes by celestial bodies, sometimes by us ourselves. And the latter exist in a twofold manner, since certain of them have [their] origin on the part of the body but certain [others] on the part of the soul. Truly, on the part of the body, as when a certain humor dominates in a man... On the part of the soul [they] have [their] origin because of a strong waking concern of the soul about something. Ecclesiastes 5:2: Dreams follow many cares. And therefore Aristotle says: Friends who are far away are concerned most about each other [rather than about other people]. It happens that the soul forms for itself an image of the beloved... In the third way, dreams have [their] origin in us from celestial bodies that alter the organs of the sensitive powers according to certain properties.

Here, Holkot presents a hierarchical system partly indebted to late-antique dream theory, but also shows himself a good Aristotelian in his emphasis on the natural causation of even "celestial" dreams. When, however, in *lectio* 202, he again defines the complete range of dream experience, he presents a hierarchy more heavily weighted toward the "higher" dream and less fully dominated by natural philosophy:

Somnia sumunt originem multipliciter. Aliquando à corpore humano, aliquando ab anima, aliquando à corporibus supercoelestibus, aliquando à spiritibus bonis, aliquando à spiritibus malis. Ex parte quidem corporis originaliter oriuntur somnia communiter in humore ... [Alia vero somnia originantur ex parte anime: vnde homines][58] solliciti, & cogitatiui, cum aliqua negocia facere cogitant frequenter somniant de eisdem ... Tertiò sunt somnia quae causantur in homine uirtute corporum supercoelestium: Nam corpora supercoelestia ... alterant corpora nostra in somno ... Quartò originantur in nobis nonnunquam somnia spiritibus bonis, sicut patet Matt. 2. de angelo quae apparuit in somnis Ioseph, & in aliis Scripturae locis. Et tale uidetur somnium Simoniadis, de quo narrat Valerius lib. 1. ca. 5 ... Quintò originantur nonnunquam somnia à malis spiritibus, sicut patet de uxore Pilati ... & à tali spiritu uidetur illud somnium causatum esse, quod narrat Valerius lib. 1, ca. 7. de Cassio Parmensi.[59]

Dreams originate in multiple ways: sometimes from the human body, sometimes from the soul, sometimes from supercelestial bodies, sometimes from good spirits, sometimes from evil spirits. Indeed, on the part of the body, dreams often arise originally in [bodily] humors ... [Other dreams truly originate on the part of the soul: whence] anxious and thoughtful [men], when they are planning to carry out some task, often dream about that same [task] ... Third, there are dreams that are caused in a man by the power of supercelestial bodies. For supercelestial bodies ... alter our bodies during sleep ... Fourth, dreams are sometimes begun in us by good spirits, as is clear in Matthew 2, concerning the angel that appeared in Joseph's sleep, and in other scriptural passages. And the dream of Simonides, about which Valerius tells in book 1, chapter 5, seems [to be] of this sort ... Fifth, sometimes dreams are begun by evil spirits, as is clear concerning Pilate's wife [Matthew 27:19] ... and that dream which Valerius tells in book 1, chapter 7, about Cassius Parmensis seems to have been caused by just such an [evil] spirit.

Holkot always remains aware of the perils attending faith in dreams, but never denies that some dreams are reliable; the skepticism that arises from both Aristotelian science and Christian theology does not alone characterize his dream theory. For Holkot, dreaming remains a complex experience: often explicable as a natural process, it can nonetheless also be inspired by supernatural forces.

At times, the late-medieval emphasis on the lower end of dream experience became very strong. Thus, Ramon Lull, in the late thirteenth century, stressed the somatic associations of dreaming even more vigorously than did Bartholomaeus, Bersuire, and Holkot.[60] Making the usual connections between hunger, thirst, humoral complexion, and the dream, he also elaborated ways in which dreaming may be involved with each of the five senses:

7 Per sensitivam [potentiam] somniant homines similitudines appetituum particularium sensuum.

8 Si oculi sunt in magna abundantia videndi, appetunt videre colores, & per illum appetitum homines, maximè si sint complexionis sanguineae, somniant propè vigilationem pulchras res; sed, si oculi magis participant cum

complexione melancholicâ, homines somniant circa profundam noctem videre turpes res.

9 Si homo de die audivit multa verba, propter consuetudinem audiendi, cùm dormiet, somniabit aliquas similitudines illorum verborum; &, si in ipso regnat sanguis, somniabit cum placito, &, si in ipso regnat melancholia, somniabit cum taedio.

10 Si in loco, in quo homo somniat, unus odor plùs regnat, quàm alius, si aër est purus aut corruptus,[61] somniabit secundùm dispositionem illius aëris res odorabiles boni vel mali odoris.

11 Si homo, qui somniat, habet indigentiam comedendi vel bibendi, vel, si una complexio est magis repleta, quàm alia, somniabit cibos, aquas, vomitum vel sudorem, & sic de aliis rebus similibus ad gustandum per dulcedinem aut amaritudinem.

12 Si corpus hominis, qui dormit, sentit frigus, somniabit res frigidas, &, si jacet in duro lecto, duras res, & sic de aliis rebus similibus ad tangendum.[62]

7 Through the sensitive [power], men dream likenesses of those things desired by the particular senses.

8 If the eyes are in a great abundance of seeing, they desire to see colors, and because of that desire, men, especially if they are of a sanguine complexion, dream beautiful things when they are about to awaken; but if the eyes share more in a melancholy complexion, men dream in the deep of night [that they] see ugly things.

9 If a man during the day has heard many words, because of the habit of hearing, when he is asleep, he will dream certain likenesses of those words; and if blood [a sanguine complexion] reigns in him, he will dream with pleasure, and if melancholy reigns in him, he will dream with loathing.

10 If, in the place in which a man dreams, one odor reigns more than another, if the air is pure or corrupt, he will dream according to the disposition of that air things that can be smelled of either a good or evil odor.

11 If the man who dreams has a need for eating or drinking, or if one complexion is more replete [in him] than another, he will dream of foods, waters, vomit, or sweat, and thus [it is] also concerning other similar things that are tasted in sweetness or bitterness.

12 If the body of the sleeping man feels a coldness, he will dream cold things, and if he lies in a hard bed, hard things, and thus [it is] also concerning other similar things that are felt by the sense of touch.

Lull thus grants sense process an unusually extensive role in dreaming; he does not, however, limit the dream to an involvement with the *potentia sensitiva* and its attendant senses. The lower "vegetative" faculty also influences the dream, as do higher faculties: *imaginativa, memoria, intellectus,* and *voluntas*.[63] Dreams are connected to the whole range of human faculties, involved with both the corporeal and incorporeal, the physical and the abstract. If Lull gives the longest portion of his discussion over to "sensitive" dreams, he nonetheless chooses to end that discussion with a strong assertion of the divinely-inspired, revelatory dream:

18 Bonus Angelus aliquando facit homines Somniare ad faciendum aliqua bona opera, ut illa procurent facere, quando vigilabunt.

19 Malus angelus facit homines somniare ad faciendum malum, ut illud faciant, quando vigilabunt.

20 DEUS in somniis revelat multas veritates hominibus, quia in dormiendo sunt magis innocentes, quàm in vigilando; & ideo bonus Angelus meliùs potest participare cum hominibus in dormiendo, quàm in vigilando, & illis revelare veritatem ex parte DEI.[64]

18 A good angel sometimes makes men dream about doing certain good works, so that they take care to do those [works] when they are awake.

19 An evil angel makes men dream about doing evil, so that they do [evil] when they are awake.

20 God reveals many truths to men in dreams, because they are more innocent while asleep than while awake, and therefore a good angel can better share with men in sleeping than in waking and reveal to them truth on the part of God.

Thus even writers intimately involved in the new, Aristotelian learning gave their attention to revelatory dreams. And certain dream theorists stood at an even greater remove from Aristotelian views than did the writers so far considered. Thomas of Cantimpré, for instance, in his thirteenth-century *Liber de natura rerum*, presents a discussion of dreams essentially void of Aristotelian lore.[65] Quoting *verbatim* from the twelfth-century *De spiritu et anima* (chapters 24–25), Thomas touches on several familiar themes:

1 Augustine's "Tria visionum genera" (pp. 92–93)
2 Augustine's suggestion that dreams can be true and false, perturbed and tranquil, and that true dreams exist in a variety of forms: "aliquando futuris omnino similia, vel aperte dicta aliquando obscuris significationibus vel quasi figurativis locutionibus prenuntiata" (p. 93)
3 ecstatic and angelic dreams, as discussed by Augustine (p. 93)
4 dreams arising from the human body and spirit, again as presented in Augustine (p. 93)
5 Macrobius's five species of dream (p. 94)

The definitions given for *oraculum, visio, sompnium, insompnium*,[66] and *fantasma* (=*visum*) are identical to those in the *De spiritu*. As in that twelfth-century work, Macrobius's treatment of *insompnium* and *fantasma* is augmented by medical lore (see "The somatic dream" in chapter 4, above). Otherwise, Thomas's dream discussion shows few traces of the "new learning." Thomas was, however, clearly familiar with Aristotle's newly available work on sleep and dreams, and with other recently translated material: in an earlier chapter, "De sompno" (1.5), he relies for his definition of sleep on Aristotle (and Pliny), and cites some rather technical material from the medical writers.[67] When it comes to discussing dreams, however, Thomas ignores Aristotle, choosing to present a compendium of Augustinian and Macrobian dream lore that emphasizes the dream's connections to both mundane and transcendent realities.

Boccaccio follows a similar path in the *Genealogiae deorum gentilium* when treating sleep and dreams.[68] In this work, with its mythological focus, Boccaccio's most important sources are the classical poets – in the chapter "De Somno," particularly Ovid, Seneca, and Virgil.[69] In his discussion of sleep, Boccaccio also cites medical and Aristotelian lore.[70] But when considering the different possible kinds of dream, he is almost wholly indebted to Macrobius. He presents Macrobius's five dream-types, citing classical or biblical examples for each. He also discusses the two gates of dreaming, and in doing so, explains at some length a theory, attributed to Porphyry, that would make all dreams ultimately true.[71] Aristotle's ideas about dreams cannot thrive in such a climate, and Boccaccio alludes to somatic theories of oneiric causation only twice, and then briefly. In his discussion of the *phantasma* (*visum*), he provides a physical explanation for the "ephialtes," and in discussing the *somnium*, he states the commonplace that true dreams are most likely to occur as morning approaches, when the dreamer is in a "sober" state.[72]

ALBERTUS MAGNUS AND VINCENT OF BEAUVAIS

To emphasize the non-Aristotelian features of late-medieval dream theory is not to deny Aristotle's importance in shaping that theory. In examining the most extensive medieval encyclopedic account of dreaming, contained in Vincent of Beauvais's *Speculum naturale*, we see how central Aristotelian doctrine had become by the mid-thirteenth century.[73] The very structure of Book 26 of Vincent's *Speculum* reflects the arrangement of material in the *Parva naturalia*: as Aristotle moves from the *De somno et vigilia* to the *De somniis* to the *De divinatione per somnum*, so Vincent discusses first sleep and waking (chapters 1–31), then dreams and related phenomena (chapters 32–80), and finally higher kinds of vision – prophecy, ecstasy, *raptus* (chapters 81–111).

The first fifty-nine chapters of Vincent's discussion come almost entirely from Albertus Magnus's heavily Aristotelian *Summa de creaturis* (questions 43–52, pp. 362–445);[74] only chapters 8, 10, and 32 derive from another source, but again an Aristotelian one, Priscianus Lydus's *Solutiones ad Chosroem*.[75] Although he rearranges his sources, occasionally bringing together material widely separated in Albert or Priscian, Vincent tends to follow the originals very closely. His treatment of sleep and waking (chapters 1–31) can be accurately described as an abridged version of the *Summa de creaturis*, question 43, "De somno et vigilia." Albert's discussion is organized around five questions originally posed by Aristotle:

1 Quid sit [somnus]?
2 Utrum animae per se vel corporis per se propria sunt [somnus et vigilia], vel communia utriusque?
3 Si communia, cujus particulae animae vel corporis sunt?
4 Propter quam causam insunt animalibus?
5 Utrum communicent omnia animalia ambobus, vel aliqua quidem somno tantum, aliqua vero vigilia tantum, aliqua vero neutro, aliqua quidem utrisque.[76]   (p. 362)

1 What is [sleep]?
2 Whether [sleep and waking] are peculiar to the soul in itself or to the body in itself, or common to both.
3 If common [to both], to which portion of the soul or body do they belong?
4 Because of what cause do they exist in animals?
5 Whether all animals share in both [sleep and waking], or indeed certain [animals] only [share in] sleep, but others only waking, and others neither, while others in fact [share in] both.

Vincent does not treat the second question, which Albert himself discusses only briefly (pp. 369–70); otherwise, he touches on most of the issues raised by Aristotle's questions and considered by Albert. Like Albert, he wholeheartedly embraces the "new science" and its physiological explanations of sleep and waking. Citing the *Summa de creaturis*, Vincent is also citing Aristotle, Avicenna, Algazel, and Alpharabius: in question 43 of Albert's work, and in Vincent's derivative discussion, such are the authorities *par excellence*.

The first part of Vincent's treatment of *dreaming* (chapters 32–61) remains similarly faithful to Albert, and similarly Aristotelian. Vincent begins this section of his work by citing Priscian's summary of Aristotle: dreams result from sensory activity, and their clarity correlates with the dreamer's physical condition (chapter 32, col. 1861).[77] In the chapter that follows, Vincent openly declares what this initial emphasis on psychological and physiological process implies – his discussion will be firmly based in Aristotelian theory:

In summa vero de somnio mouet Arist. 7. non negligendas, quaestiones. Prima siquidem quaestio est quid sit somnium videlicet in esse. Secunda vero cur dormientes quidam somniant, & quidam non. Tertia de latentibus somniis ex vi dormitionis. Quarta vtrum in somno contingat praeuidere futura. Quinta qualiter contingat futura preuidere per somnium? Sexta vtrum futura perspiciantur ab homine solum, vel causam habeant quosdam demones? Septima est, vtrum somnia fiant à natura, vel ab euentu.[78]   (chapter 33, col. 1861)

Aristotle and the late-medieval dream

Truly, in the "Summa de somnio," Aristotle raises seven questions that must not be neglected. Indeed, the first question is what the dream is, namely in its essence. Truly, the second: why certain of those who sleep dream, while certain others do not. The third: concerning dreams [that remain] hidden because of the force of sleep. The fourth: whether it may happen [that one] foresee future things during sleep. The fifth: how may it happen [that one] foresee future things through a dream? The sixth: whether future things may be perceived by man on his own or have [as their] cause certain demons? The seventh is: whether dreams occur naturally or by chance.

The ensuing discussion adheres closely to the seven Aristotelian questions and follows Albert's *Summa* faithfully:[79]

Aristotle	Albert	Vincent
1 Quid est sompnium	44 De subjecto somnii (402–10)	34 Quod somnium fit à motu simulacrorum in dormientibus (418, 421, 423)
	45 De causa somnii (410–18)	35 De causis quibus fit huiusmodi motus (423)
	46 Quid sit somnium?[80] (418–24)	36 Adhuc de eodem (420–24)
		37 An somnium passio sit intellectus (403–04)
		38 Huius quaestionis solutio (404)
		39 Qualiter somnium sit motus phantasticae virtutis (406)
		40 Qualiter somnii motus sit vt motus vertiginis (409–10)
		41 Quod somnium sit passio sensus communis (407, 409, 412)[81]
		42 De speciebus sensibilium, quae apparent in somniis (412, 414–15, 417)

2 Propter quam causam dormientes quidem sompniant, interdum vero non

47 Quare quidam non somniaverunt per totam vitam suam? (424–28)

43 De secunda quaestione Arist. circa somnium (424–25)

44 Huius Quaestionis solutio & de his qui nunquam somniant (426)

45 De illis qui iam aetate prouecti somniare incipiunt (425–27)

46 Quae phantasmata faciunt somnium (424–27)

47 Solutio praedictae quaestionis (427)

48 De somniis incertis (427–28)

---

3 Vel accidit quidem dormientibus semper sompniare, set non meminerunt, et si hoc fit propter quam causam fit

48 Quare quidam recordantur somniorum, et quidam non? (428–32)

49 De tertia quaestione Aristotelis circa somnium (428–30)

50 De somnio latente & non latente (430)

51 De deceptionibus animae in somniis (431–32)

---

4 Utrum contingat futura previdere vel non contingit

49 Utrum contingat futura praevidere in somnio? (432–33)

52 De quarta quaestione Aristotelis (432–33)

---

5 Qualiter si contingit

50 Qualiter contingat futura praevidere in somniis? (434–41)

53 De quinta quaestione eiusdem (434–36)

54 De somniis significatiuis (435–36)

55 De diuersis somniorum signis (436)

56 De reuelationibus quae fiunt in somniis (403–04, 438)

6 Utrum futura ab homine comprehendantur vel prospiciantur solum, vel quorundam daemonum habet causa	51 Utrum futura ab homine perspiciantur solum, vel quorundam daemonum habent causam? (441–43)	57 De sexta quaestione Aristotelis (441–43) 58 Cur intellectus futurorum non demonstrantur in imaginibus propriis (442–43)
7 Natura fiunt vel ab eventu	52 Utrum somnia fiant a natura vel ab eventu? (444–45)	59 De septima & ultima quaestione Aristotelis (444–45) 61 De sufficientia [di]visionis secundum ipsum (445)[82]

As the chapter headings from the *Speculum* begin to show, Vincent presents, with approval, many of Aristotle's ideas about the nature of the dream. In Aristotle, Albert, and Vincent, dreaming is "a presentation based in the movement of sense impressions, when such presentation occurs during sleep";[83] the "sensory impressions," "whether ... derived from external objects or from causes within the body," affect "the head quarters of sense-perception" (the *sensus communis*).[84] Dream images will be clear or obscure, or even absent, depending upon the individual's physiological state:

No dreams occur in sleep immediately after meals, or to sleepers who are extremely young, e.g. to infants. The internal movement in such cases is excessive, owing to the heat generated from the food ... During sleep the phantasms, or residuary movements, which are based upon the sensory impressions, become sometimes quite obliterated by the above described motion when too violent; while at other times the sights are indeed seen, but confused and weird.[85]

Similar physiological factors affect the dreamer's ability both to remember a given dream, and to recognize an ongoing dream as imagined rather than real (waking) experience.[86]

Albert and Vincent take their most strongly Aristotelian position in considering the essential nature of the dream and the processes by which it operates (Aristotle's first three questions). Here, even when they present material not directly from Aristotle, they remain faithful to the spirit of his work and its emphasis on natural phenomena:

Licet ... huiusmodi motus [i.e., motus simulacrorum in dormientibus] fiat multis de causis particularibus, tamen illae reducuntur ad quatuor principales, quae colliguntur ex dictis philosophorum. *Quarum vna est iuuentus* . . . Secunda causa est complexio frigida & sicca, sicut melancholia dominans . . . *Tertium est infirmitas*, & praecipue calida & sicca, & calidum fortissimè mouet, & siccum confortat simulachra continuando ea . . . *Quarta causa est fortissima radicatio & cogitatio circa aliquid*, & praecipue quando aliquis abstrahit se à sensibus exterioribus.[87]

(Vincent, chapters 35–36, cols. 1862–63)

Although a motion of this sort [i.e., the motion of images in those sleeping] may occur because of many particular causes, nevertheless those [causes] are reducible to four principal [ones], which are collected [here] from the sayings of the philosophers. *Of which [causes] one is youth* . . . The second cause is a cold and dry complexion, as [when] melancholy dominates . . . *Third is infirmity*, and especially a hot and dry [infirmity], for the hot very strongly moves those images, and the dry strengthens [them] so that they continue [to exist] . . . *The fourth cause is a very strong concentration and meditation on something*, and [this occurs] especially when someone abstracts himself from the external senses.

Vincent and Albert thus wholeheartedly follow newly-available explanations of the dream's mechanism of action, but when it comes to addressing Aristotle's last four questions – questions that concern not how the dream *works*, but what it might *mean* – they adopt a more complicated and cautious approach. Early in his treatment of dreaming, Albert signals that he will consider not only the "new" dream authorities, but also older, especially patristic, ones. In article one of question 44 ("Utrum somnium sit passio intellectus" [Whether the dream is a passion of the intellect]), Albert cites, alongside Aristotle, Alpharabius, Avicenna, Isaac, and Algazel (p. 403), the two most influential Christian dream theorists, and one of the most famous instances of biblical dreaming:

Gregorius et Augustinus dicunt, quod somnia sunt revelationes Angelorum. Revelatio autem haec convenientissime fit ad intellectum, sicut dicit Daniel: Quoniam *intelligentia est opus in visione* [Daniel 10:1]. (p. 403)

Gregory and Augustine say that dreams are the revelations of angels. But such revelation is made most appropriately to the intellect, as Daniel says: Because "there is need of understanding [*intelligentia*] in a vision" [Daniel 10:1].

Here, where Albert's concern is still the dream's mode of functioning and not its meaning, the import of the patristic citation is not fully addressed. He is concerned to demonstrate that dreaming is *not* in essence a "passio intellectus," but rather a "passio phantasiae [i.e., imaginationis] et sensus communis" [a passion of the phantasy (i.e., imagination) and of the common sense] (p. 409). He must, therefore, explain why the opinion expressed by Gregory and Augustine does not necessarily support classifying dreams as intellective:

Aristotle and the late-medieval dream

AD ALIUD dicendum, quod revelatio somnialis habet aliquod de esse prophetiae, et aliquid de esse somnii: et secundum hoc quod est habens esse somnii, non sistit in intellectu, sed in imaginabilibus praeparatis ad phantasiam, sicut quod Daniel vidit bestias ascendentes de mari, et Pharao spicas et boves: sed secundum quod est prophetiae, sic principaliter est in intellectu, et sic differt a somnio.　　(p. 404)

[In response] to that other [statement], it is to be said that oneiric revelation contains something of the essence of prophecy and something of the essence of the dream. And insofar as it partakes of the essence of the dream, it does not present itself in the intellect, but rather in imaginable things prepared for the phantasy, as for example Daniel saw beasts ascending from the sea, and Pharaoh [saw] ears of corn and cows. But insofar as it partakes of prophecy, to that degree is it principally in the intellect and to that degree does it differ from the dream [proper].

Albert here defers a full consideration of prophetic dream experience: "Quod autem quandoque vera intelliguntur in somniis, hoc fit quibusdam aliis de causis quae infra determinabuntur" [However, that true things are sometimes understood in dreams occurs from certain other causes (than those discussed here), which will be determined below] (p. 404).[88] Still, the patristic reference early in Albert's discussion reminds us of Christian dream theory and prepares us for the greater attention this receives as questions of the dream's meaning arise. With the discussion of Aristotle's fourth question ("Utrum contingat futura praevidere in somnio" [Whether it may happen (that one) foresee future things in a dream]), biblical and patristic references begin to proliferate. Albert cites Genesis (p. 432) and Ecclesiasticus (p. 433) in question 49 of the *Summa*; Daniel (pp. 436 and 437) and Genesis (p. 441) in question 50; "Augustinus in libro in duodecimo *super Genesim ad litteram*" (pp. 441 and 442), Matthew (pp. 441–42), Numbers (p. 442), Daniel (p. 442), 2 Maccabees (p. 442), Judges (p. 442), and "sacra Scriptura" (p. 443) in question 51; and Matthew (p. 445), Daniel (p. 445), and Gregory the Great, "in libro IV *Dialogorum*" (pp. 444–45), in question 52. Vincent follows Albert in many of these citations, referring to "scriptura diuina" and Ecclesiasticus (chapter 52, col. 1871), Genesis and Daniel (chapter 55, col. 1873, and chapter 56, col. 1874), Augustine (chapter 57, col. 1874), "sacra scriptura" (chapter 58, col. 1875), and Gregory (chapters 59–61, cols. 1875–76). Both Albert and Vincent begin, in the later sections of their discussions, to cite "*sancti* et philosophi*" [*saints* and philosophers] rather than simply "philosophi," as they have done earlier.[89]

Aristotelian "philosophers," however, continue to play an important role for both Vincent and Albert. Though Aristotle confines the dream to an explicable, "natural" realm, he does admit that dreams sometimes predict the future,[90] and Albert and Vincent carefully present his arguments in favor of predictive dreams:

Quarta quaestio Aristot. est, vtrum futura contingat in somnio praeuidere, vel non? Et patet, quod sic etiam secundum ipsum. Nam omnes inquit aestimant, aliquam assignationem futurorum habere somnia & hoc fidem importat tanquam ab experientia dictum... Idem etiam inducit rationem ab auctoritate medicorum, qui dicunt quod oportet valde somniis intendere, eo quod aliquid significent in futurum.[91]   (Vincent, chapter 52, col. 1871)

Aristotle's fourth question is: whether it may happen [that one] foresee future things in a dream, or not? And it is clear that [the answer is] yes, even according to [Aristotle] himself. For he says that all [people] judge dreams to contain a certain showing of future things, and this carries conviction, as a statement from experience... The same one [Aristotle] also introduces an argument from the authority of the physicians, who say that it is proper strongly to direct [our] attention to dreams, because these may signify something in the future.

Our two writers also cite a wealth of material in support of predictive dreams from other of the "new" authorities:

Nos autem cum sanctis, & prophetis dicimus, quod somnia frequenter aliquid signant de futuris, maximeque vt dicit Auic. quae sunt in dormitionis fine, sicut illa quae videntur in mane... Somnium tamen licet principaliter sit futurorum, tamen & preteritorum & praesentium est, quae latent cognitionem nostram, vt dicit Alpharabius.[92]   (Vincent, chapter 52, col. 1871)

We, however, with the saints and prophets, say that dreams frequently signify something concerning future things, and most of all, as Avicenna says, those [dreams] that occur at the end of sleep, as for example those that are seen in the morning... Nevertheless, the dream, though it may be principally of future things, nevertheless is also of past and present things that are hidden from our knowledge, as Alpharabius says.

When classifying predictive dreams, Vincent and Albert follow Aristotle as far as possible. They suggest, as does he, that dreams can be (1) causes of future events; (2) signs of the future; or (3) related to the future merely by accident.[93] They also identify subtypes of the first two kinds of dream that, while not fully derived from Aristotle, are nonetheless true to the spirit of Aristotelian theory.

Dreams *cause* either "ex parte corporis" or "ex parte animae." "On the part of the body," they reveal symptoms of physiological disorder masked during waking: "sicut quando aliquis videt se in igne, vel in parte, vel in toto, ex eo quod in toto vel in parte in naturali calore calefactus est" [as when someone sees himself (in a dream) either partly or fully in a fire because he has been either fully or partly heated in his natural heat]; such dreams "cause" in that the physiological problem they reveal results in a future illness (Vincent, chapter 54, col. 1872).[94] Causative dreams "on the part of the soul" are double, having to do with either "knowable" or "doable" things ("scibilia" or "operabilia"). A waking inquiry into knowledge may continue during sleep and be furthered through dreams; similarly, one may, in the *actions* of one's dream, plan out some future waking deed (Vincent, chapter 54, col. 1873).[95]

Dream *signs* in Vincent and Albert are "triplex": "in caelo, & in elementis, & in somniante" [in the heavens, and in the elements, and in the dreamer] (Vincent, chapter 55, col. 1873). The first subtype includes dreams whose significance is affected by astronomical phenomena, "secundum quod dicitur communiter à philosophis, quod aliud significant somnia in plenilunio & aliud in nouilunio" [according to that which is commonly said by the philosophers: that dreams signify one thing on the full moon and another on the new moon] (Vincent, chapter 55, col. 1873).[96] "Elemental" dreams, on the other hand, are affected by, and predict, meteorological phenomena: "aliquis pisces somnians, suspicatur futuram pluuiam, & somnians pisces mori & exiccari, interpretatur futuram serenitatem" [someone dreaming of fish conjectures future rain, and one dreaming that fish die and dry out interprets (the dream as indicating) future fair weather] (Vincent, chapter 55, col. 1873).[97] Finally, "signa" arising "ex parte somniantis" [on the part of the dreamer] "sunt dispositiones somniantium paruae, que non nisi in somno sentientur, sicut aliquis somnians ignem, interpretatur futuram iram" [are those small dispositions of dreamers that are felt only during sleep – as, for example, someone dreaming of fire interprets (it as indicating) future anger] (Vincent, chapter 55, col. 1873).[98]

The definition of such dream-types, all connected to natural processes, is clearly indebted to Aristotle. In treating the last four Aristotelian questions, however, Vincent and Albert are also guided by the spirit of patristic dream theory. Augustine, Gregory, and the Bible demand that the possibility of supernatural (divine, angelic, diabolic) dreams be addressed, and Albert and Vincent do not ignore that demand. Aristotle's typology of predictive dreams, however, leaves little room for the supernatural. "Causative" dreams and "significative" dreams *in somniante* arise from internal human process. While externally-motivated "significative" dreams – those that come about through celestial or elemental activity – transcend the human, they still fall within the realm of the natural: they do not result from the special intervention of angelic or demonic forces.

Aristotle's "accidental" dream seems even further removed from the supernatural. Resembling what occurs "whenever a person, on mentioning something, finds the very thing mentioned come to pass," the "accidental" dream "is, to him who has seen it, neither token nor cause of its [so-called] fulfilment, but a mere coincidence."[99] Despite what we might expect, however, Albert and Vincent seize on this dream of "coincidence" as an appropriate category within which to locate supernatural experience. In Aristotle, such dreams alone bear a connection to the future not attributable to a natural chain of cause and effect; in some sense, therefore, they become an appropriate locus for the transcendent. Aristotle himself says, "plurima vero accident*ia videntur*, maxime *autem* transcendentia omnia et quorum non est in *ipsis* origo set de navali *prelio* et de hiis que procul accidunt sunt" [most (prophetic dreams) truly seem (to be) coincidences, especially, moreover, all those that are "transcendent" and whose origin is not in (the dreamers) themselves, but concern (for instance) a naval battle and things that happen far away].[100] For Aristotle, the dream's "transcendence" merely signals its "accidental" quality, its position outside the realm of natural cause and within the purview of coincidence. But Albert and Vincent stand within a tradition that asserts the possibility of truly transcendent dreams, and they recognize a real transcendent source for some of the phenomena that Aristotle would call "mere coincidences":

> Accidens autem siue incursus est de his, quae procul sunt tempore vel loco, & quorum notitia super nostram videtur esse prudentiam, vt dicit philosophus, sicut est de nauali bello futuro, vel de regnis subuertendis, vel de toto mundi statu futuro sicut in somno Pharaonis, Nabuchodonosor, & Danielis. Et notitia huiusmodi somniorum non fit sine reuelatione.[101]   (Vincent, chapter 55, col. 1873)

Accident or incursion, however, concerns those things that are far off in time or place and the knowledge of which seems to be above our foresight, as the Philosopher [Aristotle] says: as for example it is concerning a future naval war, or concerning reigns to be overthrown, or concerning the whole future state of the world, as in the dream[s] of Pharaoh, Nebuchadnezzar, and Daniel. And the knowledge of dreams of this sort does not occur without revelation.

In a strange reversal, Aristotle's least reliable kind of predictive dream becomes associated with *reuelatio*.

Attempting to accommodate Christian ideas, Albert and Vincent ultimately remodel Aristotelian dream theory in striking ways. In order to argue, with Aristotle, that the predicted outcome of dreams does not occur "de necessitate" [out of necessity], they must confront the revelatory dream, which seems necessarily to come true:

1 Sunt enim somnia per revelationem divinam, ut dicunt Sancti et Philosophi: sed revelationi divinae non subest falsum: ergo nec somniis falsum suberit.
2 Item, Somnium Pharaonis et Nabuchodonosor et Danielis fuerunt prophetia de futuro: sed prophetiae non potest subesse falsum: ergo nec tali somnio.
3 Item, Tale somnium aut significat aliquid, aut nihil. Si nihil, hoc est contra Philosophos et Sanctos communiter loquentes. Si vero aliquid, hoc erit

verum: quia falsum nihil est. Si ergo erit verum, aut contingenter erit verum, aut necessario. Si contingenter, potest ergo non esse verum. Ponatur ergo, quod non eveniat: tunc illud somnium non significabit verum: et si non significat verum, nihil significat: ergo illud somnium nihil significat, sed impositum erat significare aliquid: ergo somnium quod aliquid significat, nihil significat quod est impossibile: ergo non contingenter significat verum: ergo significat necessario verum aliquid futurum.[102]　　　　　　(Albert, p. 437)

1　Truly, there are dreams [that arise] through divine revelation, as the saints and philosophers say. But falsehood does not exist in divine revelation. Therefore, neither will falsehood exist in dreams.

2　Likewise, the dream[s] of Pharaoh and Nebuchadnezzar and Daniel were prophec[ies] concerning the future. But falsehood can not exist in prophecy. Therefore, neither [can it exist in] such a dream.

3　Likewise, such a dream either signifies something or nothing. If nothing, this is contrary to the philosophers and saints, who speak in agreement. But truly, if [it signifies] something, this will be true, because falsehood is nothing. If, therefore, it is true, it will be true either contingently or necessarily. If contingently, then it *can* be not true. Therefore, let it be reckoned that it not turn out [as predicted]. Then, that dream will not signify truth. And if it does not signify truth, it signifies nothing. Therefore, that dream signifies nothing. But it was imposed that it should signify something; therefore, the dream that signifies something, signifies nothing – which is impossible. Therefore, it cannot signify truth contingently. Therefore, it signifies some future, true thing necessarily.

Such an argument can ultimately be refuted: revelation is not the immovable decree that Albert at first makes it out to be:

At vero somnium Pharaonis & Nabuchodonosor & Danielis fuerunt prophetiae secundum quid immobiles de futuro scilicet existentibus causis voluntariis, simpliciter autem non. Nam si merita voluntatis Ægyptiorum immutata fuissent, non induxisset Deus famem, similiter quod saeculum est aureum, postmodum argenteum, & postea ferreum, non aliter aestimandum est quam propter dispositionem voluntatis eorum qui sunt in saeculo, & non necessario. Somnium itaque signat aliquid scil. contingens de futuro.[103]

(Vincent, chapter 56, col. 1874)

But truly the dream[s] of Pharaoh and Nebuchadnezzar and Daniel were inexorable prophecies of the future dependent on something else [*secundum quid*], namely [on] existing voluntary causes; however, [they were] not [inexorable prophecies] simply [in and of themselves]. For if the merits of will of the Egyptians had been altered, God would not have brought about a famine. Similarly, that the age[s] of the world are gold, then soon afterwards silver, and thereafter iron, is to be judged only according to the disposition of will of those who live in the age[s] of the world, and not [as though it were] necessary. Thus, the dream signifies something about the future that is contingent.

Albert and Vincent can ultimately conclude, in fine Aristotelian fashion, that "somnia non eueniunt de necessitate, siue sint causae siue signa siue incursus futurorum accidentalis" [dreams do not come true by necessity, whether they be causes or signs or the accidental incursion of future things] (Vincent, chapter 56, col. 1874).[104] But to reach such a conclusion, the two Christian authors focus their attention firmly on the divine dreams whose very existence Aristotle would deny.

At moments, indeed, the question of necessity fades into the background and the nature of revelation itself becomes the central issue. In a discussion dependent on Augustine's distinction between intellectual and spiritual vision, Albert and Vincent distinguish two kinds of *revelatio*, the first occurring when the divine will is understood directly, the second when comprehension involves a "permixtio phantasmatum" [admixture of apparitions] (Vincent, chapter 56, col. 1873).[105] The first, since it occurs through intellectual, not spiritual, vision, "non est somnium sed prophetia" [is not a dream but rather prophecy] (Vincent, chapter 56, col. 1873);[106] the second, because it is involved with images, is true dreaming: "sine phantasmatibus non est aliquod somnium" [there is no dream without apparitions] (Vincent, chapter 56, col. 1874).[107] Vincent's treatment in particular emphasizes the revelatory dream. Toward the end of chapter 56, he abandons the question of necessity to include additional material on the "reuelatio somnialis que per Angelos fit" [oneiric revelation that occurs through angels] (col. 1874).[108] He then moves directly to Aristotle's sixth question – "vtrum futura perspiciantur ab homine solum, vel causam habeant quosdam daemones" [whether future things may be perceived by man on his own, or have (as their) cause certain demons] (chapter 57, col. 1874)[109] – where the revelatory dream again occupies a central position.

In treating this sixth question, Albert and Vincent transform Aristotle's "daemones" into Christian spirits and, influenced by Augustine, they strongly assert the role such spirits play in dreaming:

Et nos quidem dicimus quod in somniis fiunt reuelationes ab intelligentiis, quae dicuntur Angeli, fiuntque à bonis & malis iuxta sententiam Augustini.[110] Dicit enim in duodecimo lib. super Genesim: Quod per corporalem visionem ac per corporalium imagines, quae in spiritu demonstrantur, & Angeli boni instruunt & mali fallunt.[111]
                                                                    (Vincent, chapter 57, col. 1874)

And indeed, we say that revelations are caused in dreams by intelligences called angels, and they are caused by good and evil [angels], according to Augustine's statement. Truly, in the twelfth book on Genesis, he says that "By means of corporeal vision as well as by means of the images of corporeal objects revealed in the spirit, good angels instruct men and evil ones deceive them."[112]

Vincent and Albert do not, however, ignore possible objections to such a view of dreaming. If angelic "intelligentiae" are incorporeal "formae vniuersales simplices" [universal, simple forms], how can they be responsible for dreams that express themselves "in particularibus phantasmatum formis" [in the particular forms of apparitions] as "similitudines corporales" [corporeal likenesses] (Vincent, chapter 57, col. 1874)?[113] In other words, how can angelic nature communicate with a baser human nature that is not pure "intelligence," that indeed depends on images for its understanding? The answer provided by Albert and Vincent depends in part on the authority of the "new" science:[114]

Licet in Angelis sint formae simplices, tamen quia Angelus & intelligentia sunt substantiae in animas humanas agentes, vt dicunt philosophi: Formae illae sunt in eis simplices, recipiuntur ab anima vel animabus, vt particulares & corporales, & haec est solutio Alpharabii.[115]　　　　　　(Vincent, chapter 57, col. 1874)

Though the forms of the angels may be simple, nevertheless, since the angel and intelligence are substances that act on human souls, as the philosophers say, those forms are simple in them [the angels], [but] are received by the soul or souls as particular and corporeal; and this is Alpharabius's solution.

Finally, however, the view of "demonic" dreaming given by Albert and Vincent depends most fully on Christian authority: "veritas illius patet per intellectum diuinorum in sacra scriptura" [the truth of this is made clear by an understanding of the divine things in holy Scripture] (Vincent, chapter 58, col. 1875).[116] Good and evil spirits cause dreams, and those dreams, as Augustine argues and as the Bible witnesses, are involved with "particular," "corporeal" images.

In the consideration of Aristotle's fourth, fifth, and sixth questions, a tension builds between Aristotelian attention to "natural" dreams, and the assertion of supernatural, even divine, dreaming; that tension becomes, in the treatment of Aristotle's last question, outright conflict. In considering whether dreams arise naturally ("a natura") or through chance events ("ab euentu"),[117] Albert and Vincent agree with the Aristotelians that "nullum ... somnium accidit ab euentu" [no ... dream occurs by chance] (Vincent, chapter 59, col. 1875),[118] and they present at length Aristotle's arguments for wholly "natural" dreams. But here Albert and Vincent must openly come to terms with Aristotle's denial of divinely-inspired dreams, and with the conflict between that denial and other authoritative views:

Videtur autem esse contrarietas inter Gregorium & Aristotelem, quoniam Aristoteles probat somnia non esse à Deo, Gregorius dicit ea quandoque esse ab illo.[119]　　　　　　(Vincent, chapter 59, col. 1875)

There seems, however, to be an opposition between Gregory and Aristotle, since Aristotle shows that dreams are not from God, [while] Gregory says that they are sometimes from Him.

Albert and Vincent cannot support Aristotle against Gregory, and they ultimately salvage Aristotelian theory only by distorting it. First, they limit its scope, suggesting that Aristotle's denial of God's role in dreaming applies only to common or frequent dream experience:

Arist. tangit causam somnii frequentis, & hoc probat esse nature melancholicae infirmitatis, non à merito gratiae ac virtutis.[120]

(Vincent, chapter 59, col. 1875)

Aristotle touches upon the cause of the frequent dream, and he shows that this has the nature of a melancholy infirmity [and does] not [arise] on the grounds of grace and virtue.

Vincent and Albert also assert that Aristotle in certain cases admits the possibility of divine, revelatory dreams:

Dicit autem quod non semper hoc falsum est, quod somnia à Deo sint, ac per hoc innuit quandoque per diuinam reuelationem esse ab ipso.[121]

(Vincent, chapter 59, col. 1875)

He says, however, that it is not always false that dreams may be from God, and through this he approves [the idea] that [they] sometimes arise from God Himself through divine revelation.

Such an assertion misrepresents Aristotle, but the pressure of Christian dream theory is here too strong to allow Aristotle an undistorted voice.

Albert's account of dreaming ends with this diminished and deformed version of Aristotelian theory and, as it ends, attention turns away from Aristotle toward Gregory. Albert quotes the six-fold Gregorian division of dream experience (pp. 444–45), and correlates that division with a more abstract way of defining dream-types:

Quodlibet somnium est reducibile ad aliquam causam efficientem, quae causa efficiens vel est in somniante, vel extra ipsum, vel partim in ipso, et partim extra. Et si est in somniante, talis est ex parte corporis, vel ex parte animae. Et si ex parte corporis, tunc est ex ventris plenitudine vel inanitione. Si autem ex parte animae solum est in somniante, tunc est cognitio solum.[122] Si vero est extra, vel est a bonis Angelis, vel malis. Si a malis, tunc est ab illusione. Si a bonis, tunc est a revelatione. Si vero partim intra et partim extra, tunc vel erit a bonis Angelis, vel a malis. Et si a bonis, tunc est ex cogitatione et revelatione. Si a malis, tunc est ex cogitatione et illusione.[123]

(p. 445)

Any dream is traceable to a certain efficient cause, which efficient cause is either inside or outside the dreamer, or partly inside and partly outside him. And if it is inside the dreamer, such [a cause] is either on the part of the body or on the part of the soul. And if on the part of the body, then it is from either fullness or emptiness of the stomach. However, if it is in the dreamer only on the part of the soul, then [the cause] is cognition alone. If indeed it is external, it is either from good angels or from evil ones. If from evil ones, then it is from illusion. If from good ones, then it is from revelation. If indeed [the cause is] partly inside and partly outside, then it will be either from good angels or from evil ones. And if from good ones, then it is from thinking together with revelation. If from evil ones, then it is from thinking together with illusion.[124]

In addition, Albert defends Gregory's division against the charge that it is incomplete because it does not take into account certain astrological, elemental, and corporeal influences:

Gregorius non tangit nisi proxime moventia in somnio. Coelum autem et stellae et elementa non sunt moventia proxime. Per ventris enim plenitudinem et in-anitionem intelligitur omnis dispositio corporis movens in somnio.   (p. 445)

Gregory touches upon only those things acting proximately on the dream. But the sky and the stars and the elements do not act proximately. And truly, by the fullness and emptiness of the stomach, every disposition of the body that acts on the dream is to be understood.

If Albert's treatment of dreams is heavily influenced by Aristotle – the very structure of his argument is, after all, determined by Aristotle's questions – it finally presents a view in many ways distant from the Aristotelian position and closely akin to late-antique and twelfth-century theories. While he stresses the mechanisms of somatic and psychological action more strongly than do earlier writers, when it comes down to questions of significance and to defining the dream's full potential, Albert calls on patristic and biblical authorities, acknowledging a large debt to Gregory's tried-and-true system.[124] Ultimately, Albert allows the dream the same range of possibility – from the mundane to the divine and the diabolic – that we find in Augustine, Gregory, and their earlier medieval followers.

Vincent of Beauvais intensifies Albert's already strong assertion of the dream's diversity. He devotes two full chapters (60 and 61) to Gregory's dream theory, citing it even more fully than does Albert (cols. 1875–76).[125] Moreover, Vincent here considers a great deal of additional material, largely drawn from late-antique and twelfth-century sources; in doing so, he draws ever closer to the theories of Macrobius, Augustine, and Gregory.

Vincent first moves away from using Albert's *Summa de creaturis* as his source to a reliance on Jean de la Rochelle's *Summa de anima*.[126] While Jean himself was an ardent Aristotelian heavily indebted to Avicenna, Vincent quotes material taken by Jean almost exclusively from the twelfth-century *De spiritu et anima*, which in turn relies largely on Augustine and Macrobius. Thus, Vincent presents Macrobius's dream hierarchy in a form that includes the non-Macrobian medical material added to the *De spiritu*, but that is still essentially faithful to late-antique conceptions of the dream (chapter 62, cols. 1876–77).[127] Further, following Jean, Vincent explicates Macrobius's classification in a way that strongly emphasizes its double and hierarchical status:

> Aut enim videtur verum aut falsum. Si ver[u]m[128] aut videtur tectum figuris & occultum, aut videtur manifestum. Primo modo est somnium. Si vero videtur manifestum, aut videtur simpliciter, & sic est visio. Aut cum admiratione, quae accidit ex magna imaginatione alicuius personae sacrae, & sic est oraculum. Si vero videtur falsum, aut est falsitas quo ad rem visam & sic insomnium, aut est falsitas quo ad actum videndi, & sic phantasma, cum dormiens putat se videre vigilando.[129]   (Chapter 62, col. 1877)

> Truly, it [the dream] appears [as] either true or false. If true, either it appears covered and hidden in figures, or it appears manifest. In the first mode, it is a "somnium." But truly, if it appears manifest, or appears simply [*simpliciter*], then it is a "visio." Or [if it appears] with the wonder that comes from the powerful imagination of a certain sacred person, then it is an "oraculum." But truly, if it appears [as] false, either the falsity is as to the thing seen, and then [it is] an "insomnium," or the falsity is as to the act of seeing, and then [it is] a "phantasma" [i.e., *visum*], when a person who is asleep thinks that he is seeing while awake.

Dreams straddle truth and falsehood. Different kinds of false dreams are distinguishable, and true dreams can be arranged hierarchically, in order of increasing clarity and impressiveness.

In the following chapter, again citing Jean, Vincent presents another familiar way of treating dreams, as either intrinsic or extrinsic:

> Intrinseca vero duplex, scilicet curiositas anime, & appetitus corporis. *Vnde Augustinus*. sunt multa visa vsitata, quae vel à spiritu nostro multipliciter existunt, vel ex corpore quodammodo surgunt. Ex spiritu, sicut secundum studia, quae quisque exercuit, & solitas artes similitudines apparent. Ex corpore sicut si fuerimus affecti à carne vigilantes, dormientibus apparent similitudines, vt si forte esurientes aut sitientes dormiunt, epulis & potibus instanter inhiare videntur. A causa vero extrinseca visiones duobus modis accidunt in somnis. Nam vt dicit Augustinus humanum spiritum quandoque bonus assumit spiritus, & quandoque malus.[130]   (Chapter 63, col. 1877)

> Truly, the intrinsic [cause is] twofold – namely curiosity of soul and appetite of body. *Therefore Augustine* [says]: there are many wonted visions that either come forth from our spirit in multiple ways or arise from the body in some way. From the spirit, as [when] likenesses appear in accordance with the studies that one has

worked at [while awake] and [according to one's] accustomed occupations. From the body, as [when] likenesses appear [to us] while we sleep if we have been affected by the flesh while awake, as, perhaps, if hungry or thirsty [people] are sleeping, they seem [in their dreams] urgently to desire food and drink. And truly, visions occur in two ways from an extrinsic cause during sleep. For, as Augustine says, sometimes a good spirit takes a human spirit to itself, and sometimes an evil [spirit does so].

Vincent here emphasizes the intrinsic dream somewhat more strongly than the extrinsic; indeed, he next cites Priscianus Lydus on "lower" dreams (chapter 63, col. 1877).[131] But Vincent is only deferring a more extensive discussion of externally-stimulated dreams. In the following two chapters (64 and 65), he discusses angelic and demonic dreams at length, citing Augustine – via Jean – and Gregory directly.[132] External dreams arise from both good and evil motives; difficult to distinguish from each other, they must be approached with caution.[133]

In chapters 60–65, then, Vincent presents a compendium of late-antique dream lore, citing, in rapid succession, Gregory's six-tiered classification, Macrobius's five-part scheme, and patristic discussions of the angelic and the demonic. He goes on to focus attention almost exclusively on higher sorts of visionary experience, considering the following topics:

1 The means by which demons and angels affect human beings (chapters 66–74). Here, patristic writers (Augustine, Jerome, Gennadius, and Bede), the Bible, and Thomas Aquinas are the main authorities.[134]
2 Augustine's "tria genera visionum" (chapters 75–80).[135]
3 Prophecy (chapters 81–95). Aquinas, *Quaestiones disputatae de veritate*, is the main source.[136]
4 Ecstatic vision and *raptus* (chapters 96–111). Here, the discussion is drawn from Augustine and Aquinas.[137]

While the tenor of Vincent's first fifty-one chapters – the discussions of sleep and of Aristotle's first three questions on dreams – is mainly philosophical or scientific in its emphasis on explicable, natural causes, that of the last forty-six chapters is clearly theological. Here Vincent stresses those supernatural moments in which the human being approaches divinity: prophetic visions, Paul's *raptus* "in paradisum," the vision of God. Between his opening and closing discussions, Vincent treats the dream's significance (Aristotle's last four questions) and the variety of its possible incarnations (chapters 52–65). This transitional discussion involves both physical process and supernatural revelation: authoritatively examined by "sancti" and "philosophi" alike, the dream stands related both to the purely natural mechanisms of sleep, and to the rapturous experience of transcendent vision.

Dreaming in the Middle Ages

It might be argued that encyclopedias – concerned, as they are, with *preserving* information – advance older theories of dreaming not because these are still believed, but simply because they are old and "authoritative." However, when we look at those thirteenth- and fourteenth-century writers like Albertus Magnus whose thinking was most innovative and most heavily influenced by the new learning, we see a reliance on older ideas about dreaming no weaker than that of encyclopedists like Vincent of Beauvais.

In late-medieval psychological treatises, for instance, late-antique dream theory still played a central role. Such treatises proliferated in the later Middle Ages, largely in response to new ideas about the human psyche,[138] but the discussion of dreaming in such works tended to be quite conservative. Raoul de Longchamps, in the late twelfth or early thirteenth century, clearly worked with the latest sources.[139] When he discusses sleep and dreams within his treatment of *imaginatio*, he cites Aristotle "in libro *De somno et vigilia*" (pp. 52–53, 54–55, and 57–59); "Jacob filii Al-Kindi, *De somno et visione*" (p. 53); "*Libris medicinalibus*" (p. 55); "Maurus" Salernitanus, "super librum *Prognosticorum*" (p. 56); and "Galenus" (p. 57). He also addresses such Aristotelian questions as "Unde contingit quod quidam numquam somniant?" [Why it happens that certain people never dream] (p. 59).[140] Raoul chooses, nonetheless, to rely heavily on the Macrobian system of dream classification:

> Videndum est quid sit sopor sive somnium quod idem est large sumpto hoc vocabulo somnium.
> Sopor itaque est apparitio quaedam in somno adveniens et in somno recedens. Eius autem, ut habemus in Macrobio, quinque sunt: species oraculum, visio, somnium, insomnium, phantasma. (p. 53)

It is to be seen what deep sleep [*sopor*] or the dream [*somnium*] is, which [*somnium*] is the same [as *sopor*], if this word, "somnium," is taken in its largest sense.

And thus "sopor" is a certain apparition arriving in sleep and retreating in sleep. Moreover, as we have it in Macrobius, there are five species of it: *oraculum, visio, somnium, insomnium, phantasma* [i.e., *visum*].

Raoul, like other medieval writers who adopted this system, emphasizes lower dreams and their physiological involvements more strongly than does Macrobius himself: he devotes separate chapters to *insomnium*, *phantasma*, and *phialtes* [i.e., *ephialtes*], but not to Macrobius's higher dream-types. Under the pressure of Aristotelian thought, he also modifies

Macrobius's definition of *somnium* to include certain untrustworthy psychological and physiological dreams:

Dicit Commentator super librum *De somno et vigilia*: Cum praecesserint per diem motiones quaedam factae in loco imaginatorio, remanent vestigia quaedam motionum earum et in dormiente faciunt imaginationem, quae est somnium.[141]

(p. 54)

The Commentator on the book *De somno et vigilia* says: When there have preceded, during the day, certain motions produced in the seat of the imagination, certain vestiges of those motions remain and produce, in the one who is asleep, an imagination which is the "somnium."

Still, Raoul also allows for *somnia* that are externally-inspired and revelatory, if difficult to read:

Si vero spiritus illi aliquid obscure denuntient tectum figuris, velatum ambagibus, nec nisi interpretatione intelligendum, somnium stricto vocabulo dicitur. Quod ideo forsitan volunt latere spiritus, ut homines sint intenti et perspicaces in exercitatione intelligendi.

(p. 54)

Truly, if those spirits announce something obscurely – covered by figures, veiled in ambiguities, nor to be understood without interpretation – it is called a "somnium" in the strict sense of the word. Which [*somnium*] the spirits perhaps wish to be obscure so that men may be intent and acute in the exercise of [their] understanding.

Furthermore, Raoul emphasizes the transcendent quality of *visio* and *oraculum*; quoting a "Commentator super Macrobium" (perhaps Guillaume de Conches),[142] he suggests:

Quod spiritus amici humanae naturae cum non possunt hominibus colloqui in vigilia, quoniam corpora sunt suae naturae contraria, coloquuntur eis saltem in quiete dum cessant corporea sensuum officia, et transformantur in figuras corporeas apparendo eis in somno vel praedicant futura bona ut gaudeant vel innuunt mala futura ut instruant. Si ergo istud fiat a parte et ab aliqua gravi persona et certa, oraculum dicitur.

Si autem spiritus illi aliquid nuntient, quod eodem modo quo in somno apparuit in re eveniat, visio nominatur.

(p. 54)

That spirits friendly to human nature, since they cannot speak with men when they are awake (because bodies are contrary to their [the spirits'] nature), at least speak with them during sleep, when the corporeal duties of the senses cease. And [the spirits] are [then] transformed into corporeal figures to appear to [men] in [their] sleep, and they either predict future good things, so that [the men] rejoice, or signal future evils, so that they prepare [themselves]. If, then, this happens on the part of and from a certain weighty and reliable person, it is called an "oraculum."

If, however, those spirits announce something that turns out in reality in the same way that it appeared in sleep, it is named a "visio."

Despite Raoul's strong interest in lower dreams, he does not fail to emphasize the variety inherent in Macrobius's scheme. Dreams can be both mundane and transcendent; some are "interpretatione ... digna et aliquid divinationis habentia" [worthy of interpretation and containing a kind of divination], while others are "vana ... et interpretatione indigna" [vain and unworthy of interpretation] (p. 54). Discussing the two gates of dreams (p. 58) and emphasizing the dream's involvement with both body and soul (pp. 58–59), Raoul repeatedly stresses the dream's double nature.

We find a similar tendency to emphasize the important themes of late-antique dream theory in the thirteenth-century psychologist Jean de la Rochelle. Despite his general indebtedness to the new learning, in the *Summa de anima* Jean presents a discussion of dreams almost wholly composed of late-antique material.[143] He cites Macrobius's five-fold classification (f. 51ʳ; attributed by Jean to Augustine "in libro de anima et spiritu"), Gregory's six-tiered scheme (f. 51ʳ; attributed to "Jeronymus super Danielem"), and a great deal of genuine Augustinian material (f. 51ᵛ). When Jean adds to his sources, it is partly to emphasize the dream's doubleness:

Aut enim videtur verum aut falsum ... aut est in nobis. aut extra nos. Si in nobis aut ex parte corporis aut ex parte mentis ... Si causa est extra nos, tunc est ex operatione spiritualis substantie. et hoc dupliciter. aut ex operatione substantie spiritualis que est dyabolus. qui dicitur illusio. et sic est sompnium ex illusione. aut ex operatione substantie spiritualis bone. et sic dicitur fieri per revelationem.

(ff. 51ʳ⁻ᵛ)

Truly, it appears either [as] true or false ... It is either inside us or outside us. If inside us, either on the part of the body or on the part of the mind ... If the cause is outside us, then it is from the operation of a spiritual substance. And this [occurs] in two ways: either from the operation of the spiritual substance that is a devil, which is called illusion. And [if] thus, it is a dream [arising] from illusion. Or from the operation of a good spiritual substance. And [if] thus, it is said to occur through revelation.

Jean's *Summa* was very influential. As we have seen, Vincent of Beauvais used it, and as late as the fifteenth century, William of Vaurouillon, in his *Liber de anima*, followed Jean in presenting a view of dreaming largely dependent on late-antique ideas. William cites three major discussions of dreaming. The first is Macrobius's system, apparently taken from Jean;[144] the second is Gregory's scheme, attributed incorrectly, as in Jean, to "Hieronymum super secundum capitulum Danielis" [Jerome on the second chapter of Daniel];[145] the third is Averroes "in libro *De somno et vigilia*."[146] The material quoted from this last source presents the dream as an unambiguously "higher" experience than most late-antique authorities would allow. Differentiating *somnium* from *divinatio* and *prophetia*, Averroes suggests that dreams come generally "ab angelis."[147] All in all, however, William's discussion preserves the essential structure of late-antique theory. It emphasizes dream hierarchies, and stresses the dream's imaginative quality (as does most medieval psychological writing). As William suggests, the psychologist studies dreaming "ut melius imaginationis et imaginativae cognoscatur officium" [so that the function of the imagination and of the imaginative faculty may be better known].[148]

CHANGING DREAM THEORY

During the thirteenth and fourteenth centuries, dream theory changed in important ways. Aristotelian and medical works made available a fuller treatment of the physical and psychological processes involved in dreaming. Authors began to question the trustworthiness and transcendence of the dream more seriously than earlier in the Middle Ages. At the same time, however, older dream theories proved remarkably resilient. They were used to corroborate newer material – for instance, the Aristotelian emphasis on the dream's imaginative status. Authors often brought together newer and older teachings: witness the medical accretions to Macrobius's *insomnium* and *visum*. Even in texts heavily indebted to Aristotelianism, we find late-antique authorities playing important auxiliary roles (for example, in Albert's *Summa de creaturis*), or even providing the bulk of the dream lore (for example, in Jean de la Rochelle).

Even in treatments of dreaming that do not make extensive, direct use of late-antique theory, the dream's double and middle character is often strongly emphasized. Albertus Magnus, in his commentary on Aristotle's *De divinatione per somnum*, proposes an elaborate scheme for classifying visionary experience that strikes us immediately as different from the dream theory we have so far examined.[149] Still, in its general structure, Albert's scheme strongly resembles late-antique dream hierarchies.

Albert discusses only "natural" dreams, declining to address theological questions;[150] since, however, he sees many dreams as arising from heavenly movements – from the action of a "lumen" [light] that can convey the "virtutes superiorum motorum" [powers of higher movers] (p. 190) to lower creatures – Albert does allow for divinatory and transcendent dreams. The human "anima imaginativa" [imaginative soul] (p. 190) receives the celestial "lumen," or "motus," or "forma" · in images, perceiving celestial truths more or less clearly "secundum quod congruum

Dreaming in the Middle Ages

... et possibile fuerit unicuique" [according to what is appropriate and possible for each individual] (p. 190). Thirteen kinds of visionary experience result, varying in clarity and directness:

1 Dreams arise in part from human process ("a proprio corde" [from one's own heart]) and involve the "forma coelestis" [celestial form] only weakly; such dreams do not elucidate the future except "implicite et confuse" [entangledly and confusedly] and they are frequently misleading ("frequenter fallens") (p. 191).

2 Only an indistinct and confused light reaches the soul, and the images it presents are inappropriate ("inconvenientia") to the message or truth that the dream should convey (p. 191).

3 The dream's import is shown in appropriate metaphors that can be reliably interpreted (p. 191).

4 The dream is not metaphorical, but rather expresses its meaning in images of what will actually occur – "sicut res evenit" (p. 191).

5 Dream images are presented and explained by someone who appears in the dream; the explanations, however, are not explicit but rather made "in verbis et figuris" [in words and figures] (p. 191).

6 The dream images are explicitly interpreted by someone within the dream, "qui docet recte futuram visionis significationem" [who teaches correctly the future signification of the vision] (p. 191).

7 Without images, intellective truths are presented to one who is asleep (p. 192).

8 The action of the "forma coelestis" is so strong that it moves someone who is awake to see a vision; the vision, however, like the second kind of dream, is expressed "in simulacris obscuris" [in obscure images] (p. 192).

9 A waking vision, parallel to the third kind of dream, reveals future things "per formas expressas et de facili adaptabiles" [through forms clear and easily fitted (to their meaning)] (p. 192).

10 A waking vision occurs in which the images seen are also explained (p. 192).

11 A waking, imaginative vision occurs in which future and occult things are clearly understood (pp. 192–93).

12 A waking vision directly presents images of future events (p. 193).

13 "Bona occulta" [concealed good things] are revealed, which are correctly understood by the waking seer (p. 193).[151]

Albert here constructs a hierarchical description of visionary experience, of dreams, waking visions, and prophecy. Dreams (1–7) are lowest on the scale, because it takes the least celestial power to affect someone who is asleep: sleep quiets sensory process, allowing the "motus coelestis" [celestial motion] to be more easily perceived (p. 190). In waking visions (8–11), that "motus" must not only present images or ideas, but must present them in the presence of interfering data; the celestial light must be bright enough to move the soul away from its concentration on the senses (p. 192). In the last two stages of vision, true prophecy is attained, and in the final stage, the celestial signals are so strong that they display a clear message "etiam absque magna sensuum aversione" [even without a great turning away of the senses] (p. 193).

Focusing attention on just those visions that occur in sleep, we see another hierarchical scheme. The lowest kind of dream has only minimal involvement with either the imaginative or intellective powers of the soul: the "forma coelestis" touches only "virtutes motivas" [the motive powers] (p. 191). In other words, this lowest of dreams is involved with that part of the soul closest to bodily action. Indeed, like Macrobius's *insomnium*, it arises in part from internal bodily process. The highest of Albert's sleeping visions (7), on the other hand, is so distant from the bodily that it is not even involved with images (and so is not, strictly speaking, a dream). It strikes the intellect immediately with truth.

Albert arranges, between these two extreme types, a variety of intermediaries, each involved with the imagination and capable of displaying truth, however weakly. As we ascend this scale of dreaming (until we reach the fourth stage), the dream images become clearer and clearer, more and more intimately connected to the future event they predict, or to the truth they depict. The fifth and sixth dream-types are "higher" than even the clear vision of the future (4) because, in addition to presenting a truth imagistically, they include within themselves intellective material that furthers the interpretation of the dream. Moving up Albert's scale of dreams, we climb the hierarchy of human psychology from the motive, to the imaginative, to the intellective; we ascend from obscurity and unreliability to greater and greater clarity.

In sum, the structure of Albert's classification is not far removed from Augustine's three visions or Macrobius's five kinds of dream. We might, indeed, associate Albert's first dream-type with Macrobius's *insomnium*; the second and third, metaphorical representations of truth, with the *somnium*; the fourth, a clear revelation of future action, with the *visio*; and the fifth and sixth, in which a figure within the dream plays a role in explaining its meaning, with the *oraculum*.[152]

Yet Albert's system does, of course, differ from Macrobius's and from other late-antique treatments: in a way particular to medieval Aristotelianism, it emphasizes the *processes* by which dreams come into being, articulating the universal, natural movements that produce dream stimuli and the human psychology that receives those stimuli more or less clearly. New schemes like Albert's themselves became influential: in the fourteenth century, for instance, William of Aragon, in his *De pronosticatione sompniorum*, adopted and modified the Albertine system.[153] But Albert, while elaborating his own description of dreaming, did not discard what was crucial to earlier dream theory: he recognized that the dream may be both a way of discovering hidden truth and a meaningless or indecipherable message. At one extreme absolutely clear, at the other terribly obscure, the dream also exists in a variety of intermediate forms. For Albert, dreaming often arises from a source of knowledge, but in its encounters with imperfect humanity, that knowledge becomes more or less distorted. Most often, it ends up on that middle ground of the imagination where, affected by both body and intellect, truths are expressed sometimes clearly and sometimes obscurely.

6

Dreams and fiction

DREAM THEORY AND POETRY

It is difficult to define precisely the complex affiliations between the dreams found in medieval literature and the attitudes toward dreaming expressed, for instance, in dream theory or the dreambooks. Even the immensely popular *Somniale Danielis*, with its method of dream interpretation, bears a problematic relation to the dreams of medieval fiction. While Steven Fischer presents his collation of dreambook material as a "sourcebook for the interpretation of medieval literary dreams," he simultaneously warns that "there is no evidence that even one single dream in all of medieval European literature exclusively requires a dreambook for its interpretation."[1] Simone Collin, in a study of the literary use of dreambooks, concludes that "les clefs des songes et les songes tels qu'ils sont rapportés dans la littérature médiévale sont deux aspects différents et indépendants de l'onirocritique" [the dreambooks and dreams as they are reported in medieval literature are two different and independent aspects of dream interpretation].[2]

In considering the influence of the dreambooks – and certainly of more recondite theoretical material – we cannot presuppose the literary artist's familiarity with any particular idea; nor can we assume that authors would necessarily have used that dream lore with which they *were* demonstrably familiar.[3] In creating a fictional dream, the writer may have a specific theory of dreaming in mind, and may depend on that theory to create certain literary effects. But the assumption that one ancient or medieval conception of the dream (usually Macrobius's) provides a key for reading dream poetry often leads to interpretive distortions, to a narrowing of attention that may oversimplify poetic complexities. As Peden suggests:

It is undoubtedly true that mediaeval dream poetry was written in an environment in which dream theory was discussed and dreambooks consulted. But the precise nature of this environment and the way in which it conditioned creative writing demands very cautious investigation. Above all, we should not overestimate the theorists' power over the daemon of inspiration.[4]

Peden, however, perhaps shies away too absolutely from the critical use of dream theory and the dreambooks. Having suggested that Chaucer's dream poems do not depend significantly upon Macrobius, she warns firmly against emphasizing the influence of even those dream theorists whom Chaucer more clearly knew:[5]

Even his use of other theorists must be treated with caution, for it could be argued that the content of his dream poems sprang principally from literary models and his own creative imagination. The "olde bokes" provide but an *excusatio*; the dreamlike nature of his poetry lay to hand in everyday experience.[6]

Peden is certainly right to emphasize the importance of literary models in shaping Chaucer's dream poetry. Indeed, most medieval dream visions depended extensively on earlier works, and knowledge of a poem's literary antecedents of course aids our understanding of it. Still, an investigation of broader cultural contexts also enriches our reading. If we do not delimit too narrowly our view of the ways in which dream lore might affect literary works – if, for instance, we do not set our sights simply on discovering the sources of a poem's "content," and if we do not search for a strict poetic reproduction or translation of specific aspects of dream lore – we will find that a knowledge of medieval dream theory and attitudes toward dreaming helps us answer certain important questions about dream fictions.

Using what we have so far learned about medieval dreaming, we can begin to define the characteristics and possibilities of dream vision as a literary genre.[7] The pervasive ambivalence encountered in descriptions of the dream from the Bible and Plato onwards also informs dream poetry: throughout its history, dream vision exploits a double potential. Just as, in theoretical discussions, opposed, extreme kinds of dream – true and false, external and internal, good and bad – bound the range of dream experience, so extreme types of dream vision set the limits of the literary genre. On the one hand stand dream narratives consistent with the belief that the dream provides a route to higher knowledge. In these, the dreamer receives an educative vision: given oneiric access to a higher moral or eschatological realm, he or she awakens enlightened, ready to lead an improved life. Dream visions of this tradition take as their ultimate models such works as the biblical Apocalypse or Cicero's *Somnium Scipionis*.[8] At the opposite extreme stand dream visions generally corresponding to the somatic and psychological dreams of theoretical discussion. Such poems take their dreamers not to a world of transcendent knowledge, but rather back into the individual body and psyche. Instead of moving upward and outward to disclose the workings of the universe, the secrets of an afterlife, or the ways of a properly moral existence, these poems move inward into passion and downward toward the things of the world. This tradition, like that of the "higher" dream, goes back at least to Roman models – for instance, to Ovid's (or Pseudo-Ovid's) *Amores* III.v.[9]

The contrast between the Ovidian love poem and Cicero's *Somnium Scipionis* epitomizes a split found throughout the history of the dream vision. The *Somnium*, as part of Cicero's *De Republica*, addresses important public concerns, asking what constitutes proper behavior for a civic official. Furthermore, as a vision of the heavens, it examines human involvement in cosmic order, considering how earthly behavior affects the eternal life of the soul. Didactic, claiming the status of revelation, the *Somnium* instructs its dreamer (and reader) on how to live in preparation for the life to come. Ovid's poem, on the other hand, does not so much instruct as explore emotion. Instead of an ideal political or cosmic order, the dream presents a sensual garden within which the dreamer confronts the intensity of his own love. At the poem's beginning, the dreamer tries to escape the "aestus amoris" [heat of love] (36): "ipse sub arboreis vitabam frondibus aestum – / fronde sub arborea sed tamen aestus erat" [I was seeking refuge from the heat beneath the branches of the trees – though beneath the trees' branches came none the less the heat] (7–8). In contrast, as the poem ends, having been shown allegorically the infidelity of his beloved, the dreamer feels a cold emotion opposed to love's "heat." Yet, he remains immersed in emotion: "gelido mihi sanguis ab ore / fugit, et ante oculos nox stetit alta meos" [I was cold; the blood fled from my face, and before my eyes stood deep night] (45–46). His dream finally leads him not to an intellectual appreciation of his plight, but instead to an emotional, indeed visceral, response divorced from rational process.

Critics have usually defined the early tradition of the literary dream as one of serious, educative visions.[10] As the existence of the Ovidian poem suggests, however, from the tradition's beginnings, authors exploited the full range of dream possibilities. Even in strictly religious contexts, the dreams and visions recounted are not universally divine or revelatory, though they are generally treated in a serious manner. For examples of deceptive and demonic dreams, one need look no further than Gregory the Great's *Dialogues*;[11] and both divine and demonic dreams characterize Christian saints' lives. In one Old English poetic life of St. Guthlac (*Guthlac A*), the saint repeatedly encounters both angels and demons.[12] Guthlac experiences two visionary journeys – one into the heavens and one into hell – arising, unlike the revelations of the *Dream of Scipio* or the Apocalypse, from demonic action. The downward journey does not threaten Guthlac in order to reform him, as a divinely-inspired vision might (see, for example,

Strabo's *Visio Wettini*, discussed below); rather, it is intended to lead him from the path of righteousness into despair.[13] The upward journey – rather than demonstrating the insignificance of earth and the need to lead a humble life in preparation for the life to come (the sort of vision we find in the *Somnium Scipionis*) – tempts Guthlac with pride.[14] Such visions are anti-revelations, demonic temptations on the flipside of divine visionary experience.

The dreams and visions of the *Dialogues* and *Guthlac A* are not themselves fully-fledged dream visions,[15] but in medieval dream vision proper, the depiction of a wide range of visionary phenomena is also found. The poetry of the Carolingian writer, Walahfrid Strabo (809–49),[16] neatly demonstrates the doublesidedness of dream vision, even in the earlier Middle Ages.

Strabo's major poem, the *Visio Wettini*, is the elaborate, didactic account of a revelatory dream – "there came an angel to him [Wetti] sent from highest heaven" (p. 49)[17] – in which, led by the angelic guide, Wetti sees both the punishment of sinners and "the abode of blessed saints" (p. 59).[18] The angel makes explicit the significance of the dream's content, and the speaker of the poem often further expounds this teaching. The dream's didactic purpose is clear: Wetti is to return to the waking world and instruct his fellow monks on their need for reform.[19]

But while the *Visio Wettini* thus presents itself as a morally-instructive revelation, it also – if marginally – suggests the possibility of other kinds of vision. Before his long dream, having just fallen into a light sleep,[20] Wetti encounters "the spirit of guile ... dressed as a priest" (p. 46).[21] The devil threatens Wetti with torture, and "while the evil spirit ma[kes] these dire threats ... a horde [of demons] in hideous array" rushes into the room (p. 47).[22] Wetti is terrified, but he is defended within the dream: "Divine assistance came swiftly. He saw seated in the cell some radiant monks, whose bodies emitted streams of light" (p. 47).[23] The demons flee, and the dream shifts from a demonic to an angelic mode: before he wakes, Wetti briefly converses with an angel.

Through this preliminary dream, Strabo reminds us of the emphasis in Christian thought on both demonic and angelic visions.[24] And in the midst of Wetti's longer *visio*, Strabo recounts a third dream that also calls to mind the possibility of dreams that are not revelatory. Wetti's angel tells him about a certain bishop who could have helped the soul of an abbot escape its purgatorial punishments "in accordance with the instructions which the abbot had given when he appeared to a cleric in a dream" (p. 53).[25] The cleric's dream is veridical, but the bishop refuses to believe it:

Thinking these were the empty lies of an ordinary dream [*soliti mendacia inania somni*], [he] did not give the instructions serious consideration and ignored the love he owed his brother... When the bishop later heard the whole story from the cleric's own mouth, he said, "This I believe was mere fantasy [*fantasmata*]; so I give no credence to the imaginary message [*verbis fictis*]."[26] (pp. 53–54)

Though Strabo here asserts the divine nature of this particular dream, he simultaneously reminds us of other, "lying" dreams – and of the difficulty involved in discerning the true nature of any dream.

The two short dreams included in the *Visio Wettini* raise, and begin to answer, questions about the genre of the *Visio* itself: they help define the place of Strabo's main narrative within the gamut of possible dreams and dream poems. The demonic dream briefly enacts an experience radically opposed to Wetti's later revelation, and thus sets off the angelic *visio* as something special, indeed miraculous. The cleric's dream, set within the main narrative, serves a similar purpose: by raising the specter of "ordinary," "lying," "fantastic" dreams, it makes Wetti's vision, by contrast, all the more enlightening.[27]

Strabo thus calls to mind, within the *Visio Wettini*, the full range of oneiric experience as presented by the dream theorists, making clear which portion of the range most interests him. But if Strabo here concentrates on revelation, in another poem, the short "De quodam somnio ad Erluinum,"[28] he depicts a radically different kind of dream. This second poem stands in sharp contrast to the *Visio Wettini*, though at first seeming to promise a divine revelation much like Wetti's. An impressive eagle, associated explicitly with the realm of the gods, appears, cutting through obscurities in a way that suggests enlightenment: "Cum subito tenebras, fama est, Iovis armiger altas / Decutiens, oculis visus adesse viri" [When suddenly, rumor has it, the armsbearer of Jove, shaking off the deep darkness, seemed to be present to the eyes of the man (i.e., the dreamer)] (5–6).[29]

Intensifying the expectation of revelation, Strabo's eagle lifts the dreamer up into the heavens.[30] The move toward the divine, however, has an unexpected effect, evoking not wonder but terror. No eager student of celestial mysteries, Strabo's dreamer does not want to fly; he is a "new Daedalus" (13) not because of any daring or ingenuity, but because of his fear (13–14): "Ales ad alta volat, timidumque per aera portat, / Donec terrorem purior aethra dedit" [The winged one flies to the heights and carries the timid man through the air, until the purer ether gave terror] (11–12).

The subsequent actions of the dreamer more than fulfill the expectations raised by his unheroic response to flight: he declares – in comically inflated language – that he is about to vomit (15–18) and proceeds to do so (21–22). The eagle, disgusted by the actions of his charge, announces that the heavenly trip is over:

> Hic aquila: "Absurdum est divinis sedibus," inquit,
>   "Inserere, aspergat qui loca celsa lue.
> Ergo redi et strati sordes intende relapsus,
>   Nec rursus speres sordibus astra sequi."　　　　　　(23–26)

Here the eagle says: "It is absurd to introduce to the divine abode one who would sprinkle the lofty places with plague. Therefore, return, and, fallen back, examine the filth of [your] blanket. Nor should you again hope to pursue the stars with filth."

The dreamer awakens to find that he has in fact vomited all over his bed: "Evigilans, quicquid supero sibi visus ab axe / Fundere, per lectum repperit ire suum" [Waking up, he found that whatever had seemed to him (before) to pour out from the high heavens had (instead) gone onto his bed] (27–28).

While Strabo's *Visio Wettini* grew out of a tradition – literary and theoretical – of angelically-inspired dreams, his "De quodam somnio ad Erluinum" depends upon an opposed tradition of physically-motivated ones. A digestive disorder seems to stand at the root of this dream, and it is with the working-out of that disorder that the dream is finally concerned. Awakening covered with physical matter, the dreamer finds himself – quite unlike Wetti – intellectually and spiritually unchanged; instead, he has been reaffirmed, even rebaptized, in his corporeality.

It is hard to imagine a poem in spirit more distant from the seriously didactic *Visio Wettini* than the "Ad Erluinum." Yet, the two poems are similar in form: both start from the premise of a dream; both are imaginative (in the Augustinian sense of the word), working through the presentation of vivid "likenesses"; and both recount a journey. Although generically-related, the two poems nonetheless move in opposite directions: one upward toward enlightenment, the other down into physicality. Already in the ninth century, these two paths were available to the writer of dream poetry; the divine and mundane dreams of theoretical discussion could both be put to literary use.[31]

Exploiting the opposite poles of medieval dream hierarchies, revelatory and meaningless, or deceptive, dream fictions represent the ideal boundaries of the genre of dream vision. Only in the most extreme cases, however, is an ideal higher or lower vision unambiguously realized. Earthly visions, even when they strongly affirm physicality, like the "Ad Erluinum," often suggest at least the *potential* for heavenward movement:

at the start of Strabo's poem, we anticipate the penetration of divine mysteries. The "courtly love" vision, even when only revealing the dreamer's erotic entanglements, frequently calls to mind (for instance, through the language of a "religion of love") transcendent realities. Inversely, there is often a pull downward in revelatory visions. When, in the *Visio Wettini*, Wetti briefly resists his angel's command to make public what he has seen, we are diverted from the wonders of the other world and reminded of the human being's weakness, his distance from an ideal of moral action (pp. 63–64; lines 656–79). Similarly, in the Middle English *Pearl*, the dreamer's naïve, uncomprehending questions prevent the poem from ever fully transcending earthly perspectives. Movement toward an understanding of religious mysteries rarely proceeds unimpeded in medieval dream poetry; the fictional dreamer is, after all, human and fallible.

We cannot, in practice, completely separate divine and mundane visions from each other: the threat of failed vision often lies beneath the surface of the revelatory dream poem, as the suggestion of revelation often inheres in works of the "lower" tradition. The tension between the transcendent and the mundane, central to medieval dream theory, creeps into even the most fully divine or earthly dream visions.

In poems like Strabo's *Visio Wettini* and "Ad Erluinum," of course, higher and lower elements are radically out of balance; we have no difficulty identifying the main upward or downward thrust of such poems. In certain dream visions, however, mundane and celestial qualities are more evenly matched. Such "middle visions" powerfully exploit the double nature of the dream, locating themselves midway between the two poles of the literary genre. As in Macrobius's *somnium*, compact of fiction and truth, as also in Gregory the Great's ambivalent dream, combining external *revelatio* and internal *cogitatio*, the tension of higher and lower elements in the middle dream vision remains unresolved. Poems of this tradition simultaneously evoke opposed ideas about the nature of dreaming, and, by doing so, situate themselves to explore areas of betweenness – the realms that lie between the divine and the mundane, the true and the false, the good and the bad. They place their readers in a position similar to that of Gregory the Great's dreamer, unable finally to pin down the poem's status as revelation or deception, unable unambiguously to define its direction of movement as upward or downward.

As with higher and lower visions, the middle vision has a long history. We have seen that Lucian, in the second century, called on conflicting explanations of the dream to help create a complicated ambiguity. The didactic point of his "Dream" – that "those who are young" should "take the better direction and cleave to education"[32] – is supported by Lucian's assertion of the dream's divine authority. But when Lucian questions the dream's transcendent nature, raising the possibility of its psychological motivation, we begin to doubt the reliability of the poem's ostensible message. What kind of faith can we have in the teaching of a disturbed dream? Caught between the claim of divine inspiration and the suggestion of the dream's unreliability, we cannot finally be sure how to read Lucian's fiction.

The middle vision is part of the dream vision genre throughout the Middle Ages, but it becomes especially important in later medieval literature. A poem as influential as the *Roman de la rose* uses the dream form to navigate a middle course between full involvement in earthly love and detachment from, even condemnation of, physical passion. Chaucer's dream poems, Boccaccio's *Corbaccio*, and Langland's *Piers Plowman* are all middle visions, evoking the possibility of revelation even as they nervously question their own reliability.

In the later Middle Ages, new philosophical and theological movements tended to push God and the human being ever further apart, emphasizing the gap between divine action and human understanding.[33] This situation elicited various responses: on the one hand, a mysticism that sought superrational unity with God; on the other, a science that concentrated its attention more and more fully on the mundane realm accessible to human reason. The late-medieval popularity of the middle vision can be read as one additional reaction to the perception of a growing distance between humanity and divinity. As demonstrated by medieval dream theory, the dream remained, throughout the Middle Ages, associated with both earth and heaven. In choosing to represent a dream, an author also chose to depict a realm located between the divine and the mundane. Definable as neither a miraculous revelation nor merely a psychosomatic dream, the middle vision involves both higher and lower portions of the cosmos, taking place on a field of action neither confined to earth nor hopelessly beyond human reach. Navigating a course between unambiguously upward- and downward-looking visions, the middle vision offers a way of exploring the connections between the world in which we find ourselves and the transcendent realm for which we yearn.

THE SELF-REFLEXIVITY OF DREAM VISION:
DREAMS, FICTIONS, MIRRORS

The structure of medieval dream hierarchies suggests a way of defining the overall structure of the dream vision genre: the habit of mind that advances a theoretical classification of higher, lower, and middle dream-types expresses itself as well in a hierarchy of dream fictions. Such a hierarchical definition of dream vision is further bolstered by medieval treatments of fiction itself: for the Middle Ages, it was not only the dream that was potentially double in its significance and moral value, but also poetry. Involved in the middleness of imagination, the poetic, like the oneiric, dwells in a region between body and intellect, wedding ideas to a sensible and pleasurable form.[34]

Theorists of the dream and of literature recognize, sometimes explicitly, the parallel complexity of oneiric and literary realms. Thus, Petrarch uses the dream as a way of defining both the common view that poems are unreliable and his own belief in their value and truth:

When a person who is asleep is touched with laurel his dreams come true. Which makes it singularly appropriate for poets, who are said to be wont to sleep upon Parnassus, as Persius has it: "Nec in bicipiti somniasse Parnaso" [*Satires*, Prologue, 2–3] and the rest. This is said covertly to show that truth is contained in poetic writings which to the foolish seem to be but dreams – the poet's head being wreathed with the leaves that make dreams come true.[35]

In a more systematic way, Macrobius also brings fiction and dream together, creating a complicated parallel between the two. The first three chapters of Macrobius's *Commentary* form a preface to the work, having as their unifying motive the proof that Cicero's *Somnium Scipionis* deserves serious philosophical attention. The third chapter, as we have seen, treats dreaming, arguing that Cicero's *Somnium* "embraces the three reliable types" (I.iii.12) of dream by means of which "we are gifted with the powers of divination" (I.iii.8). Macrobius thus successfully distinguishes Scipio's dream from dreams "not worth interpreting" (I.iii.3). The goal in the two preceding chapters is similar: there Macrobius also defends the philosophical status of the *Somnium Scipionis*. These first two chapters, however, address not the *Somnium*'s identity as dream, but instead its position as fictional construct.[36] Promising to refute the Epicurean claim "that philosophers should refrain from using fiction since no kind of fiction has a place with those who profess to tell the truth" (I.ii.4), Macrobius argues, with his usual penchant for moderation, that "Philosophy does not discountenance all stories nor does it accept all" (I.ii.6), and suggests that "in order to distinguish between what it rejects as unfit to enter its sacred precincts and what it frequently and gladly admits, the points of division must needs be clarified" (I.ii.6). In essence, Macrobius here proposes to classify fictions much as, in the following chapter, he will classify dreams.

Macrobius proceeds to derive a five-part literary hierarchy strikingly similar to his dream classification. On one end of the literary scale stand fictions with absolutely no basis in truth, serving not at all "to encourage the reader to good works" (I.ii.7);[37] such fictions are clearly inappropriate to philosophical discourse, and Macrobius relegates them "to children's nurseries" (I.ii.8). At the opposite pole are narratives that attempt to reach the realm of divinity and divine ideas. In Macrobius's view, however, God and Mind "pass the bounds of speech" and "those of human comprehension" (I.ii.14): "it is a sacrilege for fables to approach this sphere" (I.ii.16). When philosophers consider "the Supreme God and Mind, they shun the use of fabulous narratives" (I.ii.14).[38]

Between these two extremes lies an interim literary class, itself divisible in three. All three intermediate fictions "draw the reader's attention to certain kinds of virtue" (I.ii.9), but not all are acceptable for philosophy. "The fables of Aesop," for instance, in which "the setting and plot are fictitious" (I.ii.9), are "inappropriate to philosophical treatises" (I.ii.10). However, other intermediate fictions, *narrationes fabulosae*, rest "on a solid foundation of truth, which is treated in a fictitious style" (I.ii.9). These fictions too can be subdivided, "for there is more than one way of telling the truth when the argument is real but presented in the form of a fable" (I.ii.10):

> Either the presentation of the plot involves matters that are base and unworthy of divinities and are monstrosities of some sort (as, for example, gods caught in adultery, Saturn cutting off the privy parts of his father Caelus and himself thrown into chains by his son and successor), a type which philosophers prefer to disregard altogether; or else a decent and dignified conception of holy truths, with respectable events and characters, is presented beneath a modest veil of allegory.[39]
>
> (I.ii.11)

This last "is the only type of fiction approved by the philosopher who is prudent in handling sacred matters" (I.ii.11).

Macrobius's classification of fictions differs in certain ways from his treatment of dreams, most notably in the suggestion that fiction can reach too high into the realm of divinity; no such suggestion is made for the dream.[40] Still, Macrobius gives us a hierarchy of fictions, arranged according to their increasing proximity to truth, to the realm of pure idea:

1 fables impiously attempting to approach the sphere of God and Mind	inappropriate to philosophy
2 *narrationes fabulosae*, presenting a "decent and dignified conception of holy truths"	appropriate to philosophy
3 *narrationes fabulosae*, presenting "matters that are base and unworthy of divinities"	inappropriate to philosophy

4 fables in which "both the setting and plot are   inappropriate to philosophy
fictitious"

5 "fables that promise only to gratify the ear"   inappropriate to philosophy

Macrobius thus depicts dream and fiction as occupying parallel realms: each includes "higher" and "lower" types, and each allows for intermediate combinations of the "high" and the "low." Both dream and fiction are "double" experiences, and both are capable of bridging the opposed terms of falsehood and truth. Moreover, in his literary as well as his oneiric discussion, Macrobius gives middle experience his most concentrated attention. Only fictions occupying an appropriate intermediate ground – marrying the proper content ("a decent and dignified conception of holy truths, with respectable events and characters") to the proper form ("a modest veil of allegory") – pass muster for philosophical use. This interim sort of fiction of course closely resembles Macrobius's middle dream, the *somnium*, which "conceals with strange shapes and veils with ambiguity the true meaning of the information being offered" (I.iii.10).[41]

At least certain medieval readers took Macrobius's close association of dreams and fictions to heart. Pascalis Romanus, in reproducing Macrobius's five-fold dream system, draws an extraordinarily explicit connection between the hierarchy of dreams and a hierarchy of literary forms:

Est itaque fantasia tamquam fabula, insompnium velud proverbium vel parabola, visio tamquam hystoria, oraculum ut prophecia, sompnium allegoria.[42]

Thus the *phantasm* [i.e., *visum*] is like a fable, the *insomnium* just like a proverb or parable, the *visio* like history, the *oraculum* like prophecy, the *somnium* allegory.

Pascalis's literary typology clearly differs from that of Macrobius, but the close association between dreams and verbal constructs is certainly indebted to the *Commentary*. Pascalis, like Macrobius, emphasizes the allegorical quality of the *somnium*:

In sompnio vero ... a rebus aliis allegorice et per figuras res futuras significantes, res eventure cernuntur.[43]

In the *somnium* truly ... the things that are to happen are perceived allegorically by means of other things and through figures that signify future things.

Enigmatic dreams and figural literature call each other to mind. And more strikingly, *every* kind of dream evokes, for Pascalis, a literary analogue: as dreams range from the unreliable to the undeniably true, so literature exists in a realm between the wholly fabulous and the prophetic. We thus see, in Pascalis, a survival, even a strengthening, of Macrobius's association of the oneiric and the fictional.

The parallel hierarchies of fiction and dream suggest that, when dreams are used fictionally, the resulting dream fictions will themselves constitute a hierarchy of higher, lower, and middle types; as suggested above, we may describe the genre of dream vision as just such a hierarchy. The parallel between dream and fiction also has important implications for defining the central concerns of dream vision. The dream fiction, by representing in the dream an imaginative entity like fiction itself, often becomes self-reflexive. Dream vision is especially liable to become metafiction, thematizing issues of representation and interpretation.[44]

That dreaming is recognized as an especially appropriate vehicle for considering literary issues is suggested by the very vocabulary a dream theorist like Pascalis Romanus uses. Frequently employing words like "tegumentum," "integumentum," "tectum," "figura," "involucrum," and "ambages," standard vocabulary in medieval literary theory,[45] Pascalis also strongly invokes the biblical language underlying medieval allegoresis. He cites the formula, "littera occidit, spiritus autem vivificat" [the letter killeth, but the spirit quickeneth] (2 Corinthians 3:6),[46] and goes on to define the proper way of reading dreams in a passage that also applies in a more general way to the reading of allegory:

Cum diversa videris et per nocturnam quietem variis anima tua fuerit exagitata terroribus vel incitata promissis ea contempne que superficies sompnii tenet et ad sapientiam divinam atque misterium quod introrsus latet astuta mente recurre, et quod sompnio vel visione per enigma monstratur, sagaci ratione discerne, ut quicquid alii velud in fantasmate vident, tu lucido cordis oculo conspicias. Nam plerumque et in divina scriptura maxime veteri que umbram sompnii naturalis continet, id ipsum facere compellimur ut non ymaginem et corpus littere sed spiritum et significatam veritatem perscrutemur.[47]

When you have seen diverse things, and your soul has been chased about, in [its] nocturnal rest, by various terrors or [has been] roused by promises, contemn those things which the surface of the dream holds and, with an astute mind, hasten to the divine wisdom and mystery that lies hidden inwards, and discern, with keen reason, that which is shown through enigma in the dream or vision, so that whatever others see as though in a phantasm, you may behold with the clear eye of the heart. For generally, and in divine scripture, most of all in the Old [Testament], which contains the shadow of the natural dream, we are compelled to do this very thing: that we investigate not the image and body of the letter but rather the spirit and the truth [that is] signified.

The association thus made between literary and oneiric interpretation is not an anomaly. Elsewhere, we also see a thorough interpenetration of the languages of dream theory and literary study. Albertus Magnus repeatedly suggests that dreams communicate "metaphorice" [metaphorically].[48] William of Aragon, influenced by Albert, differentiates dreams that predict the future "per convenientem metaphoram" [through appropriate metaphor] from those that are more directly prophetic, acting "sine integumento metaphore" [without the covering of metaphor].[49] And John of Salisbury, in his *Policraticus*, treats dream phenomena in the context of a more general consideration of "signs."[50] His examination of the significance of dreams is tied up with an interest in polysemy, and particularly in linguistic ambiguity.[51]

When, in the fourteenth century, Robert Holkot stressed the uncertainty of dream interpretation – "somniorum diuinationi indulgere est multum periculosum ... propter diuersitatem significationis in somniis: potest enim somnium aequivoce & aequaliter multa significare" [to indulge in dream divination is very perilous . . . because of the diversity of signification in dreams: indeed, a dream can equivocally and equally signify many things] – he did so in a long tradition that associated the "equivocal" dream with enigmatic signs of all sorts, especially with fictions.[52] When the author of a dream vision like *The Pilgrimage of the Lyfe of the Manhode* essentially identifies the processes of writing and dreaming – "I haue sett it in writinge in þe wise þat I mette it ... If þis metinge I haue not wel ymet, I preye þat to riht it be corrected of þilke þat kunne bettere meete, or þat bettere mown make it" – we should not be surprised.[53]

Framing his or her poem as a dream, the medieval author focused attention on a human experience clearly linked to literary process, and the reader of a dream vision was prepared for a poem that, examining dream experience, might also examine its own status as poetry. Both "higher" and "lower" dream visions could be self-reflexive. Thus, the Middle English *Pearl* concentrates its attention self-consciously on problems of understanding, asking how the human being can properly interpret, and convey to others, a superhuman experience. On the other hand, dream poems of a "lower," earthly love often reflected on the liaisons between poetry and passion, the lover and the poet. The middle vision, however, provided authors with especially rich possibilities for self-reflexive narrative. In a poem like Chaucer's *Book of the Duchess*, the sustained ambiguity of the middle vision produces a work whose complex form forcefully calls attention to itself and to its own processes of movement. Depicting a dream whose status *vis-à-vis* truth is ambiguous, such a dream vision focuses attention on that aspect of literature most problematic for the Middle Ages – its position between truth and falsehood. The middle vision offered writers a chance to explore, in the ambiguities of dream experience, anxieties about the ambiguity of literary art.

This view of the dream vision as self-reflexive receives support from the striking and pervasive medieval association between dreams and that premier instrument of self-examination, the mirror.[54] Calcidius treats dreams and mirrors side by side, including each within a larger discussion of the senses and of visual images.[55] The Arabic philosopher Algazel explicitly associates true dreams with a process of mirroring.[56] Raoul de Longchamps's consideration of the dream is occasioned by the "triplex speculum" [threefold mirror] of Alain de Lille's *Anticlaudianus*.[57] Nature, in Jean de Meun's *Roman de la rose*, follows her discourse on mirrors with a discussion of dreams.[58] And of course, in Guillaume de Lorris's portion of the *Roman*, the mirror of Narcissus plays a central role in the lover's dream.[59] In fact, mirrors often have a prominent place within literary dreams – for instance, in Dante's dream of Leah,[60] in Deguileville's *Pelerinage de la vie humaine*,[61] and in Langland's *Piers Plowman*.[62] At the end of Alain de Lille's *De planctu naturae*, the dream and the mirror are nearly equated: "When the mirror with these images and visions was withdrawn, I awoke from my dream and ecstasy and the previous vision of the mystic apparition left me."[63] And in Chaucer's *Squire's Tale*, the mirror is identified as the *cause* of Canace's dream: "And in hire sleep, right for impressioun / Of hire mirour, she hadde a visioun."[64] Often, mirror and dream serve as parallel or complementary modes of self-knowledge. In Chaucer's *Knight's Tale*, Arcite decides to return to Athens, disguising his identity, after he dreams and after he looks in a mirror.[65] Toward the end of Gower's *Confessio Amantis*, an "Avision" (VIII.2805) and the mirror scene that follows it reveal to Amans his release from love.[66] Cresseid's fall into leprosy in Henryson's *Testament of Cresseid* is announced in a dream and confirmed by a mirror.[67]

When we encounter a fictional dream, then, we are likely to associate it with specular self-examination, and when we encounter the dream vision's first-person narrative, we may expect (because of the dream's association with both mirrors and fictions) a literary work that examines, as though in a mirror, its own imaginative (oneiric, poetic, and specular) status.[68] But while the strong connection between dreams and mirrors thus strengthens our view of the dream poem as self-reflexive, it also helps qualify that view, allowing us to define with greater precision *how* exactly the dream vision's self-reflexivity operates. For the Middle Ages, mirrors were not solely agents of self-examination, and medieval dream poetry, even at its most self-conscious, is not narrowly self-concerned or solipsistic. The goal of looking into a mirror *is* in part self-knowledge, and the dream poem does mirror itself, examining its own constructs and movement. Medieval mirrors, however, serve not only to reflect the self, but also to reveal information about the world beyond the self.[69] Similarly, the self-conscious dream poem is not independent of the external reality or truth that it attempts to represent. In its self-reflexive movements, dream vision raises not only self-contained formal questions, but also questions about how literature grasps and represents real and true entities existing outside a strictly poetic realm. The dream poem's self-reflexivity, in other words, often leads it into questions of epistemology.

When Henryson's Cresseid discovers that she will be "lyke ane lazarous" (343), and when Chaucer's Arcite realizes his need to return to Emily, they do not do so in a state of isolated self-consideration. In these situations dreams serve not only as reflections of psychology, but also as revelations of divine will: it is Mercury who directs Arcite back to Athens, and the pagan gods who show Cresseid their anger and promise to punish her. The mirrors that follow each of the two dreams confirm not only the individual's internal state, but also an external, and apparently divine, judgment. What might be presented as moments of pure self-discovery are instead represented as complex, compact of internal reflection and external revelation.

Dreams, fictions, and mirrors all involve "higher" and "lower" forces. Like dreams and poems, the mirror reaches both upward and downward, both into and beyond the individual self. Intimately involved with image-making, the mirror is, like other complex, imaginative entities, both "double" and "middle." As Frederick Goldin suggests:

> The mirror . . . reflects the world that Plato defined and that the Neoplatonists transmitted to the Middle Ages. As the mirror is made of matter, it has the capacity of matter to receive the image of ideal forms. From this root idea three distinct developments are possible.
>
> We can stress the ideality of the image and ignore the materiality of the mirror. Then we praise the mirror for its clarity . . .
>
> We can reverse this emphasis and stress the mirror's essential passivity. Then we condemn it as a snare of vain images that seduce us with a false beauty and leave us with nothing . . .
>
> We can consider both matter and form together. The mirror awakens our consciousness of the ideal by translating it into sensible images. It shows us an image of sensible Beauty in the beauty of a momentary body. But that image is fleeting, it has no substance; and we must learn to leave the mirror behind and to love a beauty that is invisible and immutable.[70]

In its search for knowledge, the human being may become involved with each of these three aspects of the mirror, but with radically different results. Gazing into "the mirror of matter" means accepting the images of corporeal things as real and valuable in themselves; yet doing so neglects truths that transcend the physical. Medieval writers often define this material mirror as one of sterile *self*-examination, commonly associating it with the myth of Narcissus.[71] In the words of the *Ovide Moralisé*:

Let him understand by Narcisus those who delight madly, senselessly, the haughty, the presumptuous, who misuse temporal goods, who see themselves and take delight in the false mirrors of this world . . . It is the perilous mirror in which the proud look upon themselves, who covet earthly delights . . . It is the deceiving fountain, which makes the faint and mutable image seem real and permanent.[72]

Immersion in the image of a corporeal self that is fleeting and corruptible results in a failure to recognize the self's affiliations with higher, spiritual being. Narcissistic mirrors, reflecting only the deceptive world of appearances, give access to a knowledge that is limited and ultimately vain.

The mirror, however, can also figure the highest of epistemological processes. Holy Scripture, properly read, is a mirror reflecting divine truth.[73] The Book of Nature mirrors the workings of divinity insofar as the creation images the mind of its Creator.[74] And as a creature made in God's image, the human soul, directing its gaze upward, is a mirror of the divine.[75] The close association between reliable knowledge and the mirror shows itself strikingly in the common use of *Speculum* or *Mirror* as the title for works – like Vincent of Beauvais's *Speculum Maius* or the *Mirror of Magistrates* – seen as giving access to a truth beyond the reach of everyday experience.[76]

The mirror may trap us in narcissism, but it may also allow us to enter a world of unaccustomed knowledge. Sometimes, as in the *Pilgrimage of the Lyfe of the Manhode*, it plays both roles.[77] In this long dream vision, the mirror figures prominently in the iconography of Oiseuce (Idleness) and Orgoill (Pride), personifications partly responsible for the dreamer–pilgrim's entrapment in worldly snares.[78] On the other hand, another kind of mirror pulls the dreamer away from such entanglements. The first image of the dream – "þe citee of Jerusalem," to which the pilgrim is "stired to go" (20) – presents itself "in a miro*ur*" (20),[79] and a second mirror (situated on the pilgrim's "burdoun" of Esperaunce) reiterates the lofty goal of pilgrimage:

On þe ende an hy was a pomelle of a ro*u*nd miro*ur*, shynynge and fair, in whiche cleerliche men mihten see al þe cuntre þat was fer. þer was no regio*u*n so fer þat þerinne men ne mihten seen it, and þer*e* I sygh þilke citee to whiche I was exited to gon: riht as I hadde seyn it and ap*er*seyued it bifore in þe miro*ur*, also in þe pomelle I syh it, wherof I was fayn.   (1870–76)

While mirrors, like dreams and fictions, may figure two extreme positions – both the snares of Oiseuce/Orgoill and the transcendent goal of pilgrimage – they more often than not confront us with ambivalence. Because they frame images, mirrors, even at their most "ideal," continue to be affiliated with the lower realm of sense. The mirror of Scripture itself functions by means of stories and figures whose truth becomes apparent only through allegoresis.[80] In the *Pilgrimage*, the mirror on the pilgrim's "burdoun" reflects not only his heavenly goal, but also his personal situation. It mediates between the divine and the earthly; in fact, at one point it is equated to the supreme mediator, "Ihesu Crist": "The hye pomel is Ihesu Crist þat is as þe lettere seith a mirour þat is withoute spot" (2009–10).[81] In this mirror we see ourselves – "eche wyght may see his visage" (2011) – but not in order to admire, idly and proudly, what we see. Rather, the mirror serves to put the self, and the world, into proper perspective: "in whiche [mirour] al þe world may mire him wel and considere him, for al þe world þerinne mired is nouht as greet as aas in a dee" (2011–13). Recognizing our own smallness in this mirror, we also perceive our potential greatness – our capacity for entering "Jerusalem." Ideally, as in the mirror of Christ, we move from the material to the spiritual, but in any case we *begin* in the realm of matter.

Writers of the Middle Ages had an acute sense of human epistemological limitation and potentiality – of the possibility of understanding the transcendent realm of Idea, as well as the need, in human learning, for something the senses could grasp.[82] Even while pointing toward the ineffable, mirrors accommodate the senses; fictions and dreams present their truths dressed up in images. In medieval epistemology, transcendent knowledge can be gained through an examination of the mundane,[83] and, beginning with introspection, knowledge of the superhuman can be attained.[84] In a waking vision, Julian of Norwich looks intently inward to find not just herself, but an "endlesse" world of divinity:

And then oure good lorde opynnyd my gostely eye and shewde me my soule in þe myddys of my harte. I saw þe soule so large as it were an endlesse warde, and also as it were a blessyd kyngdom; and by the condicions þat I saw there in I vnderstode þat it is a wurschypfulle cytte, in myddes of that cytte (sitts) oure lorde Jhesu, very god and very man, a feyer person and of large stature, hyghest bysschope, most solempne kynge, wurschypfullest lorde. And I saw hym clothyd solemply in wurschyppes. He syttyth in þe soule evyn ryghte in pees and rest, and he rulyth and ȝe(m)yth hevyn and erth and all that is.[85]

Julian later makes explicit the epistemological assumptions underlying her vision, suggesting that knowledge of higher truth comes through both introspection and the inspection of lower things:

Al thyng that he [God] hath made shewyth his lordschyppe, as vnderstandyng was gevyn in the same tyme by example of a creature that is led to se grete noblynesse and kyngdoms longyng to a lorde; and when it had sene all the nobylnes beneth, than mervelyng it was steryd to seke vppe aboue to that hygh place where the lorde dwellyth, knowyng by reson þat hys dwellyng is in the wurthyest place. And thus I vnderstonde truly that oure soule may never haue rest in thyng þat is beneth it selfe. And whan it comyth aboue alle creatures in to it selfe, yett may it not abyde in the beholdyng of it selfe; but alle þe beholdyng is blyssydfully sett in god, that is the maker, dwellyng ther in, for in mannes soule is his very dwellyng.[86]

The sudden blossoming in Julian's heart of a transcendent kingdom – the movement from individual soul to Christ's "endlesse warde" – forcefully dramatizes the intimate relation between self-examination and broader epistemological process. Entities that themselves stand between body and idea – mirrors, dreams, fictions – are especially conducive to the leap from the mundane to the transcendent, from self-knowledge to metaphysical insight. While we may become trapped in the snares of the lower world – the mirror of Narcissus, the corporeal images of dreams, the seductive formal embodiments of the literary – the consideration of lower reality need not be an end in itself. Ideally, as for Julian, self-examination opens out into "hevyn and erth and all that is." The oneiric and specular self-scrutiny of Arcite and Cresseid reveals, beyond individual psychology, external forces at work shaping human fate.

It must be emphasized, however, that the epiphanic movement of Julian's "showing" is an *ideal*. Often the results of human desire for knowledge are far more equivocal: higher knowledge may be only obliquely glimpsed; corporeality may stand in the way of full and clear understanding. Dream fictions explore both the successes and failures of the human search for knowledge. Because dreams and fictions are, like the mirror, simultaneously involved in materiality and abstraction, when dream fiction turns inward to consider itself, it is often confronted by a crucial epistemological question: *how* can human knowledge lift itself out of the material to contemplate a higher reality?

NICOLE ORESME'S *TRACTATUS DE COMMENSURABILITATE VEL INCOMMENSURABILITATE MOTUUM CELI*

The middle dream vision often exploits the dream's transcendent associations to promise access to a knowledge otherwise unattainable, but it also often frustrates such a promise. Poised between an eternal, divine realm and a material world offering no stable knowledge, the middle vision finds itself perfectly positioned to explore the tension between human desire for enlightenment, and the human obstacles to that desire. Fictions and dreams are both possible, if uncertain, routes to knowledge, and in its self-reflexive movement, the dream vision represents and probes the human being's difficult striving after truth.

Many late-medieval dream visions – Chaucer's *House of Fame*, Langland's *Piers Plowman*, Boccaccio's *Corbaccio* – concern themselves with the problem of knowledge, but the self-conscious exploration of epistemology is perhaps most striking in a dream vision less well-known than these, the Latin prose dream that brings Nicole Oresme's scientific treatise, the *Tractatus de commensurabilitate vel incommensurabilitate motuum celi*, to its close.[87]

In the *Tractatus*, Oresme concerns himself with a technical matter: the commensurability or incommensurability of the motions of the celestial bodies.[88] If motions are commensurable, the ratio between them is a rational number; if incommensurable, their ratio is irrational. As Oresme argues, "it is necessary that all celestial motions be either mutually commensurable, or that some be mutually incommensurable" (I.62–64, p. 181), and in the first two parts of his tripartite work, he examines the mathematical and astronomical consequences of these two possibilities: "we shall see, in the first part of this work, what [consequences] follow if they are [assumed] commensurable; and, in the second part, what follows if they are incommensurable" (I.64–66, p. 181).

For Oresme, a great deal rides upon the decision between these two cosmic options: they have vastly different implications for a view of universal order and of the forces controlling that order. The popular notion of a Great Year[89] – "in certeyn yeres space / That every sterre shulde come into his place / Ther it was first"[90] – depends upon the assumption of commensurability (I.821–23, p. 243). No such orderly recurrence is possible if we assume incommensurability. Incommensurable motion, however, leads to its own wondrous order:

On the assumption of the incommensurability and eternity of motions, it is truly beautiful to contemplate how such a configuration as an exact conjunction occurs only once through all of infinite time, and how it was necessary through an eternal future that it occur in this [very] instant with no conjunction like it preceding or following.   (II.307–11, p. 273)

As the consequences, both mathematical and cosmic, of commensurable and incommensurable motions are neatly laid out in the first two parts of Oresme's work, the underlying question – which of the two possibilities correctly describes the universe – becomes more and more pressing. Oresme promises, early on, that the third section of the *Tractatus* will resolve just this issue: "we shall investigate what has been assumed – that is, whether they are commensurable or not" (I.66–67, p. 181). And arriving at the "tertia pars" of the *Tractatus*, we are ready to move beyond its earlier *sic* and *non* to the promised investigation of assumptions and discovery of truth:

Since two of the three things that I proposed have [now] been completed by concluding each of them conditionally from two contradictory hypotheses – namely, [1] what follows if all the celestial motions are mutually commensurable, and [2] what follows if some are incommensurable – the third thing remains to be considered because the understanding, not yet fully satisfied, seeks more discussion until the issue can be terminated categorically.   (III.1–6, p. 285)

We may now expect Oresme to proceed in his usual discursive mode and decide the central question of the *Tractatus* by mathematical proof and reasoned argument. Instead, surprisingly, Oresme shifts to a narrative mode, indeed, to dream narrative: "Ecce mihi, quasi sompniatori, visus est Apollo, musis et scientiis comitatus" [As one having a dream, I saw Apollo accompanied by the Muses and Sciences] (III.9–10, p. 285). But if the shift is surprising, it is also promising. After all, mathematical proof and reasoned argument have so far yielded equally convincing cases for each of Oresme's opposed "hypotheses." Perhaps the problem now needs to be examined from a different angle; in any case, the dream provides a radically new perspective.

No longer confined to the realm of human endeavor, the dreamer–mathematician meets, and converses with, a divine figure perfectly appropriate to the issues thus far raised by the *Tractatus*. As god of the sun, Apollo is himself associated with the celestial bodies whose motion is at issue; as ruler of the "Muses and Sciences," he represents the very disciplines that underlie Oresme's discourse. This god should speak with authority on both mathematical and astronomical questions. Indeed, Apollo explicitly promises revelation: "Then Apollo, smiling, saw the Muses and Sciences standing around and ordered them to do this [inform the dreamer],[91] saying 'Teach him what he asks' [*docete hunc quod ipse petit*]" (III.49–50, p. 289). Arithmetic and Geometry, personifications of Oresme's own mathematical instruments, eagerly answer Apollo's call, rising to instruct the dreamer.

The dream thus promises a revealed solution to the central question of the *Tractatus*, but its opening is not unambiguous. Prerequisite to Apollo's pledge of divine instruction is the recognition that human means of attaining knowledge are themselves inadequate for resolving the problem at hand. As the dream opens, Apollo "rebuke[s]" (III.10, p. 285) the dreamer:

You should understand that exactness transcends the human mind [*Nosce precisas humanum transcendit ingenium*] . . . With reference to the authority of Ptolemy, al-Battani says that "[even] on the excellence of such instruction, so noble [and] so heavenly, it is not possible for anyone to understand the truth exactly [*veritatem ad unguem comprehendere non est cuiquam possibile*]." (III.12 and 18–20, pp. 285–87)

Apollo's argument forces the dreamer into agreement, and the response he gives to the god extends our awareness of the limitations of scientific method, the method so far employed by the *Tractatus*:

I understand, then, my dear father,[92] that it is not given to human powers to discover such things unless furnished with some principle assumed beforehand. And now I know that the judgment of the senses cannot attain exactness. But [even] if the senses could attain such exact knowledge, one could not know whether he had judged rightly, since an insensible [or undetectable] addition or subtraction could alter a ratio but would not change the judgment. Therefore, I do not vainly presume that the aforesaid problem is solvable by mathematical demonstration. (III.32–37, p. 287)

The dreamer here admits that he cannot proceed any further on his own; his mathematical approach cannot work without "some principle assumed beforehand," that is, without the assumption of either commensurability or incommensurability. But even as he makes this admission, he refuses to give up the search for truth:

But, oh immortal gods who know all things, why did you make the very nature of men such that they desire to know, and then deceive or frustrate this desire by concealing from us the most important truths [*Sed o dii immortales, qui noscis omnia, cur fecistis quod homines natura scire desiderant et fraudato desiderio vel frustrato nobis absconditis optimas veritates*]? ... If, then, we are unable to know many things by discovering them for ourselves, I beseech you to disclose to me, with good grace, your teachings concerning this one doubt [*Si itaque per inventionem nostram multa scire non possumus, oro ego ut hoc unum dubium per vestram doctrinam mihi de benigna gratia reseretur*]. (III.38–40 and 47–49, pp. 287 and 289)

It is only now that Apollo makes his promise of revelation, and what has preceded that promise radically qualifies it. Even as we move toward the expected vision of truth, we become aware that such a vision is necessarily exceptional, a transcendence of normal human powers of perception made necessary by their deficiencies: "Nosce precisas humanum transcendit ingenium" (III.12). The human being, unaided, cannot arrive at the kind of exact knowledge that Apollo promises. The revelatory dream is a last resort.

In emphasizing the contrast between the promise of divine revelation and the limitations of human ability, Oresme begins to suggest that his purpose in presenting the dream is not simply to provide a definitive answer to a vexing question, but also to explore the relation between divine and human ways of knowing. Moreover, Oresme is not satisfied simply with pitting the (in)capacities of human reason against the mysterious universal powers that transcend those capacities: he does not present a brilliant revelatory vision in stark contrast to the uncertainties of the earlier, "human" sections of the *Tractatus*. Instead, in a move typical of the middle vision, he begins to qualify and question even Apollo's explicit promise of revelation.

Apollo urges Arithmetic and Geometry to instruct the dreamer, but earlier in the dream, in his exposition of human weakness, he has called these very disciplines into question: "And so the ratio of these motions is unknown, and neither arithmetic nor geometry will lead you to a knowledge of it" (III.23–24, p. 287). In fact, as soon as Arithmetic and Geometry begin speaking, they disagree, restating the central question of the *Tractatus* rather than moving palpably closer to its solution: "And immediately Arithmetic said: 'All the celestial motions are commensurable.' Geometry, rising, contradicted her and said: 'On the contrary, some celestial motions are incommensurable'" (III.50–52, p. 289). At the very moment when Apollo has led us to expect straightforward exposition – "docete hunc quod ipse petit" (III.50) – we move instead, with Apollo's complicity, into the realm of dispute: "quasi litis contestatione, iussit Apollo utramque partem[93] rationibus defendere suam causam" [Apollo ordered each side to defend their cause with reasoned arguments, as if they were litigants in a law court] (III.53–54, p. 289).

The bulk of Oresme's dream is taken up by the dispute between Arithmetic and Geometry, and as long as the two personifications speak, the dream provides, instead of the promised revelation, a reenactment of the central problem of Oresme's treatise. The very form of the dispute – not a true dialogue but two long orations set side by side – mirrors the contrastive structure of the first two parts of the *Tractatus*, in which the need to decide between commensurability and incommensurability was first implicitly articulated.[94]

However, the dream dispute does not just replay Oresme's earlier consideration. Ironically, the discourse of Arithmetic and Geometry is far less mathematical than what has preceded it – so much so that, when the dispute ends, the dreamer is moved to comment:

And what do they really contribute with their rhetorical persuasions [*rethoricis persuasionibus*] or sophistical proofs [*topicis probationibus*], [they who habitually use only demonstrations, spurning every other kind of argument]?[95] Why do they adopt the method of more uncertain knowledge – a method to which they are unaccustomed [*Cur incertioris scientie modum eis insolitum acceperunt*]?

(III.470–74, p. 323)

Arithmetic and Geometry *do* try, in their debate, to move beyond the method and conclusions of the first two sections of the *Tractatus*, proposing reasons why either commensurability or incommensurability would be preferable from a cosmic point of view.[96] In other words, they try to second-guess the divine forces controlling universal order:

[Arithmetic:] Indeed, the opposite conclusion of our sister, Geometry, seems to deprive us of divine goodness, diminish the perfection of the world, destroy the beauty of the heavens, bring harm to mankind, cause ignorance, and detract from the beauty of the whole universe of beings . . . It seems unworthy and unreasonable that the divine mind should connect the celestial motions, which organize and regulate the other corporeal motions, in such a haphazard relationship, when, indeed, it ought to arrange them rationally and according to a rule.

(III.61–65 and 67–69, pp. 289–91)

[Geometry:] The heavens would glitter with even greater splendor if the bodies were commensurable and their motions incommensurable, or if some motions were commensurable and others incommensurable, where all are regular [and uniform], than if all were commensurable. By mixing together irrationality and regularity, the regularity would be varied by the irrationality, and the irrationality, with regularity bound to it, would not be deprived . . . Now whether or not an irrational ratio is more noble [than a rational ratio], an harmonious union of them is more excellent than a separate [and independent] uniformity.

(III.332–37 and 340–41, pp. 311–13)

However, as the dreamer recognizes when the debate ends, neither Geometry nor Arithmetic can provide any sure "demonstration." Trying to decide the issue of commensurability, they move into uncertain territory – "incertioris scientie modum" (III.473) – where, as Apollo has predicted, they have no special efficacy: "neither arithmetic nor geometry will lead you to a knowledge of it [the ratio of these motions]" (III.23–24, p. 287).

The debate itself, rather than providing the definitive answer that Apollo has promised, focuses attention again and again on the *problem* of attaining knowledge. And in its irresolution, the dispute of the sciences demonstrates the inadequacy of not just one, but several kinds of (human) proof: although both Arithmetic and Geometry rely on "rhetorical persuasions" rather than mathematical "demonstrations," they employ two very different argumentative strategies. Arithmetic's is almost wholly an argument from authority, in which the effect depends not on subtlety (or even consistency) of thought, but on the piling up of impressive quotations from Plato, Aristotle, Macrobius, Boethius, Apuleius, "Hermes," and others. Geometry, when she begins her oration, distinguishes herself from Arithmetic on the basis not only of what she will argue, but also of *how* she will argue it:

Oh father, our sister, lavish with words and spare in good judgment, filling your divine ears with long digressions, has demonstrated nothing effectually . . . I believe her side is less probable and will show this with stronger arguments and far less special pleading [*fortioribus licet paucioribus persuasionibus*].[97]

(III.324–25 and 327–28, p. 311)

Elsewhere, Geometry comments explicitly, and damningly, on Arithmetic's use of authority: "we say that, in virtue of such mutually conflicting witnesses [*testibus invicem discordibus*], she ought not to be believed" (III.368–69, p. 315; see also III.416–18, p. 317). Geometry, in fact, relies more sparingly on authority than does her "sister." She uses logic instead (coming closer than Arithmetic to the practices of mathematical proof; see III.420–34, p. 319), and at several crucial points appeals to experience (even, one might say, experiments):

A ratio of tones does not vary as a ratio of velocities, for whether a string or a drum is struck strongly or weakly, slowly or quickly, nothing is changed by this.

(III.375–78, p. 315)

Nor, indeed, are their [poetic philosophers'] statements compatible with the phenomena observed thus far by astronomers.

(III.418–19, p. 317; my addition)

While Geometry's case for the incommensurability of celestial motions seems finally more measured and convincing than Arithmetic's – it is, as Edward Grant argues, clearly with incommensurability that Oresme's own sentiments lie[98] – neither side can be definitively proven, as Geometry herself tacitly admits in the conclusion of her oration:

Consequently, with regard to any two motions whose ratio is unknown to us, it is more probable that that ratio is irrational than rational – provided that no other consideration intervenes that was not taken into account in what has already been discussed.   (III.463–66, p. 321)

The best conclusion that the dream debate can provide is a "probable" one, and as Geometry herself argues, "nothing prevents certain false propositions from being more probable than certain true ones" (III.326–27, p. 311). Human modes of proof – Arithmetic's citation of authority, Geometry's logic and appeals to experience – do not lead to a definitive answer.

Oresme brings us to consider the limitations of human knowledge not only in the form and method of the dream debate, but also in its content; as Arithmetic realizes, the question of commensurability itself has important implications for an assessment of the human ability to know:

I will now show how great a blindness is produced in men who deny that the celestial motions are proportioned by numbers. For if this were true, no one could

Dreams and fiction

ever foresee [*precognoscere*] aspects, or predict [*predicere*] conjunctions, or learn of effects beforehand [*previdere*]. Indeed, astronomy would lie hidden [from us] in every age, unknown and even unknowable [*incognita ac etiam inscibilis*], as was shown before; it would no longer be counted among the mathematical disciplines. But if the celestial velocities are incommensurable, why did the maker of the world "give to man an uplifted face and bade him stand erect and turn his eyes to heaven?" "Of what avail that man derived his intelligence from above, [that he has held up his head to heaven]?"[99]   (III.262–69, p. 305)

Arithmetic here echoes the dreamer's earlier dismay over the frustration of human knowledge:

But, oh immortal gods who know all things, why did you make the very nature of men such that they desire to know, and then deceive or frustrate this desire by concealing from us the most important truths?   (III.38–40, p. 287)

Indeed, the debate between the two sister sciences can be read not only as a recasting of the scientific conflict of the *Tractatus*, but also as a partial reenactment of the epistemologically-concerned discussion between the dreamer and Apollo with which the dream opens. Responding to Arithmetic's comments on knowledge, Geometry presents an alternative view of the proper relation between human intellect and truth – a view closely related to that earlier expressed by Apollo:

Furthermore, those who object that man would be ignorant [of celestial motions if these motions were incommensurable] are unconvincing. For it is enough to know beforehand that a future conjunction, or eclipse, of this mobile falls below a certain degree, minute, second, or third; nor is it necessary to predict the exact point or instant of time [in which these will occur], since, as Pliny says, "the measure of the heavens is not reducible to inches." And according to Ptolemy, we are unable to determine the exact truth in such matters [*non possumus in talibus comprehendere veritatem ad unguem*]. In these matters, then, anyone who announces results that are free of noticeable error would seem to have determined things adequately and beautifully. But if men knew all motions exactly, it would not be necessary to make further observations, or to record the celestial revolutions with attentive care. As far as such excellent things are concerned, it would be better that something should always be known about them, while, at the same time, something should always remain unknown, so that it may be investigated further. For such an inquiry, acquired with a sweet taste, would divert noble minds from terrestrial things and, with their desire continually aroused, totally engage and engross those [already] occupied in so respectable an exercise of high-minded endeavor.
                    (III.435–48, pp. 319–21)

Directly echoing Apollo's earlier "veritatem ad unguem comprehendere non est cuiquam possibile" (III.19–20),[100] Geometry here turns the uncertainty that follows upon incommensurability (and by implication, the even more radical uncertainty that results from an inability to decide between commensurability and incommensurability) into something to be celebrated. In her view, it is necessary and proper that human knowledge be limited; otherwise, it would cease to be human:

If, however, these motions were known punctually, and this Great [or Perfect] Year were possible, then, surely, all things to come, and the whole order of future events could be foreseen by men, who could then construct a perpetual almanac based on all the effects of the world. They would become like immortal gods. But it is the gods, not men, who know future times and moments, which are subject to the divine power alone. Indeed, it would be very repugnant that men should come to know about future events beforehand. It seems arrogant of them to believe that they can acquire a foreknowledge of future contingents, only some of which are subject to celestial powers.[101]   (III.448–56, p. 321)

The dream debate finally goes a remarkably short distance toward a solution of the scientific problem of the *Tractatus*, but it leads deeply into a consideration of the epistemological concerns surrounding that problem. Defining the possibilities and limitations of human investigation into heavenly phenomena becomes, as Oresme himself recognizes, one of the central purposes of the *Tractatus*:

Therefore, lest those who are eager to pursue so noble a study [as astronomy] either despair before such great difficulty, or, believing that they know things about the motions of the stars which cannot be known by man, deceive themselves and others with rash impudence, I have written this little book on the commensurability of the celestial motions.   (Prol.39–42, p. 175; my addition)

Still, what finally is to be made of Apollo's promise of revelation? Despite the unresolved nature of the dispute between Arithmetic and Geometry, Apollo, as the debate ends, is satisfied with its outcome: "Scarcely had Geometry finished what she had proposed, when, behold, Apollo, believing himself adequately informed, ordered silence" (III.467–68). The dreamer, however, remains dissatisfied with where his dream has taken him:

And I, not without reason, was astonished and confounded at the novelty of so many things, so that these thoughts occurred to me. Since every truth seemed consonant with each side, in what sense are these disagreements the parents of truth [*Cum cuicumque vero consonet omne verum, cur sunt discordes iste veritatis parentes*]?   (III.468–70, pp. 321–23)

Apollo, sensing the dreamer's disappointment, renews his promise of revelation:

Perceiving the thought in my mind, father Apollo said: "Do not seriously believe that there is a genuine disagreement [*veram esse discordiam*] between these most illustrious mothers of evident truth [*evidentis veritatis*]. For they amuse themselves and mock the stylistic mode of an inferior science [*inferioris scientie stilum*]. In conversing [*fabulando*] with them, we also jestingly adopt the manner [*formam*] of doubt in our judgments. But we shall see the advances and causes [*Processusque et causas*] of these things, for straightaway we shall announce the truth in the form of a judgment [*in figura iudicii veritatem*]." (III.474–79, p. 323)

This final exchange between the dreamer and Apollo serves to emphasize, one last time, the gap between human and divine knowledge which the dream debate has so consistently dramatized. Apollo considers himself "adequately informed" (III.468, p. 321), while the dreamer is "astonished and confounded" (III.469, p. 323). The dreamer displays confusion and ignorance, while Apollo can read the dreamer's very thoughts. Still, as Apollo promises, revelation is finally at hand; divine knowledge will finally become accessible to human intellect:

With the most ardent desire did I await his determination, but, alas, the dream vanishes, the conclusion is left in doubt, and I am ignorant of what Apollo, the judge, has decreed on this matter [*Cumque summo desiderio sententiam expectarem, et ecce sompnus abiit, dubia conclusio restat et ipse nescio quid super hoc iudex decrevit Apollo*].
(III.479–81, p. 323)

As the scribe of one of the *Tractatus* manuscripts (dated 1401) exclaims: "Ecce finem sine fine" [Behold an ending without an ending].[102] The promise of revelation is finally renewed only to make its frustration all the more powerful.

In Oresme's *Tractatus*, Apollo's promise of cosmic revelation leads not to revelation, but to a self-reflexive consideration of the possibilities and limitations of scientific inquiry. On the middle ground of the dream, Oresme examines the complicated interplay between humanity, searching for truth but often frustrated in that search, and the cosmos, partly open to examination yet partly hidden and enigmatic. Oresme's dream articulates that middle region where the "desire to know" meets the barriers of human limitation and cosmic inscrutability.

7

Dreams and life

Dreaming is an anomalous experience, a kind of consciousness present only during unconsciousness, and, as the anthropologist Mary Douglas suggests, anomalies are often perceived as both a locus of danger and a source of power.[1] Medieval discussions clearly recognize the power of the dream – its ability, in predicting the future, to escape temporal constraints; its potential access to a divine realm – but they also treat the dream as dangerous. Not only legal proscriptions against dream divination but the dreambooks themselves – by making dream experience regular, predictable, interpretable – work toward containing the dream's dangers. Dream theory, in its long history, may be read as an attempt to control the dream's dangerous power through codification. An experience that is, dizzyingly, divine, demonic, angelic, psychological, and somatic is made less strange if viewed not as *one* experience, but as divisible into distinct types, each attributable to a particular cause – whether angelic or demonic, internal or external. Dream theorists themselves, however, do not erase the dream's anomalies, as shown by the recognition of hybrid kinds of dream and the perception that, in practice, dreams may defy classification. Moreover, literary works often forcefully exploit the dream's anomalies, presenting dream fictions that fit neatly into no single category, and that therefore articulate important questions about the connections between (or breachings of) the categories themselves. Works like Oresme's *Tractatus* ask, for instance, what relation divine revelation bears to more mundane means of attaining knowledge.[2] Thus, alongside the desire to understand and control the dream, is found a refusal to oversimplify dream experience, a refusal to make it either merely vain or wholly significant. The dream's complexity is asserted even when such an assertion frustrates the impulse toward neat categorization.

Having examined the response of medieval philosophy, theology, science, literature, and law to the anomalies of dream experience, one final, and perhaps most difficult, question must now be confronted: how did real dreamers treat their dreams? There can, of course, be no simple answer. Different dreamers, of distinct social status, education, and experience, must have used their dreams in varying ways, but only the dreams of those able to record their experience, and only the dreams they thought worthy of preservation, survive. Moreover, the material available is always written and thus always subject to the distortions of writing: the shape of autobiographical dreams is often influenced, for instance, by the conventions of hagiography. Still, we do have, in autobiography, rich dream narratives that provide at least a partial view of how individuals responded to their "real-life" dreams.[3] In such accounts, there is a remarkable use of the dream's anomalies. Intimately linked to the dreaming self, reflecting its most private thoughts, and yet also potentially separate from that self, capable of providing external revelation, autobiographical dreams are often presented as questioning the very assumptions that govern a dreamer's life. In other words, they may offer a radically new reading of that life from a perspective both intimate to the dreamer, and distinct from his or her normal means of perception.

Thus, in an autobiography like that of Guibert de Nogent (c. 1115), dreams and visions appear especially at pivotal points in the history of the self, when the whole course of life comes under reexamination.[4] Guibert's mother withdraws from secular life only after a dream convinces her that she should do so (I.14, Benton, p. 73; Bourgin, p. 47); her later decision to become a nun also depends upon a revelatory vision (II.4, Benton, pp. 133–34; Bourgin, pp. 117–18).[5] Similarly, Guibert's choice of vocation is intimately linked to dreaming. His education begins as the result of one of his tutor's dreams:

At night when he was sleeping in his room . . . the figure of a white-headed old man, of very dignified appearance, seemed to lead me in by the hand through the door of the room. Halting within hearing, while the other looked on, he pointed out his bed to me and said, "Go to him, for he will love you very much." When he dropped my hand and let me go, I ran to the man, and as I kissed him again and again on the face, he awoke and conceived such an affection for me that putting aside all hesitation . . . he agreed to go to my mother and live in her house [and become Guibert's teacher].[6]   (I.4, Benton, pp. 45–46; Bourgin, p. 13)

Later, at a crucial point in Guibert's literary career – when he has fallen excessively in love with the pagan poets and with "versemaking" (I.17, Benton, p. 87; Bourgin, p. 64) – the tutor has another significant dream:

As he slept, there appeared to him the following vision: an old man with beautiful white hair – in fact that very man, I dare say, who had brought me to him at the beginning and had promised his love for me in the future – appeared to him and

said with great severity, "I wish you to give account to me for the writings that
have been composed; however, the hand which wrote them is not his who wrote."

(I.17, Benton, p. 87; Bourgin, pp. 64–65)

This dream takes as its subject Guibert's entire life: in its representation
of "that very man . . . who had brought me to him at the beginning," it calls
to mind the past course of Guibert's career, even as it focuses attention on
Guibert's "obscene" compositions, on his present (fallen) condition. At
the same time, the dream is a revelation of the future, suggesting an
ultimate rejection of frivolous, debased poetry:

> We mourned and were joyful in Thy hope, on the one hand seeing Thy displeasure
> in that fatherly rebuke, and on the other thinking from the meaning of the vision
> that confidence in some amendment of my frivolity was to come. For when the
> hand that wrote the letters was said not to be his who wr[o]te them, without doubt
> it meant that the hand would not continue in such shameful activity.

(I.17, Benton, p. 88; Bourgin, p. 65)

The dream suggests Guibert's imminent literary conversion,[7] and it comes
to play a crucial role in his self-definition. In the introduction to his
Tractatus de incarnatione contra Judaeos, Guibert retells the dream as a way of
explaining how he came to write such a pious work:

> Cum puer essem et sub paedagogo agerem, accidit me quasdam admodum
> saeculares litterulas dictitasse; quod cum magister idem aegre tulisset, dormienti
> astitit cano persona capite, dicens: Volo mihi rationem de litteris reddas,
> verumtamen manus quae scripsit non est illius personae quae scripsit. Quod cum
> esset mihi ab ipso relatum, animadverti quod aliquid mihi internae lucis
> impenderet Deus, ut manus mea piis serviret operibus.[8]

> When I was a boy and acted under [the direction of] a tutor, it happened that I had
> composed certain very worldly, trivial writings. When that same master had
> reacted with displeasure to this fact, a white-headed person stood by him while he
> was sleeping, and said: "I wish you to give account to me for [these] writings;
> however, the hand which wrote [them] is not [the hand] of the person who wrote."
> When this [thing] was related to me by him [the tutor], I became aware that God
> was meting out some internal light to me, so that my hand might serve pious
> works.

The association thus made between dreaming and the moment of an
essential change in the way one sees the world is not unique to Guibert. In
Augustine's *Confessions*, an essential model for medieval autobiographers,
Monica's dream of the rule, despite occurring long before Augustine's
actual conversion, nonetheless plays a role central to that conversion:

> She saw herself standing on a certain wooden rule, and a shining youth coming
> towards her, cheerful and smiling upon her, herself grieving, and overwhelmed

152

with grief. But he having . . . enquired of her the causes of her grief and daily tears, and she answering that she was bewailing my perdition, he bade her rest contented, and told her to look and observe, "That where she was, there was I also." And when she looked, she saw me standing by her in the same rule.[9]

(III.11.19, p. 47)

Monica's dream correctly predicts the outcome of Augustine's long search for meaning, foreseeing his final acceptance of Christianity. The dream, however, does not look *only* toward an ideal future; it demands interpretation, and indeed is read in two radically different ways:

When she had told me this vision, and I would fain bend it to mean, "That she rather should not despair of being one day what I was;" she presently, without any hesitation, replies; "No; for it was not told me that, 'where he, there thou also;' but 'where thou, there he also.'" I confess to Thee, O Lord . . . that Thy answer, through my waking mother, – that she was not perplexed by the plausibility of my false interpretation, and so quickly saw what was to be seen, and which I certainly had not perceived, before she spake, – even then moved me more than the dream itself, by which a joy to the holy woman, to be fulfilled so long after, was for the consolation of her present anguish, so long before foresignified.

(III.11.20, pp. 47–48)

Even as they point to Augustine's ultimate place with the Christian Monica, the dream and its two opposed interpretations dramatize the state of conflict between mother and son, emphasizing the interpretive gap separating the two. The dream demonstrates both the final goal of Augustine's search, and the great distance he must traverse before attaining that goal. And in Augustine's response to his mother's confident interpretation of the dream – "Thy answer, through my waking mother . . . even then moved me more than the dream itself" – Augustine is seen beginning to "move" in the right direction.

Significantly, "almost nine years" later (III.11.20, p. 48), immediately after his conversion, Augustine recalls Monica's dream and its meaning. Having heard the command, "Tolle, lege," and having read the scriptural passage (Romans 13:13–14) that finally enables him to see the world with a clarity akin to Monica's own, Augustine goes to his mother to report what has happened:

We tell her; she rejoiceth: we relate in order how it took place; she leaps for joy, and triumpheth, and blesseth Thee . . . For Thou convertedst me unto Thyself, so that I sought neither wife, nor any hope of this world, standing in that rule of faith, where Thou hadst shewed me unto her in a vision so many years before.

(VIII.12.30, pp.171–72)

Newly empowered with the ability to read the world through the lens of faith and Scripture, Augustine recalls Monica's dream and proclaims its truth; in doing so he leaves behind, once and for all, his former self of "false interpretation" (III.11.20, p. 47). The reminiscence of the dream and the final recognition of its true meaning coincide with a radical change in Augustine's way of reading the world.

HERMANN OF COLOGNE'S *OPUSCULUM DE CONVERSIONE SUA*

The dream's affinity for moments of interpretive crisis shows itself quite generally in medieval autobiography; dreams often attend an individual's radical reassessment of the self and the world. The correlation between dreaming and the revision of interpretive assumptions is especially striking in one mid-twelfth-century autobiography, the *Opusculum de conversione sua*, written by Hermann of Cologne, a convert from Judaism to Christianity.[10]

Hermann's conversion account is, in one sense, simple and straightforward: it proceeds chronologically, and in it Hermann singlemindedly concentrates attention on the course of his growing involvement in Christianity. He details the circumstances of his first encounter with the Christian faith (chapter 2),[11] and carefully chronicles his developing intellectual and affective attachment to the new religion (chapters 3–9). Throughout the first half of his account, Hermann harbors doubts about conversion (chapters 3–4 and 9), hovering between Judaism and Christianity. Indeed, his progress toward "truth" is halted for a time by obstacles that the Jewish community sets in his path (chapter 10). Soon, however, Hermann is back on the "right" track (chapter 11), and aided by the prayers of two especially devout women, he receives an illumination that turns him once and for all away from his native religion (chapter 12). From here, despite the continued opposition of the Jewish community (chapters 14–16), and despite Hermann's early reluctance to make his conversion public (chapter 16), the narrative moves forward ineluctably (chapters 13–20). Hermann becomes a catechumen (chapter 17), is baptized, taking a new name (chapter 19), and finally renounces secular life to enter the Premonstratensian order (chapter 20).[12]

But while Hermann's narrative follows a predictable course, it is not the uncomplicated – essentially oral and anecdotal – account that certain critics would make it.[13] Hermann does more in the *Opusculum* than simply report events; he also explains their coherence, how they fit into an overarching trajectory that leads from the "errors" of Judaism to the "truth" of Christianity.[14] Not content with merely describing the pattern of his life, Hermann probes more deeply, trying to explain what exactly it means to reject Judaism for Christianity.

For Hermann, as for Augustine, conversion involves learning to read the world and written words in new ways,[15] and in explaining his conversion experience, he returns repeatedly, even obsessively, to the theme of reading. It is, in fact, the distinctively Christian way of reading Holy Scripture, the allegorical interpretation of the "old law," that first impresses Hermann when he encounters the teaching of Bishop Ekbert of Münster:

Ibi itaque audiebam *scriba*m *doctu*m *in regno celorum de thesauro suo nova et vetera profer*entem [Matthew 13:52], et vetus scilicet testamentum ad novum referendo et novum ex veteri idonea satis ratione approbando. Legalium quoque mandatorum quedam, ut sunt: *Non mechaberis; non furtum facies; non falsum testimonium dices; honora patrem et matrem* [Exodus 20:14, 15, 16, 12], ad solam littere superficiem tenenda esse docebat; quedam autem, qualia sunt: *Non arabis in bove simul et asino* [Deuteronomy 22:10]; et *non coques edum in lacte matris sue* [Exodus 23:19, 34:26; Deuteronomy 14:21], supervacua quantum ad litteram asserens, ad sensus allegoricos pulcherrima nichilominus ratione transferebat.

(Chapter 2, pp. 73–74)

And thus, there I heard "a scribe instructed in the kingdom of heaven bringing forth out of his treasure new things and old" [Matthew 13:52], and namely in referring the Old Testament to the New and in proving the New from the Old by quite appropriate reasoning. He also taught that certain of the legal mandates – such as, "Thou shalt not commit adultery," "Thou shalt not steal," "Thou shalt not bear false witness," "Honour thy father and thy mother" [Exodus 20:14, 15, 16, 12] – are to be kept on the literal level alone, while certain others – which are of this sort: "Thou shalt not plough with an ox and an ass together" [Deuteronomy 22:10], and "Thou shalt not boil a kid in the milk of his dam" [Exodus 23:19, 34:26; Deuteronomy 14:21] – he asserted [to be] superfluous as far as the letter is concerned; nevertheless, with most beautiful reason, he referred [these] to allegorical senses.

From this introduction to allegory, Ekbert proceeds, presumably for Hermann's benefit, to assert directly the superiority of such an interpretive method to the opposed, erroneous, Jewish way of reading:

Iudeis tamquam brutis quibusdam iumentis sola in his littera velut palea contentis, Christiani ut homines ratione utentes spirituali intelligentia velut dulcissima palee medulla reficerentur. (Chapter 2, p. 74)

[While] Jews, like certain brute beasts of burden, are contented, in these things, by the letter alone, like unto chaff, Christians, as men who use reason, may be refreshed by a spiritual understanding, like unto the most sweet kernel within the chaff.

The contrast thus established remains prominently displayed throughout the *Opusculum*. Jews inspect only the outside of things, penetrating no deeper than the "littera velut palea." Deaf and blind to true (inner) meaning,[16] they see no further than the veil of appearances:

Scis equidem, teste apostolo, *usque in hodiernum diem, cum legitur* Iudeis *Moyses, velamen positum est super cor eorum* [2 Corinthians 3:15]. Hoc audiens et, unde verbi huius occasio tracta foret, optime tamquam in veteri testamento exercitatus intelligens, vehementer expavi, reputans ne forte, sicut filii quondam Israel clarificatam in monte Moysi faciem non nisi velo mediante quibant aspicere, sic ego misticum Mosaice legis intellectum nequaquam, velut interpositis quibusdam carnalium figurarum umbris, clara mentis acie possem attingere.[17]

(Chapter 11, p. 104)

Indeed you know, with the apostle as witness, [that] "even until this day, when Moses is read" by the Jews, "the veil is put upon their heart" [2 Corinthians 3:15]. Hearing this and understanding whence the occasion for this saying might be drawn, because [I was] very well trained in the Old Testament, I became powerfully frightened, reckoning that perhaps, just as formerly the children of Israel were unable without a mediating veil to look at Moses's face, enlightened on the mountain, I too might be unable to arrive by any means at a mystic comprehension of the Mosaic law with the clear sight of the mind, as though certain shadows of carnal figures [had been] interposed.

Judaism necessarily presents a barrier to understanding, blocking out the light of truth with its own darkness:

Sed miser ego more *aspidis surde et obturantis aures suas* [Psalms 57:5] suavissime incantationis sue verba auribus cordis non percipiebam, ac mentualibus oculis, quos iudaice cecitatis caligo obduxerat, lumen veritatis intueri non poteram.

(Chapter 4, pp. 82–83)

But I, miserable, after the manner of "the deaf asp that stoppeth her ears" [Psalms 57:5], did not perceive with the ears of the heart the words of his most pleasant incantation, but with lying eyes, which the murk of Jewish blindness had covered, I was not able to gaze at the light of truth.

Before his conversion, Hermann himself sometimes speaks for Judaism and its exegetical practices. Thus, debating with Rupert of Deutz over problems of representation and interpretation (chapter 3–4),[18] Hermann – still bound by the conceptual framework of Judaism – defends literal reading of the "old law" (chapter 3, pp. 77–78) and attacks Christian faithlessness to the scriptural letter (chapter 3, p. 78). In particular, he denounces Christian "worship" of images ("ydolatria"), especially the image of the crucified Christ (chapter 3, pp. 78–79). Responding to Hermann, Rupert, as might be expected, exposes the "errors" of Jewish literalism. He demonstrates how the Old Testament, read typologically, validates Christian practices (chapter 4, pp. 79–80 and 82), and shows that the crucifix is not an idol, but a symbol whose visible form calls to mind the invisible truth of Christ's sacrifice (chapter 4, p. 80).[19]

Hermann, however, is unconvinced; as long as he remains a Jew, he obstinately clings to literal reading, or, when this fails, resorts to distorted, sophistical reasoning:

Cumque multa mihi de Christi adventu ex lege et prophetis proferrent testimonia, ego soli littere pertinacissime innitens ea de Christo vel predicta non fuisse contendebam vel, si hec negare non poteram, sinistra ea qualibet interpretatione pervertebam, aut certe, si neutrum manifesta conclusus ratione valebam, callida eos tergiversatione per ambages verborum ad aliam mihi solvendam questionem circumducebam. (Chapter 9, p. 97)

And when they brought forth to me many testimonies from the law and the prophets about the advent of Christ, I, most stubbornly depending on the letter alone, either contended that those things had not been predicted about Christ; or, if I was unable to deny these things, I perverted them by some left-handed interpretation; or, certainly, if, constrained by manifest reason, I was not able [to follow] either of these [courses], I led them around by a skillful evasion, through the windings of words, to a different question to be solved by me.

Hermann's interpretive blindness and duplicity here mark his distance from Christianity; his interpretive insight elsewhere shows him moving steadily away from Judaism. Indeed, the progress of Hermann's conversion is measured largely in such terms: Hermann figures the journey from Judaism to Christianity as a movement from obtuse, material ways of reading toward enlightened, spiritual exegesis. At the opening of his narrative, though well-versed in Hebrew literature (chapter 2, p. 74), Hermann describes himself as unread ("illectus," chapter 2, p. 73). From his final (Christian) perspective, Hermann is only a reader insofar as he is a Christian reader. The "illiterate" Hermann, however, quickly shows himself apt for Christian learning. Even in his earliest exposure to Christianity, he is able, at least at moments, to read the old law allegorically:

Sciens etiam animalia non ruminantia a lege inter immunda deputari, quecumque mihi ex illius [Ekeberti] predicatione audita placuerant, in ventrem memorie sepius mecum ruminanda transmisi, Christianis autem ea me, que dicebantur, attentissime audientem magno cum stupore intuentibus, et num sermo mihi episcopalis placuisset sciscitantibus, partim minus, partim amplius placere respondi.[20]
(Chapter 2, p. 74)

Also knowing that nonruminating animals are counted by the law among the unclean, whatever things had pleased me [that I] heard in his [Ekbert's] preaching, I transmitted to the stomach of [my] memory to be often ruminated on by me. However, when the Christians looked at me listening, most attentively and with great wonder, to those things that were said, and when they asked whether the bishop's discourse had pleased me, I responded that it pleased partly less [and] partly more.

From such a hesitant, but promising, start, Hermann becomes more and more "literate," and more and more allegorically "ruminative." He quickly, even miraculously, learns to read Latin:

Clericorum etiam sepe scholas ingrediens libros ab eis accepi, in quibus singulorum elementorum proprietates diligenter considerans et vocabula sagaciter investigans, cepi subito cum ingenti audientium stupore litteras sillabis et sillabas dictionibus nullo docente copulare sicque in brevi scientiam legendi scripturas assecutus sum. Quod ne forte alicui incredibile videatur, non hoc mihi sed Deo, cui nichil impossibile est, asscribatur.[21]   (Chapter 2, p. 76)

Also, often entering the schools of the clerics, I received books from them, in which, diligently considering the properties of the individual letters and sagaciously investigating the words, I suddenly began, to the vast wonder of those listening, to couple letters into syllables and syllables into utterances, with no one teaching [me]. And thus in a short time I attained the ability to read writings. Which (lest by chance it appear incredible to anyone) is to be ascribed not to me but to God, to whom nothing is impossible.

The ease with which Hermann masters the written language of Christianity anticipates his special aptitude for the religion as a whole, including its distinctive ways of interpreting sacred texts.

The education in exegetical practices that Hermann receives is not the *only* factor in his movement toward Christianity.[22] Still, the moment of conversion *is* intimately involved with the ongoing narrative of interpretive progress. Conversion comes as a sudden splash of light, turning Hermann away from the darkness of Judaism toward Christian clarity:

Tanta repente cordi meo christiane fidei claritas infulsit, ut ab eo totius pristine dubietatis et ignorantie tenebras penitus effugaverit.   (Chapter 12, p. 108)

Such a brightness of Christian faith suddenly shone in my heart, that it completely drove away from it [my heart] the darkness of all earlier doubt and ignorance.

From this point on, Hermann no longer hesitates about the validity of allegorical reading: what the Old Testament presents "visibiliter," Hermann interprets as significant "invisibiliter," in relation to the life of the spirit (chapter 19, p. 120).

In the dialectic between Christian and Jewish ways of reading, dreams play a crucial role. Before converting, as he worries about whether to become a Christian, Hermann prays fervently for divine revelation, asking for a dream that will guide him in making his religious choice:

Cepi iterum, sicut prius crebris eum precibus implorare, ut mihi *veritatis viam*, sicut sancto quondam Danieli somniorum misteria [Daniel 7:1ff.], nocturna visione dignaretur revelare.   (Chapter 8, p. 94)

Dreams and life

I began again, as before, to beseech Him with frequent prayers, that He would deign to reveal to me, in a nocturnal vision, "the way of truth," as once [He revealed] the mysteries of dreams to the blessed Daniel [Daniel 7:1ff.].

But although Hermann here shows himself sincere in his desire for guidance – he adds to his prayers a strenuous three-day fast[23] – he is consistently denied revelation:

Mane autem expergefactus cernensque caliginosam noctem rutilo sole illustrari, gemebam graviter et ultra quam dici vel credi potest dolebam, quod tali exemplo a vero *sole iustitie* [Malachi 4:2] Christo non meruissem illuminari.

(Chapter 8, p. 95)

However, when I awakened in the morning and perceived that murky night was illuminated by the golden sun, I moaned gravely and mourned, beyond what can be said or believed, that, [despite] such a precedent [the sun illuminating the night], I had [still] not merited to be illuminated by the true "sun of justice" [Malachi 4:2], Christ.

Hermann does not yet "merit" the illumination that will allow him to escape the "iudaice cecitatis caligo" [murk of Jewish blindness] (chapter 4, p. 83). He has already learned something about Christian ways of reading the world (witness his figural interpretation of the sun), but he is still beset by doubts, and still involved in deceptions – "horrenda infidelitatis caligine involutum" [wrapped up in the horrible murk of infidelity] (chapter 8, p. 95). Hermann must learn more about Christianity before he can receive unambiguous revelation.

The moment of conversion itself finally provides the sort of illuminated experience that Hermann desires, and later, in a scene clearly echoing his earlier striving after revelation, Hermann is granted a *dream* that is unambiguous in its significance:

Vidi somnium sicut visu ita et relatu dulcissimum. *Vidi* versus orientem *ce*lum *apert*um [Acts 7:55], cuius imaginaria,[24] que mihi per visum apparebat structura, auro purissimo per totum fuerat ornata. Ubi dominum Iesum sublimi in solio et paterna maiestate potentissime atque, honorificentissime vidi residentem atque sceptri vice triumphale sue crucis signum super dextrum humerum tenentem. Cui, ut mihi videbatur, cum excellentissimis eius amicis assistens ineffabili contempla-tionis sue suavitate inestimabiliter delectabar. (Chapter 18, pp. 116–17)

I saw a dream most sweet in both the seeing and the telling. "I saw" toward the east "the heavens opened" [Acts 7:55], whose imaginary structure, which appeared to me in the vision, had been completely adorned with most pure gold. Where I saw the Lord Jesus sitting, most powerfully and in greatest honor, on a sublime throne and in paternal majesty, and holding above His right shoulder the triumphal sign of His cross in place of a scepter. In whom, as it seemed to me, I was inestimably delighted, standing with His most excellent friends in the ineffable sweetness of their contemplation.

Hermann's dream shows him the ultimate goal of Christian life – the beatific vision of Christ – and provides a foretaste of the eternal "delight" that lies in his future.

As the dream continues, however, it also shows Hermann the error that he has left behind and the horrible end to which Jewish life *would* have brought him:

Ecce duo amite mee filii, quorum alter Nathan, alius Ysaac vocabatur, post tergum meum prepeti gressu transibant, ut ex ipso eorum transitu liquido animadvertentibus daretur intelligi, illam eis beatitudinem non ad solatium, sed ad supplicium esse demonstratam, ut eo ipso intus in animo torquerentur, quod illa, quam cernebant, sanctorum gloria perfrui non merebantur.   (Chapter 18, p. 117)

Behold, the two sons of my paternal aunt, one named Nathan and the other Isaac, were passing behind my back on a swift course, so that it might be made understandable to those looking on, by the fact of their fluid passing-by, that that beatitude was shown to them not as a solace but as a punishment, so that inwardly in the soul they might be tortured by the very fact that they did not deserve to enjoy the glory of the saints that they perceived.

Behind himself, Hermann sees his past blindness, and in an exchange that calls to mind his pre-conversion debates,[25] he speaks, now with convincing Christian authority, of Jewish error and of proper interpretation:

O miseri et infelices, numquid non istud, quod super humerum Christi videtis, crucis signum illam nunc vobis Ysaie ad mentem reducit prophetiam: *Cuius imperium super humerum eius* [Isaiah 9:6]? Huic vos olim de Christo prophetie per meam exhortationem credere contempsistis, quam ecce ad perpetuam confusionem vestram impletam aspicitis.   (Chapter 18, p. 117)

O wretched and unhappy ones, does that sign of the cross, which you see above the shoulder of Christ, not now recall to your mind that prophecy of Isaiah's: "Whose government is upon his shoulder" [Isaiah 9:6]? Formerly you did not deign to believe, at my exhortation, this prophecy about Christ, which behold you [now] see fulfilled to your perpetual confusion.

In the other world of this dream, the truth of Hermann's position, and of Christian exegesis, must be admitted, and the dire consequences of Judaism made evident:

Illi [duo Judaei] vero nimio pavore circumdati vix mihi paucis humili et suppressa voce responderunt, dicentes: Vera quidem, o nepos, sed nimis heu sero nobis sunt probata que memoras, quoniam amisso salutaris spatio penitentie sine spe consequende salutis eterne destinati sumus gehenne. Vix verbum compleverant statimque de medio facti sunt, impleta in eis scriptura, que ait: *Tollatur impius, ne videat gloriam Dei* [Isaiah 26:10].   (Chapter 18, p. 117)

Truly, those [two Jews], enveloped by a great trembling, responded to me with difficulty, saying in few words in a humble and suppressed voice: O nephew, indeed true, but alas much too late for us, are the proven [things] that you call to mind, since, with the time for saving penitence gone, we are destined, without hope of future salvation, to eternal Gehenna. Hardly had they completed that word when immediately they were put out of the way – that scripture fulfilled in them which says: "Let the wicked be removed, lest he see the glory of the Lord" [Isaiah 26:10].

Hermann's dream provides, as in Augustine and Guibert, a way of figuring the whole course of a life. It glances back at Hermann's (Jewish) past, and recognizes his present position of (Christian) authority; further- more, it forecasts his other-worldly fate and contrasts that fate with the inevitable damnation of the Jews. As Hermann realizes when he awakens – recalling his earlier unrequited desire for revelation – the dream measures his spiritual progress from unenlightened Judaism to Christian illlumination:

Expergefactus itaque et recordatus, quantis aliquando precibus et lacrimis ieiuniorumque frequentia talem celitus pro mea illuminatione visionem impetrare sategeram, cepi in his que videram gaudio spirituali superabundare debitasque Deo pro tam suavi visione, qua in eius fide roborari merueram, grates exsolvere.

(Chapter 18, pp. 117–18)

And thus having awakened and remembered with how many prayers and tears and with [what] frequency of fasting I once had enough to do to obtain such a vision from heaven for my illumination, I began to overflow with spiritual joy for those things that I had seen and to pay God back the thanks owed for such a pleasant vision, by which I had merited to be made strong in His faith.

Hermann's dream allows him confidently to survey his life – to gaze down from a secure, authoritative perspective and judge the experience of conversion. Such an unambiguous revelation, the *Opusculum* seems to say, comes only to Christians; in any case, it comes to Hermann only after he has given himself fully to Christianity. But Hermann has another sort of dream – ambiguous in its significance and susceptible to a variety of possible interpretations – long before his conversion (chapters 1 and 21). The dream occurs when Hermann is thirteen years old[26] and still unexposed to Christianity. While the later, revelatory dream offers a retrospective, and unequivocal, view of the conversion experience, Hermann's adolescent dream is proleptic – "proventura mihi Deus gratie sue beneficia iocundis- simo huiuscemodi visionis demonstravit presagio" [God, by the most pleasant presage of a vision of this sort, indicated the benefits of his grace that were to come forth for me] (chapter 1, p. 70) – anticipating the course of his life. While the two dreams thus differ radically in kind from each other, each in its own way participates intimately in the exploration of interpretive process central to Hermann's self-examination. If Hermann's dream of the other world provides a summary of the changes made in moving from Judaism to Christianity, his earlier dream dramatizes the *need* for change, defining Hermann's initial position – "adhuc iudaice infidelitatis nexibus tenerer irretitus" [hitherto I was held entangled in the bonds of Jewish infidelity] (chapter 1, p. 70) – and simultaneously suggesting the end toward which Hermann's life will move.

Indeed, Hermann's adolescent dream literally encompasses the whole of the conversion narrative. It is the first event recounted in the *Opusculum*, and Hermann self-consciously returns to it as he brings his work to its close.[27] This enigmatic dream – in which Hermann is honored by the emperor at a spectacular feast, receiving as gifts a white horse, a golden girdle, a purse containing seven coins, and the inheritance of a recently deceased prince – because it demands interpretation, and because it actually receives radically different interpretations from Jews and Christians, provides Hermann with an especially powerful emblem of the interpretive changes around which his life pivots.

From the very beginning, Hermann understands that his dream is significant:

In huius itaque visionis iocunditate evigilans, licet puer essem, non tamen levitate puerili ea que tam insolita videram, inania esse iudicavi, sed magnum aliquid ratus eorum mihi portendi presagio. (Chapter 1, p. 71)

And thus awakening in the pleasantness of this vision, though I was a boy, nevertheless I did not judge in childish levity that these so unaccustomed things that I had seen were empty, but reckoned that something great was portended for me by their prediction.

Since he is a Jewish boy, however, Hermann has access only to Jewish means of interpretation; going to one of his relatives, a man of great authority among the Jews (chapter 1, p. 71), Hermann receives a reading of the dream that, in its emphasis on the material and worldly, is clearly inadequate:

Relatumque ei per ordinem somnium, ut mihi, quomodo nosset, interpretaretur, oravi. *Qui* ea sola *que carnis sunt sapi*ens [Romans 8:5] quandam mihi secundum carnis felicitatem dictavit coniecturam, per equum magnum et candidum significari dicens, quod nobilem ac speciosam uxorem sortiturus, per nummos marsupio inclusos, quod multas divitias habiturus, per celebratum cum imperatore convivium, quod plurimum honorabilis inter Iudeos essem futurus.[28]

(Chapter 1, pp. 71–72)

And I told him the dream, related in order, so that he might, insofar as he knew how, interpret [it] for me. "Who, minding" only those things "that are of the flesh" [Romans 8:5], expressed for me a certain interpretation according to the felicity of the flesh, saying that by the great, shining white horse it was signified that I was destined to have a noble and beautiful wife; by the coins enclosed in the purse, that I would have much wealth; by the feast celebrated with the emperor, that I would be most honorable among the Jews.

This first reading of the dream defines the starting point of Hermann's narrative. And in the narrator's retrospective recognition of the inadequacy of this initial reading – in Hermann's ultimate judgment of Judaism by the standards of New Testament reading (Romans 8:5) – we catch a glimpse of where the story will end:

Sed hanc visionem multo post evidentius divina in me gratia spiritualibus beneficiis adimplevit, sicut et eiusdem postmodum visionis interpretatio indicabit et rei ipsius effectus comprobabit.   (Chapter 1, p. 72)

But much later, divine grace [working] in me fulfilled this vision more clearly with spiritual benefits, as both the interpretation of this same vision will presently indicate and the outcome of the event itself will confirm.

In the discrepancy between Hermann the thirteen-year-old Jewish boy and Hermann the Christian narrator who perceives spiritual meanings that formerly eluded him, we find marked out the ground that the account of conversion must cover.[29]

The *Opusculum* thus traces the process by which Hermann's Jewish ways of reading are Christianized, and Hermann makes gradual progress in the faith throughout his account. But in order to confirm that progress – to measure more dramatically how far Hermann has finally come – the end of the story returns to Hermann's adolescent dream and its interpretation.

It is only after Hermann converts, is baptized, and becomes a priest that he fully understands his early dream:

Gradatim ad ordines canonicos ascendi, donec ad sacerdotalis excellentie dignitatem perveni. Tunc itaque primo visum ante meam conversionem somnium in prima huius opusculi fronte insertum, quid in me futurum presignaverit, intellexi, cuius sicut superius promisi, interpretationem explicabo.   (Chapter 20, p. 122)

By degrees I ascended to canon's orders, until I attained to the dignity of priestly excellence. And then, for the first time, I understood the dream I saw before my conversion, inserted at the very beginning of this little work, which presignified for me what was to come, and of which, as I promised above, I will [now] unfold the interpretation.

Granted the illumination necessary to Christian exegesis, Hermann can now give an elaborate allegorical reading of his dream that drives home its significance for his *spiritual* life. The emperor signifies the "celestial king"; the powerful prince who dies is Lucifer; the white horse stands for the grace of baptism, the belt for restraint of the flesh, the seven coins for the gifts of the "septiform" Spirit. The dream, which at first seems to point to success in the material world, finally reveals itself as a veiled anticipation of Hermann's withdrawal from the temptations of Jewish carnality:

Ego nitido illo balteo, id est continentie robore precinctus, regio equo insedi, quia *gratia* baptismi *in me vacua non fuit* [1 Corinthians 15:10], sed quod equi indicat usus, eam cum Dei adiutorio spirituali exercitio semper excolere et ad bonum usum inflectere laboravi. Christum quoque regem secutus sum, *mundum* et *que in mundo sunt* [1 John 2:15] contempnendo nec solum mea omnia, verum etiam et meipsum pro eius amore abnegando, faciens hoc, quod ipse de se testatur: *Non* veni, inquiens, *fac*ere *voluntatem meam, sed eius, qui misit me* [John 6:38], patris.

(Chapter 21, p. 124)

I, girded with that shining belt, that is with the strength of continence, sat on the regal horse, because the "grace" of baptism "in me hath not been void" [1 Corinthians 15:10], but rather (which the use of the horse indicates) I always labored, with the aid of God, to cultivate that [grace] with spiritual exercise and to turn [it] to good use. I also followed Christ the king in despising "the world" and "the things which are in the world" [1 John 2:15], and in abnegating not only all of my things but also even myself for love of Him, doing that which He Himself witnesses about Himself, saying: I came "not to do my own will, but the will of him that sent me" [John 6:38], [the will] of the Father.

The end of the *Opusculum* returns to the work's opening event, and radically transforms that event. The extent of the transformation, the extent to which the dream's perceived significance has changed, provides a yardstick for what has happened in Hermann's life as a whole. All those changes to which Hermann has been subject are summed up finally in the exaggerated contrast between Jewish and Christian ways of reading the dream. The uncertain "rumination" of Hermann's first, slow steps toward Christianity (see above) becomes at last a confident consideration of Christian doctrine:

Olus, quod in mensa regia manducare mihi visus sum, Christi arbitror designare evangelium . . . Ad regale [i]gitur convivium olus manducare, est sacerdotem dominico altari assistentem sancti evangelii precepta sollerter atque subtiliter considerando velut in ore cordis ruminare.

(Chapter 21, p. 125)

I judge that the vegetables, which, at the royal table, I seemed to myself to chew on, designate the gospel of Christ . . . To chew on vegetables at the royal feast, therefore, is [for] the priest assisting at the church altar to ruminate, as though in the mouth of [his] heart, in considering skillfully and acutely the precepts of holy gospel.

Susceptible to either a mundane, literal reading, or a divine, allegorical one, Hermann's enigmatic dream provides a ground upon which two radically different approaches to the world are explored. Hermann the proselyte, of course, finally embraces the "higher" reading of his dream, using it and its interpretation to justify in part the radical religious change he has undergone. Still, the twice-interpreted dream itself stands unresolved between the materiality of its images, read materially by the Jews, and the spirituality of Hermann's final, Christian interpretation. Thus the dream and the two readings it receives encapsulate the interpretive problem central to the *Opusculum*; they also stand as an appropriate emblem for the complexity of the medieval dream.

Notes

INTRODUCTION

1 Freud's work is so clearly accepted as the origin of contemporary views of dreaming that one author can state, incorrectly but with no hesitation, that "Sigmund Freud was the first to propose that dreams had a function" – Kim A. McDonald, "Medical Researchers Investigate Dreams for Clues to Patients' Emotional and Physical Health," *The Chronicle of Higher Education*, July 13, 1988, p. A5.

2 For a study of how different contemporary psychological schools – Freudian, Jungian, Culturalist, Object Relational, Phenomenological, and Gestalt – would interpret the same set of dreams, see James L. Fosshage and Clemens A. Loew (eds.), *Dream Interpretation: A Comparative Study*, revised edition (New York: PMA, 1987).

3 Sigmund Freud, *The Interpretation of Dreams* [*Die Traumdeutung*; first edition, 1900], James Strachey (trans. and ed.) (New York: Avon Books, 1965), p. 647.

4 J. Allan Hobson and Robert W. McCarley, "The Brain as a Dream State Generator: An Activation-Synthesis Hypothesis of the Dream Process," *The American Journal of Psychiatry* 134 (1977), 1335–48; the quotations are from pp. 1346 and 1347. See also the authors' earlier critique of the neurobiological bases of Freud's dream theory: McCarley and Hobson, "The Neurobiological Origins of Psychoanalytic Dream Theory," *The American Journal of Psychiatry* 134 (1977), 1211–21.

5 See especially Hobson and McCarley, "Brain as a Dream State Generator," pp. 1336 and 1346, and the authors' reply to criticism of their theory in "Letters to the Editor," *The American Journal of Psychiatry* 135 (1978), 617–18. Still, the psychiatric community quite clearly read Hobson and McCarley as attacking the significance of dreams; see "Letters to the Editor," pp. 613–15, and John C. Nemiah, "Children of an Idle Brain?" *The American Journal of Psychiatry* 135 (1978), 1530.

6 Hobson and McCarley, "Brain as a Dream State Generator," p. 1336.

7 Francis Crick and Graeme Mitchison, "The Function of Dream Sleep," *Nature* 304 (1983), 111–14; the quotations are from p. 111.

8 *Ibid.*, p. 114.

9 On some post-medieval anticipations of the newest, most radically physiological theories of dreaming, see Peretz Lavie and J. Allan Hobson, "Origin of Dreams: Anticipation of Modern Theories in the Philosophy and Physiology of the Eighteenth and Nineteenth Centuries," *Psychological Bulletin* 100 (1986), 229–40.

10 See, for instance, *Grandma's Lucky Number Dream Book* (Baltimore: Grandma's Candle Shop, 1979). For pictures of "lucky number dream books" contemporary with Freud, see Robert Wayne Pelton, *The Complete Book of Dream Interpretation* (New York: Arco, 1983), pp. 6–7 and 23.

11 See, for instance, Zolar, *Zolar's Encyclopedia and Dictionary of Dreams* (New York: Arco,

1963); *The Mystic Dream Book: 2500 Dreams Explained* (New York: Arco, 1983 [1963]); Gustavus Hindman Miller, *Ten Thousand Dreams Interpreted, or What's in a Dream: A Scientific and Practical Exposition* (Chicago: Rand McNally, 1980); and Pelton, *Complete Book*. Miller's treatment seems, from topical references made in the introduction, to date from the turn of the twentieth century.

12 Pelton, *Complete Book*, p. v.

13 See especially *ibid.*, pp. 3–20; and Miller, *Ten Thousand Dreams*, pp. 7–9 and 19. Pelton cites Horney, Adler, and Fromm on pp. 29, 72, and 91 respectively; Zolar, *Zolar's Encyclopedia*, cites Freud on p. vii.

14 Miller, *Ten Thousand Dreams*, p. 9; and Pelton, *Complete Book*, p. 5. In his introduction, Pelton borrows generously from Miller. For Aristotle's statement, see chapter 2 below.

15 Freud, *Interpretation of Dreams*, p. 659. Freud also treats predictive dreams on pp. 39 and 97; in both places, he interestingly refuses to close the door on the possibility of premonitory dream experience.

16 *Ibid.*, pp. 659–60. The German citation is from *Die Traumdeutung*, in *Gesammelte Werke*, vols. II–III (London: Imago, 1942), p. 626.

17 C.G. Jung, *Memories, Dreams, Reflections*, revised edition, Aniela Jaffé (recorder and ed.), Richard and Clara Winston (trans.) (New York: Vintage Books, Random House, 1965), p. 300.

18 *Ibid.*, p. 301.

19 *Ibid.*, p. 316. This last citation follows Jung's account of a premonitory dream: "Several months before my mother's death, in September 1922, I had a dream which presaged it" (p. 315).

20 Stephen LaBerge, *Lucid Dreaming* (New York: Ballantine Books, 1985), p. 7.

21 *Ibid.*, p. 268. Later, LaBerge speculates more generally on transcendence (p. 272).

22 The recent work of cultural historians like Jacques LeGoff (*L'Imaginaire médiéval: Essais* [Paris: Gallimard, 1985]) and A.J. Gurevich (*Categories of Medieval Culture*, G.L. Campbell [trans.] [London: Routledge and Kegan Paul, 1985] and *Medieval Popular Culture: Problems of Belief and Perception*, János M. Bak and Paul A. Hollingsworth [trans.] [Cambridge: Cambridge University Press; and Paris: Éditions de la Maison des Sciences de l'Homme, 1988]) toward defining particular medieval habits of mind points in promising directions for the study of attitudes toward dreaming. For work especially pertinent to the medieval dream, see Gurevich, *Medieval Popular Culture*, pp. 104–52; Gurevich, "Oral and Written Culture of the Middle Ages: Two 'Peasant Visions' of the Late Twelfth–Early Thirteenth Centuries," *New Literary History* 16 (1984), 51–66; LeGoff, *L'Imaginaire médiéval*, pp. 265–330; LeGoff, "Dreams in the Culture and Collective Psychology of the Medieval West," in *Time, Work, and Culture in the Middle Ages*, Arthur Goldhammer (trans.) (Chicago and London: University of Chicago Press, 1980), pp. 201–04; LeGoff, "Le Christianisme et les rêves (IIe–VIIe siècles)," in Tullio Gregory (ed.), *I sogni nel medioevo*, Seminario Internazionale, Rome, 2–4 October 1983 (Rome: Edizioni dell'Ateneo, 1985), pp. 169–218; Michel Aubrun, "Caractères et portée religieuse et sociale des 'Visiones' en Occident du VIe au XIe siècle," *Cahiers de Civilisation Médiévale: X^e–XIIe Siècles* 23 (1980), 109–30; Peter Burke, "L'Histoire sociale des rêves," *Annales: Economies, Sociétés, Civilisations* 28 (1973), 329–42; and Carolly Erickson, *The Medieval Vision: Essays in History and Perception* (New York: Oxford University Press, 1976).

23 See Gurevich's comment, in *Medieval Popular Culture*, that "the stereotypical form that visions received from many authors was the sole possible method of describing and realizing them": "This did not reduce the vision to a purely 'literary' composition – in

the modern meaning based on the opposition of life and literature. For already the visionary himself, attempting to communicate the secrets he had experienced in the Other World, could not help clothing his visions in traditional forms known to him" (pp. 125–26). Adam Davy, *Adam Davy's Five Dreams About Edward II*, F.J. Furnivall (ed.), EETS, OS 69 (London: N. Trübner, 1878), provides an interesting case in which the presentation of "actual" dreams is clearly indebted to religious texts and to the traditions of patronage poetry.

I DREAMBOOKS AND THEIR AUDIENCES

1 See, for instance, St. Jerome's dream-journey to "the judgment seat of the Judge," Jerome, Letter 22, to Eustachium, in *The Principal Works of St. Jerome*, W.H. Fremantle (trans.), A Select Library of Nicene and Post-Nicene Fathers of the Catholic Church, second series, 6 (New York: The Christian Literature Company; and Oxford and London: Parker, 1893), chapter 30, pp. 35–36; and see Sulpitius Severus's dream of St. Martin, Sulpitius Severus, Letter 2, to Aurelius, in *The Works of Sulpitius Severus*, Alexander Roberts (trans.), A Select Library of Nicene and Post-Nicene Fathers of the Christian Church, second series, 11 (New York, 1894; rpt. Grand Rapids, Mich.: Wm. B. Eerdmans, 1978), pp. 19–21.

2 See also Genesis 20:3–7; Numbers 12:6–8; Judges 7:13–15; 3 Kings [= 1 Kings, RSV] 3:5–15; Esther 10:5 and 11:3–12; Job 33:15–16; Ecclesiasticus 34:6; Joel 2:28; 2 Maccabees 15:11–16; Matthew 2:12; and Acts 2:17 and 16:9. In addition, the New Testament Apocalypse, while not explicitly a dream, was often read in the Middle Ages as representing experience closely akin to dreaming.

3 Latin citations of the Bible are from the *Biblia sacra iuxta Vulgatam versionem*, revised edition, 2 vols., Robertus Weber (ed.) (Stuttgart: Württembergische Bibelanstalt, 1975). English versions are from *The Holy Bible*, translated from the Latin Vulgate [Douay-Rheims version] (Baltimore, 1899; rpt. Rockford, Ill.: Tan Books, 1971). For other biblical warnings against faith in dreams, see Leviticus 19:26; Deuteronomy 13:1–5; 2 Paralipomenon [= 2 Chronicles, RSV] 33:6; Ecclesiastes 5:2 and 5:6; Ecclesiasticus 34:1–7; Isaiah 29:7–8 and 56:10; Jeremiah 23:25–32, 27:9, and 29:8–9; and Zechariah 10:2.

4 For helpful overviews of the three kinds of manual, see Max Förster, "Beiträge zur mittelalterlichen Volkskunde IV," *Archiv für das Studium der neueren Sprachen und Literaturen* 125 (1910), 39–70, esp. pp. 39–40; Walther Suchier, "Altfranzösische Traumbücher," *Zeitschrift für französische Sprache und Literatur* 65 (1943–44), 129–67, esp. pp. 135–67; and Steven R. Fischer, *The Dream in the Middle High German Epic* (Bern: Peter Lang, 1978), pp. 23–29. For a valuable discussion of the larger tradition of "ancient and medieval dream-books," see Lynn Thorndike, *A History of Magic and Experimental Science*, II (New York: Macmillan, 1923), pp. 290–302. In my discussion of the dreambooks I adopt the English terminology used by Fischer.

5 E. Sievers, "Bedeutung der Buchstaben," *Zeitschrift für deutsches Alterthum* 18 (1875), 297.

6 Unless otherwise indicated, all translations are my own.

7 Förster, "Die altenglischen Traumlunare," *Englische Studien* 60 (1925–26), 67–68.

8 See Förster, "Mittelalterliche Orakelalphabete für Psalterwahrsagung," *Forschungen und Fortschritte* 4 (1928), 204–06. Note also the association between a text, the moment of awakening, and prophecy, affirmed twice in the discussion of dreams in the Talmud,

The Babylonian Talmud, Maurice Simon (trans.), I. Epstein (ed.) (London: The Soncino Press, 1935–48), I, part 5 [*Seder Zera'im*]: "R. Joḥanan said: If one rises early and a Scriptural verse comes to his mouth, this is a kind of minor prophecy" (*Berakoth* 55b; compare *Berakoth* 57b).

9 See Förster, "Beiträge zur mittelalterlichen Volkskunde III," *Archiv für das Studium der neueren Sprachen und Literaturen* 121 (1908), 32–33.

10 See the texts in Emanuel Svenberg, *De Latinska Lunaria: Text och Studier* (Göteborg: Elanders, 1936), pp. 24–83, 96–99, and 100–02; Förster, "Vom Fortleben antiker Sammellunare im Englischen und in anderen Volkssprachen," *Anglia* 67–68 (1944), 1–171, esp. pp. 16–19, 79–129, 136, 137–43, 148–58, and 160–63; Svenberg, *Lunaria et Zodiologia Latina* (Göteborg: Elanders, 1963), pp. 41, 42–43, and 60–71; and the facsimiles in Maurice Hélin, *La Clef des songes: Fac-similés, notes et liste des éditions incunables* (Paris, 1925; rpt. Geneva: Slatkine Reprints, 1977), pp. 9–12, 41, and 43–45. For the distinction between *lunaria specialia* and *lunaria collectiva*, see Svenberg, *Lunaria et Zodiologia*, p. 5. As Erik Wistrand, "Lunariastudien," *Göteborgs Högskolas Arsskrift* 48, no. 4 (1942), 1–41, suggests, collective lunars probably arose "through the compilation of specialized lunars" [durch Kompilation von Speciallunaria] (p. 17).

11 See Förster, "Beiträge III"; Förster, "Die altenglischen Traumlunare"; and Lawrence T. Martin, *Somniale Danielis: An Edition of a Medieval Latin Dream Interpretation Handbook* (Frankfurt: Peter Lang, 1981), pp. 13–60.

12 See Förster, "Die altenglischen Traumlunare," pp. 92–93; Förster, "Das älteste kymrische Traumbuch (um 1350)," *Zeitschrift für celtische Philologie* 13 (1921), 86–92; and Förster, "Beiträge IV," p. 40n.

13 Martin, *Somniale Danielis*, pp. 97, 114, and 119.

14 Quoted from Svenberg, *De Latinska Lunaria*, pp. 24–28. See also other of the *lunaria collectiva*, in Svenberg, *De Latinska Lunaria* and *Lunaria et Zodiologia*, and in Förster, "Vom Fortleben."

15 Förster, "Mittelalterliche Orakelalphabete," p. 205; Anton E. Schönbach, "Bedeutung der Buchstaben," *Zeitschrift für deutsches Alterthum* 34 (1890), 1; Schönbach, "Zu Zs. 17, 84," *Zeitschrift für deutsches Alterthum* 18 (1875), 81; and Suchier, "Altfranzösische Traumbücher," p. 162.

16 Schönbach, "Bedeutung der Buchstaben," p. 2.

17 Martin, *Somniale Danielis*, pp. 95–96. There are also Hebrew dreambooks that associate themselves with both Joseph and Daniel; see Franco Michelini Tocci, "Teoria e interpretazione dei sogni nella cultura ebraica medievale," in Gregory (ed.), *I sogni nel medioevo*, pp. 279–86.

18 The dreamlunar also sometimes affiliated itself with Daniel. See the *explicit* of the Latin collective lunar with Old English gloss printed by Förster, "Vom Fortleben," p. 129: "Finiunt somnia Danielis prophete" (glossed as "endiað swefnu witiȝan"). And see the introduction to the Middle English prose lunar also presented by Förster, "Vom Fortleben," p. 138: "Here foloyth a prophitable 7 a commodius treatise, compendiusly schowyng þe interpretacion or deposicions of the dremys of Danyell þe prophete by the reuelacion of þe angyl of God 7 fyrst of þe dayes of þe mone 7 of þe condicions 7 propertyes." Elsewhere, the dreamlunar is so closely affiliated in the manuscripts with the dreambook proper that the two works are designated by a common (authenticating) title – "Somniale Danielis." See, for instance, Alf Önnerfors, *Mediaevalia: Abhandlungen und Aufsätze* (Frankfurt: Peter Lang, 1977), p. 40; Hélin, *La Clef des songes*, pp. 9–13; Martin, *Somniale Danielis*, pp. 28, 30, and 46; and Lynn Thorndike and Pearl

Kibre, *A Catalogue of Incipits of Mediaeval Scientific Writings in Latin* (Cambridge, Mass.: Mediaeval Academy of America, 1963), cols. 837–38.

19 For lists of manuscripts and printed editions of the dream alphabet, see *ibid.*, cols. 4–5; Thorndike, *History*, II, pp. 294–95; Förster, "Beiträge IV," p. 40; Hélin, *La Clef des songes*, p. 47; and Martin, *Somniale Danielis*, pp. 34, 36, 56, and 58. For lists of the languages into which the dream alphabet was translated, see Förster, "Mittelalterliche Orakelalphabete," p. 204; and Suchier, "Altfranzösische Traumbücher," p. 161. See Sievers, "Bedeutung der Buchstaben" (1875), and Schönbach, "Bedeutung der Buchstaben," for editions of the Latin dream alphabet. Wolfram Schmitt, "Ein deutsches Traumbüchlein aus dem späten Mittelalter," *Studia Neophilologica* 37 (1965), 98–99; Steinmeyer, "Bedeutung der Buchstaben," *Zeitschrift für deutsches Alterthum* 17 (1874), 84; and Schönbach, "Bedeutung der Buchstaben" and "Zu Zs. 17, 84," print German versions. Schönbach, "Bedeutung der Buchstaben," compares two Latin and three German texts. In addition, Sievers, "Bedeutung der Buchstaben," *Zeitschrift für deutsches Alterthum* 21 (1877), 189–90, edits an Old English version, and Jules Camus, "Notices et extraits des manuscrits français de Modène," *Revue des Langues Romanes* 35 (1891), 205–06, and "Un Manuscrit namurois du XVe siècle," *Revue des Langues Romanes* 38 (1895), 36, and Suchier, "Altfranzösische Traumbücher," p. 162, present French texts.

20 Thorndike and Kibre, *Catalogue of Incipits*, col. 838; Thorndike, *History*, II, pp. 294–95; and Förster, "Die altenglischen Traumlunare," pp. 62–63.

21 *Ibid.*

22 For Latin editions, see Svenburg, *De Latinska Lunaria* and *Lunaria et Zodiologia*; Kr. Kålund (ed.), *Alfraeði Islensk: Islandsk Encyklopaedisk Litteratur*, I (Copenhagen: S.L. Møllers, 1908), pp. 84–89; and Richard Wünsch, "Volkskundliche aus alten Handschriften," *Hessische Blätter für Volkskunde* 2, no. 2 (1903), 89–90. And see the "Expositio sompniorum secundum omnes dies lunae" [exposition of dreams according to all the days of the moon] from Michael Scot's *Liber introductorius*, printed in Tullio Gregory, "I sogni e gli astri," in Gregory (ed.), *I sogni nel medioevo*, pp. 136–37, n. 69. Förster, "Die altenglischen Traumlunare," edits a Latin version of the specialized dreamlunar, along with the Old English translations, and in his "Vom Fortleben," he edits a Latin collective lunar with Old English gloss (pp. 79–129), two other Latin versions (pp. 16–19 and 160–63), a Middle English prose redaction (pp. 138–43), and parts of Middle English verse (p. 136), Middle High German prose (pp. 148–50), Netherlandish verse (p. 150), French verse and prose (pp. 151–54), Provençal prose (p. 155), and Middle Welsh prose (pp. 155–59) versions. (Förster gives references to more complete editions of those texts which he only partially presents.) Hélin, *La Clef des songes*, pp. 9–12, 41, and 43–45, prints facsimiles from five *lunaria* published, along with the *Somniale Danielis*, in the late fifteenth century. On even later dreamlunars – Modern English texts related to the medieval *lunaria collectiva* and Scandinavian versions in eighteenth-century manuscripts – see Förster, "Vom Fortleben," pp. 144–46 and 150–51.

23 Martin, *Somniale Danielis*, pp. 13–62.

24 André Paradis, "Les Oniromanciens et leurs traités des rêves," in Guy-H. Allard (ed.), *Aspects de la marginalité du Moyen Age* (Montreal: Les Editions de l'Aurore, 1975), p. 121.

25 Förster, "Das älteste kymrische Traumbuch," p. 60.

26 See Martin, *Somniale Danielis*, p. 1.

27 On the incunabula, see Hélin, *La Clef des songes*, pp. 91–99. Modern editions of the *Somniale Danielis* include: Thomas Wright and James Orchard Halliwell (eds.), *Reliquiae Antiquae: Scraps from Ancient Manuscripts*, I (London: William Pickering, 1841; rpt. New York: AMS Press, 1966), pp. 261–68 [Middle English verse]; Graffunder, "Daniels Traumdeutungen. Ein mittelalterliches Traumbuch in deutschen Versen," *Zeitschrift für deutsches Altertum und deutsche Litteratur* 48 (1907), 507–31 [German verse]; Förster, "Beiträge zur mittelalterlichen Volkskunde II," *Archiv für das Studium der neueren Sprachen und Literaturen* 120 (1908), 302–05 [Old English]; Förster, "Beiträge IV" [Latin and Old English]; Förster, "Beiträge zur mittelalterlichen Volkskunde V," *Archiv für das Studium der neueren Sprachen und Literaturen* 127 (1911), 31–84 [Middle English verse and prose; Latin]; Förster, "Beiträge zur mittelalterlichen Volkskunde IX," *Archiv für das Studium der neueren Sprachen und Literaturen* 134 (1916), 264–93 [Old English]; Förster, "Das älteste kymrische Traumbuch" [Middle Welsh]; Hélin, *La Clef des songes* [Latin, French, and German incunabula]; Suchier, "Altfranzösische Traumbücher" [French prose and verse]; Curt F. Bühler, "Two Middle English Texts of the *Somnia Danielis*," *Anglia* 80 (1962), 264–73 [Middle English]; B.S. Cron, *A Medieval Dreambook* (London: The Gogmagog Press, 1963) [Latin]; Josef Werlin, "Das Traumbuch des Armen Nikolaus von Prag," *Stifter-Jahrbuch* 8 (1964), 195–208 [German]; E.O.G. Turville-Petre, "An Icelandic Version of the *Somniale Danielis*," in Allan H. Orrick (ed.), *Nordica et Anglica: Studies in Honor of Stefán Einarsson* (The Hague and Paris: Mouton, 1968), pp. 19–36 [Old Norse]; Gerhart Hoffmeister, "Rasis' Traumlehre: Traumbücher des Spätmittelalters," *Archiv für Kulturgeschichte* 51 (1969), 137–59 [Latin]; Martin, "The Earliest Versions of the Latin *Somniale Danielis*," *Manuscripta* 23 (1979), 131–41 [Latin]; Martin, *Somniale Danielis*, pp. 95–212 [Latin]; Fischer, *The Complete Medieval Dreambook: A Multilingual, Alphabetical Somnia Danielis Collation* (Bern and Frankfurt: Peter Lang, 1982) [a collation of twenty-three Latin, French, English, and German versions]; and Jutta Grub, *Das lateinische Traumbuch im Codex Upsaliensis C664 (9. Jh.): Eine frühmittelalterliche Fassung der lateinischen Somniale Danielis-Tradition* (Frankfurt: Peter Lang, 1984) [Latin]. On the early-modern popularity of dreambooks, see Önnerfors, *Mediaevalia*, pp. 46–48, and Grub, *Das lateinische Traumbuch*, pp. xxviii–xxix.

28 Stephanus Baluzius (ed.), *Capitularia regum francorum*, I (Paris: Ex Typis Francisci-Augustini Quillan, 1780), reprinted in Joannes Dominicus Mansi (ed.), *Sacrorum conciliorum nova et amplissima collectio*, XVIIB (Paris: Hubert Welter, 1902; rpt. Graz, Austria: Akademische Druck-u. Verlagsanstalt, 1960), col. 518. I have emphasized the direct verbal echoes of Deuteronomy in the quotation, and in my translation have followed as far as possible the language of the Douay-Rheims version of Deuteronomy. Charles Henry Lea cites related legal material, *Materials Toward a History of Witchcraft*, Arthur C. Howland (ed.) (Philadelphia: University of Pennsylvania Press, 1939), I, pp. 138–39; and Giulio Guidorizzi notes late-antique legislation, both civil and ecclesiastical, against dream divination, "L'interpretazione dei sogni nel mondo tardoantico: oralità e scrittura," in Gregory (ed.), *I sogni nel medioevo*, p. 152. Guidorizzi argues that it was in Late Antiquity that divination became "illecito, sospetto, demoniaco" [illicit, suspect, demonical]: "la logica dell'indovino divenne qualcosa di particolare, di sconnesso, in contrapposizione non solo con la cultura, ma anche con la razionalità ufficiale" [the diviner's logic became something singular, disconnected, in opposition not only to the culture, but also to official rationality] (p. 158).

29 Baluzius, *Capitularia regum francorum*, col. 1143.

30 The *Decretum* was compiled in the mid-twelfth century (*c.* 1140) and formed, along with Pope Gregory IX's *Decretales* (1234), the *Sext* (1298), and the *Clementinae* (1317), the core of late-medieval canon law. As Leonard E. Boyle, "The Curriculum of the Faculty of Canon Law at Oxford in the First Half of the Fourteenth Century," *Oxford Studies Presented to Daniel Callus* (Oxford: Oxford Historical Society, 1964), pp. 135–62, suggests, although the position of the *Decretum* in the law curriculum at Oxford was becoming less central at the beginning of the fourteenth century, it continued to be taught there. The *Decretum*'s standing in continental schools of law was apparently even firmer than it was at Oxford. See also the article on canon law in the *New Catholic Encyclopedia* (New York: McGraw-Hill, 1967), III, pp. 41–45.

31 I cite Gratian's *Decretum* from Aemilius Friedberg's revision of Aemilius Ludovicus Richter's edition, *Corpus iuris canonici*, part 1 (Leipzig: Ex Officina Bernhardi Tauchnitz, 1879), giving references parenthetically in my text.

32 The "sortes sanctorum," like the dream alphabet, made prognostic use of the psalter and of randomly-determined letters or numbers. See Johannes Bolte, "Anhang. Zur Geschichte der Losbücher," *Georg Wickrams Werke*, IV (Tübingen: Gedruckt für den litterarischen Verein in Stuttgart, 1903), p. 319; and Förster, "Mittelalterliche Orakelalphabete," p. 205.

33 This law is reaffirmed frequently in later medieval legal collections: see Gregory IX's *Decretales*, in Richter and Friedberg (eds.), *Corpus iuris canonici*, part 2, book 5, section [*titulus*] 21, chapter 1; the Council of Trent, in Edmond Martène and Ursin Durand (eds.), *Thesaurus novus anecdotorum* (Paris: Lutetiae Parisiorum, 1717; rpt. New York: Burt Franklin, 1968), IV, p. 257; and the synod of Nantes, *Thesaurus novus anecdotorum*, IV, p. 947.

34 The Latin text shifts from the plural ("inquirunt," "adtendunt," "sciant") to the singular ("paganum," "apostatam," "abeuntem," "inimicum," "emendatus," "reconcilietur"). In my translation, I maintain the plural throughout for the sake of fluency.

35 Interestingly, Martin describes one manuscript of the *Somniale* where references to Daniel's authorship seem to have been censored: "the . . . prologue begins *Incipit sompniale prophete*, with an erasure following *sompniale*, probably striking out an abbreviation for *Danielis*. The explicit is *Explicit sompniale prophete*, again with a space or an erasure after *sompniale*. All of this strongly suggests that the attribution was deliberately expunged by the scribe, perhaps because of criticism of this attribution, like that of John of Salisbury" (*Somniale Danielis*, p. 17). For John of Salisbury's criticism, see *Policratici sive de nugis curialium et vestigii philosophorum libri viii*, Clemens C.I. Webb (ed.) (Oxford: Clarendon Press, 1909), book 2, chapter 17, and Joseph B. Pike's translation, *Frivolities of Courtiers and Footprints of Philosophers* (Minneapolis: The University of Minnesota Press; and London: Oxford University Press, 1938), p. 84: "The dream interpreter which is inscribed with the name of Daniel [*coniectorium, qui nomine Danielis inscribitur*] is apparently lacking in the weight which truth carries, when it allows but one meaning to one thing. This matter really needs no further consideration since the whole tradition of the activity is foolish and the circulating manual of dream interpretation [*uagus coniectorum liber*] passes brazenly from hand to hand of the curious."

36 See Richard Scholz, *Unbekannte kirchenpolitische Streitschriften aus der Zeit Ludwigs des Bayern (1327–1354)*, 2 vols. (Rom: Verlag von Loescher, 1911, 1914), I, pp. 191–97, for a discussion of Agostino's work, and II, pp. 481–90, for excerpts from the text. In chapter 20, Agostino concludes that, though "divinatio facta per sompnia . . .

provenire potest" [the divination made by means of dreams . . . can come about], "ipsorum interpretatio est humana superstitio et ut in pluribus dyabolica illusio" [their interpretation is a human superstition and, as in many cases, a diabolic illusion] (p. 483). At the conclusion of his work, Agostino similarly recognizes both the possibility of reliable divination and the illicit nature of its use: "Quamvis igitur superius fecerimus mentionem de multis modis divinandi, quorum aliquos diximus veritatem posse habere, nulli tamen christiano licet per divinationem aliquam veritatem exquirere" [Although we have thus made mention above of many modes of divining, some of which we said can possess truth, nevertheless it is not permitted to any Christian to seek out any truth through divination] (p. 490).

37 Nicole Oresme, "Nicole Oresme: Quaestio contra divinatores horoscopios," S. Caroti (ed.), *AHDLMA* 43 (1976), 201–310, p. 221; but see also pp. 216–17, where Oresme recognizes the possibility of using Aristotle to support an opposing argument.

38 Schmitt, "Ein deutsches Traumbüchlein," p. 97. For a similar marginal notation in a dreambook manuscript, see Önnerfors, *Mediaevalia*, p. 40: "am Rande hat eine spätere Hand, vermutlich die eines kleingläubigen Humanisten, hinzugefügt: *N.B. Sunt superstitiosa deliramenta*" [in the margin, a later hand, probably that of a skeptical humanist, has added: *N.B. These are superstitious absurdities*].

39 See especially the first few chapters – "The Cult of Relics," "The Saints and their Relics," and "The Pursuit of the Miraculous" – in Jonathan Sumption, *Pilgrimage: An Image of Mediaeval Religion* (London: Faber and Faber, 1975).

40 See Carlo Ginzburg, *The Cheese and the Worms: The Cosmos of a Sixteenth-Century Miller*, John and Anne C. Tedeschi (trans.) (Baltimore: Johns Hopkins University Press, 1980), and *The Night Battles: Witchcraft and Agrarian Cults in the Sixteenth and Seventeenth Centuries*, John and Anne C. Tedeschi (trans.) (Baltimore: Johns Hopkins University Press, 1983).

41 Also note Gurevich's more general claim that "Only in a certain symbiosis with learned tradition could medieval popular tradition exist" (*Medieval Popular Culture*, p. 38).

42 See, Förster, "Die altenglischen Traumlunare," pp. 58–62; "Das älteste kymrische Traumbuch," pp. 56–61; and "Die Kleinliteratur des Aberglaubens im Altenglischen," *Archiv für das Studium der neueren Sprachen und Literaturen* 110 (1903), 358. Önnerfors would revise Förster's version of the dreambook's history, but he too accepts the notion of a Greek original; see *Mediaevalia*, p. 35. E. de Stoop, "Onirocriticon du prophète Daniel dedié au roi Nabuchodonosor," *Revue de Philologie de Littérature et d'Histoire Anciennes* 33 (1909), 93–111, edits a late, and corrupt, Greek text of the *Somniale Danielis*. For an ancient Assyrian dreambook that resembles in certain ways the *Somniale Danielis*, and that may bear some genetic relation to European dreambooks, see A. Leo Oppenheim, *The Interpretation of Dreams in the Ancient Near East, With a Translation of an Assyrian Dream-Book*, Transactions of the American Philosophical Society NS, 46, part 3 (1956), 256–307.

43 See Martin's brief discussions of changes in the content of the *Somniale Danielis* over the centuries: "Earliest Versions," pp. 137–38, and *Somniale Danielis*, pp. 10–12.

44 For interesting comments on the dreambooks' audience, see Paradis, "Les Oniroman-ciens," pp. 125–26. Paradis finally suggests that "l'interprétation des rêves n'est tout au plus qu'un jeu plus ou moins gratuit de société, qu'une occasion de distractions amusantes" [the interpretation of dreams is at most nothing but a more or less gratuitous game of society, nothing but an occasion for amusing distractions] (p. 126). Such a view does not, I believe, adequately account for the sometimes impassioned

objections to dreambooks and their use. But see Paradis's suggestion that "L'opposition aux *clefs du songe* n'est somme toute qu'une opposition de forme, qu'une opposition de principe" [the opposition to the dreambooks is finally nothing but an opposition of form, an opposition of principle] (p. 126).

45 See Hoffmeister, "Rasis' Traumlehre," pp. 144–46 and 152–59.

46 See Graffunder, "Daniels Traumdeutungen," pp. 516–17.

47 See Martin, *Somniale Danielis*, pp. 41–42 and 50–51.

48 See *ibid.*, pp. 17–18 and 37–38.

49 *Ibid.*, p. 36.

50 See the *Summa de creaturis*, in Albertus Magnus, *Opera omnia*, XXXV, August Borgnet (ed.) (Paris: Apud Ludovicum Vivès, 1896), *quaestio* 50, p. 440. In addition to this citation of the "dreambook proper," we find references to the lunar interpretation of dreams in Albert's commentary on Aristotle's *De divinatione per somnum*, in Borgnet (ed.), *Opera omnia*, IX, p. 179, and in the *Summa de creaturis*, p. 436. The last reference is reproduced by Vincent of Beauvais, *Speculum naturale* (Douai: Ex Officina Typographica et Sumptibus Balthazaris Belleri in Circino Aureo, 1624; rpt. Graz, Austria: Akademische Druck-u. Verlagsanstalt, 1964), book 26, chapter 55, col. 1873.

51 Guibert de Nogent, *Self and Society in Medieval France: The Memoirs of Abbot Guibert of Nogent (1064?–c. 1125)*, John F. Benton (ed.), C.C. Swinton Bland (trans.) [revised by Benton] (New York: Harper and Row, 1970), p. 101. Early critics tended to emphasize Guibert's "rationalism"; more recently others have taken pains to point out the sometimes superstitious bases of his skeptical attitudes. See especially Benton's introduction to Guibert's memoirs, pp. 8 and 28–30.

52 For instance, see Margery Kempe, *The Book of Margery Kempe*, Sanford Brown Meech and Hope Emily Allen (eds.), EETS, OS 212 (London: Oxford University Press, 1940), book 1, chapter 16, where Kempe confers with the Archbishop of Canterbury:

> Sche schewyd þis worshepful lord hir maner of leuyng & swech grace as God wrowt in hyr mende & in hir sowle to wetyn what he wold say þerto, ȝyf he fond any defawte eyþyr in hyre contemplacyon er in hir wepyng. & sche teld hym also þe cawse of hyr wepyng and þe maner of daly[awns] þat owyr Lord dalyid to hyr sowle. And he fond no defawt þerin but a-prevyd hir maner of leuyng & was rygth glad þat owyr mercyful Lord Cryst Ihesu schewyd swech grace in owyr days, blyssed mot he be. (pp. 36–37)

53 See, for instance, *ibid.*, book 1, chapter 33:

> & sithyn sche schewyd hym þe secret thyngys of reuelacyonys & of hey contemplacyons, & how sche had swech mend in hys Passyon & so gret compassyon whan God wolde ȝeue it þat sche fel down þerwyth & myth not beryn it. þan sche wept bittyrly, sche sobbyd boistowsly & cryed ful lowde & horybly þat þe pepel was oftyn-tymes aferd & gretly astoyned, demyng sche had ben vexyd wyth sum euyl spiryt er a sodeyn sekenes, not leuyng it was þe werk of God but raþar sum euyl spiryt, er a sodeyn sekenes, er ellys symulacyon & ypocrisy falsly feyned of hir owyn self. (p. 83)

54 See John of Salisbury, *Policraticus*, book 2, chapters 14–17.

55 Francis X. Newman, "Somnium: Medieval Theories of Dreaming and the Form of Vision Poetry," dissertation, Princeton University, 1963, pp. 135–42. See also the comments of Kathryn L. Lynch, *The High Medieval Dream Vision: Poetry, Philosophy, and Literary Form* (Stanford: Stanford University Press, 1988), pp. 75–76.

56 Simone Collin-Roset, "Le *Liber thesauri occulti* de Pascalis Romanus (un traité d'interprétation des songes du XIIe siècle)," *AHDLMA* 30 (1963), 111–98; the citation is from book 1, chapter 1, p. 145.

57 Förster, "Beiträge V," p. 46.

58 Giraldus Cambrensis, *Expugnatio Hibernica: The Conquest of Ireland*, A.B. Scott and F.X. Martin (eds. and trans.) (Dublin: Royal Irish Academy, 1978), book 1, chapter 42, pp. 118–19; see also Giraldus's *Itinerary Through Wales*, Richard Colt Hoare (trans.), W. Llewelyn Williams (ed.) (London: J.M. Dent; and New York: E.P. Dutton, 1908), book 2, chapter 2, pp. 102–03.

2 THE DOUBLENESS AND MIDDLENESS OF DREAMS

1 Lucian, "The Dream, or Lucian's Career," A.M. Harmon (ed. and trans.), Loeb Classical Library: Lucian, 3 (London: William Heinemann; and New York: G.P. Putnam's Sons, 1921), p. 219. Subsequent references to this translation will be given parenthetically in my text.

2 The association of seasonal change with variations in the frequency and reliability of dreams is a commonplace of classical and medieval dream theory. See Newman's discussion in "Somnium," pp. 271–72 and 279–81, and, for particular instances, see Pliny the Elder, *Natural History*, Harris Rackham, W.H.S. Jones, and D.E. Eichholz (eds. and trans.), Loeb Classical Library (Cambridge, Mass.: Harvard University Press; and London: William Heinemann, 1947–63), VIII, book 28, chapter 14, section 54, pp. 39–41; Tertullian, *On the Soul [De anima]*, in Edwin A. Quain (trans.), *Apologetical Works*, The Fathers of the Church: A New Translation, 10 (Washington, D.C.: The Catholic University of America Press, 1950), chapter 48, section 1, p. 286; and John of Salisbury, *Policraticus*, book 2, chapter 15, Pike (trans.), p. 78. The Icelandic *Gísla saga*, far removed in time and place from Lucian, suggests that "dreams come on again, as soon as the nights grow long" (*The Saga of Gisli*, George Johnston [trans.] [Toronto: University of Toronto Press, 1963], p. 36).

3 Artemidorus, *The Interpretation of Dreams: The Oneirocritica of Artemidorus*, Robert White (trans.) (Park Ridge, N.J.: Noyes Press, 1975), p. 21. On Artemidorus's place in the dream discourse of Late Antiquity, see Guidorizzi, "L'interpretazione dei sogni." And for interesting discussion of Artemidorus's treatment of erotic dreams, see Michel Foucault, *The Care of the Self: The History of Sexuality*, III, Robert Hurley (trans.) (New York: Vintage Books, Random House, 1986), pp. 3–36; and John J. Winkler, *The Constraints of Desire: The Anthropology of Sex and Gender in Ancient Greece* (New York and London: Routledge, 1990), pp. 23–44.

4 See Plato, *Timaeus*, R.G. Bury (ed. and trans.), Loeb Classical Library: Plato, 7 (London: William Heinemann; and Cambridge, Mass.: Harvard University Press, 1952), esp. 45–46 and 71–72, and *The Republic*, 2 vols., Paul Shorey (ed. and trans.), Loeb Classical Library (Cambridge, Mass.: Harvard University Press; and London: William Heinemann, 1946, 1956), esp. 571–72; Aristotle, *De somno et vigilia, De somniis [De insomniis]*, and *De divinatione per somnum*, included together in the *Parva naturalia*, in W.D. Ross (ed.), J.I. Beare and G.R.T. Ross (trans.), *Works*, III (Oxford: Clarendon Press, 1931); Cicero, *De divinatione*, in William Armstead Falconer (ed. and trans.), *De senectute, De amicitia, De divinatione*, Loeb Classical Library (London: William Heinemann; and New York: G.P. Putnam's Sons, 1923), esp. book 1, chapters 20–30 for the case in favor of oneiric divination, and book 2, chapters 58–72 for the case

against; and Lucretius, *De rerum natura, Of the Nature of Things*, William Ellery Leonard (trans.) (New York: E.P. Dutton, 1957), book 4, lines 720–819 and 909–1049. For overviews of classical treatments of dreaming and for further bibliography, see E.R. Dodds, *The Greeks and the Irrational* (Berkeley: University of California Press, 1951), pp. 102–34; Newman, "Somnium," pp. 1–58; C.A. Behr, *Aelius Aristides and the Sacred Tales* (Amsterdam: Adolf M. Hakkert, 1968), pp. 171–95; and A.H.M. Kessels, "Ancient Systems of Dream-Classification," *Mnemosyne* series 4, 22 (1969), 389–424.

5 Plato, *Timaeus* 71E–72C, Bury (ed. and trans.). Shorey asserts, in his edition of the *Republic* (II, p. 337n.), that Plato's comments on divination in the *Timaeus* are ironic. But for an opposed view, see Behr, *Aelius Aristides*, p. 173, and see Dodds's brief discussion, *The Greeks and the Irrational*, p. 120.

6 Plato, *Republic* 571C, Shorey (ed. and trans.).

7 I cite Beare's translation of Aristotle, *Parva naturalia*.

8 Synesius of Cyrene, *De insomniis*, in Augustine Fitzgerald (trans.), *The Essays and Hymns of Synesius of Cyrene* (London: Oxford University Press, 1930), II, pp. 326–59; the passage cited is on p. 347. For the original Greek text, see Synesius of Cyrene, *De insomniis, PG* 66, cols. 1281–320. According to Newman, "Somnium," Synesius's treatise on dreams is "the most extended treatment of the subject by a Christian of the patristic period, but a work virtually unknown to later centuries" (p. 115). Despite Synesius's lack of influence, it is clear that extreme assertions of the value of dream experience, similar to his, were sometimes made by others. See my discussion of Calcidius. For further information on Synesius's *De insomniis* and his peculiar brand of Neoplatonism, see Newman, "Somnium," pp. 115–18; Jay Bregman, *Synesius of Cyrene: Philosopher–Bishop* (Berkeley: University of California Press, 1982), pp. 145–54; Christian Lacombrade, *Synésios de Cyrène: Hellène et Chrétien* (Paris: Société d'Edition "Les Belles Lettres," 1951), pp. 150–69; and Guidorizzi, "L'interpretazione dei sogni," pp. 153–55. On the complex and obscure history of the "gates of dreams," see Ernest Leslie Highbarger, *The Gates of Dreams: An Archaeological Examination of Vergil, Aeneid VI, 893–899* (Baltimore: The Johns Hopkins Press, 1940). References to the gates became commonplace in the Middle Ages; see, for example, the casual mention in Hermann of Carinthia, *De essentiis: A Critical Edition with Translation and Commentary*, Charles Burnett (ed.) (Leiden and Cologne: E.J. Brill, 1982), pp. 178–79.

9 See Synesius, *De insomniis*, Fitzgerald (trans.), II, pp. 341–42 and 349–50.

10 *Ibid.*, p. 332.

11 I quote from Thomas Taylor's 1821 translation, reprinted as *Iamblichus on the Mysteries of the Egyptians, Chaldeans, and Assyrians*, third edition (London: Stuart and Watkins, 1968). See Newman's discussion of Iamblichus, "Somnium," pp. 66–67.

12 Iamblichus, *On the Mysteries*, p. 115.

13 *Ibid.*

14 *Ibid.*

15 *Ibid.*, p. 119.

16 For the Latin text of Macrobius, see Iacobus Willis (ed.), *Commentarii in Somnium Scipionis* (Leipzig: B.G. Teubner, 1963). I will quote from William Harris Stahl (trans.), *Commentary on the Dream of Scipio* (New York: Columbia University Press, 1952), citing book, chapter, and section numbers parenthetically in my text. I have used two Latin editions of Calcidius's *Commentary*: Ioh. Wrobel (ed.), *Platonis Timaeus interprete Chalcidio cum eiusdem commentario* (Leipzig: B.G. Teubner, 1876); and J.H. Waszink (ed.), *Timaeus a Calcidio translatus commentarioque instructus* (London: Warburg Institute;

and Leiden: E.J. Brill, 1962). I follow Waszink, except where noted, citing chapter numbers from his edition parenthetically in my text. No full English translation of Calcidius's *Commentary* exists, though portions have been translated in J. den Boeft, *Calcidius on Demons (Commentarius ch. 127–136)* (Leiden: E.J. Brill, 1977); den Boeft, *Calcidius on Fate, His Doctrine and Sources* (Leiden: E.J. Brill, 1970); and J.C.M. van Winden, *Calcidius on Matter, His Doctrine and Sources: A Chapter in the History of Platonism* (Leiden: E.J. Brill, 1959). Where possible, I cite these translations; otherwise, I have translated the Latin myself. A useful epitome of Calcidius's discussion of dreams is given by Waszink, "Die sogenannte Fünfteilung der Träume bei Chalcidius und ihre Quellen," *Mnemosyne* third series, 9 (1940), 65–85.

17 Newman, "Somnium," p. 66. Later, Newman modifies his position, suggesting that "these classifications were more than mere devices of reconciliation; they also permitted their makers to stress what they clearly felt to be the true significance of dreams" (p. 77).

18 For an overview of source studies on Macrobius, see Stahl's introduction to his translation of the *Commentary*, pp. 23–39 and 87–88. For more detailed discussion of the sources of Macrobius's treatment of dreams, see Phil. M. Schedler, "Die Philosophie des Macrobius und ihr Einfluss auf die Wissenschaft des christlichen Mittelalters," *Beiträge zur Geschichte der Philosophie des Mittelalters* 13, no. 1 (1916), 1–159, esp. 83–85; Karl Mras, "Macrobius' Kommentar zu Ciceros Somnium. Ein Beitrag zur Geistesgeschichte des 5. Jahrhunderts n. Chr.," *Sitzungsberichte der preussischen Akademie der Wissenschaften: Philosophisch-historische Klasse* (1933), 232–86, esp. 237–38; Claes Blum, *Studies in the Dream-Book of Artemidorus: Inaugural Dissertation* (Uppsala: Almquist and Wiksells, 1936), pp. 52–71; Pierre Courcelle, *Late Latin Writers and Their Greek Sources*, Harry E. Wedeck (trans.) (Cambridge, Mass.: Harvard University Press, 1969 [1948]), pp. 35–36; Kessels, "Ancient Systems," pp. 395–414; Jacques Flamant, *Macrobe et le Néo-Platonisme latin, à la fin du IVe siècle* (Leiden: E.J. Brill, 1977), pp. 161–64; and P.W. van der Horst, "Macrobius and the New Testament: A Contribution to the Corpus Hellenisticum," *Novum Testamentum* 15 (1973), 220–32, esp. 221–22. Blum and Kessels also discuss the sources of Calcidius's dream theory. Waszink, "Die sogenannte Fünfteilung," treats mainly Calcidius, but includes a comparison to Macrobius. For further speculation on Macrobius's sources, see B.W. Switalski, "Des Chalcidius Kommentar zu Plato's Timaeus: Eine historisch–kritische Untersuchung," *Beiträge zur Geschichte der Philosophie des Mittelalters* 3, no. 6 (1902), 1–113, esp. 36–37, 44–45, and 50–51; and den Boeft, *Calcidius on Demons*, p. 52.

19 See Blum, *Studies*, p. 56; Kessels, "Ancient Systems," pp. 413–14; and Flamant, *Macrobe*, pp. 161–62.

20 Dreams, like Macrobius's *insomnium*, that arise from our daily activities were recognized by many classical (and medieval) authors. See Martine Dulaey's discussion in *Le Rêve dans la vie et la pensée de Saint Augustin* (Paris: Etudes Augustiniennes, 1973), pp. 98–102. As Dulaey suggests, the idea that dreams arise from reminiscences of daily life "est devenue le lieu commun le plus répandu de la psychologie antique du rêve" [became the most widespread commonplace of ancient dream psychology] (p. 98).

21 Interestingly, in certain traditions, dreams like the *visum*, experienced in a state between sleep and waking, seem to have had a special divine status. See Iamblichus, *On the Mysteries*: "But the dreams which are denominated *theopemptoi* or *sent from God* . . . take place either when sleep is leaving us, and we are beginning to awake, and then we hear a certain voice which concisely tells us what is to be done; or voices are heard by us,

between sleep and waking, or when we are perfectly awake" (p. 115). See also Dodds, *The Greeks and the Irrational*, pp. 113 and 128, n. 62.

22 John of Salisbury, *Policraticus*, book 2, chapter 15, Pike (trans.), p. 81.

23 Calcidius here somewhat oversimplifies Aristotle's dream theory, but he does capture the Aristotelian insistence on naturally-explicable dreams.

24 On Calcidius's dubious ascription of one particular view of dreams to Heraclitus, see H. Diels (ed.), *Die Fragmente der Vorsokratiker*, second edition (Berlin: Weidmannsche Buchhandlung, 1906), I, p. 61; and M. Marcovich (ed.), *Heraclitus: Greek Text with a Short Commentary* (Merida, Venezuela: The Los Andes University Press, 1967), pp. 580–83. Diels suggests that the passage cited by Calcidius actually comes from Posidonius's (lost) commentary on the *Timaeus* (p. 61); Marcovich concurs (p. 582).

25 Most scholars consider that this passage refers to a *third* authoritative position on dreams, whereas I suggest that it represents a further comment on the Heraclitean–Stoic point of view discussed in chapter 251. For the more common view, see Switalski, "Des Chalcidius Kommentar," pp. 50–51; and Waszink, "Die sogenannte Fünfteilung," p. 66. Chapter 252 is made difficult not only by the indefiniteness of "hi" and "qui," but also by disagreements among the manuscripts and editors; see the textual notes in Wrobel (ed.), *Platonis Timaeus*, p. 284, and Waszink (ed.), *Timaeus*, p. 261. I here follow Waszink in reading "parte" (rather than Wrobel's "partes"); otherwise, I adopt Wrobel's reading. Waszink reads, "Hi quoque parte abutentes sententiae pro solida perfectaque scientia," at the end of chapter 251, and begins chapter 252 with a new sentence, "Sunt qui . . ." The use of the subjunctive "putent," though, makes more sense if the clause beginning "hi quoque" is correlated to the following "qui" clause [They also are wrongly using . . . (they) who would consider that . . .]. If, however, we follow Waszink and take "Sunt qui . . ." as the main clause of an independent sentence, the subjunctive is slightly puzzling; the indicative, "Sunt qui . . . putant" – "there are those who consider" – would serve at least as well as the subjunctive, "Sunt qui . . . putent" – "there are those who would consider." If, indeed, paragraph 252 is meant to present a third authoritative view of dreams, we would expect it to be in the indicative (as a point of view objectively existing), as are the views of Aristotle and Heraclitus in paragraphs 250 and 251. In any case, the mixing of human *intellectus* with divine *intellegentia*, described in paragraph 252, closely resembles Heraclitus's claim of a connection between human and divine *ratio*. If the later discussion is meant to bring a third philosophical position into play, that position is nonetheless close to Heraclitus – asserting at least as radical a merging of the divine and the human realms.

26 Calcidius treats such dreams in chapters 249 and 253. In the former, he comments on *Timaeus* 45E–46A; in the latter, he quotes the more expansive discussion of dreams from *Republic* IX, suggesting that here Plato means to expound more fully the Timaean doctrine: "Quippe in his perfecte docuit, quod perfunctorie posuit in Timaeo" [Indeed, in these (passages from *Republic* IX) he taught perfectly that which he put forward perfunctorily in the *Timaeus*] (253).

27 Here Calcidius translates from Plato, *Republic* 571C–D.

28 Here Calcidius translates from *ibid.*, 571D–572B.

29 In chapter 254, Calcidius translates passages from Plato's *Crito* (44A–B) and *Phaedo* (60E–61B), and from the *Epinomis* ("Is liber qui Philosophus inscribitur" [The book that is entitled "The Philosopher"]), a work often falsely attributed to Plato. For the *Crito* and *Phaedo*, see Harold North Fowler (ed. and trans.), Loeb Classical Library:

Plato, 1 (London: William Heinemann; and Cambridge, Mass.: Harvard University Press, 1947); for the *Epinomis*, see W.R.M. Lamb (ed. and trans.), Loeb Classical Library: Plato, 8 (London: William Heinemann; and New York: G.P. Putnam's Sons, 1927), pp. 423–87. On Calcidius's use of the *Epinomis*, see den Boeft, *Calcidius on Demons*, p. 52.

30 Calcidius's citation here is incorrect. The passage quoted (on Socrates's *daimon*) comes not from the *Euthydemus*, but from the *Theages* (128D), a work almost certainly not by Plato; see Lamb (ed. and trans.), Loeb Classical Library: Plato, 8, pp. 341–83.

31 On Calcidius's treatment of this *vox*, see Waszink, "La Théorie du langage des dieux et des démons dans Calcidius," in Jacques Fontaine and Charles Kannengiesser (eds.), *Epektasis: Mélanges patristiques offerts au Cardinal Jean Daniélou* (Paris: Beauchesne, 1972), pp. 237–44.

32 Certainly, later writers often consider the waking vision to be a "higher" kind of revelation than the dream. Most strikingly, see Albertus Magnus's thirteen grades of visionary experience in *De somno et vigilia*, Borgnet (ed.), *Opera omnia*, IX, pp. 191–93 (discussed in chapter 5 below); and see William of Aragon's similar system of classification, in Roger A. Pack, "De pronosticatione sompniorum libellus Guillelmo de Aragonia adscriptus," *AHDLMA* 33 (1966), 237–92.

33 See chapters 127–36 for Calcidius's most complete discussion of the role "diuinae potestates" or "daemones" play in mediating between the transcendent and the mundane. This portion of Calcidius's *Commentary* is translated by den Boeft in *Calcidius on Demons*.

34 Most considerations of Calcidius's dream thought center on this last section of his discussion, and especially on his fivefold classification of dreams as *somnium, uisum, admonitio, spectaculum*, and *reuelatio*. Attempts to define a one-to-one correspondence between this fivefold scheme and that of Macrobius have been especially common. See Blum, *Studies*, p. 58; Mras, "Macrobius' Kommentar," p. 237; Switalski, "Des Chalcidius Kommentar," p. 45; and Behr, *Aelius Aristides*, pp. 176–77. Waszink, "Die sogenannte Fünfteilung," pp. 72–73, and Kessels, "Ancient Systems," pp. 401–06, however, suggest that detailed correspondences between the two systems of dream classification do not exist. I agree; still, the *general* similarity of structure between the two schemes is striking.

35 Waszink, "Die sogenannte Fünfteilung," pp. 74–76, considers and rejects the possibility that the phrase "Hebraica philosophia" refers to biblical dream lore; he proposes instead that Calcidius here refers to Philo Judaeus's work on dreams. See also Blum, *Studies*, p. 59, and Kessels, "Ancient Systems," p. 401.

36 See Waszink's slightly different reading of Calcidius's scheme, "Die sogenannte Fünfteilung," p. 68:

> Es werden also drei Traumarten angenommen: solche, die aus einer Einwirkung auf die Seele von aussen her stammen, solche, die von dem *logikon* herrühren, das entweder ungestört oder den *pathe* unterworfen ist, und zuletzt solche, die durch die *divinae potestates* der Seele zur Belehrung oder Bestrafung vorgeführt werden.

> Thus, three species of dreams are admitted: those that arise from an influence on the soul from without; those that originate in the *logikon* (reason), which is either undisturbed or subject to *pathe* (passion); and finally those that through *divinae potestates* (divine powers) are brought before the soul for its instruction or punishment.

37 *Ibid.*, p. 83.

38 Waszink concludes that the *spectaculum* was probably, in Calcidius's sources, a dream emanating directly from God, but that, following Porphyry's lead, Calcidius interposed between God and the dreamer the intermediate "coelestes potestates" so central to Neoplatonism ("Die sogenannte Fünfteilung," pp. 82–83). Waszink further suggests that Calcidius's failure to name the source of the *reuelatio* comes from his reluctance to assert an immediately divine dream (p. 83). This would, of course, be consistent with Calcidius's earlier objections to dream theories that claim too direct a link between the human and the divine (chapters 251–52).

39 See A.O. Lovejoy, *The Great Chain of Being: A Study of the History of an Idea* (Cambridge, Mass.: Harvard University Press, 1964 [1936]), esp. pp. 24–66.

40 Stahl's translation here incorrectly reads "Mind." The original reads: "cum ex summo deo mens, ex mente anima fit, *anima* vero et condat et vita compleat omnia quae sequuntur."

41 Lovejoy comments that this passage "was probably one of the chief vehicles through which" the complex of ideas involved in the Chain of Being "was transmitted to medieval writers" (*Great Chain of Being*, p. 63). On Macrobius's expression of the Neoplatonic doctrine of "emanation," see Flamant, *Macrobe*, pp. 494–529.

42 The translation of this passage is den Boeft's, *Calcidius on Demons*, p. 131.

43 See Plato, *Timaeus* 41D, 42E–43A, 44D, 69C–D, 73B–E, 88C–89A, and 90C–D. Macrobius says: "physici mundum magnum hominem et hominem brevem mundum esse dixerunt" [Philosophers called the universe a huge man and man a miniature universe] (II.xii.11). Calcidius expresses much the same idea in similar language: "opinor hominem mundum breuem a ueteribus appellatum" [I believe that man was called a miniature universe by the ancients] (202). See also Calcidius, chapters 101, 187, 213, and 231–33. For an extensive general discussion of the idea of microcosm and macrocosm, see Rudolf Allers, "Microcosmus from Anaximandros to Paracelsus," *Traditio* 2 (1944), 319–407.

44 Macrobius elsewhere describes the movement of the soul in more detail (I.xii), making explicit the comparison of individual soul and World-Soul. On Macrobius's account of the soul's descent from heaven, see Flamant, *Macrobe*, pp. 523–24 and 540–65; M.A. Elferink, *La Descente de l'âme d'après Macrobe* (Leiden: E.J. Brill, 1968); and Herman de Ley, *Macrobius and Numenius: A Study of Macrobius, In Somn., I, c. 12*, Collection Latomus, 125 (Brussels: Latomus, Revue d'Etudes Latines, 1972).

45 The translation is from den Boeft, *Calcidius on Fate*.

46 Compare Lynch's conclusion that "because dreams occur while man is in the body and yet seem to lead him to a knowledge that transcends bodily limitations, they have a special relevance to the thinker who seeks to explore the threshold between body and spirit" (*High Medieval Dream Vision*, p. 64).

3 THE PATRISTIC DREAM

1 Artemidorus presents a similar subdivision of allegorical dreams; see *Interpretation of Dreams*, book 1, pp. 16–17.

2 Nevertheless, as Macrobius makes clear in discussing Agamemnon's dream (*Iliad*, book 2, lines 5ff.), even higher dreams may contain ambiguities (I.vii.4–6).

3 Augustine's relation to Neoplatonism is ambivalent in a way unlike that of Calcidius or Macrobius; see, for instance, his discussion of Porphyry's treatment of theurgy –

Augustine, *Concerning the City of God against the Pagans*, Henry Bettenson (trans.) (Harmondsworth: Penguin Books, 1972), book 10, chapters 9–11, pp. 383–90. Elsewhere, Augustine admits a similarity between Christian and Neoplatonic ideas, but also calls attention to the deficiencies of non-Christian thought (see, for instance, *City of God*, book 10, chapter 29, p. 414). Augustine's debt to Neoplatonism has provided an extraordinarily fertile ground for scholarly work. For some of this work, see Paul Henry, *Plotin et l'Occident* (Louvain: Spicilegium Sacrum Lovaniense, 1934), pp. 63–145; J. Wytzes, "Bemerkungen zu dem neuplatonischen Einfluss in Augustins 'De Genesi ad literam,'" *Zeitschrift für die neutestamentliche Wissenschaft und die Kunde der älteren Kirche* 39 (1940), 137–51; Jean Pépin, *"Ex Platonicorum persona": Etudes sur les lectures philosophiques de saint Augustin* (Amsterdam: Adolf M. Hakkert, 1977); Courcelle, *Late Latin Writers*, pp. 149–223; A.H. Armstrong, "St. Augustine and Christian Neoplatonism," in R.A. Markus (ed.), *Augustine: A Collection of Critical Essays* (Garden City, N.Y.: Anchor Books, Doubleday, 1972), pp. 3–37; and Eugene TeSelle, "Porphyry and Augustine," *Augustinian Studies* 5 (1974), 113–47. Many more such studies could be cited. For works that consider the Neoplatonic component of Augustine's theory of dreaming more directly, see John H. Taylor, "The Meaning of *Spiritus* in St. Augustine's *De Genesi*, XII," *The Modern Schoolman* 26 (1948–49), 211–18; Dulaey, *Le Rêve*, esp. pp. 73–88; and R.A. Markus, "The Eclipse of a Neo-Platonic Theme: Augustine and Gregory the Great on Visions and Prophecies," in H.J. Blumenthal and R.A. Markus (eds.), *Neoplatonism and Early Christian Thought: Essays in Honour of A.H. Armstrong* (London: Variorum Publications, 1981), pp. 204–11.

4 See Augustine, *City of God*, book 22, chapter 8, pp. 1035 and 1038.

5 See Augustine, *Confessions*, E.B. Pusey (trans.) (London and Toronto: J.M. Dent; and New York: E.P. Dutton, 1907), book 3, chapter 11, section 19, p. 47; and see my discussion in chapter 7 below.

6 See Augustine, *De Genesi ad litteram*, John Hammond Taylor (trans.), *The Literal Meaning of Genesis* (New York and Ramsey, N.J.: Newman Press, 1982), vol. II, XII.30.58, p. 221:

> Men in their waking hours think of their troubles . . . and so in their sleep, too, they frequently dream of something they need . . . When they happen to go to sleep hungry and thirsty, they are often after food and drink with open mouth. Now, in my opinion, when these objects are compared with the revelations of angels, they ought to be assigned the same relative value that we give, in the corporeal order, to earthly bodies in comparison with celestial bodies.

In my text, I cite Taylor's translation; parenthetical references give book, chapter, and section numbers along with page numbers from vol. II of Taylor. For the Latin text, see *De Genesi ad litteram libri duodecim*, Iosephus Zycha (ed.), Corpus Scriptorum Ecclesiasticorum Latinorum, XXVIII, section 3, part 1 (Prague and Vienna: F. Temsky; and Leipzig: G. Freytag, 1894). See Dulaey, *Le Rêve*, pp. 98–102, for a discussion of mundane dreams in Augustine, his predecessors, and his contemporaries.

7 Augustine's epistemology has been the subject of extensive study. For an overview, see R.A. Markus, "Marius Victorinus and Augustine," in Armstrong (ed.), *Cambridge History of Later Greek and Early Medieval Philosophy* (Cambridge: Cambridge University Press, 1970), esp. pp. 362–79. For more detailed discussion, see Etienne Gilson, *The Christian Philosophy of Saint Augustine*, L.E.M. Lynch (trans.) (New York: Random House, 1960), esp. pp. 25–184; Ronald H. Nash, *The Light of the Mind: St. Augustine's*

Theory of Knowledge (Lexington, Kentucky: The University Press of Kentucky, 1969); and Marcia L. Colish, *The Mirror of Language: A Study in the Medieval Theory of Knowledge*, revised edition (Lincoln and London: University of Nebraska Press, 1983). For a good introduction to the epistemological concerns of *De Genesi* XII, see Matthias E. Korger, "Grundprobleme der augustinischen Erkenntnislehre: Erläutert am Beispiel von *De Genesi ad litteram* XII," *Recherches Augustiniennes* 2 (1962), 33–57.

8 On Augustine's unusual use of the word "spiritus" in the *De Genesi*, see Taylor, "The Meaning of *Spiritus*." Augustine himself comments, at the end of book XII, on his use of unorthodox terminology (XII.37.70, pp. 230–31). Remarks made in the *City of God* (book 10, chapter 9, p. 384) suggest that the distinction between "spirit" and "intellect" has an ultimately Neoplatonic origin. See also Pépin, *"Ex Platonicorum persona"*, p. 261; and Korger, "Grundprobleme," pp. 41–43.

9 The scheme of the three visions also appears elsewhere in Augustine's work, both implicitly and explicitly. See, for instance, *City of God*, book 10, chapter 9, p. 384; *Letters* 9, 159, and 162, Wilfrid Parsons (trans.), The Fathers of the Church: A New Translation, 12, 20 (New York: Fathers of the Church, 1951); and *De Trinitate libri xv*, W.J. Mountain (ed.), Corpus Christianorum, series latina, 50, 50A (Turnholt: Typographi Brepols Editores Pontificii, 1968), IX.6.11 (translated by Arthur West Haddan, *On the Holy Trinity*, A Select Library of the Nicene and Post-Nicene Fathers of the Christian Church, 3 [Buffalo: The Christian Literature Company, 1887], p. 130). See also Taylor's translation of the *De Genesi* (p. 304, n. 25) for references to the three visions in the first eleven books of that work. For critical considerations of Augustine's treatment of vision in the *De Genesi*, and for suggestions of Neoplatonic influence, see Korger, "Grundprobleme"; Newman, "Somnium," pp. 110–15; and Markus, "Eclipse."

10 Augustine differentiates "true images [*ueras imagines*], representing the bodies that we have seen and still hold in memory," from "fictitious images [*fictas imagines*], fashioned by the power of thought": "My manner of thinking about Carthage, which I know, is different from my manner of thinking about Alexandria, which I do not know" (XII.6.15, p. 186). Elsewhere, Augustine calls the "true image" *phantasia* and the "fictitious image" *phantasma* (see, for instance, *De Trinitate* VIII.6.9). For discussion of this distinction, see Murray Wright Bundy, *The Theory of Imagination in Classical and Mediaeval Thought* (Urbana, Ill.: The University of Illinois, 1927), pp. 89–90, 158, 193–94, and 260; Sheila Delany, *Chaucer's House of Fame: The Poetics of Skeptical Fideism* (Chicago and London: The University of Chicago Press, 1972), pp. 61–62; Nash, *Light of the Mind*, p. 55; and Dulaey, *Le Rêve*, pp. 93–96. Pépin, *"Ex Platonicorum persona"*, pp. 261–63, argues that the differentiation of *phantasia* and *phantasma*, and Augustine's use of Alexandria as an example of *phantasma*, have Porphyrian sources; see also Willy Theiler, *Porphyrius und Augustin* (Halle [Saale]: Max Niemeyer, 1933), pp. 37–38.

11 As Nash, *Light of the Mind*, suggests, in Augustine's thought "there is a similarity between the structure of being and the structure of knowing":

> Augustine's ontology consists of an hierarchical structure of reality with God, its creator, at the apex and the world of bodies at the lowest level. His epistemology finds man beginning with sensation but attempting to climb by way of reason to the eternal ideas in the mind of God. (p. 5)

12 This definition of spiritual vision clearly resembles Neoplatonic descriptions of intermediate phenomena; see Markus, "Eclipse," p. 205. As TeSelle, "Porphyry and Augustine," points out:

Augustine's understanding of mediation is similar to the "law of the mean" that was made into a systematic principle by [the Neoplatonists] Iamblicus and Proclus that two entities which are doubly disjunct, having the opposed characteristics x and y, not-x and not-y respectively, can be related only through a mean which is compatible with at least one aspect of each of the extremes (x and not-y, or not-x and y). (p. 125)

13 See also Augustine, *Letters* 162 (to Evodius).

14 The distinction of tranquil and troubled dreams calls to mind Calcidius's discussion of dreams "quae iuxta cogitationes rationabilis animae partis *uel purae atque immunis a perturbatione uel in passionibus positae oboriuntur*" (256; my emphasis). See the discussion in chapter 2 above.

15 See Dulaey, *Le Rêve*, pp. 89–93, for a discussion of Augustine's differentiation of dream-types and for a schematic comparison of Augustine, Macrobius, and Calcidius similar to the one I present. Despite the parallels between the three late-antique schemes, I do not mean to suggest a neat one-to-one correspondence between the various kinds of dream that each of the authors distinguishes. Augustine's tripartite division of true dreams in fact corresponds relatively closely to Macrobius's distinction of *visio*, *oraculum*, and *somnium*, but there are problems matching up Augustine and Calcidius. Although one might describe Calcidius's *reuelationes* as dreams "futuris omnino similia" and his *admonitiones* as dreams "aperte dicta," the *uisum* does not clearly resemble Augustine's third, figurative, dream (but see Dulaey, *Le Rêve*, pp. 91–92, esp. p. 92, n. 15). In addition, Calcidius's waking vision, the *spectaculum*, has no counterpart in Augustine's scheme. Again, as in comparing Macrobius and Calcidius (see chapter 2, n. 34 above), the most important thing to note is the general, structural similarity among the three systems.

16 Augustine, *De Trinitate* IX.4.7. See also Augustine, *Letters* 159 and 162.

17 I cite H. Browne's translation of the *De cura*, *On Care to Be Had for the Dead*, A Select Library of the Nicene and Post-Nicene Fathers of the Christian Church, 3 (Buffalo: The Christian Literature Company, 1887), pp. 537–51; for the Latin text, see *De cura pro mortuis gerenda*, PL 40, cols. 591–610. As Dulaey suggests (*Le Rêve*, p. 146), the *De cura* was written mainly to combat popular beliefs associating dreams with actual visitations from the realm of the dead; see Dulaey's general discussion of the role that popular or cultic ideas played in forming Augustine's dream thought (pp. 141–225). See also the exchange of letters between Augustine and Evodius, *Letters* 158 and 159.

18 The "Eulogius" whom Augustine here mentions is probably Favonius Eulogius, author of the *Disputatio de Somnio Scipionis*, Roger-E. van Weddingen (ed. and trans.), Collection Latomus, 27 (Brussels: Latomus, Revue d'Etudes Latines, 1957). See van Weddingen's introduction, pp. 5–6, and Dulaey, *Le Rêve*, p. 79.

19 Augustine, *De cura* 13, Browne (trans.), pp. 545–46.

20 *Ibid.*, 12, Browne (trans.), p. 545.

21 *Ibid.*

22 *Ibid.*

23 As Nash, *Light of the Mind*, suggests, "Augustine's point is that truth cannot be derived from sensation; it can only be imposed on sensation by a mind that is aware of eternal truth" (p. 122).

24 For the distinction between "use" and "enjoyment," see Augustine's *De doctrina christiana*, D.W. Robertson (trans.), *On Christian Doctrine* (Indianapolis: Bobbs-Merrill, 1958), I.iii–v.3–5, pp. 9–10.

25 See Augustine's discussion of rapture, *De Genesi* XII.26.53–54, pp. 216–17. Intellectual rapture presents "a direct vision and not . . . a dark image" (XII.26.54, p. 217); the direct intellectual vision of God is, however, extremely rare (XII.27.55, pp. 218–19).

26 See the discussions of Synesius, and Plato and Calcidius in chapter 2 above.

27 See the discussion of Augustine above.

28 Colish, *Mirror of Language*, comments that one of Augustine's "favorite ideas" is "the interdependence of morality and cognition" (p. 37).

29 Compare Augustine's discussion in the *Confessions* X.30.41–42. The attitude of Christian theorists toward wet-dreams provides a telling gauge of the extent to which volition was seen to be involved in the dream. For the most part, theorists followed Augustine's authoritative treatment, but with certain significant modifications and deviations. See, for instance, Thomas Aquinas, *Summa theologiae*, Thomas Gilby (ed.) (n.p.: Blackfriars, 1968), vol. XLIII, II(2).q.154.a.5, pp. 122–27. For a harsher view, see Innocent III, *On the Misery of the Human Condition*, Donald R. Howard (ed.), Margaret Mary Dietz (trans.) (Indianapolis and New York: Bobbs-Merrill, 1969), book 1, chapter 24, pp. 27–28.

30 Tertullian, *On the Soul* [*De anima*], chapter 45, section 4, Quain (trans.), p. 281. Tertullian's most extensive discussion of sleep and dreams is found in chapters 43–49 of the *De anima*; for the Latin text, see Tertullian, *Opera*, part 2: Opera Montanistica, Waszink (ed.), Corpus Christianorum, series latina, 2 (Turnholt: Typographi Brepols Editores Pontificii, 1954).

31 In chapter 47 of the *De anima*, Tertullian treats dreams caused by demons, by God, and by the soul itself; he then, somewhat obscurely, suggests that some dreams fit none of these three categories: "Ea autem, quae neque a deo neque a daemonio neque ab anima uidebuntur accidere, et praeter opinionem et praeter interpretationem et praeter enarrationem facultatis, ipsi proprie ecstasi et rationi eius separabuntur." Quain translates: "Finally, those dreams which cannot be attributed to God, or the Devil, or the soul itself, since they are beyond expectation, or any ordinary explanation, or even of being intelligibly related, will have to be placed in a special category as arising from ecstasy and its attendant circumstances" (p. 286). On the difficulties of Tertullian's dream classification, see Behr, *Aelius Aristides*, p. 175, n. 11a; Behr proposes a very different reading of this passage from Quain's, in fact denying the existence of a fourth class of dreams in Tertullian's system.

32 Tertullian, *De anima*, chapter 47, section 3, Quain (trans.), p. 286. Behr, *Aelius Aristides*, argues that Tertullian's "tertia species" "is the well known, non-predictive dream activity of the mind" (p. 175, n. 11a); however, others cited by Behr read it as "a prophetic class."

33 The passage cited is from Gregory the Great's *Dialogues* IV.50.2; compare his *Moralia in Iob* VIII.24.42. Most of Gregory's discussion of dreams appears identically in *Dialogues* IV.50–51 and *Moralia in Iob* VIII.24.42–43; the two passages do, however, diverge near their respective endings. Unless otherwise noted, I quote from the *Dialogues*, Adalbert de Vogüé (ed.), Sources Chrétiennes, 265 (Paris: Les Editions du Cerf, 1980), and translations are by Odo John Zimmerman, *Dialogues*, The Fathers of the Church: A New Translation, 39 (New York: Fathers of the Church, 1959). I have used Marc Adriaen's edition of the *Moralia in Iob*, Corpus Christianorum, series latina, 143 (Turnholt: Typographi Brepols Editores Pontificii, 1979), and the English translation from the Library of Fathers of the Holy Catholic Church, *Morals on the Book of Job*, I (Oxford: John Henry Parker; and London: F. and J. Rivington, 1844).

34 See Markus, "Eclipse."

35 See Iamblichus's hierarchical organization of "Gods," "angels," and "daemons," in *On the Mysteries*, esp. section 2; Calcidius's demonology, esp. chapters 131–35, den Boeft (trans.), *Caldicius on Demons*; and Augustine, *City of God*, book 10, chapter 11, pp. 386–90. Christian angelology and demonology owe a great deal to Neoplatonic discussions of demonic action: see especially a work like Pseudo-Dionysius the Areopagite's *Celestial Hierarchy, La Hiérarchie céleste*, Günther Heil (ed.), Maurice de Gandillac (trans.), Sources Chrétiennes, 58 (Paris: Les Editions du Cerf, 1958). Pépin has suggested that Augustine's treatment of angels is specifically indebted to Neoplatonic demonology; see *"Ex Platonicorum Persona"*, pp. xvii and 29–37.

36 But, in Macrobius, even potentially helpful dreams can be misleading. See the treatment of Agamemnon's dream (I.vii.4–6).

37 Quain translates here, rather too loosely, "the Devil" (p. 285). The Latin reads: "Definimus enim (1) *a daemoniis* plurimum incuti somnia ... (2) A deo autem, pollicito scilicet et gratiam spiritus sancti in omnem carnem et sicut prophetaturos, ita et somniaturos seruos suos et ancillas suas" (chapter 47, sections 1–2).

38 Tertullian, *De anima*, chapter 47, sections 1–2, Quain (trans.), p. 285.

39 Gregory, *Dialogues* IV.50.3, Zimmerman (trans.), p. 261; see *Moralia* VIII.24.42. Gregory cites Ecclesiasticus 34:7 and Leviticus 19:26 as scriptural evidence of demonic dreams and notes especially the association of such dreams with divination.

40 Gregory, *Dialogues* IV.50.4, Zimmerman (trans.), p. 261; see *Moralia* VIII.24.42. I have slightly revised Zimmerman's translation. The biblical reference is to Matthew 2:13–14. Gregory cites, as another example of *reuelatio*, the Old Testament Joseph's dream (Genesis 37:5–10).

41 Gregory cites biblical authority – Ecclesiastes 5:2; Daniel 2:29 and 31 – to establish the authenticity of his mixed dream-types (*Dialogues* IV.50.4–5, Zimmerman [trans.], pp. 261–62; see *Moralia* VIII.24.42). Compare the citation of Daniel 2:29 in the Talmud: "R. Samuel b. Nahmani said in the name of R. Jonathan: A man is shown in a dream only what is suggested by his own thoughts, as it says, *As for thee, Oh King, thy thoughts came into thy mind upon thy bed*" (*Berakoth* 55b).

42 Tertullian, *De anima*, chapter 47, section 2, Quain (trans.), p. 285.

43 *Ibid.*, chapter 47, section 1, p. 285.

44 *Ibid.*

45 Gregory, *Dialogues* IV.50.6, Zimmerman (trans.), p. 262. This passage does not appear in the *Moralia*, but the idea expressed is implicit in Gregory's discussion there of the actions of the "malignus spiritus" (VIII.24.43).

46 Tertullian, *De anima*, chapter 47, section 2, Quain (trans.), pp. 285–86.

47 *Ibid.*, p. 285.

48 *Ibid.*, chapter 47, section 1; I cite my own translation. Quain, p. 285, translates the passage somewhat loosely: "But, when they deliberately set out *to delude us with favors* ..."

49 Gregory, *Moralia* VIII.24.43; the translation is that of the Library of Fathers of the Holy Catholic Church, pp. 449–50. This passage is not found in the *Dialogues*.

50 See Gregory, *Dialogues* IV.50.2, Zimmerman (trans.), p. 261: "The first two ways [dreams of the stomach] we all know from personal experience. The other four we find mentioned in the Bible." See also *Moralia* VIII.24.42.

51 Gregory, *Dialogues* IV.50.1, Zimmerman (trans.), p. 261. There is no parallel passage in the *Moralia*.

52 Compare Deuteronomy 18:10 ("qui arioles sciscitetur et observet somnia" [any one ...

that consulteth soothsayers, or observeth dreams]) and Leviticus 19:26 ("non augurabimini nec observabitis somnia" [you shall not divine nor observe dreams]). And see chapter 1 above.

53 Gregory, *Dialogues* IV.50.6, Zimmerman (trans.), p. 262. This passage does not appear in the *Moralia*.

54 Gregory, *Dialogues* IV.50.6, Zimmerman (trans.), p. 262.

55 *Ibid.*, IV.51, p. 262.

56 *Ibid.*, IV.50.6, p. 262; see *Moralia* VIII.24.43.

57 The problem of "discernment" or *discretio* became very important in the Middle Ages. Thus, Margery Kempe repeatedly consulted her spiritual advisers to confirm that her dreams and visions were not demonic temptations but rather divinely-inspired. For a general overview of the topic, see the article on "Discernement des esprits," *Dictionnaire de spiritualité: Ascétique et mystique, doctrine et histoire* (Paris: Beauchesne, 1957), III, cols. 1222–91. For interesting late-medieval treatments, see Heinrich von Langenstein [Henry of Hesse], *"Unterscheidung der Geister": Lateinisch und deutsch: Texte und Untersuchungen zu Übersetzungsliteratur der Wiener Schule [De discretione spirituum]*, Thomas Hohmann (ed.) (Munich: Artemis, 1977); and *The Chastising of God's Children*, Joyce Bazire and Eric Colledge (eds.) (Oxford: Basil Blackwell, 1957), pp. 177–82.

58 I cite H.J. Thomson's edition and translation, Prudentius, *Liber Cathemerinon*, Loeb Classical Library: Prudentius, 1 (London: William Heinemann; and Cambridge, Mass.: Harvard University Press, 1949), giving line numbers parenthetically in my text. On Prudentius, see F.J.E. Raby, *A History of Christian–Latin Poetry* (Oxford: Clarendon Press, 1927), pp. 44–71, esp. pp. 44–49, on the *Cathemerinon*. On the treatment of dreaming in the *Cathemerinon*, see Newman, "Somnium," pp. 106–07.

59 Prudentius refers to Genesis 40 and 41 (Joseph), and to the Apocalypse.

60 Compare the hymn for Compline in the Daily Office, "Te lucis ante terminum," in A.S. Walpole (ed.), *Early Latin Hymns* (Cambridge: Cambridge University Press, 1922; rpt. Hildesheim: Georg Olms Verlagsbuchhandlung, 1966), p. 299, esp. lines 5–9: "procul recedant somnia / et noctium phantasmata, / hostemque nostrum conprime / ne polluantur corpora" [let dreams and the apparitions of night retreat far away, and hold back our enemy lest (our) bodies be defiled].

61 Gregory, *Dialogues* IV.50.6, Zimmerman (trans.), p. 262; see *Moralia* VIII.24.43.

4 FROM THE FOURTH TO THE TWELFTH CENTURY

1 For discussions of the poem's opening passage, see Walter Clyde Curry, *Chaucer and the Mediaeval Sciences*, revised edition (New York: Barnes and Noble, 1960), pp. 196–97 and 202–03; Wolfgang Clemen, *Chaucer's Early Poetry*, C.A.M. Sym (trans.) (London: Methuen, 1963; and New York: Barnes and Noble, 1964), pp. 73–75; C.S. Lewis, *The Discarded Image: An Introduction to Medieval and Renaissance Literature* (Cambridge: Cambridge University Press, 1964), pp. 54 and 63–64; B.G. Koonce, *Chaucer and the Tradition of Fame: Symbolism in The House of Fame* (Princeton, N.J.: Princeton University Press, 1966), pp. 46–57; J.A.W. Bennett, *Chaucer's Book of Fame: An Exposition of 'The House of Fame'* (Oxford: Clarendon Press, 1968), pp. 1–5; Francis X. Newman, "*Hous of Fame*, 7–12," *English Language Notes* 6 (1968), 5–12; Delany, *Chaucer's House of Fame*, pp. 36–47; Enrico Giaccherini, "Una crux chauceriana: I sogni nella *House of Fame*," *Rivista di letterature moderne e comparate* 27 (1974), 165–76; and A.C. Spearing, *Medieval Dream-Poetry* (Cambridge: Cambridge University Press, 1976), pp. 73–76. Also see

John M. Fyler's notes in Geoffrey Chaucer, *The Riverside Chaucer*, third edition, Larry D. Benson (general ed.) (Boston: Houghton Mifflin, 1987), p. 978.

2 I cite Fyler's edition of the *House of Fame*, *Riverside Chaucer*, giving line numbers parenthetically in my text.

3 The narrator's "turne us every drem to goode" may have been a commonplace in Middle English; see, for instance, the comparable phrase in *Havelok the Dane*, Walter Hoyt French and Charles Brockway Hale (eds.), *Middle English Metrical Romances* (New York: Prentice-Hall, 1930): "Iesu Crist, þat made mone, / þine dremes turne to joye" (lines 1314–15). We also find interesting parallels further afield, in the Near-Eastern rituals discussed by Oppenheim, *Interpretation of Dreams*, pp. 295–307: "Change the dream I had into a good one!" (p. 300). See also the Talmud – "As thou didst turn the curse of the wicked Balaam into a blessing, so turn all my dreams into something good for me" (*Berakoth* 55b) – and the Jewish ritual of "turning a dream to good," described by Joshua Trachtenberg, *Jewish Magic and Superstition: A Study in Folk Religion* (New York: Atheneum, A Temple Book, 1970), pp. 247–48.

4 For an overview of the "Platonisms" influential in the Middle Ages, see Stephen Gersh, "Platonism – Neoplatonism – Aristotelianism: A Twelfth-Century Metaphysical System and its Sources," in Robert L. Benson and Giles Constable (eds.), *Renaissance and Renewal in the Twelfth Century* (Cambridge, Mass.: Harvard University Press, 1982), pp. 512–34, esp. the useful bibliography, pp. 532–34.

5 J.D.A. Ogilvy, *Books Known to the English, 596–1066* (Cambridge, Mass.: Mediaeval Academy of America, 1967), p. 196.

6 Alison M. Peden, "Science and Philosophy in Wales at the Time of the Norman Conquest: A Macrobius Manuscript from Llanbadarn," *Cambridge Medieval Celtic Studies* 2 (1981), 21–45.

7 See, for instance, Günter Glauche, *Schullektüre im Mittelalter* (Munich: Arbeo, 1970), pp. 69, 93–94, and 96; Jeanne Vielliard, "Le Registre de prêt de la bibliothèque du collège de Sorbonne au XVᵉ siècle," in Jozef Ijsewijn and Jacques Paquet (eds.), *The Universities in the Later Middle Ages* (Leuven: Leuven University Press, 1978), pp. 276–92, esp. p. 291; and J.A.W. Bennett, *Chaucer at Oxford and at Cambridge* (Toronto: University of Toronto Press, 1974), p. 67.

8 I count, in Manitius's list – *Handschriften antiker Autoren in mittelalterlichen Bibliothekskatalogen*, Karl Manitius (ed.), *Zentralblatt für Bibliothekswesen*, Beihefte, 67 (Leipzig: Otto Harrassowitz, 1935; rpt. Nendeln, Liechtenstein: Kraus Reprint; and Wiesbaden: Otto Harrassowitz, 1968), pp. 227–32 – twenty-one German, twenty-six French, twenty-one British, sixteen Italian, and six Spanish references to either the *Somnium Scipionis*, or *Macrobius de somnio Scipionis*. For a somewhat different count, see Stahl's introduction to his translation of Macrobius's *Commentary* (p. 60).

9 Thorndike, *History*, I, p. 544.

10 Macrobius, *Opera quae supersunt*, Ludwig von Jan (ed.) (Quedlinburg and Leipzig: Typis et Sumptibus Godofredi Bassii, 1848–52), I, pp. lxii–lxxix.

11 Peden, "Macrobius and Medieval Dream Literature," *Medium Ævum* 54 (1985), 61.

12 Macrobius, *Commentary*, Stahl (trans.), p. 60. Macrobius's works remained popular and influential in the Renaissance. See Flamant, *Macrobe*, p. 1, and the more specialized studies of C.R. Ligota, "L'Influence de Macrobe pendant la Renaissance," in *Le Soleil à la Renaissance: Science et mythes* (Brussels: Presses Universitaires de Bruxelles; and Paris: Presses Universitaires de France, 1965), pp. 463–82; Michael D. Mc. Gaha, "The Influence of Macrobius on Cervantes," *Revue de Littérature Comparée* 53 (1979), 462–69;

and Robert K. Presson, "Two Types of Dreams in the Elizabethan Drama, and their Heritage: *Somnium Animale* and the Prick-of-Conscience," *Studies in English Literature* 7 (1967), 239–56.

13 Manitius, *Handschriften*, pp. 173–76. The list includes thirty-five German, thirty-five French, thirty British, nine Italian, and three Spanish citations.

14 Calcidius, *Timaeus*, Waszink (ed.), pp. cvi–cxxxi. Seventy-nine manuscripts contain the translation alone, fourteen contain just the commentary, and forty-four contain both. Three of these manuscripts were produced in the ninth century, three in the tenth, twenty-four in the eleventh, forty-seven in the twelfth, sixteen in the thirteenth, ten in the fourteenth, and thirty-four in the fifteenth and early sixteenth. (In making this calculation, I have included manuscripts that Waszink attributes to the borderline between two centuries – only five of the 137 – in the count for the later of the two centuries.) In addition to these manuscripts, which, even when fragmentary, contain sizable portions of Calcidius's text, Waszink lists seven "codices fragmenta minora exhibentes" [volumes containing minor fragments] (pp. cxxviii–cxxx).

15 See Glauche, *Schullektüre*, pp. 69, 74, 93, and 96. Calcidius's *Timaeus* long continued to be a major source of Platonic thought in Western Europe; see Pearl Kibre, "The Intellectual Interests Reflected in Libraries of the Fourteenth and Fifteenth Centuries," *Journal of the History of Ideas* 7 (1946), 257–97, esp. p. 283.

16 A *Versio Timaei Platonis* is found in BM Harl. 2610, which probably dates from the tenth century, but the manuscript is of doubtful provenance; see Ogilvy, *Books Known to the English*, p. 109.

17 See "Die handschriftliche Überlieferung der Werke des heiligen Augustinus," Österreichische Akademie der Wissenschaften, Philosophisch–historische Klasse, Sitzungsberichte (Vienna): Manfred Oberleitner, I, part 1, "Italien: Werkverzeichnis," 263 (1969); Franz Römer, II, part 1, "Grossbritannien und Irland: Werkverzeichnis," 281 (1972); Römer, III, "Polen. Anhang: Die Skandinavischen Staaten. Dänemark–Finnland–Schweden," 289 (1973); Johannes Divjak, IV, "Spanien und Portugal. Werkverzeichnis. Verzeichnis nach Bibliotheken," 292 (1974); Rainer Kurz, V, part 1, "Bundesrepublik Deutschland und Westberlin, Werkverzeichnis," 306 (1976). The list includes forty-five manuscripts in Italy; forty-three in Great Britain and Ireland; nineteen in West Germany; eleven in Spain and Portugal; three in Poland; and one in Scandinavia. Manuscript collections in other countries have not yet been surveyed. See also Taylor's translation of Augustine's *De Genesi*, I, pp. 12–13.

18 Thorndike, *University Records and Life in the Middle Ages* (New York: Columbia University Press, 1944), p. 113.

19 Ogilvy, *Books Known to the English*, p. 88.

20 Neil R. Ker, "Oxford College Libraries before 1500," in Ijsewijn and Paquet (eds.), *Universities*, p. 297. For the late medieval popularity of Augustine's works, see also Kibre, "Intellectual Interests," p. 279.

21 Ogilvy, *Books Known to the English*, pp. 150 and 152–53.

22 Thorndike, *University Records*, p. 112; and Ker, "Oxford College Libraries," p. 297.

23 Gregory, *Moralia*, Adriaen (ed.), p. xiv; the list of manuscripts is on pp. xiv–xxix. Most of the manuscripts surveyed do not contain the whole of the *Moralia*, but almost 200 manuscripts do include book VIII, which contains Gregory's discussion of dreams.

24 Kibre, "Intellectual Interests," p. 279.

25 Georg Dufner, *Die Dialoge Gregors des Grossen im Wandel der Zeiten und Sprachen* (Padua: Antenore, 1968), p. 37.

26 The quotation is from de Vogüé's Sources Chrétiennes edition of Gregory's *Dialogues*, CCLI, p. 164. See also de Vogüé on the "Diffusion médiévale de l'œuvre," CCLI, pp. 141–43.

27 The list that follows is based on information provided in Dufner, *Die Dialoge*, pp. 38–45 and 50–189. Several vernacular translations of the *Moralia* were also made; see Claude Dagens, *Saint Grégoire le Grand: Culture et expérience chrétiennes* (Paris: Etudes Augustiniennes, 1977), p. 441.

28 For an overview of Augustine's influence, see Cayré, "Note complémentaire: 'Augustinisme,'" *Dictionnaire de théologie catholique, Tables générales*, I (Paris: Letouzey, 1951), cols. 317–24. For more specific suggestions about the importance of the *De Genesi ad litteram*, see S. Viarre, "Le Commentaire ordonné du monde dans quelques sommes scientifiques des XIIe et XIIIe siècles," in R.R. Bolgar (ed.), *Classical Influences on European Culture: Proceedings of an International Conference Held at King's College, Cambridge, April 1974* (Cambridge and New York: Cambridge University Press, 1976), pp. 204 and 210; Gersh, "Platonism – Neoplatonism – Aristotelianism," pp. 526 and 528; Peden, "Macrobius," pp. 59 and 62; Newman, "Somnium," pp. 172–77; Curry, *Chaucer and the Mediaeval Sciences*, p. 213; and M.D. Chenu, "Spiritus: Le Vocabulaire de l'âme au XIIe siècle," *Revue des Sciences Philosophiques et Théologiques* 41 (1957), 209–32, esp. pp. 211, 217, 218, and 226.

For an overview of Gregory's influence, see Dagens, *Saint Grégoire le Grand*, pp. 16–17 and 441–43. On the medieval legacy of the *Dialogues*, see Dufner, *Die Dialoge*, esp. pp. 29–38. For the most intensive study of the influence of the *Moralia*, see the series of articles by René Wasselynck: "Les Compilations des 'Moralia in Job' du VIIe au XIIe siècle," *RTAM* 29 (1962), 5–32; "Les 'Moralia in Job' dans les ouvrages de morale du haut Moyen Age latin," *RTAM* 31 (1964), 5–31; "Extraits du 'Remediarum Conversorum' du Pierre de Londres," *RTAM* 32 (1965), 121–32; "L'Influence de l'exégèse de S. Grégoire le Grand sur les commentaires bibliques médiévaux (VIIe–XIIe s.)," *RTAM* 32 (1965), 157–204; and "La Présence des Moralia de S. Grégoire le Grand dans les ouvrages de morale du XIIe siècle," *RTAM* 35 (1968), 197–240.

For work on Macrobius's influence in the Middle Ages, see the important early studies of Schedler, "Die Philosophie des Macrobius," and Pierre Duhem, *Le Système du monde: Histoire des doctrines cosmologiques de Platon à Copernic*, 10 vols. (Paris: Hermann, 1913–59), and Stahl's summary of this work in the introduction to his translation of Macrobius's *Commentary*. See also the following more specialized studies: Henry, "La Doctrine plotinienne de Macrobe sur les vertus chez quelques auteurs médiévaux," in *Plotin et l'Occident*, pp. 248–50; Pierre Courcelle, "La Postérité chrétienne du Songe de Scipion," *Revue des Etudes Latines* 36 (1958), 205–34; William H. Stahl, "Dominant Traditions in Early Medieval Latin Science," *Isis* 50 (1959), 95–124; Edouard Jeauneau, *"Lectio philosophorum": Recherches sur l'école de Chartres* (Amsterdam: Adolf M. Hakkert, 1973), pp. 267–308; Hubert Silvestre, "Note sur la survie de Macrobe au Moyen Age," *Classica et Mediaevalia* 24 (1963), 170–80; Silvestre, "Une Adaptation du commentaire de Macrobe sur le Songe de Scipion dans un manuscrit de Bruxelles," *AHDLMA* 29 (1962), 93–101; Charles Dahlberg, "Macrobius and the Unity of the *Roman de la Rose*," *Studies in Philology* 58 (1961), 573–82; Joseph A. Dane, *"Integumentum* as Interpretation: Note on William of Conches' Commentary on Macrobius (I, 2, 10–11)," *Classical Folia* 32 (1978), 201–15; Lewis, *Discarded Image*, pp. 60–69; Peden, "Science and Philosophy"; Gersh, "Platonism – Neoplatonism – Aristotelianism";

Peden, "Macrobius"; and C.H.L. Bodenham, "The Nature of the Dream in Late Medieval French Literature," *Medium Ævum* 54 (1985), 74–86.

The study of Calcidius's influence has, to date, been more limited; see Gersh, "Platonism – Neoplatonism – Aristotelianism," p. 533. Scholars, however, generally agree that Calcidius's effect on high- and late-medieval thought was at least as important as that of Macrobius; see Macrobius, *Commentary*, Stahl (trans.), p. 46, and Etienne Gilson, *La Philosophie au Moyen Age: Des origines patristiques à la fin du XIVe siècle*, second edition (Paris: Payot, 1944), p. 117. We find Calcidius influencing much the same authors as Macrobius, for instance, Guillaume de Conches, John of Salisbury, Bernardus Silvestris, and Alain de Lille. For further work on Calcidius's influence, see Lewis, *Discarded Image*, pp. 49–60; Calcidius, *Calcidius on Matter*, van Winden (trans.), pp. 2–4; Jeauneau, *"Lectio philosophorum"*, pp. 195–264; and Duhem, *Le Système du monde*.

29 Isidore of Seville, *Sententiarum libri tres*, PL 83, col. 669.

Pseudo-Isidore of Seville, *Sententiarum liber quartus*, PL 83, col. 1163. On the spurious book of sentences, see *Isidoriana, sive in editionem operum S. Isidori Hispalensis prolegomena*, PL 81, cols. 228–29: "opera vel spuria vel suspecta."

Tajo of Saragossa, *Sententiarum libri quinque*, PL 80, cols. 919–21.

Rabanus Maurus, *Commentariorum in Ecclesiasticum libri decem*, PL 109, cols. 1005–07.

30 The quotation is from the *New Catholic Encyclopedia*, VII, p. 675. See also Paul Séjourné, *Le Dernier Père de l'Eglise: Saint Isidore de Séville: Son rôle dans l'histoire du droit canonique* (Paris: Gabriel Beauchesne, 1929), esp. pp. 495–98 for information on the manuscript tradition of Isidore's works. Isidore adds a category to Gregory's six-part scheme, distinguishing dreams that arise "(1) ex saturitate [from satiety], (2) seu inanitione [or from emptiness] . . . (3) ex propria cogitatione [from one's own thinking] . . . (4) illusione [from illusion] . . . (5) supernae revelationis mysterio [from the mystery of supernal revelation] . . . (6) cogitatione simul et illusione [from thinking combined with illusion], (7) atque item cogitatione et revelatione" [and likewise from thinking and revelation] (*PL* 83, col. 669). Later writers often followed Isidore in including thought itself as a separate cause of dreams.

31 Richard Hazelton, "Chaucer and Cato," *Speculum* 35 (1960), 369.

32 Newman, "Somnium," p. 95n.

33 See Otloh of St. Emmeram, *Liber visionum tum suarum, tum aliorum*, PL 146, col. 341: "quarum omnium genera visionum multifarie in sacra reperiuntur Scriptura, maxime tamen in libro quarto Dialogorum a beato Gregorio prolata" [the types of all these visions are found in many places in holy Scripture, but most of all (they are) brought forward by St. Gregory in the fourth book of the Dialogues].

34 Pascalis Romanus, *Liber thesauri occulti*, book 1, chapters 1 and 3, pp. 143 and 151.

35 Bonaventure, *Commentaria in quatuor libros Sententiarum magistri Petri Lombardi*, in *Opera omnia*, II (Quarracchi: Ex Typographia Collegii S. Bonaventurae, 1885), book 2, *dist*. 7, part 2, article 1, question 3, *ad* 3, p. 195. Here, Bonaventure distinguishes dreams that arise "ex dispositione corporis" [from a disposition of the body], "ex sollicitudine mentis" [from an anxiety of the mind], "ex illusione diabolica" [from diabolic illusion], "ex revelatione angelica" [from angelic revelation], and "ex visitatione divina" [from divine visitation]. Bonaventure quotes Gregory more directly elsewhere in his *Commentary on the Sentences* (book 2, *dist*. 25, part 2, single article, question 6, p. 621), and he also makes use of material from Augustine's *De Genesi ad litteram*.

36 Onulf, *Vita Popponis abbatis Stabulensis*, Georgius Heinricus Pertz (ed.), Monumenta

Germaniae Historica, Scriptores, 11 (Hanover: Impensis Bibliopolii Aulici Hahniani, 1854), pp. 310–11.

Alain de Lille, *Liber sententiarum ac dictorum memorabilium*, PL 210, col. 256.

Thomas of Froidmont [Thomas of Beverly], *Liber de modo bene vivendi, ad sororem*, PL 184, col. 1300. On the false ascription to Bernard and the attribution to Thomas, see the *Dictionnaire de spiritualité*, I, col. 1500, and P. Glorieux, *Pour revaloriser Migne: Tables rectificatives*, Mélanges de Science Religieuse, 9, cahier supplémentaire (Lille: Facultés Catholiques, 1952), p. 74; on Thomas, see the *Dictionnaire des auteurs cisterciens*, Emile Brouette, Anselme Dimier, and Eugène Manning (eds.) (Rochefort: Abbaye Notre-Dame de St. Rémy, 1977), II, cols. 681–82.

Caesarius of Heisterbach, *The Dialogue on Miracles*, H. von E. Scott and C.C. Swinton Bland (trans.) (London: Routledge, 1929), II, book 8, chapter 4, pp. 4–5.

Thomas de Chobham, *Summa confessorum*, F. Broomfield (ed.) (Louvain: Editions Nauwelaerts; and Paris: Béatrice-Nauwelaerts, 1968), pp. 483–84.

Albertus Magnus, *Commentarius in Danielem*, in Borgnet (ed.), *Opera omnia*, XVIII, p. 476; *Summa de creaturis*, in Borgnet (ed.), *Opera omnia*, XXXV, pp. 444–45.

Jean de la Rochelle [John of Rupella], *Summa de anima*, Bibliothèque Nationale, MS Latin 6686.A, ff. 51^{r-v}.

Vincent of Beauvais, *Speculum naturale*, book 26, chapters 60–61, cols. 1875–76.

Johannis Michaelis, *In Danielem*, in Thomas Aquinas, *Opera omnia*, Roberto Busa (ed.) (Stuttgart: Frommann-Holzboog, 1980), VII, chapter 2, p. 311, cols. 2–3. Busa attributes this commentary to Johannis, but see also Martin Grabmann, "Die Werke des hl. Thomas von Aquin: Eine literarhistorische Untersuchung und Einführung," third edition, *Beiträge zur Geschichte der Philosophie und Theologie des Mittelalters* 22, nos. 1–2 (1949), p. 396.

Albert of Orlamunde, *Philosophia pauperum, sive Isagoge in libros Aristotelis Physicorum, De caelo et mundo, De generatione et corruptione, Meteororum et De anima*, a compendium of material from Albertus Magnus's commentary on Aristotle, is included in Borgnet's edition of Albert's *Opera omnia*, V; the Gregorian material is on p. 520. See Martin Grabmann, "Die Philosophia Pauperum und ihr Verfasser Albert von Orlamunde. Ein Beitrag zur Geschichte des philosophischen Unterrichtes an den deutschen Stadtschulen des ausgehenden Mittelalters," *Beiträge zur Geschichte der Philosophie des Mittelalters* 20, no. 2 (1918), 1–56, for the argument that Albert of Orlamunde is the author. For a summary of the debate over authorship, see George C. Reilly, *The Psychology of Saint Albert the Great Compared with that of Saint Thomas* (Washington, D.C.: The Catholic University of America, 1934), pp. 4–5.

William of Vaurouillon, "The *Liber de Anima* of William of Vaurouillon O.F.M.," Ignatius Brady (ed.), *Mediaeval Studies* 10 (1948), 224–97, and 11 (1949), 247–307; for Gregory's classification, see 11 (1949), 276–77.

It is clear that these authors often did not take Gregory's scheme directly from Gregory. In Johannis Michaelis and Caesarius of Heisterbach, the system presented seems to derive ultimately from Isidore's adaptation of Gregory. Albertus Magnus, in the *Summa de creaturis*, ascribes the six-fold scheme to Gregory, but elsewhere (in the commentary on Daniel) he refers it to a "Glossa"; Jean de la Rochelle and William of Vaurouillon, following Jean, ascribe Gregory's scheme to Jerome.

37 For William of Wadington's *Manuel des péchés*, see Robert Mannyng of Brunne, *Robert of Brunne's "Handlyng Synne," A.D. 1303, With Those Parts of the Anglo-French Treatise on Which it was Founded, William of Wadington's "Manuel des Pechiez"*, Frederick J. Furnivall

(ed.), EETS, OS 119 (London: Kegan Paul, Trench, Trübner and Co., 1901), pp. 14–17, lines 1125–214. On the disputed authorship of the Anglo–Norman poem, see E. J. Arnould, *Le Manuel des péchés: Etude de littérature religieuse anglo-normande (XIIIme siècle)* (Paris: E. Droz, 1940), pp. 245–53.

> For the *Handlyng Synne* itself, see Robert Mannyng of Brunne, *Handlyng Synne*, Idelle Sullens (ed.) (Binghamton, N.Y.: State University of New York at Binghamton, 1983), lines 379–478.

> Richard Rolle, *The Form of Living*, in C. Horstmann (ed.), *Yorkshire Writers: Richard Rolle of Hampole, an English Father of the Church, and his Followers*, I (London: Swan Sonnenschein; and New York: Macmillan, 1895), pp. 15–16. On the *Form of Living*, see Hope Emily Allen, *The Writings Ascribed to Richard Rolle Hermit of Hampole and Materials for His Biography* (New York: D.C. Heath, 1927), pp. 256–68; and John A. Alford, "Richard Rolle and Related Works," in A.S.G. Edwards (ed.), *Middle English Prose: A Critical Guide to Major Authors* (New Brunswick, N.J.: Rutgers University Press, 1984), pp. 35–60. Spearing, *Medieval Dream-Poetry*, suggests that Rolle's dream classification was "translated with certain modifications" from the *Liber de modo bene vivendi* (p. 57), but this is unlikely: the *Liber*'s listing of dreams is in the Isidorian format, while Rolle's is in the Gregorian.

> Peter Idley, *Instructions to His Son*, Charlotte d'Evelyn (ed.) (Boston: D.C. Heath; and London: Oxford University Press, 1935), book 2, lines 384–432, esp. 391–408. Idley's source is Mannyng's *Handlyng Synne*.

38 See chapter 3, note 9, above.

39 For more on the dissemination of Augustine's three visions, see A. J. Minnis, "Langland's Ymaginatif and Late-Medieval Theories of Imagination," *Comparative Criticism: A Yearbook* 3 (1981), 71–103, esp. 92–94.

40 Alain de Lille, *Summa de arte praedicatoria*, PL 210, col. 126. For more on Alain's treatment of dreams, see the discussion of "Twelfth-century dream hierarchies" in this chapter below; Newman, "Somnium," pp. 142–55; and Lynch, *High Medieval Dream Vision*, pp. 50–51.

41 See Curry, *Chaucer and the Mediaeval Sciences*, pp. 207–09 and 213–14; as Curry's discussion makes clear, however, this division of dreaming has not only Augustinian, but also Aristotelian (and particularly Avicennan) sources.

42 Isidore of Seville, *Etymologiarum libri XX*, PL 82, col. 286.

43 *Libri Carolini*, Monumenta Germaniae Historica, Concilia, supplement to vol. II (Hanover and Leipzig: Bibliopolii Hahniani, 1924), pp. 160–61. Theodulf of Orleans is probably the author of the *Libri Carolini*, though Alcuin is also a candidate for authorship. On the problem of attribution, see the *New Catholic Encyclopedia* articles on Theodulf and Alcuin; Ann Freeman, "Theodulf of Orleans and the *Libri Carolini*," *Speculum* 32 (1957), 663–705; Freeman, "Further Studies in the *Libri Carolini*," *Speculum* 40 (1965), 203–89; and Luitpold Wallach, *Alcuin and Charlemagne: Studies in Carolingian History and Literature* (Ithaca: Cornell University Press, 1959), esp. pp. 4, 169–77, and 224–25.

> Alcuin, *Commentariorum in Apocalypsin libri quinque*, PL 100, col. 1089.

44 Clarenbaldus of Arras's *Tractatulus* is edited by Nikolaus M. Häring in "The Creation and Creator of the World according to Thierry of Chartres and Clarenbaldus of Arras," *AHDLMA* 22 (1955), 137–216; the Augustinian material is on p. 202.

> *De spiritu et anima*, chapter 24: PL 40, cols. 796–98; Erasmo Leiva and Benedicta Ward (trans.), *Treatise on the Spirit and the Soul*, in Bernard McGinn (ed.), *Three Treatises*

on Man: A Cistercian Anthropology (Kalamazoo, Mich.: Cistercian Publications, 1977), p. 218. Migne attributes the *De spiritu* to Augustine, and twentieth-century scholars have sometimes accepted this attribution; see, for instance, Curry, *Chaucer and the Mediaeval Sciences,* pp. 213 and 341, and J. Stephen Russell, *The English Dream Vision: Anatomy of a Form* (Columbus: Ohio State University Press, 1988), pp. 64–65. But it was already recognized as spurious by some medieval writers; see the Thomistic *reportatio, De concordantiis suiipsius,* in Aquinas, *Opera omnia,* Busa (ed.), VI, p. 586, col. 2. The *De spiritu* has been attributed by some to Alcher of Clairvaux (see Glorieux, *Pour revaloriser Migne,* p. 27), but this attribution has also been disputed: see McGinn's introduction to *Three Treatises on Man,* pp. 64–67. The *De spiritu* was an extremely popular work; Oberleitner, *et al.,* "Die handschriftliche Überlieferung," list 247 manuscripts.

Richard of St. Victor, *Adnotatiunculae elucidatoriae in Joelem prophetam, PL* 175, col. 355; and *In Apocalypsim Joannis libri septem, PL* 196, cols. 686–87. See also Richard's discussion of dreaming in the *De eruditione hominis interioris libri tres,* book 1, chapters 1–2 and 19, and book 2, chapter 2, *PL* 196, cols. 1229–34, 1261–63, and 1299–301. Spearing, *Medieval Dream-Poetry,* discusses some of this material, pp. 116–18. Brief sections from the *Commentary on Joel* are translated by Clare Kirchberger in Richard of St. Victor, *Selected Writings on Contemplation* (New York: Harper and Brothers, 1955), pp. 253–56. Migne attributes the *Commentary on Joel* to Hugh of St. Victor; for the ascription to Richard, see Glorieux, *Pour revaloriser Migne,* p. 67, and Häring, "Commentary and Hermeneutics," in Benson and Constable (eds.), *Renaissance and Renewal,* p. 192.

Gilbert of Poitiers's *De discretione animae, spiritus et mentis* is edited by Häring, "Gilbert of Poitiers, Author of the 'De Discretione animae, spiritus et mentis' Commonly Attributed to Achard of Saint Victor," *Mediaeval Studies* 22 (1960), 148–91; the Augustinian material appears on pp. 184–85 and throughout. The text has commonly been attributed to Achard; while Häring makes a strong case for Gilbert's authorship, J. Châtillon, for one, is not convinced. See his "Achard de Saint Victor et le 'De discretione animae, spiritus et mentis,'" *AHDLMA* 31 (1964), 7–35.

45 Albertus Magnus, *Summa de creaturis,* in Borgnet (ed.), *Opera omnia,* XXXV, p. 441; *Enarrationes in Evangelium Lucae,* in Borgnet (ed.), *Opera omnia,* XXII, p. 41; and *Enarrationes in Apocalypsim sancti Joannis,* in Borgnet (ed.), *Opera omnia,* XXXVIII, p. 474.

Thomas of Cantimpré, *Liber de natura rerum: Editio princeps secundum codices manuscriptos,* part 1: Text, H. Boese (ed.) (Berlin and New York: Walter de Gruyter, 1973), pp. 92–93.

Caesarius of Heisterbach, *Dialogue on Miracles,* II, book 8, chapter 1, pp. 1–2.

Aquinas, *Summa theologiae;* see esp. II(2).q.173.a.3 and II(2).q.174.a.1.

Pseudo-Aquinas, *Super Apocalypsim,* in Busa's edition of Aquinas, *Opera omnia,* VII, prologue, p. 721, col. 3. On the spurious ascription to Aquinas, see Grabmann, "Die Werke," p. 396.

Pseudo-Aquinas, *De humanitate Jesu Christi Domini Nostri,* again in Busa's edition of Aquinas, *Opera omnia,* VII, article 1, p. 688, cols. 1–2. On the attribution to Aquinas, see Grabmann, "Die Werke," p. 398.

Hugh of St. Cher (?), *Super Apocalypsim,* in Busa's edition of Aquinas, *Opera omnia,* VII, prologue, pp. 217–18, and chapter 1, pp. 220–21. Busa tentatively attributes this work of Pseudo-Aquinas to Hugh; on the problem of authorship, see also Grabmann, "Die Werke," p. 396.

Jean de la Rochelle, *Tractatus de divisione multiplici potentiarum animae: Texte critique avec introduction notes et tables*, Pierre Michaud-Quantin (ed.) (Paris: Librairie Philosophique J. Vrin, 1964), part 2, chapter 16, p. 86, and chapter 53, p. 131; and *Summa de anima*, Bibliothèque Nationale, MS Latin 6686.A, ff. 37ᵛ–38ʳ.

Vincent of Beauvais, *Speculum naturale*, book 26, chapters 75–80, cols. 1885–89.

Nicolaus de Gorran, *In septem epistolas canonicas*, in Busa's edition of Aquinas, *Opera omnia*, VII, number 3, chapter 1, p. 381, col. 3, and number 4, chapter 4, p. 393, col. 1. On the authorship of this commentary, see Grabmann, "Die Werke," p. 396.

Johannis Michaelis, *In Danielem*, in Busa's edition of Aquinas, *Opera omnia*, VII, chapter 10, p. 323, col. 3.

Petrus Johannis Olivi, *Postilla in librum Geneseos*, in Busa's edition of Aquinas, *Opera omnia*, VII, chapter 2, p. 492, col. 2. On the question of authorship, see Grabmann, "Die Werke," p. 396.

46 William of Vaurouillon, *Liber de anima*, *Mediaeval Studies* 11 (1949), 256–57.
 The Chastising of God's Children, Bazire and Colledge (eds.), pp. 169–72.

47 Guillaume de Conches, *Glosae super Platonem*, Edouard Jeauneau (ed.) (Paris: Librairie Philosophique J. Vrin, 1965), p. 243; see the discussion of "Twelfth-century dream hierarchies" in this chapter below. Guillaume may also be dependent here on the Macrobian categories of *oraculum*, *visio*, and *somnium*.

48 For citations of the *De Genesi*, see Aquinas, *Summa theologiae*, I.q.84.a.8; I.q.94.a.4; I.q.111.a.3; II(2).q.154.a.5; and II(2). q.172.a.1. For use of the *De cura*, see I.q.89.a.8 and Suppl.q.69.a.3.

49 Ailred of Rievaulx, *De anima*, C.H. Talbot (ed.), *Mediaeval and Renaissance Studies* (The Warburg Institute, University of London), supplement 1 (1952), pp. 132–42.

50 Macrobius, *Commentary*, Stahl (trans.), p. 42; see also Lewis, *Discarded Image*, p. 63.

51 Peden, "Macrobius," esp. pp. 61–62 and 65.

52 Onulf, *Vita Popponis*, p. 311. See Peden, "Macrobius," p. 62.

53 John of Salisbury, *Policraticus*, book 2, chapter 15, Pike (trans.), pp. 75–81.
 Pascalis Romanus, *Liber thesauri occulti*, book 1, chapters 8–14, pp. 156–62.
 De spiritu et anima, chapter 25, *PL* 40, col. 798, Leiva and Ward (trans.), pp. 220–21.

54 Raoul de Longchamps [Radulphus de Longo Campo], *In Anticlaudianum Alani commentum*, Jan Sulowski (ed.) (Wrocław: Zakład Naradowy Imienia Ossolińskich Wydawnictwo Polskiej Akademii Nauk, 1972), chapters 50–58, pp. 53–58.

55 Albertus Magnus, *Commentarius in Danielem*, in Borgnet (ed.), *Opera omnia*, XVIII, pp. 468, 473, and 476–77; and *Enarrationes in Matthaeum*, in Borgnet (ed.), *Opera omnia*, XX, pp. 49–50. For the *De fato*, sometimes ascribed to Aquinas, see Busa's edition of Aquinas's *Opera omnia*, VII, article 1, argument 8, p. 47, col. 3. On the attribution of this work to Albert, see Grabmann, "Die Werke," p. 399.

56 Albert of Orlamunde, *Philosophia pauperum*, in Borgnet's edition of Albertus Magnus, *Opera omnia*, V, p. 520.
 Thomas de Chobham, *Summa confessorum*, pp. 481–83. Thomas's explanation of *oraculum*, *visio*, and *somnium* is interesting and somewhat eccentric.
 Vincent of Beauvais, *Speculum naturale*, book 26, chapter 62, cols. 1876–77.
 Thomas of Cantimpré, *Liber de natura rerum*, p. 94.
 Jean de la Rochelle, *Summa de anima*, Bibliothèque Nationale, MS Latin 6686.A, f. 51ʳ.
 Johannis Michaelis, *In Danielem*, in Busa's edition of Aquinas, *Opera omnia*, VII, chapter 2, p. 311, col. 3.

57 See Macrobius, *Commentary*, Stahl (trans.), p. 44, summarizing Schedler's work.

58 This last ascription is made in the chapter heading (chapter 62) of the Douai edition of Vincent's *Speculum*.

59 Giovanni Boccaccio, *Genealogiae deorum gentilium* (Venice, 1494; rpt. New York and London: Garland Publishing, 1976), book 1, chapter 31, "De somno decimoseptimo Herebi filio."

　　Guido da Pisa, *Expositiones et glose super Comediam Dantis, or Commentary on Dante's Inferno*, Vincenzo Cioffari (ed.) (Albany, N.Y.: State University of New York Press, 1974), pp. 18–19.

60 William of Vaurouillon, *Liber de anima*, *Mediaeval Studies* 10 (1948), 242, and 11 (1949), 275–76. Like Vincent of Beauvais, William is here also heavily indebted to Jean de la Rochelle.

61 Adelard of Bath, *De eodem et diverso*, H. Willner (ed.), *Beiträge zur Geschichte der Philosophie des Mittelalters* 4, no. 1 (1903), p. 13. On Adelard's use of Calcidius's *Timaeus*, see Margaret Gibson, "Adelard of Bath," pp. 10–11, and Alison Drew, "The *De eodem et diverso*," pp. 17–18, both in Charles Burnett (ed.), *Adelard of Bath: An English Scientist and Arabist of the Early Twelfth Century*, Warburg Institute Surveys and Texts, 14 (London: The Warburg Institute, University of London, 1987).

62 Guillaume de Conches, *Glosae super Platonem*, pp. 242–43; *De philosophia mundi*, PL 172, col. 94; and *Dragmaticon*, Stanford University Libraries, MS M412, ff. 74^{r-v}. On the Stanford *Dragmaticon* manuscript, see Thomas C. Moser, Jr., "A Science for a King: William of Conches and the *Dragmaticon*," *The Imprint of the Stanford Libraries Associates* 10 (1984), 4–11.

63 See Collin-Roset, "Le *Liber thesauri occulti*," p. 128, on Pascalis's connections with Chartres; on his use of "Plato" (Calcidius), see p. 129. For Calcidian dream lore in Pascalis, see *Liber thesauri occulti*, book 1, chapter 3, p. 148, book I, chapter 7, pp. 155–56, and book 1, chapter 11, p. 160.

64 Francesco Petrarca, *Le familiari*, Vittorio Rossi (ed.) (Florence: G.C. Sansoni, 1934), II, book 5, letter 7, p. 22; translated by Aldo S. Bernardo, *Rerum familiarium libri [Letters on Familiar Matters]* (Albany, N.Y.: State University of New York Press, 1975), I, p. 251.

65 The suggestion is C.S. Lewis's, *Discarded Image*, p. 54. See also Joseph E. Grennen, "Chaucer and Chalcidius: The Platonic Origins of the *Hous of Fame*," *Viator* 15 (1984), 237–62, for a broader argument about the dependence of Chaucer's poem on Calcidius's Platonism.

66 For treatments of the twelfth-century renaissance, and for further bibliography, see Winthrop Wetherbee, *Platonism and Poetry in the Twelfth Century: The Literary Influence of the School of Chartres* (Princeton, N.J.: Princeton University Press, 1972); Brian Stock, *Myth and Science in the Twelfth Century: A Study of Bernard Silvester* (Princeton, N.J.: Princeton University Press, 1972); and Benson and Constable (eds.), *Renaissance and Renewal*.

67 The quotations are from Winthrop Wetherbee's introduction to his translation of Bernardus Silvestris, *The Cosmographia of Bernardus Silvestris* (New York and London: Columbia University Press, 1973), p. 10.

68 Peden, "Macrobius," pp. 61–62 and 64–65; see also Stahl's introduction to his translation of Macrobius's *Commentary*, p. 43. On the Calcidius manuscripts, see note 14 above.

69 See, for instance, Wetherbee, *Platonism and Poetry*, pp. 32–34 and 54–55; and Jerome Taylor's introduction to his translation of Hugh of St. Victor, *The Didascalicon of Hugh*

of St. Victor: A Medieval Guide to the Arts (New York and London: Columbia University Press, 1961).

70 The quotation is from Wetherbee's translation of Bernardus Silvestris, *Cosmographia*, p. 90; compare Macrobius, *Commentary* I.xiv.6–7 (cited above, pp. 32–33). For the Latin text, see Bernardus Silvestris, *De mundi universitate, libri duo, sive Megacosmus et microcosmus*, Carl Sigmund Barach and Johann Wrobel (eds.) (Innsbruck: Verlag der Wagner'schen Universitaets-Buchhandlung, 1876); Peter Dronke has reedited Bernardus's work, *Cosmographia* (Leiden: E.J. Brill, 1978).

71 Bernardus Silvestris, *Cosmographia*, Wetherbee (trans.), p. 91.

72 See, for instance, *De spiritu et anima*, chapters 4, 11, and 33, Leiva and Ward (trans.), pp. 185, 196, and 230.

73 See Taylor's introduction to Hugh of St. Victor, *Didascalicon*.

74 Hugh of St. Victor, *Didascalicon*, book I, chapter 6, Taylor (trans.), pp. 52–53. For the Latin text, see Hugh of St. Victor, *Didascalicon: De studio legendi: A Critical Text*, Charles Henry Buttimer (ed.) (Washington, D.C.: The Catholic University Press, 1939).

75 For the relation between Nature and the main mediative agent of earlier Platonic–Neoplatonic thought, the World-Soul, see George D. Economou, *The Goddess Natura in Medieval Literature* (Cambridge, Mass.: Harvard University Press, 1972), pp. 1–27 and 58–103.

76 On "summae de anima," see Wetherbee's introduction to Bernardus Silvestris, *Cosmographia*, p. 2.

77 Godefroy of St. Victor, *Microcosmus*, Philippe Delhaye (ed.) (Lille: Facultés Catholiques; and Gembloux: J. Duculot, 1951). See also Godefroy's *Fons philosophiae*, Pierre Michaud-Quantin (ed.) (Namur: Godenne, 1956), translated by Edward A. Synan, *The Fountain of Philosophy* (Toronto: Pontifical Institute of Mediaeval Studies, 1972); the *De spiritu et anima*; and William of St. Thierry, *The Nature of the Body and the Soul*, Benjamin Clark (trans.), in McGinn (ed.), *Three Treatises on Man*, esp. prologue, p. 103, book 1, chapter 3, p. 109, and book 2, chapter 2, p. 128.

78 Bernardus Silvestris, *Cosmographia*, Wetherbee (trans.), p. 121.

79 Compare Augustine, *De Genesi* XII.24.51, Taylor (trans.), p. 214:

> Spiritual vision can be reasonably and naturally said to occupy a kind of middle ground between intellectual and corporeal vision. For I suppose that a thing which is not really a body, but like a body, can be appropriately said to be in the middle between that which is truly a body and that which is neither a body nor like a body.

80 *De spiritu et anima*, chapter 14, Leiva and Ward (trans.), pp. 201–02.

81 Isaac of Stella, *Letter on the Soul*, Bernard McGinn (trans.), in McGinn (ed.), *Three Treatises on Man*, chapter 12, pp. 165–66.

82 See chapter 3, notes 3 and 12, above.

83 Onulf, *Vita Popponis*, p. 311.

84 Pascalis Romanus, *Liber thesauri occulti*, book 1, chapter 2, p. 147, and book 1, chapter 4, p. 152.

85 See John of Salisbury, *Policraticus*, book 2, chapters 14 and 17, Pike (trans.), pp. 75 and 86–87.

86 See *De spiritu et anima*, chapters 24–27, Leiva and Ward (trans.), pp. 217–23.

87 Thomas de Chobham, *Summa confessorum*, p. 483.

88 For a fine consideration of the connections between twelfth- and thirteenth-century dream theory and the new physical sciences of the later Middle Ages (particularly astronomy), see Gregory, "I sogni e gli astri."

89 Leo Tuscus's dreambook remains unedited. See Antoine Dondaine, "Hugues Ethérien et Léon Toscan," *AHDLMA* 19 (1952), 67–134; Charles H. Haskins, "Leo Tuscus," *Byzantinische Zeitschrift* 24 (1923–24), 43–47; Haskins, *Studies in the History of Mediaeval Science* (New York: Frederick Ungar, 1960 [1924]), pp. 215–18 (Haskins edits Leo's preface, pp. 217–18); and Marie-Thérèse d'Alverny, "Translations and Translators," in Benson and Constable (eds.), *Renaissance and Renewal*, p. 438.

90 For the translation of al-Kindi, *Liber de somno et visione*, see Albino Nagy, "Die philosophischen Abhandlungen des Ja'qub ben Ishaq al-Kindi," *Beiträge zur Geschichte der Philosophie des Mittelalters* 2, no. 5 (1897).

91 On Pascalis's connections to Greek and Arabic traditions, and on the relation between his use of Pseudo-Achmet and that of Leo Tuscus, see Collin-Roset's introduction to the *Liber thesauri occulti*, pp. 125–37.

92 See d'Alverny, "Translations and Translators," pp. 422–26, 435, and 444–45. For Aristotle's *De anima*, see Kenelm Foster and Silvester Humphries (eds. and trans.), *De anima, In the Version of William of Moerbeke and the Commentary of St. Thomas Aquinas* (New Haven: Yale University Press, 1951). For Avicenna's *De anima*, see S. van Riet (ed.), *Avicenna latinus: Liber de anima seu Sextus de naturalibus*, 2 vols. (Louvain: Editions Orientalistes; and Leiden: E. J. Brill, 1968; Louvain: E. Peeters; and Leiden: E. J. Brill, 1972). Lynch, *High Medieval Dream Vision*, presents a good reading of Avicenna's dream psychology (pp. 65–69).

93 See, for instance, Aristotle, *De anima* II.1.235–44, Foster and Humphries (eds. and trans.), pp. 173–74.

94 See Macrobius, *Commentary* II.xiv–xvi, Stahl (trans.), pp. 227–43.

95 See Aristotle, *De anima* II.4–III.8.

96 On *spiritus* in the medical tradition, see James J. Bono, "Medical Spirits and the Medieval Language of Life," *Traditio* 40 (1984), 91–130; and Curry, *Chaucer and the Mediaeval Sciences*, pp. 203–07. Such material was adopted, for instance, by William of St. Thierry, *Nature of the Body and the Soul*, book 1, chapter 4, Clark (trans.), pp. 111–12; and by the author of the *De spiritu et anima*, chapter 20, Leiva and Ward (trans.), p. 213.

97 Peden, "Macrobius," emphasizes this aspect of twelfth-century dream theory; for a different view, see Newman's discussion, "Somnium," pp. 129–84.

98 See Collin-Roset's introduction to the *Liber thesauri occulti*, pp. 125–37; and see Peden, "Macrobius," p. 65.

99 Pascalis Romanus, *Liber thesauri occulti*, book 1, chapter 10, p. 158.

100 *Ibid.*, pp. 158–59.

101 *Ibid.*, book 1, chapter 9, p. 157.

102 *De spiritu et anima*, chapter 25, Leiva and Ward (trans.), p. 221.

103 *Ibid.*

104 See Algazel, *Algazel's Metaphysics: A Mediaeval Translation*, J.T. Muckle (ed.) (Toronto: St. Michael's College, 1933), II.v.6, pp. 190–91; Avicenna, *Liber canonis* (Venice, 1507; rpt. Hildesheim: Georg Olms Verlagsbuchhandlung, 1964), book 1, *fen* 2, doctrine 3, chapters 3, 4, 6, 7, ff. 42^r–43^r; and Hoffmeister, "Rasis' Traumlehre," pp. 140–42, 145–46, 147–49, and 150–52. On the translation activities of Gerard of Cremona and his school, see d'Alverny, "Translations and Translators," pp. 452–54, and on the translation of Algazel, see pp. 444–46. Marta Fattori, "Sogni e temperamenti," in

Gregory (ed.), *I sogni nel medioevo*, pp. 87–109, and Gianfranco Fioravanti, "La 'scientia sompnialis' di Boezio di Dacia," *Atti della Accademia delle Scienze di Torino: II. Classe di scienze morali, storiche e filologiche* 101 (1966–67), 329–69, esp. 347–50, discuss the tradition of humoral dreams. For some additional medieval uses of the tradition, see Pascalis Romanus, *Liber thesauri occulti*, book 1, chapter 1, pp. 143–44; Boethius of Dacia, *On Dreams*, John F. Wippel (trans.) (Toronto: Pontifical Institute of Mediaeval Studies, 1987), pp. 74–76; and Chaucer, *Nun's Priest's Tale, Canterbury Tales* VII.2923–69, in *Riverside Chaucer*.

105 Adelard of Bath, *De eodem et diverso*, p. 13.

106 See, for instance, Avicenna, *Avicenna latinus: Liber de anima*, II, part 4, chapter 2, p. 32. A statement of the clarity and purity of morning dreams is also, however, available in a patristic source like Tertullian's *De anima* (chapter 48).

107 See, for instance, Dante, *Inferno* 26.7: "Ma se presso al mattin del ver si sogna . . ." [But if near morning our dreams are true . . .]. I cite the edition and translation of Charles S. Singleton, *The Divine Comedy* (Princeton, N.J.: Princeton University Press, 1970). For more on the tradition of reliable morning dreams, see Charles Speroni, "Dante's Prophetic Morning-Dreams," *Studies in Philology* 45 (1948), 50–59.

108 See Peden, "Macrobius," pp. 64–65.

109 John of Salisbury, *Policraticus*, book 2, chapter 15, Pike (trans.), p. 76.

110 Pascalis Romanus, *Liber thesauri occulti*, book 1, chapter 11, p. 160.

111 *Ibid.*, book 1, chapter 7, p. 156. See also book 1, chapter 3, p. 148.

112 *Ibid.*, book 1, chapter 2, p. 147.

113 *Ibid.*, book 1, chapter 7, pp. 155–56. Compare Calcidius's first summary scheme of dream-types, discussed in chapter 2 above; and see Collin-Roset's notes to the *Liber*, pp. 155–56.

114 Guillaume de Conches, *Glosae super Platonem*, p. 242.

115 *Ibid.*, p. 243. Compare Guillaume's *De philosophia mundi* IV.22, *PL* 172, col. 94, and his revision of the *De philosophia*, the *Dragmaticon*, Stanford University Libraries, MS M412, f. 74ᵛ.

116 *De spiritu et anima*, chapter 23, Leiva and Ward (trans.), pp. 216–17.

117 John of Salisbury, *Policraticus*, book 2, chapter 14, Pike (trans.), p. 75. Compare Macrobius, *Commentary* I.iii.6 and I.iii.17–20.

118 See John of Salisbury, *Policraticus*, book 2, chapter 17, Pike (trans.), p. 86; and *De spiritu et anima*, chapters 23, 24 and 27, Leiva and Ward (trans.), pp. 216, 219, and 222–23.

119 See Matthew 27:19.

120 Honorius of Autun, *Elucidarium*, in Yves Lefèvre, *L'Elucidarium et les lucidaires: Contribution, par l'histoire d'un texte, à l'histoire des croyances religieuses en France au Moyen Age* (Paris: E. de Boccard, 1954), p. 452. For an interesting reading of Honorius's work, see the chapter entitled "The *Elucidarium*: Popular Theology and Folk Religiosity in the Middle Ages," in Gurevich's *Medieval Popular Culture*, pp. 153–75.

121 Hildegard of Bingen, *Causae et curae*, Paulus Kaiser (ed.) (Leipzig: Teubner, 1903), pp. 82–83 and 143.

122 *Ibid.*, pp. 82–83.

123 *Ibid.*, p. 83. Compare the more morally-neutral treatment of wet dreams in Augustine (discussed in chapter 3 above; see esp. note 29); and see *De spiritu et anima* (following Augustine), chapter 23, Leiva and Ward (trans.), p. 216.

124 Hildegard of Bingen, *Causae et curae*, p. 143.

125 See, for instance, al-Kindi, *De somno et visione*, Nagy (ed.), pp. 20–23.

126 Richard of St. Victor, *Adnotatiunculae elucidatoriae in Joelem*, PL 175, cols. 355–56.

127 Alain de Lille, *Summa de arte praedicatoria*, PL 210, col. 126.

128 John of Salisbury, *Policraticus*, book 2, chapter 16, Pike (trans.), p. 83.

129 Guillaume de Conches, *Glosae super Platonem*, p. 242.

130 *Ibid.*, p. 243.

131 Compare Augustine, *De Genesi* XII.18.39, cited above, pp. 38–39.

132 John of Salisbury, *Policraticus*, book 2, chapter 15, Pike (trans.), p. 81.

133 See, for instance, *De spiritu et anima*, chapters 24–26, Leiva and Ward (trans.), pp. 218–22.

134 *De spiritu et anima*, chapter 33, Leiva and Ward (trans.), p. 231.

135 Ailred of Rievaulx, *De anima*, p. 135.

136 Ailred, for instance, suggests that the pain imagined in a dream, while not really experienced by the body, is nonetheless real pain, because truly felt (*De anima*, p. 136). And Ailred proposes that imaginative dreams, while they may mislead us, may also educate (p. 142).

137 Richard of St. Victor, *Adnotatiunculae elucidatoriae in Joelem*, PL 175, cols. 355–56. See Newman's discussion, "Somnium," pp. 175–76.

138 Alain de Lille, *Summa de arte praedicatoria*, PL 210, col. 126.

139 *Ibid.*, col. 196.

140 *Ibid.*, cols. 195–96.

141 *Ibid.*, cols. 195–96.

142 *Ibid.*, col. 195.

143 *Ibid.*, col. 196.

144 Parenthetical page numbers refer to the text of Gilbert's *De discretione* edited by Häring, "Gilbert of Poitiers."

5 ARISTOTLE AND THE LATE-MEDIEVAL DREAM

1 See Isidore of Seville, *Sententiae*, PL 83, col. 670: "Somnia similia sunt auguriis, et qui ea intendunt, revera augurari noscuntur." The association between dreaming and augury is, of course, ultimately biblical, and is perpetuated in canon law; see chapter 1 above.

2 See Ecclesiasticus 34:2. As Russell, *English Dream Vision*, notes (p. 68), Ecclesiasticus 34 inspires, in Rabanus Maurus's ninth-century *Commentarii in Ecclesiasticum*, a discussion of dreams similar in certain ways to that of the *Liber de modo bene vivendi*; for Rabanus's discussion, see PL 109, cols. 1005–08.

3 See Ecclesiasticus 34:5.

4 Thomas of Froidmont, *Liber de modo bene vivendi*, PL 184, col. 1301. On the question of authorship and on Thomas of Froidmont [Beverly], see chapter 4, note 36, above.

5 Thomas uses the version of Gregory's scheme found in Isidore's *Sentences*. Compare Thomas, *Liber de modo bene vivendi*, PL 184, col. 1300, to Isidore, *Sententiae*, PL 83, col. 669.

6 Thomas of Froidmont, *Liber de modo bene vivendi*, PL 184, col. 1300.

7 See, for instance, Alain de Lille, *Liber sententiarum*, PL 210, col. 256, who cites Ecclesiasticus 34:2, Leviticus 19:26, and Numbers 23:23 as authorities, and Richard Rolle, *The Form of Living*, p. 16, who cites Ecclesiastes 5:6.

8 S.D. Wingate, *The Mediaeval Latin Versions of the Aristotelian Scientific Corpus, with Special Reference to the Biological Works* (London: The Courier Press, 1931), pp. 48–52;

d'Alverny, "Translations and Translators," p. 436; and Bernard G. Dod, "Aristoteles latinus," in Norman Kretzmann, Anthony Kenny, Jan Pinborg, and Eleonore Stump (eds.), *The Cambridge History of Later Medieval Philosophy: From the Rediscovery of Aristotle to the Disintegration of Scholasticism, 1100–1600* (Cambridge: Cambridge University Press, 1982), pp. 47, 50–51, and 76. The medieval translations are available in modern editions: Aristotle, *De somno et vigilia liber, adiectis veteribus translationibus et Theodori Metochitae commentario,* H.J. Drossaart Lulofs (ed.) (Leiden: Burgersdijk and Niermans – Templum Salamonis, 1943), and *De insomniis et De divinatione per somnum: A New Edition of the Greek Text with the Latin Translations,* 2 vols., H.J. Drossaart Lulofs (ed.) (Leiden: E.J. Brill, 1947).

9 Wingate, *Mediaeval Latin Versions,* pp. 92–93; and Dod, "Aristoteles latinus," pp. 49, 63–64, and 76. For more on the Latin versions, see Aristotle, *De somno et vigilia,* Drossaart Lulofs (ed.), pp. xi–xix.

10 Wingate, *Mediaeval Latin Versions,* pp. 48 and 121–22; Dod, "Aristoteles latinus," pp. 49, 59, and 76; and d'Alverny, "Translations and Translators," pp. 455–57. A modern edition of the Latin Averroes is available, *Compendia librorum Aristotelis qui Parva naturalia vocantur,* Emily Ledyard Shields (ed.), Corpus Commentariorum Averrois in Aristotelem, versio latina, 7 (Cambridge, Mass.: The Mediaeval Academy of America, 1949), as is a modern English translation, *Epitome of Parva Naturalia,* Harry Blumberg (trans.), Corpus Commentariorum Averrois in Aristotelem, versio anglica, 7 (Cambridge, Mass.: The Mediaeval Academy of America, 1961).

11 See the series of articles by C.H. Lohr, "Medieval Latin Aristotle Commentaries," *Traditio* 23 (1967), 313–413; 24 (1968), 149–245; 26 (1970), 135–216; 27 (1971), 251–351; 28 (1972), 281–396; 29 (1973), 93–197; and 30 (1974), 119–44.

12 Citations of Aristotle here are from Beare's translation of the *Parva naturalia,* in Ross (ed.), *Works,* III.

13 Peden, "Macrobius," p. 67; see also pp. 65–66.

14 Bodenham, "Nature of the Dream," p. 75. Bodenham concludes that, "As the mind in sleep knows only itself, at least in the context of Aristotle's *Parva Naturalia,* the events in the narrative [of the *Roman de la rose*] must be the substance of the mind that dreamt them" (p. 76). However, Avicenna and the other Aristotelians newly translated into Latin, though "schooled in the Aristotelian view of things," were often far more willing than Aristotle himself to admit the possibility of an external and divine component of dream experience. For Avicenna's most extensive treatment of dreaming, see *Avicenna latinus: Liber de anima,* van Riet (ed.), part 4, chapter 2, pp. 12–34, and part 4, chapter 1, pp. 4–5. See also Lynch's reading of Avicenna's dream theory, *High Medieval Dream Vision,* pp. 65–69.

15 See, for instance, the recent claim that Macrobius's "was the authoritative classification for dreams for over a millennium" (Russell, *English Dream Vision,* p. 62). Critics earlier than Peden and Bodenham have also sometimes objected to an overemphasis on the importance of Macrobian dream theory; see Curry, *Chaucer and the Mediaeval Sciences,* pp. 195 and 202–03.

16 Boethius of Dacia, *On Dreams,* Wippel (trans.), p. 75. For the Latin text, see Boethius of Dacia, *De somniis,* in Nicolaus Georgius Green-Pedersen (ed.), *Opera,* VI, part 2 (Copenhagen: Gad, 1976): "non tamen nego quin angelus vel diabolus possit dormienti vel infirmo secundum veritatem apparere divina voluntate" (p. 389).

17 Fioravanti, "La 'scientia sompnialis,'" pp. 366 and 369. Fioravanti's discussion is exceptionally full and perceptive. He explores Boethius's indebtedness to Aristotle (pp.

339–45) and to a more general "schola peripatetica" (pp. 345–51). He also contrasts Boethius's dream theory with that of other Aristotelians (particularly Albertus Magnus and Averroes) who fail to confine the significant dream to a natural realm as fully as does Boethius (pp. 351–69).

18 Adam of Buckfield, *In De somno et vigilia, In De somniis, In De divinatione per somnum*, in Aquinas, *Opera omnia*, Busa (ed.), VII, pp. 14–20. On the question of authorship, see Grabmann, "Die Werke," pp. 396–97.

19 Adam of Buckfield, *In De divinatione*, sections [*lectiones*] 1–2, p. 19, cols. 2–3. Compare Aristotle, *De divinatione*, Drossaart Lulofs (ed.) [*vetus translatio*]: "et aliorum animalium sompniant quedam, missa a deo utique non *sunt* sompnia, neque facta huius gratia" [and certain of the other animals dream; clearly (therefore) dreams are not sent by God nor do they occur by His grace] (463b, p. 38); "*infimi* enim homines previdentes sunt et recte sompniantes, tanquam non deo mittente" [truly, the most inferior men can foresee (things) and dream correctly, as though God does not send (dreams)] (463b, p. 40); "et ideo accidit passio hec quibuslibet et non prudentissimis" [and therefore this passion happens to anyone and not to the most prudent] (464a, pp. 42–44).

20 Roger Bacon, *Compendium studii theologiae*, H. Rashdall (ed.), British Society of Franciscan Studies, 3 (Aberdeen: Typis Academicis, 1911), p. 33.

21 See Wippel's introduction to Boethius of Dacia, *On Dreams*, p. 23. The proposition constitutes article 33 of the Condemnation of 1277 (177 in Mandonnet's numbering). See also the discussion of the Condemnation in Gregory, "I sogni e gli astri," pp. 142–43.

22 Petrarca, *Rerum memorandarum libri*, Giuseppe Billanovich (ed.) (Florence: G.C. Sansoni, 1943), p. 222.

23 *Ibid.*, p. 223. Compare Petrarch's similar comments in *Le familiari*, book 5, letter 7, Bernardo (trans.), I, pp. 251–52:

> I agree in this with my Cicero as I do in so many other things. However, I do so without obstinacy and am ready to alter my agreement with him if anything more certain should appear ... If you should wish to hear me dealing with this matter in a more elaborate fashion, I have in hand a book entitled *Liber memorandarum rerum*.

24 Albertus Magnus, *De somno et vigilia*, in Borgnet (ed.), *Opera omnia*, IX, book 3, treatise 1, chapter 1, p. 178.

25 *Ibid.*

26 *Ibid.*, book 3, treatise 1, chapter 12, p. 195. See also book 3, treatise 2, chapter 9, p. 207.

27 Petrarca, *Le familiari*, book 5, letter 7, Bernardo (trans.), p. 251.

28 *Ibid.*

29 I cite Bartholomaeus Anglicus, *On the Properties of Things: John Trevisa's Translation of Bartholomaeus Anglicus De proprietatibus rerum: A Critical Text*, M.C. Seymour (ed.) (Oxford: Clarendon Press, 1975); parenthetical page numbers refer to this edition. I have consulted the Latin text, *Liber de proprietatibus rerum*, in the 1505 Strasbourg edition. "The first important encyclopedia of the Middle Ages" (*The Catholic Encyclopedia* [New York: Robert Appleton, 1907], II, p. 313), Bartholomaeus's work was completed *c.* 1240–50; Trevisa's Middle English translation is dated 1398.

30 See Aristotle, *De divinatione* 463b, Drossaart Lulofs (ed.), pp. 38–39. And compare Lucretius, *De rerum natura*, book 4, lines 987–93.

31 In this last statement, Bartholomaeus recalls Gregorian dream lore (perhaps in Isidore of Seville's version).

32 See chapter 4, p. 72, and note 104, above.

33 Compare Macrobius's *insomnium* (*Commentary* I.iii.4); and see chapter 2, note 20, above.

34 See Macrobius, *Commentary* I.iii.4.

35 See Aristotle, *De somniis* 461a and 462b, Drossaart Lulofs (ed.), pp. 20–21 and 30–31.

36 See Genesis 30:37–43 and 31:10–13.

37 See Augustine, *De Genesi* XII.13.28 and XII.18.39, Taylor (trans.), pp. 196 and 203–04. Bartholomaeus recognizes explicitly his debt to the *"super Genesim libro 12°"* (pp. 336–37).

38 See *ibid.*, XII.12.25 and XII.24.51, pp. 193 and 214.

39 See *ibid.*, XII.18.39, pp. 203–04.

40 Encyclopedic discussions of the dream that I do not treat include Michael Scot, *Liber introductorius* (early thirteenth century); Henri Bate, *Speculum divinorum et quorundam naturalium* (composed between 1286 and 1305); and the *Compendium philosophiae* (early fourteenth century). Thorndike, *Michael Scot* (London: Thomas Nelson, 1965), pp. 89–90, summarizes Scot's discussion of dreaming, which seems, on the whole, to emphasize somatic and physical process more strongly than does Bartholomaeus in his *De proprietatibus*; see also Peden's comments, "Macrobius," p. 65. Bate's discussion of dreaming in the seventeenth part of his *Speculum*, which appears to be quite extensive, remains unedited, but E. van de Vyver provides a "Tabula capitulorum" in vol. I of his (incomplete) edition, *Speculum divinorum et quorundam naturalium, Edition critique* (Louvain: Publications Universitaires; and Paris: Béatrice-Nauwelaerts, 1960), pp. 35–36; see also Henri Bate, *Speculum divinorum et quorundam naturalium* (*Etude critique et texte inédit*), G. Wallerand (ed.) (Louvain: Institut Supérieur de Philosophie de l'Université, 1931), pp. 24–25. The discussion of dreams in the fifth book of the *Compendium philosophiae* also remains unedited, but, again, a list of chapter headings is available; see Michel de Boüard, *Une Nouvelle Encyclopédie médiévale: Le Compendium philosophiae* (Paris: E. de Boccard, 1936), p. 189.

41 Peden, "Macrobius," p. 65.

42 I cite the 1730–31 Cologne edition of Pierre Bersuire [Petrus Berchorius], *Opera omnia* (Apud Petrum Pütz). The discussion of dreams in the *Reductorium morale, De proprietatibus rerum* is found in II, book 4, chapter 20, pp. 76–77; the *Dictionarium morale* entry, "Somniare. Somnium," is in VI, pp. 112–13. I provide volume and page numbers parenthetically in my text.

43 Such a statement has interesting implications for dream fictions: if a dream itself mistakes the sign for the signified, what of an imaginary (fictional) dream?

44 Robert Holkot, *In librum Sapientiae regis Salomonis praelectiones CCXIII* (Basel: Jacobus Ryterus, 1586). *Lectiones* 82, 89, 103, 192, and 202 all contain material on sleep and dreams.

45 Robert A. Pratt, "Some Latin Sources of the Nonnes Preest on Dreams," *Speculum* 52 (1977), 538–70. It has also been proposed that Chaucer knew Vincent of Beauvais's treatment of dreaming, discussed below. See Pauline Aiken, "Vincent of Beauvais and Dame Pertelote's Knowledge of Medicine," *Speculum* 10 (1935), 281–87.

46 Holkot, *In librum Sapientiae*, *lectio* 192, p. 632. Compare Aristotle, *De somno et vigilia* 457b.

47 Holkot, *In librum Sapientiae*, *lectio* 202, p. 665. Compare Aristotle, *De somniis* 461a–62a.

48 See, for instance, Holkot, *In librum Sapientiae*, *lectio* 192, p. 632: "Somnus in Sacra scriptura signat peccatum, & dormiens peccatorem" [In sacred Scripture, sleep signifies sin and the sleeper (signifies) the sinner].

49 *Ibid., lectio* 103, p. 351. The verse quotation is from the *Disticha Catonis*; see the Middle English version, Benet Burgh (trans.), *Parvus Cato, Magnus Cato*, Fumio Kuriyagawa (ed.) (Tokyo: Seijo University, 1974), p. 32, and see Hazelton, "Chaucer and Cato," on the ways in which Cato was used in the medieval schools.

50 Holkot, *In librum Sapientiae, lectio* 202, p. 667. Holkot goes on to quote Ecclesiasticus 34.

51 *Ibid.*

52 *Ibid.* Compare Aristotle, *De divinatione* 463b.

53 Holkot, *In librum Sapientiae, lectio* 202, p. 667.

54 *Ibid., lectio* 103, pp. 348–49. Compare Aristotle, *De divinatione* 463b.

55 Holkot, *In librum Sapientiae, lectio* 103, p. 350.

56 See Aristotle, *De divinatione* 464a.

57 Holkot, *In librum Sapientiae, lectio* 103, pp. 350–51.

58 The 1586 Basel edition is here deficient. I have supplied the missing text from the 1509 Venice edition, Robert Holkot, *Super librum Sapientie, lectio* 201 [= 202 in the Basel edition], p. 171.

59 Holkot, *In librum Sapientiae, lectio* 202, pp. 665–66. For the dreams of Simonides and Cassius Parmensis, see Valerius Maximus, *Factorum et dictorum memorabilium libri I–IV*, I, Fabricius Serra (ed.) (Pisa: Giardini, 1986), book 1, chapter 7, pp. 45–47. Note the care with which Holkot cites both biblical and classical examples of the last two dream-types. His is surely a system concerned with bringing together Christian and classical thought.

60 Ramon Lull [Raymundus Lullus], *Liber proverbiorum, Opera*, VI (Mainz, 1737; rpt. Frankfurt: Minerva, 1965), p. 368.

61 Compare Bartholomaeus Anglicus, *De proprietatibus rerum*, Seymour (ed.), p. 338 (cited p. 91 above).

62 Lull, *Liber proverbiorum*, p. 368.

63 *Ibid.* The organization of Lull's treatment recalls the structure of the medieval *Summae de anima*.

64 Lull, *Liber proverbiorum*, p. 368.

65 Thomas of Cantimpré, *Liber de natura rerum*, book 2, chapter 13, Boese (ed.), pp. 92–94. I cite page numbers from Boese's edition parenthetically in my text.

66 "Insompnium" has been left out of Thomas's list of the five kinds of dream: "Omnium que sibi videre videntur dormientes quinque sunt genera, videlicet oraculum, visio, sompnium . . . fantasma" [There are five kinds of all those things that sleepers seem to themselves to see: namely, the *oraculum, visio, sompnium . . . fantasma*] (p. 94). (Compare the *De spiritu et anima*, PL 40, col. 798: "Omnium quae sibi videre videntur dormientes, quinque sunt genera; videlicet, oraculum, visio, somnium, insomnium, et phantasma.") The definition of *insompnium* is nevertheless intact, but instead of beginning, "Insomnium est," as in the *De spiritu*, it reads "*Ut* sompnium est" – at least in Boese's edition. Since the apparatus to that edition is still unpublished (see Boese's foreword, pp. vii–ix), it is impossible to determine how common the reading "Ut sompnium" is. (Paleographically, of course, *Ut sompnium* would be an easy error for *Insompnium*.) As the text currently stands, the definition of *insompnium* appears to be a continuation of the definition of *sompnium*; the reader of the text, however, knowing that there are *five* "genera" of dreams, might assume that Thomas meant to distinguish two kinds of "sompnium" – one that conveys truth through "figures," and one that arises from psychological and physiological disturbance. In any case, Thomas preserves the full *range* of possible dream experience that we find in Macrobius.

67 Thomas mentions dreaming in this chapter only to cite Aristotle's discussion of the relation between age and dreams. Compare Thomas, *Liber de natura rerum*, p. 18, to Aristotle, *De somniis* 461a and 462b, Drossaart Lulofs (ed.), pp. 20–21 and 30–31.

68 Boccaccio, *Genealogiae*, book 1, chapter 31. Compare the brief "thoughts about dreams" in Giovanni Boccaccio, *De casibus illustrium virorum*, Louis Brewer Hall (ed.) (Paris, 1520; rpt. Gainesville, Florida: Scholars' Facsimiles and Reprints, 1962), book 2, ff. 20^{r-v} (pp. 65–66), translated by Louis Brewer Hall, *The Fates of Illustrious Men* (New York: Frederick Ungar, 1965), pp. 64–65.

69 He cites Ovid, *Metamorphoses*, book 11, lines 623–25, 595–615, and 634–44; Seneca, *Hercules furens*, lines 1065–78; and Virgil, *Aeneid*, book 4, lines 3–4 and book 6, lines 893–96. I have consulted Ovid, *Metamorphoses*, 2 vols., Frank Justus Miller (ed. and trans.), Loeb Classical Library (Cambridge, Mass.: Harvard University Press; and London: William Heinemann, 1960); Seneca, *Seneca's Tragedies*, I, Frank Justus Miller (ed. and trans.), Loeb Classical Library (London: William Heinemann; and New York: G.P. Putnam's Sons, 1917); and Virgil, *Aeneid*, 2 vols., H. Rushton Fairclough (ed. and trans.), Loeb Classical Library (Cambridge, Mass.: Harvard University Press; and London: William Heinemann, 1934–35).

70 Boccaccio, *Genealogiae*, book 1, chapter 31, f. 14^r: "Somnus secundum quosdam est intimi ignis coertio: & per membra mollita: & labore relaxata diffusa quies. secundum uero alios est quies animalium uirtutum: cum intentione naturalium" [According to some, sleep is a restraint of the inmost fire, and a rest diffused through limbs weakened and eased from labor. But truly, according to others, it is a rest of the animal powers with an intensification of the natural (powers)]; "Filius ergo Herebi Noctisque dicitur somnus: quia a uaporibus humidis e stomacho surgentibus: & opilantibus arterias: & quieta obscuritate causetur" [Sleep is therefore called the son of Erebus (son of Chaos, brother of Night) and Night: since it may be caused by humid vapors rising out of the stomach and obstructing the arteries, and by a quiet darkness].

71 Boccaccio, *Genealogiae*, book 1, chapter 31, f. 14^v. The discussion expands on Macrobius's citation of Porphyry (*Commentary* I.iii.17–20).

72 Boccaccio, *Genealogiae*, book 1, chapter 31, ff. 14^{r-v}.

73 I will cite (parenthetically) chapter and column numbers from book 26 of Vincent's *Speculum naturale*. For an introduction to the scholarship on Vincent's work, see Jean Schneider, "Vincent de Beauvais – Orientation bibliographique," *Spicae: Cahiers de l'Atelier Vincent de Beauvais*, I (Paris: Editions du Centre National de la Recherche Scientifique, 1978), pp. 7–29, and Schneider, "Communication: Recherches sur une encyclopédie du XIIIe siècle: Le *Speculum majus* de Vincent de Beauvais," *Académie des Inscriptions et Belles-Lettres – Comptes Rendus* (1976), 174–89. On the sources of Vincent's *Speculum*, see E. Boutaric, "Vincent de Beauvais et la connaissance de l'antiquité classique au treizième siècle," *Revue des Questions Historiques* 17 (1875), 5–57; Roberto Valentini, "Vincenzo di Beauvais e la conoscenza della letteratura cristiana in Francia nella prima metà del secolo XIII," *"Didaskaleion": studi filologici di letteratura cristiana antica* 4 (1915), 109–67 (rpt. Amsterdam: John Benjamins, N.V., 1968); P. Parthenius Minges, "Exzerpte aus Alexander von Hales bei Vinzenz von Beauvais," *Franziskanische Studien* 1 (1914), 52–65; and Ludwig Lieser, "Vinzenz von Beauvais als Kompilator und Philosoph: Textkritische Untersuchung der Zitate aus den antiken und patristischen Literatur im Speculum naturale, Buch 23 bis 27 (Seelenlehre)," Inaugural-Dissertation, University of Cologne, 1927. Minges and Lieser discuss the sources of *Speculum naturale*, book 26. Lieser also considers the relationship between

Vincent's "Platonic–Augustinian" sources and his "Aristotelian–Peripatetic" ones (pp. 9–10 and 26–27).

74 Albertus Magnus, *Summa de creaturis*, in Borgnet (ed.), *Opera omnia*, XXXV. I cite page numbers from this edition parenthetically in my text. On Albert as Vincent's source, see Lieser, "Vinzenz von Beauvais," pp. 8–9.

75 Priscianus Lydus, *Solutionum ad Chosroem liber*, I. Bywater (ed.), Supplementum Aristotelicum, I, part 2 (Berlin: Typis et Impensis Georgii Reimer, 1886), pp. 39–104. The material Vincent uses is contained in chapters 2 and 3 of Priscian (pp. 52–63). On Priscian, see Bywater's introduction; J.T. Muckle, "Greek Works Translated Into Latin Before 1350 (Continuation)," *Mediaeval Studies* 5 (1943), 102–14; and Peden, "Macrobius," pp. 60 and 71. On Vincent's use of Priscian, see Lieser, "Vinzenz von Beauvais," p. 25.

76 Compare the almost identical list of questions in Aristotle, *De somno et vigilia*, Drossaart Lulofs (ed.) [*vetus translatio*], p. 1*.

77 Compare Priscianus Lydus, *Solutiones*, pp. 59–62.

78 See Aristotle, *De somno et vigilia*, Drossaart Lulofs (ed.) [*vetus translatio*], p. 1*, for a list of essentially the same seven questions. These questions, stated at the beginning of the *De somno et vigilia*, are answered in the *De somniis* (questions 1–3) and the *De divinatione per somnum* (questions 4–7).

79 In the chart that follows, I list Aristotle's seven questions alongside the corresponding questions (44–52) from Albert's *Summa de creaturis* and the corresponding chapter headings (34–61) from book 26 of Vincent's *Speculum naturale*. Following each of Albert's questions, I provide page numbers from Borgnet's edition of the *Summa de creaturis*; and following the chapter headings from Vincent, I give the page numbers from Albert's *Summa* on which source material for Vincent's discussion may be found.

80 Each of the first three questions in Albert addresses the issue of the dream's "essence," raised by Aristotle's first question. See Albert, *Summa de creaturis*, p. 402.

81 Chapter 41 is incorrectly labelled "CAPVT XL" in the Douai edition (col. 1865).

82 Chapter 60, which I have not included in my chart, marks Vincent's first major departure from the source material of Priscian and Albert. But in chapter 61, Vincent briefly reverts to the *Summa de creaturis*. Here, he discusses Gregory's system for classifying dreams, which comes up in chapter 59 and which he quotes in full in chapter 60. In the Douai edition, chapter 61 is erroneously entitled, "De sufficientia visionis secundum ipsum"; I have emended "visionis" to "*divisionis*." See Vincent's text: "patet ex parte causarum sufficientia diuisionis somniorum secundum Gregorium" [the sufficiency of Gregory's division of dreams according to their causes is evident] (col. 1876).

83 Aristotle, *De somniis* 462a, Beare (trans.).

84 *Ibid.*, 460b–61a. Compare Vincent, *Speculum naturale*, book 26, chapter 34, col. 1861, and chapter 40, col. 1864; and Albert, *Summa de creaturis*, pp. 418, 421, and 409.

85 Aristotle, *De somniis* 461a, Beare (trans.). See Vincent, *Speculum naturale*, book 26, chapter 45, col. 1867, and chapter 48, col. 1869; and Albert, *Summa de creaturis*, pp. 426–27 and 428.

86 Aristotle, *De somniis* 461b–62b; Vincent, *Speculum naturale*, book 26, chapters 49–51, cols. 1869–71; and Albert, *Summa de creaturis*, pp. 428–32.

87 *Ibid.*, pp. 423–24. Aristotle himself does not list these four causes of dreams together; they are, however, consistent with his explanation of the mechanisms of dreaming.

88 Vincent recognizes that Albert here raises an issue more appropriately considered later

in the discussion of dreaming. When he adapts this portion of the *Summa* ("An somnium passio sit intellectus?" chapters 37–38, cols. 1863–64), Vincent leaves out the reference to "revelationes Angelorum," instead incorporating this material into a later chapter whose explicit subject is revelation ("De reuelationibus quae fiunt in somniis," chapter 56, col. 1874).

89 See Albert, *Summa de creaturis*, pp. 433 and 437; and Vincent, *Speculum naturale*, book 26, chapter 52, col. 1871, and chapter 54, col. 1872.

90 See p. 18 above.

91 See Albert, *Summa de creaturis*, p. 432, and Aristotle, *De divinatione* 462b and 463a.

92 See Albert, *Summa de creaturis*, p. 433, and Avicenna, *Avicenna latinus: Liber de anima*, p. 32.

93 Vincent, *Speculum naturale*, book 26, chapter 54, col. 1872, and Albert, *Summa de creaturis*, p. 435. Compare Aristotle, *De divinatione* 462b–63a.

94 See Albert, *Summa de creaturis*, p. 435, and Aristotle, *De divinatione* 463a.

95 See Albert, *Summa de creaturis*, p. 436, and Aristotle, *De divinatione* 463a.

96 See Albert, *Summa de creaturis*, p. 436, and see the discussion of the dreamlunar in chapter 1 above.

97 See Albert, *Summa de creaturis*, p. 436. Aristotle's brief discussion of "weather-signs, e.g., those of rain or wind" (*De divinatione* 463b, Beare [trans.]), is probably an ultimate source for the treatment of "elemental" dreams in Albert and Vincent.

98 See Albert, *Summa de creaturis*, p. 436. Aristotle, *De divinatione* 463a, discusses somatically- and psychologically-stimulated predictive dreams.

99 *Ibid.*, 463b, Beare (trans.).

100 Aristotle, *De divinatione per somnum* 463a–b, Drossaart Lulofs (ed.) [*vetus translatio*], p. 38; my translation.

101 See Albert, *Summa de creaturis*, p. 436. In a passage not reproduced by Vincent, Albert goes even further in defining the position of transcendent dreams. Replying to the suggestion that "somnium non sit ab intelligentiis separatis, quae dicuntur Angeli" [the dream may not be from the separate intelligences that are called angels] (p. 435), Albert essentially replaces the accidental dream with the revelatory: "Ad ultimum dicendum, quod omnia somnia illa quae non manifestantur in signis corporalibus vel causis, supra nostram sunt prudentiam, ut dicit Philosophus, et sunt revelationes ab intelligentiis traditae humanis animabus" [To the last (statement) it must be said that all those dreams that are not manifested in corporeal signs or in causes are above our knowledge, as the Philosopher (Aristotle) says, and are revelations handed down from intelligences to human souls] (p. 437). For another interesting modification of the Aristotelian "accidental" dream, see Albert's *De fato*, in Aquinas, *Opera omnia*, Busa (ed.), VII, article 1, argument 8, p. 47, col. 3.

102 This portion of the argument is left out of the *Speculum naturale*. Vincent, however, does not avoid the argument itself. See the discussion below.

103 Albert, *Summa de creaturis*, p. 438.

104 *Ibid.*

105 *Ibid.*

106 *Ibid.* Compare Augustine's treatment of prophecy, *De Genesi* XII.9.20, cited above.

107 Albert, *Summa de creaturis*, p. 438.

108 This material is derived from earlier in Albert's discussion (p. 404). See note 88 above.

109 Albert, *Summa de creaturis*, p. 441.

110 *Ibid.*, p. 442.

111 *Ibid.*, p. 441. See Augustine, *De Genesi* XII.14.29.

112 Within my translation, I cite, in slightly modified form, Taylor's translation of Augustine, *De Genesi* XII.14.29, p. 197.

113 Albert, *Summa de creaturis*, p. 442. Similar questions are often posed in the writings indebted to Aristotelianism; see Gregory, "I sogni e gli astri," pp. 119–21, and Tocci, "Teoria e interpretazione dei sogni," p. 267.

114 Aristotle's own positions on dreaming were often questioned by the Arabic Aristotelians, allowing writers like Albert and Vincent to bring together more easily Aristotelian and Christian theories; see Gregory's comments on Arabic Aristotelianism and its reassertion of the importance of the divinatory dream ("I sogni e gli astri," p. 118).

115 Albert, *Summa de creaturis*, p. 443.

116 *Ibid.*

117 The chance involved in *eventus* is not the same as the chance of Aristotle's accidentally-predictive dreams. "Coincidental" dreams are *predictive* by chance; they do not, however, arise out of chance processes, but rather from the normal (natural) functioning of physiology and psychology.

118 Albert, *Summa de creaturis*, p. 445.

119 *Ibid.*

120 *Ibid.*; see Aristotle, *De divinatione* 464a–b.

121 Albert, *Summa de creaturis*, p. 445. Borgnet's edition of the *Summa* here reads: "Dicit enim, quod non semper hoc est falsum, quod somnia *non* sunt a Deo: et per hoc innuit quandoque somnia esse per revelationem divinam" [He says, truly, that it is not always false that dreams are *not* from God, and through this he approves (the idea) that dreams sometimes arise through divine revelation] (my emphasis). The additional "non" confuses the passage; still, even if the "non" is authorial, Albert, in the second half of the statement, affirms Aristotle's partial approval of divine dreams.

122 "Cognitio solum" probably derives from Isidore of Seville's version of Gregory's scheme (*Sententiae*, PL 83, col. 669); see chapter 4, note 30, above.

123 It is most likely that Albert here borrowed from Jean de la Rochelle's *Summa de anima*, Bibliothèque Nationale, MS Latin 6686.A, ff. 51ʳ⁻ᵛ.

124 Another thirteenth-century writer, St. Bonaventure, explicitly signals his own movement away from "philosophical" authorities toward Christian ones in the discussion of dreams contained in his *Commentaria in quatuor libros Sententiarum*, book 2, *dist.* 7, part 2, article 1, question 3, *ad* 3, p. 195: "quidquid de hoc senserint philosophi, quorum positiones longum esset hic retexere, quod de eis dicit sacra Scriptura indubitanter est tenendum" [whatever the philosophers may have thought about this – and it would be long to unravel their positions here – that which sacred Scripture says about them (dreams) is to be held without doubt].

125 Vincent borrows from Gregory's *Moralia* to supplement the material Albert cites from the *Dialogues*. On Vincent's use of Gregory, see Lieser, "Vinzenz von Beauvais," pp. 7 and 34–35.

126 On Vincent's indebtedness to Jean, see Lieser, "Vinzenz von Beauvais," p. 8, and Minges, "Exzerpte aus Alexander von Hales," p. 53.

127 Compare Jean de la Rochelle, *Summa de anima*, f. 51ʳ, and the *De spiritu et anima*, chapter 25, *PL* 40, col. 798, Leiva and Ward (trans.), pp. 220–21.

128 The Douai edition here reads "ver*m*."

129 I have not found a parallel passage in the *De spiritu et anima*. The source passage in Jean

de la Rochelle, *Summa de anima*, f. 51ʳ, may be *generally* indebted to Augustine (via the *De spiritu*); see *De spiritu*, chapter 24, PL 40, col. 797, and Augustine, *De Genesi* XII.18.39 (cited above, pp. 38–39). On Vincent's indebtedness to Augustinian material, see Lieser, "Vinzenz von Beauvais," pp. 7 and 26–31. The distinction made at the end of the passage between the object of perception and the act of perception itself is a familiar one in late-antique and medieval philosophy: see, for instance, Boethius, *The Consolation of Philosophy*, V.E. Watts (trans.) (Harmondsworth: Penguin Books, 1969), book 5, prose 4, pp. 155–59; and Peter Abelard, *A Dialogue of a Philosopher with a Jew, and a Christian*, Pierre J. Payer (trans.) (Toronto: Pontifical Institute of Mediaeval Studies, 1979), p. 131.

130 Jean de la Rochelle, *Summa de anima*, f. 51ᵛ. See *De spiritu*, chapter 24, PL 40, col. 797, Leiva and Ward (trans.), p. 219; and Augustine, *De Genesi* XII.30.58, Taylor (trans.), p. 221, Zycha (ed.), pp. 424–25.

131 See Priscianus Lydus, *Solutiones*, p. 62.

132 For the Augustinian material, see Jean de la Rochelle, *Summa de anima*, f. 51ᵛ; *De spiritu et anima*, chapter 27, PL 40, col. 799, Leiva and Ward (trans.), pp. 222–23; Augustine, *De Genesi* XII.13.28–XII.14.29, Taylor (trans.), pp. 196–97, Zycha (ed.), pp. 398–99. For the Gregorian material, see Gregory, *Moralia*, book 8, chapter 43 and *Dialogues*, book 4, chapter 50.

133 Vincent further quotes Augustine on the "discretio spirituum" in *Speculum naturale*, book 26, chapter 99, cols. 1905–06.

134 In chapters 66–73, Vincent cites the following sources by name: "Augustinus in libro de diuinatione daemonum" (chapter 66); see Augustine, *De divinatione daemonum liber unus, PL* 40, col. 586. "Hieronimus super Mathaeum lib. 2" (chapter 67); see Jerome, *Commentariorum in evangelium Matthaei ad Eusebium libri quatuor, PL* 26, cols. 112–13. "Gennadius in lib. de diffinitionibus Ecclesiasticorum dogmatum" (chapter 69); see Gennadius, *Liber de ecclesiasticis dogmatibus, PL* 58, col. 999. "Beda super actus Apostolorum" (chapter 69); see Bede, *Super Acta apostolorum expositio, PL* 92, col. 954. "Hieronimus ubi sup." (chapter 70); see Jerome, *Commentarii in evangelium Matthaei, PL* 26, col. 113. On these sources, see Lieser, "Vinzenz von Beauvais," pp. 35–36. I have not been able to discover Vincent's source or soures for the remaining material in these chapters. Collections of *Sententiae* often consider the character of demonic and angelic action; see, for an early and influential example, Isidore of Seville's *Sentences, PL* 83, col. 661 (compare Vincent, chapter 67). Indeed, I suspect that much of the material in chapters 66–73 may be taken from a commentary on the second book of Peter Lombard's *Sentences*. Certain of the material in Vincent seems *ultimately* to be derived from Peter. Thus, Peter quotes the same portions of Gennadius and Bede that Vincent does in chapter 69 (col. 1880) (though Peter attributes the Gennadius text to Augustine); see Peter Lombard, *Sententiarum libri quatuor, PL* 192, col. 669. See also Albertus Magnus, *In secundum librum Sententiarum*, Borgnet (ed.), *Opera omnia*, XXVII, pp. 178–79.

The whole of Vincent's chapter 74 is taken from Thomas Aquinas, *Quaestiones disputatae de veritate* [*QDV*], question 11, article 3, in Busa (ed.), *Opera omnia*, III, p. 75. For a translation of the *QDV*, see Aquinas, *Truth*, 3 vols., Robert W. Mulligan, James V. McGlynn, and Robert W. Schmidt (trans.) (Chicago: Henry Regnery, 1952–54). On Vincent's indebtedness to Aquinas, see Minges, "Exzerpte aus Alexander von Hales," pp. 61–64, and Lieser, "Vinzenz von Beauvais," p. 8. For a brief discussion of Aquinas's complex treatment of prophecy in the *QDV*, see Gregory, "I sogni e gli astri," pp. 133–35.

135 Vincent's sources are as follows:

chapter 75: Augustine, *De Genesi* XII.6.15, XII.8.19, and XII.9.20–XII.10.21, Taylor (trans.), pp. 185–86, 188–89, and 190–91, Zycha (ed.), pp. 387, 390–91, and 392.

chapter 76: *Ibid.*, XII.16.32–33 and XII.24.51, Taylor (trans.), pp. 199–201 and 213–14, Zycha (ed.), pp. 401–03 and 416–17.

chapter 77: *Ibid.*, XII.11.22–24, Taylor (trans.), pp. 191–93, Zycha (ed.), pp. 392–95.

chapter 78: *Ibid.*, XII.25.52 and XII.14.29, Taylor (trans.), pp. 215–16 and 197, Zycha (ed.), pp. 417–18 and 399.

chapter 79: *Ibid.*, XII.14.30–XII.15.31, Taylor (trans.), pp. 197–99, Zycha (ed.), pp. 399–401.

chapter 80: *Ibid.*, XII.30.58–XII.32.61, Taylor (trans.), pp. 221–24, Zycha (ed.), pp. 424–27.

136 Vincent's sources are as follows:

chapter 81: Aquinas, *QDV* 12.1, p. 76; Augustine, *De Genesi* XII.9.20, Taylor (trans.), pp. 189–90, Zycha (ed.), p. 391; and Jerome, *Commentariorum in Isaiam prophetam libri duodeviginti*, *PL* 24, col. 19. I have not been able to identify the source(s) for additional material in this chapter.

chapter 82: Aquinas, *QDV* 12.1, pp. 76–77.

chapter 83: *Ibid.*, 12.4, pp. 79–80.

chapter 84: *Ibid.*, 12.4–5, pp. 79–80.

chapter 85: *Ibid.*, 12.6, pp. 80–81.

chapter 86: *Ibid.*

chapter 87: *Ibid.*, 12.7, pp. 81–82.

chapter 88: *Ibid.*, 12.8, p. 82.

chapter 89: *Ibid.*, 12.9, p. 83.

chapter 90: *Ibid.*, pp. 82–83.

chapter 91: *Ibid.*, p. 83.

chapter 92: *Ibid.*, 12.12, p. 85.

chapter 93: *Ibid.*, pp. 85–86.

chapter 94: *Ibid.*, 12.13, p. 86.

chapter 95: *Ibid.*

137 Vincent's sources are as follows:

chapter 96: Augustine, *De Genesi* XII.12.25–XII.13.27, Taylor (trans.), pp. 193–95, Zycha (ed.), pp. 395–98.

chapter 97: *Ibid.*, XII.18.40–XII.20.42, Taylor (trans.), pp. 204–06, Zycha (ed.), pp. 407–09.

chapter 98: *Ibid.*, XII.20.42–43, XII.22.45, and XII.22.48, Taylor (trans.), pp. 206–07, 209–10, and 211, Zycha (ed.), pp. 409–10, 412, and 414.

chapter 99: *Ibid.*, XII.13.28–XII.14.29, XII.17.34, and XII.26.53, Taylor (trans.), pp. 196–97, 201, and 216, Zycha (ed.), pp. 398, 403, and 418–19.

chapter 100: *Ibid.*, XII.26.54–XII.28.56 and XII.34.67, Taylor (trans.), pp. 216–19 and 228, Zycha (ed.), pp. 419–23 and 432.

chapter 101: Aquinas, *QDV* 13.1, p. 87.

chapter 102: *Ibid.*

chapter 103: *Ibid.*, 13.2, p. 88.

chapter 104: *Ibid.*, 13.3, p. 89.

chapter 105: *Ibid.*, pp. 88–89.

chapter 106: *Ibid.*, p. 89.

chapter 107: *Ibid.*, 13.4, p. 90.

chapter 108: *Ibid.*, pp. 89–90.

chapter 109: *Ibid.*, 13.5, p. 90.

chapter 110: *Ibid.*, pp. 90–91.

chapter 111: *Ibid.*, 13.2, p. 88.

138 See Peden, "Macrobius," p. 65.

139 Raoul de Longchamps, *In Anticlaudianum Alani commentum*; the discussion of the "virtutes animae" and of dreaming occurs on pp. 43–61. I cite page numbers parenthetically in my text.

140 See Aristotle, *De somniis* 461a and 462b.

141 I have not been able to identify the Aristotelian "Commentator" to whom Raoul here refers; see Sulowski's note in his edition of Raoul, *In Anticlaudianum*, p. 54.

142 See *ibid.*

143 Much of this material is taken from the *De spiritu et anima*, and most of it is quoted in Vincent of Beauvais, *Speculum naturale*. See the discussion of Vincent above. I cite folio numbers from Bibliothèque Nationale, MS Latin 6686.A parenthetically in my text.

144 William, however, cites both Macrobius and Augustine as sources for this material, where Jean had referred it only to Augustine; see *Liber de anima*, *Mediaeval Studies* 11 (1949), 275. William also refers to Macrobius's scheme earlier in the *Liber*, *Mediaeval Studies* 10 (1948), 241–42.

145 William of Vaurouillon, *Liber de anima*, *Mediaeval Studies* 11 (1949), 276. See Brady's note on the attribution to Jerome.

146 *Ibid.*, 277.

147 *Ibid.* For the Latin source, see Averroes, *Compendia librorum Aristotelis qui Parva naturalia vocantur*, p. 95: "Dicunt enim quod sompnia sunt ab angelis et divinationes a demonibus et prophetie a Deo, aut cum medio aut sine medio" [they say, truly, that dreams are from angels and divinations from demons and prophecies from God, either with or without an intermediary].

148 William of Vaurouillon, *Liber de anima*, *Mediaeval Studies* 11 (1949), 277. See also p. 275.

149 Albert's commentary is found in vol. IX of Borgnet's edition of the *Opera omnia*; parenthetical page references are to this edition. Some of the same material is presented in part 6 of [Pseudo-]Albertus Magnus, *Liber de apprehensione*, Borgnet (ed.), *Opera omnia*, V, esp. pp. 611–14 for the thirteen grades of visionary experience. See Gregory's discussion of Albert's system, "I sogni e gli astri," pp. 121–33.

150 See pp. 88–89 above.

151 Differing grades of spiritual and intellectual vision are recognized by Augustine, *De Genesi* XII.29.57, Taylor (trans.), p. 220. However, Albert's system perhaps most closely resembles the hierarchical treatment of "grades of prophecy" presented by the Jewish Aristotelian, Moses Maimonides, *The Guide of the Perplexed*, Shlomo Pines (trans.) (Chicago: University of Chicago Press, 1963), part 2, chapter 45, pp. 395–403. See Colette Sirat's discussion of Maimonides, *Les Théories des visions surnaturelles dans la pensée juive du Moyen-Age* (Leiden: E.J. Brill, 1969), pp. 136–46. Maimonides's discussion of prophecy fits into broader Neoplatonic and Aristotelian traditions within Jewish philosophy; it is also related to the thought of Arabic Aristotelians such as Avicenna and Averroes. See Sirat, esp. pp. 61–88 and 126–58.

152 That Albert was familiar with Macrobius's classification of dreams is clear. See chapter 4, note 55, above. That Albert was thinking of Macrobius when he composed his commentary on Aristotle's *De divinatione* is also evident: in discussing the seventh

kind of vision, he mentions the "Somnium Scipionis" (p. 192). Influenced by Albert, William of Vaurouillon later associated Macrobius with the idea of a "lumen" that more or less clearly illuminates dreams; see his *Summa de anima, Mediaeval Studies* 10 (1948), 241–42.

153 Pack, "De pronosticatione sompniorum," pp. 258–60 and 262–64. The treatise is sometimes ascribed to Arnald of Villanova or to "frater Albertus" (presumably Albertus Magnus). See the discussion of William's work in Gregory, "I sogni e gli astri," pp. 137–41. For a fifteenth-century use of the "De pronosticatione," see Roger A. Pack, "A Treatise on Prognostications by Venancius of Moerbeke," *AHDLMA* 43 (1976), 311–22, esp. 311–12, 314, and 320.

6 DREAMS AND FICTION

1 Fischer, *Complete Medieval Dreambook*, p. 9; and see Fischer's bibliography of critical attempts to apply the medieval dreambooks to the interpretation of literary dreams (p. 169, n. 25).

2 Simone Collin, "L'Emploi des clefs des songes dans la littérature médiévale," *Bulletin Philologique et Historique*, II (1967) (Paris: Bibliothèque Nationale, 1969), pp. 851–66; the citation is from p. 866. Also see Önnerfors, *Mediaevalia*, on the influence works like the *Somniale Danielis* may have exerted on Germanic literature (pp. 48–57); and for interesting discussions of the relation between literary dreams and various kinds of dream lore, see the work of Klaus Speckenbach: "Von den Troimen. Über den Traum in Theorie und Dichtung," in Helmut Rücker and Kurt Otto Seidel (eds.), *"Sagen mit Sinne": Festschrift für Marie-Luise Dittrich zum 65. Geburtstag* (Göppingen: Alfred Kümmerle, 1976), pp. 169–204, and "Form, Funktion und Bedeutung der Träume im *Lancelot-Gral-Zyklus*," in Gregory (ed.), *I sogni nel medioevo*, pp. 317–55.

3 Thus, Boccaccio must have known Macrobius's five-fold system for classifying dreams, since he quotes it in his *Genealogiae* (see the discussion of Boccaccio in chapter 5 above); however, whether Boccaccio meant to evoke Macrobian theory in his literary dream visions is more difficult to ascertain.

4 Peden, "Macrobius," p. 70.

5 On the possible sources of Chaucer's dream lore, see, for instance, Aiken, "Vincent of Beauvais"; Hazelton, "Chaucer and Cato," esp. pp. 368–69 and 371–73; and Pratt, "Some Latin Sources."

6 Peden, "Macrobius," p. 69.

7 The best study of the genre as a whole remains Spearing's *Medieval Dream-Poetry*. Lynch's recent *High Medieval Dream Vision* is an especially full and perceptive treatment of a subgenre of dream poem. Other recent examinations of the genre include Russell, *English Dream Vision*, and Christiane Marchello-Nizia, "La Rhétorique des songes et le songe comme rhétorique dans la littérature française médiévale," in Gregory (ed.), *I sogni nel medioevo*, pp. 245–59.

8 While not, strictly speaking, a *dream* vision, the Apocalypse strongly influenced medieval dream narrative. See, for instance, the imagery of the Middle English *Pearl*, or even Chaucer's *House of Fame*. As Newman points out, "Somnium," pp. 114–15 and 171–77, the Apocalypse is closely related to the dream in Augustinian thought: both figure as kinds of spiritual vision.

9 I cite Ovid, *Heroides and Amores*, Grant Showerman (ed. and trans.), Loeb Classical Library (Cambridge, Mass.: Harvard University Press; and London: William

Heinemann, 1958), giving line numbers parenthetically in my text. Ovid's authorship of the poem is disputed; for the sake of convenience, I will refer to the author as Ovid. Newman briefly discusses the influence of this short poem, "Somnium," pp. 236 and 243–44.

10 See, for instance, Constance B. Hieatt, *The Realism of Dream Visions: The Poetic Exploitation of the Dream-Experience in Chaucer and His Contemporaries* (The Hague and Paris: Mouton, 1967), pp. 20–22. Spearing, in examining the early tradition of dream vision, also emphasizes "higher," educative visions, though his discussion is more complete and subtle than Hieatt's; he admits, for instance, the presence of "lower" elements even in serious, didactic visions (*Medieval Dream-Poetry*, p. 24).

11 Gregory's six-fold division of dream experience in book IV of the *Dialogues* is surrounded by anecdotal accounts of dreams and visions, and his theoretical discussion is followed immediately by the story of a misleading dream that its recipient erroneously believes to be reliable.

12 George Philip Krapp and Elliott Van Kirk Dobbie (eds.), *The Exeter Book*, The Anglo–Saxon Poetic Records, 3 (New York: Columbia University Press, 1936), pp. 49–72.

13 See *Guthlac A*, lines 557–76.

14 See *ibid.*, lines 412–20.

15 Gregory's *Dialogues* and the genre of the saint's life, however, were extremely popular in the Middle Ages and exerted important influences on dream-frame narrative.

16 For treatments of Strabo, see Max Manitius, *Geschichte der lateinischen Literatur des Mittelalters*, Handbuch der klassischen Altertums-Wissenschaft, 9, no. 2 (Munich: C.H. Beck'sche Verlagsbuchhandlung, 1911), I, pp. 302–14; Raby, *History of Christian–Latin Poetry*, pp. 183–89; and Önnerfors, *Mediaevalia*, pp. 58–201.

17 I quote from Walahfrid Strabo, *Walahfrid Strabo's Visio Wettini: Text, Translation, and Commentary*, David A. Traill (ed. and trans.) (Bern: Herbert Lang; and Frankfurt: Peter Lang, 1974), giving page numbers parenthetically in my text. The Latin, in Traill's edition, reads: "caelorum e culmine missus / Angelus . . . venit" (lines 294–95).

18 The Latin reads: "beatorum . . . Sedes" (lines 545–46).

19 See Traill (ed. and trans.), *Walahfrid Strabo's Visio Wettini*, pp. 63–66 and lines 656–734.

20 See *ibid.*, line 207: "Conclusis oculis penitus dormire nequibat" [closed his eyes, but had not yet been able to fall into a deep sleep] (p. 46). This line might be read as implying that Wetti is still awake (see the reading in Jacques LeGoff, *The Birth of Purgatory*, Arthur Goldhammer [trans.] [Chicago: The University of Chicago Press, 1984], p. 116), but Wetti clearly awakens later on ("Evigilat," line 262). Perhaps we are meant to connect Wetti's initial brief vision with dreams like Macrobius's deceptive *visum*, said to occur in a state between sleep and waking.

21 The Latin reads: "Spiritus ecce doli . . . / Clericus in specie" (lines 208–09).

22 The Latin reads: "Ille igitur dum tanta minans promittit" (line 221); "Turba . . . / . . . tetro agmine" (lines 222–23).

23 The Latin reads: "divina cito advenit clementia cursu: / Viderat in cella monachos sedisse nitentes, / Forma quibus radians" (lines 237–39).

24 It is interesting to note that Wetti, in response to the demons' terrifying assault, asks "to have read to him the last words in Gregory's work called the *Dialogus*" (p. 49) [Exposcitque legi sibi verba novissima sancti / Gregorii in scripto quod noscitur illius esse / Dialogus] (lines 283–85), a work that, of course, explicitly treats both angelic and demonic dreams. Wetti's reading matter is again referred to toward the beginning of his longer vision (lines 299–301).

25 The complete Latin passage reads: "Angelus haec addit, quidam quod praesul eundem / Deberet precibus factisque iuvare benignis, / Ante dies multos ceu demandaverat ipsi / Legato ostensus, quem tunc per somnia ferre / Hortatur sibi dicta patri" (lines 400–04).

26 The Latin reads: "Sed episcopus ille / Esse ratus soliti mendacia inania somni / Ludendo excepit dispecto fratris amore ... Post haec antistes dum cuncta ex ore ferentis / Audiit, 'Haec,' inquit, 'fantasmata credo fuisse / Idcircoque fidem verbis non commodo fictis'" (lines 404–06 and 428–30). Because he misreads the dream, the bishop is severely punished (lines 407–09 and 432–34); the episode thus serves to dramatize the dangers inherent in a failed "discretio somniorum."

27 The account of the cleric's dream, by presenting a misinterpreted veridical dream – and emphasizing the painful consequences of misinterpretation – also legislates (by contrast) the proper way to *read* Wetti's revelatory vision.

28 Walahfrid Strabo, "De quodam somnio ad Erluinum," Ernst Dümmler (ed.), Monumenta Germaniae Historica, Poetae Latini Aevi Carolini, 2 (Berlin: Weidmann, 1884), pp. 364–65; I cite line numbers from this edition parenthetically in my text. See Newman's brief discussion of the poem, "Somnium," pp. 243–44. Newman suggests an indebtedness to [Pseudo-]Ovid's *Amores*, book 3, poem 5 – Strabo's poem begins with an echo of the Ovidian opening, "Nox erat" – that would support reading the poem as participating in a tradition of "lower" dream visions going back at least to [Pseudo-]Ovid.

29 The appearance of the eagle calls to mind a third of Strabo's dream poems – "Ad eandem [i.e., Iudith imperatricem] de quodam somnio," Ernst Dümmler (ed.), Monumenta Germaniae Historica, Poetae Latini Aevi Carolini, 2, pp. 379–80. In this poem, we see *God* performing much the same action as Strabo's eagle: "deus, prisci *atra* timoris / *Nubila decutiens*" [God, *shaking off* the *dark clouds* of ancient fear] (11–12; my emphasis).

30 We also encounter the dream of eagle-borne flight in such later medieval works as Dante's *Purgatorio* and Chaucer's *House of Fame*. The tradition grows out of classical myth, especially the story of Ganymede; see *Purgatorio* 9.22–24, and line 589 of the *House of Fame*. The similarity between the poems of Strabo and Chaucer is quite striking, especially the burlesque tone of each. But Strabo was not popular in the late Middle Ages (Traill [ed.], *Visio Wettini*, pp. 17–18), and it seems unlikely that Chaucer knew his work. The similarities between the two poems are probably best ascribed to a use of similar traditions.

31 For similar suggestions of a double tradition in the medieval dream vision, see Phillip Whitcomb Damon, "Twelfth Century Latin Vision Poetry," dissertation, University of California, Berkeley, 1952, who discusses "a substantial body of twelfth century Latin verse in which the motif of the visionary journey is turned to a variety of purely secular uses" (p. 145); and Karl Forstner, "Das Traumgedicht Baudris von Bourgeuil (Carmen 37)," *Mittellateinisches Jahrbuch* 6 (1970), 45–57, esp. 54–55.

32 Lucian, "The Dream, or Lucian's Career," p. 231.

33 On the importance of philosophical and theological movements for late-medieval English poetry, see Laurence Eldredge, "Chaucer's *Hous of Fame* and the *Via Moderna*," *Neuphilologische Mitteilungen* 71 (1970), 105–19; Delany, *Chaucer's House of Fame*; Russell A. Peck, "Chaucer and the Nominalist Questions," *Speculum* 53 (1978), 745–60; Janet Coleman, *Piers Plowman and the Moderni* (Rome: Edizioni di Storia e Letteratura, 1981); and Holly Wallace Boucher, "Nominalism: The Difference for Chaucer and Boccaccio," *Chaucer Review* 20 (1985–86), 213–20.

34 For one important treatment of medieval esthetics, see Edgar de Bruyne, *Etudes d'esthétique médiévale* (Brussels: "De Tempel," 1946).

35 Francesco Petrarca, "Coronation Oration," in Ernest Hatch Wilkins (trans.), *Studies in the Life and Works of Petrarch* (Cambridge, Mass.: The Mediaeval Academy of America, 1955), p. 311.

36 Macrobius thus treats the *Somnium Scipionis* according to the rules of both philosophical *fiction* and *real-life* dream, but the implicit contradiction – between artistic construct and "real" experience – does not appear to concern him. See Charlotte Nell Cook Morse, "William Dunbar: His Vision Poetry and the Medieval Poetic Tradition," dissertation, Stanford University, 1969:

> [Macrobius] was among the first critics to recognize the value of the dream as a fictional device, apart from the worth of an actual dream for divination. His criticism bridged the gap between the dream as an everyday real occurrence and the dream as a purposeful invention of philosophers and poets, deliberately shaped to create meaning. (pp. 48–49)

Macrobius's willingness to treat a dream that he admits is fictional as though it were actual demonstrates how strongly he identified oneiric and fictional realms. Interestingly, Macrobius's contemporary, Favonius Eulogius, in prefatory remarks to his *Disputatio de Somnio Scipionis* (chapter 1, section 1, p. 13), brings fiction and dream together in a manner reminiscent of Macrobius.

37 Examples of such "fables" include "the comedies of Menander and his imitators, or the narratives replete with imaginary doings of lovers in which Petronius Arbiter so freely indulged and with which Apuleius, astonishingly, sometimes amused himself" (I.ii.8).

38 Instead of using "fables" to discuss God and Mind, the philosopher "resort[s] to similes and analogies" (I.ii.14).

39 Macrobius's definition of allegorical fiction is echoed repeatedly in the Middle Ages. See Petrarca, "Coronation Oration," pp. 306–07, and Boccaccio, *Genealogy of the Gods*, book 14, chapter 7, in Charles G. Osgood (ed. and trans.), *Boccaccio on Poetry* (Indianapolis and New York: Bobbs-Merrill, 1956 [1930]), pp. 39 and 157.

40 The difference here probably arises from a sense of the *volitional* component in the production of fiction. An author can *try* to fictionalize a realm not appropriately subject to the rules of fiction, breaching decorum; but a dreamer, granted a divine dream, does not *will* the revelations he or she receives. The dreamer is not personally responsible for the oneiric penetration of divine mysteries; rather, any such penetration reflects divine will.

41 See Spearing, *Medieval Dream-Poetry*, p. 10: "The precise terms used by Macrobius about the *somnium* are of special interest in implying that such dreams are 'natural' equivalents to the artifice of allegory, and thereby explaining why allegorical fictions so often come to be set in dreams." See also Lynch, *High Medieval Dream Vision*, pp. 66 and 74–75, and Ralph Howard Bloch, "A Study of the Dream Motif in the Old French Narrative," dissertation, Stanford University, 1970, p. 268.

42 Pascalis Romanus, *Liber thesauri occulti*, book 1, chapter 14, p. 160. Lynch comments briefly on this material, *High Medieval Dream Vision*, p. 74. The omission of a modifier – "tamquam," "velud," "ut" – between "somnium" and "allegoria" makes the connection between the two seem stronger than is the link between the other types of dream and their fictional analogues; rather than an analogy, Pascalis here seems almost to imply an *identity* between the middle dream and allegorical fiction.

43 Pascalis Romanus, *Liber thesauri occulti*, book 1, chapter 14, p. 161.
44 See Spearing's suggestion that

> a dream-poem, from the fourteenth century on, is a poem which has more fully
> realized its own existence as a poem . . . It . . . does not take for granted its own
> existence, but is continuously aware of its own existence and of the need,
> therefore, to justify that existence . . . The dream-poem becomes a device for
> expressing the poet's consciousness of himself as poet and for making his work
> reflexive. (*Medieval Dream-Poetry*, pp. 4–6)

See also Lynch's discussion, *High Medieval Dream Vision*, pp. 71–76.
45 See the following instances in Pascalis Romanus, *Liber thesauri occulti*:
tegumentum
Book 1, chapter 1, p. 141: "elegi tegumentum aptamque revelationem describere
videlicet sompnium"
Book 1, chapter 2, p. 147: "dedit eis Deus per tegumentum sompnii futura conspicere"
integumentum
Book 1, chapter 14, p. 160: "apperte et sine aliquo integumento debere prospicere
futura"
tectum
Book 1, chapter 13, p. 160: "tectum figuris et velatum ambagibus"; compare
Macrobius, *Commentary* I.iii.10.
figura
Book 1, chapter 3, p. 147: "Sompnium itaque est figura quam ymaginatur dormiens,
vel sompnium est ymaginatio in animo dormientis im-
pressa que comprehendit figuras aliquas vel ymaginatur"
Book 1, chapter 14, p. 161: "allegorice et per figuras"
Book 2, chapter 5, p. 169: "ostenditur figuris dormientibus"
involucrum
Book 1, chapter 1, p. 142: "amplius per enigmata et involucrum quam facie ad faciem
aliquid cernunt"
ambages
Book 1, chapter 13, p. 160: "tectum figuris et velatum ambagibus"; compare
Macrobius, *Commentary* I.iii.10.
Book 1, chapter 14, p. 160: "per ambages velata investiga(n)tur ab anima"
46 Pascalis Romanus, *Liber thesauri occulti*, book 1, chapter 1, p. 145.
47 *Ibid.*, p. 146.
48 Albertus Magnus, *De somno et vigilia*, Borgnet (ed.), *Opera omnia*, IX, pp. 179–85.
49 Pack, "De pronosticatione sompniorum," p. 259.
50 Significantly, John's definition of the sign emphasizes its middle (imaginative)
character: "A sign is something that makes an impression upon the senses and in
addition has some significance" (*Policraticus*, book 2, chapter 14, Pike [trans.], p. 74).
51 See especially John of Salisbury, *Policraticus*, book 2, chapters 16–17.
52 Holkot, *In librum Sapientiae, lectio* 202, p. 667.
53 *The Pilgrimage of the Lyfe of the Manhode*, Avril Henry (ed.), EETS, OS 288 (London:
Oxford University Press, 1985), pp. 174–75.
54 On the importance of the mirror in classical and medieval accounts of self-knowledge,
see Pierre Courcelle, *Connais-toi toi-même de Socrate à Saint Bernard*, 2 vols. (Paris: Etudes
Augustiniennes, 1974–75), pp. 22, 32, 49–51, 61, 71–72, 77–78, 176, 281, and 288. And

for a more general treatment of the medieval mirror, see Herbert Grabes, *The Mutable Glass: Mirror-Imagery in Titles and Texts of the Middle Ages and English Renaissance*, Gordon Collier (trans.) (Cambridge: Cambridge University Press, 1982). The most recent work on medieval mirrors, Edward Peter Nolan, *Now Through a Glass Darkly: Specular Images of Being and Knowing from Virgil to Chaucer* (Ann Arbor: The University of Michigan Press, 1990), appeared too late to be used in the present study.

55 Calcidius, *Commentary*, chapters 249–56, on dreams, and chapters 257–59, on mirrors. On the discussion of dreams, see chapter 2 above.

56 Algazel, *Algazel's Metaphysics* II.v.5, p. 189.

57 On Raoul's discussion of dreams in his *In Anticlaudianum*, see my treatment of "The medieval psychologists" in chapter 5 above. Raoul's exegesis of Alain's lines – "Dextra manus triplicis speculi triplicata nitore / Splendet" [Her right hand is resplendent, aflame with the brightness of a threefold mirror] (Alain de Lille, *Anticlaudianus*, Robert Bossuat [ed.] [Paris: J. Vrin, 1955], book 1, lines 450–51; translated by James J. Sheridan as *Anticlaudianus, or the Good and Perfect Man* [Toronto: Pontifical Institute of Mediaeval Studies, 1973], p. 63) – includes chapters 41–65; the dream discussion comprises chapters 49–60. Alain himself presents an interesting discussion of mirrors in his *Summa de arte praedicatoria*; see note 70 below.

58 Guillaume de Lorris and Jean de Meun, *Le Roman de la rose*, Daniel Poirion (ed.) (Paris: Garnier-Flammarion, 1974), lines 18043–286 (on mirrors) and 18287–514 (on dreams).

59 *Ibid.*, lines 1432–680.

60 Dante, *Purgatorio* 27.94–114. On a pervasive pattern of Narcissus/mirror imagery in the *Divine Comedy*, see Kevin Brownlee, "Dante and Narcissus (*Purg.* xxx, 76–99)," *Dante Studies* 96 (1978), 201–06, esp. 205–06, n. 7.

61 I have not been able to consult Stürzinger's rare Roxburghe Club edition (1893) of the first version (1330–31) of Deguileville's *Pelerinage*; no modern edition of the second version of the poem (1355) exists. Two Middle English renderings are, however, available in the Early English Text Society series: John Lydgate's *The Pilgrimage of the Life of Man*, F. J. Furnivall (ed.), EETS, ES 77, 83 (London: Kegan Paul, Trench, Trübner and Co., 1899, 1901) [dated 1426, a translation of Deguileville's second version]; and *The Pilgrimage of the Lyfe of the Manhode* [dated *c.* 1400, an anonymous prose translation of the first French version]. Mirrors appear at lines 317–22, 5990–6012, 6698–712, 7085–92, 11643, 14001–03, 14715–62, 19717–22, 22254, 22343–54, 22371–518, and 24800–04 of Lydgate's version, and at lines 19–21, 1743–52, 1870–76, 2009–14, 3687–88, 3960–61, 4373–91, 4849–50, 5753–55, and 7257–59 of the prose *Pilgrimage*. See V. A. Kolve, *Chaucer and the Imagery of Narrative: The First Five Canterbury Tales* (Stanford: Stanford University Press, 1984), pp. 51–53, for a discussion of the poem and some of its mirrors.

62 In the C Version of *Piers*, there are two "mirrors of Middle-earth"; see William Langland, *Piers Plowman by William Langland: An Edition of the C-Text*, Derek Pearsall (ed.) (Berkeley and Los Angeles: University of California Press, 1979 [1978]), XI.171 and XIII.131. The B Version contains only one of the two mirrors; see Langland, *Piers Plowman: The B Version: Will's Visions of Piers Plowman, Do-Well, Do-Better and Do-Best*, George Kane and E. Talbot Donaldson (eds.) (London: University of London, Athlone Press, 1975), XI.9, corresponding to C.XI.171. The mirror of C.XIII.131 is, in the B text, the "*mountaigne* that Mydelerd hy3te" (XI.315; my emphasis). Neither mirror appears in the A Version or in the Z Text; see Langland, *Piers Plowman: The A Version: Will's Visions of Piers Plowman and Do-Well*, George Kane (ed.) (London:

216

University of London, Athlone Press, 1960), and Langland, *Piers Plowman: The Z Version*, A.G. Rigg and Charlotte Brewer (eds.), Studies and Texts, 59 (Toronto: Pontifical Institute of Mediaeval Studies, 1983). For a reading of the mirrors of the C Version, see Steven F. Kruger, "Mirrors and the Trajectory of Vision in *Piers Plowman*," *Speculum* 66 (1991), 74–95.

63 Alain de Lille, *The Plaint of Nature*, James J. Sheridan (trans.) (Toronto: Pontifical Institute of Mediaeval Studies, 1980), p. 221.

64 Chaucer, *Canterbury Tales* V.371–72, *Riverside Chaucer*.

65 *Ibid.*, I.1380–407; the dream is at lines 1380–98 and the mirror at lines 1399–407. Neither dream nor mirror comes from Chaucer's major source, Boccaccio's *Teseida*. See Vincent J. DiMarco's note to lines 1384–92, *Riverside Chaucer*, p. 832.

66 John Gower, *The English Works of John Gower*, 2 vols., G.C. Macaulay (ed.), EETS, ES 81, 82 (London: Kegan Paul, Trench, Trübner and Co., 1900–01); the "Avision" is at *Confessio Amantis* VIII.2440–807, the mirror at VIII.2810–57. Gower's tale of Virgil's mirror (*Confessio Amantis* V.2031–224) also brings mirrors and dreams together; here, the destruction of Rome's truth-telling mirror depends on a series of fabricated dreams.

67 Robert Henryson, *The Poems of Robert Henryson*, Denton Fox (ed.) (Oxford: Clarendon Press, 1981); the dream is at lines 141–347 of the *Testament of Cresseid*, the mirror at lines 347–50.

68 Alexander Neckam, *De naturis rerum libri duo*, Thomas Wright (ed.) (London: Longman, Green, Longman, Roberts, and Green, 1863), book 2, chapter 154, p. 239, explicitly associates the mirror with processes of literary interpretation:

> Dum integrum est speculum, unica uno solo inspiciente resultat imago; frangatur in plures vitrum, quot sunt ibi fractiones, tot resultabunt imagines. Sic et in Sacra Scriptura, quot sunt expositiones, totidem relucent intelligentiae. Sed, mira res! subtrahe plumbum suppositum vitro, jam nulla resultabit imago inspicientis. Subtrahe et fundamentum fidei, jam teipsum in Sacra Scriptura non videbis dilucide. Potest et per plumbum intelligi peccatum. In speculo igitur Sacrae Scripturae minus limpide teipsum cernes, nisi te esse peccatorem fatearis. Si enim dixerimus quia peccatum non habemus, nos ipsos seducimus, et veritas in nobis non est.

> While a mirror is whole, one sole image is reflected to the single one looking into it; should the glass be broken into many (pieces), as many images will be reflected as there are fragments there. Thus also in sacred Scripture: just as many understandings shine forth as there are expositions. But – a wondrous thing! – take away the lead placed under the glass, and then no image of the one looking into [the mirror] will be reflected. Likewise, take away the foundation of faith, and then you will not see yourself clearly in sacred Scripture. By the lead, sin can also be understood. Accordingly, you will perceive yourself less clearly in the mirror of sacred Scripture, if you do not confess yourself to be a sinner. Truly, if we have said that we do not have sin, we lead ourselves astray, and truth is not within us.

69 The information revealed by the mirror may pertain to the natural world (see, for instance, Guillaume de Lorris and Jean de Meun, *Le Roman de la rose*, lines 18046–54 and 18061–77) or to supernatural verities. The association between mirrors and a knowledge of the highest realities is, of course, ultimately biblical; see 1 Corinthians 13:12, and Wisdom 7:26.

70 Frederick Goldin, *The Mirror of Narcissus in the Courtly Love Lyric* (Ithaca, N.Y.: Cornell

University Press, 1967), pp. 4–5. See also Ritamary Bradley, "Backgrounds of the Title *Speculum* in Mediaeval Literature," *Speculum* 29 (1954), 112, citing the triple mirrors of Alain de Lille's *Summa de arte praedicatoria* (*PL* 210, cols. 118–19). Alain's treatment of mirrors parallels his discussion of dreams (cols. 126–27 and 195–96; see "Twelfth-century dream hierarchies" in chapter 4 above).

71 See Goldin, *Mirror of Narcissus*, pp. 6–7 and 20; and Grabes, *Mutable Glass*, pp. 118–19 and 134–36. For further discussion of the associations between Narcissus's mirror and "the theme of earthly impermanence," see R.E. Kaske, "*Piers Plowman* and Local Iconography," *Journal of the Warburg and Courtauld Institutes* 31 (1968), 164, and Joseph S. Wittig, "'Piers Plowman' B, Passus IX–XII: Elements in the Design of the Inward Journey," *Traditio* 28 (1972), 235.

72 Cited in Goldin, *Mirror of Narcissus*, pp. 64–65; see also Grabes, *Mutable Glass*, p. 109.

73 See Bradley, "Backgrounds of the Title *Speculum*," pp. 102–03, 105, and 109–13; Goldin, *Mirror of Narcissus*, pp. 5 and 9–13; Grabes, *Mutable Glass*, pp. 76 and 93–95; and see the passage cited from Alexander Neckam in note 68 above.

74 See Ernst Robert Curtius, *European Literature and the Latin Middle Ages*, Willard R. Trask (trans.) (Princeton, N.J.: Princeton University Press, 1973 [1953]), pp. 319–26, for an important discussion of the Book of Nature. Curtius calls our attention to Alain de Lille's striking identification of the creation as a book, picture, and mirror in one: "Omnis mundi creatura, / Quasi liber, et pictura / Nobis est, et speculum. / Nostrae vitae, nostrae mortis, / Nostri status, nostrae sortis / Fidele signaculum" [Each creature of the world is for us a sort of book and picture and mirror. Of our life, of our death, of our state, of our fate, a trustworthy sign] (*PL* 210, col. 579). The idea of the cosmos as mirror of an ideal realm is of course ultimately Platonic. Among the Neoplatonists, Macrobius's depiction of creation as a process of sequential mirrorings is especially noteworthy:

> Since Mind emanates from the Supreme God and Soul from Mind, and [Soul], indeed, forms and suffuses all below with life, and since this is the one splendor lighting up everything and visible in all, like a countenance reflected in many mirrors arranged in a row, and since all follow on in continuous succession, degenerating step by step in their downward course, the close observer will find that from the Supreme God even to the bottommost dregs of the universe there is one tie, binding at every link and never broken. This is the golden chain of Homer. (*Commentary* I.xiv.15)

75 For a wide-ranging consideration of the idea that the soul is a mirror in which God can be known, see Hans Leisegang, "La Connaissance de Dieu au miroir de l'âme et de la nature," *Revue d'Histoire et de Philosophie Religieuses* 17 (1937), 145–71. See also Grabes, *Mutable Glass*, pp. 88–89.

76 See Bradley, "Backgrounds of the Title *Speculum*," and Grabes, *Mutable Glass*.

77 See the comments in Avril Henry, "þe Pilgrimage of þe Lyfe of þe Manhode: The Large Design, with Special Reference to Books 2–4," *Neuphilologische Mitteilungen* 87 (1986), 229–36, esp. 236. In citing the *Pilgrimage*, I will follow Henry's EETS edition, giving line numbers parenthetically in my text. For additional material pertinent to the mirror's doubleness, see the "Agyographe" episode in Lydgate's *Pilgrimage* (lines 22283–518), not contained in the anonymous Middle English prose translation.

78 See the *Pilgrimage*, lines 3686–88, 3958–61, and 4373–91. Interestingly, Oiseuce's use of the mirror is associated with her enjoyment of vain fictions (3686–93), and Orgoill's

mirror is clearly connected to the myth of Echo and Narcissus (4388–91). For further medieval associations between vicious self-concern and mirrors, see Guillaume de Lorris and Jean de Meun, *Le Roman de la rose*, line 557 (Guillaume's Oiseuse is clearly the model for the Oiseuce of the *Pilgrimage*); Meg Twycross, *The Medieval Anadyomene: A Study in Chaucer's Mythography* (Oxford: Basil Blackwell, Society for the Study of Mediaeval Languages and Literature, 1972), pp. 24 and 82–92; Morton W. Bloomfield, *The Seven Deadly Sins: An Introduction to the History of a Religious Concept, with Special Reference to Medieval English Literature* (East Lansing: Michigan State College Press, 1952), pp. 104 and 442; and Kaske, "*Piers Plowman* and Local Iconography," pp. 163–66, esp. 164, n. 14.

79 The initial, specular imaging of the goal of the pilgrimage is recalled as the pilgrim finally nears that goal: "þou art at þe wiket and at þe dore þat þou seygh sumtime in þe mirro*ur*" (7257–59).

80 See Goldin, *Mirror of Narcissus*, pp. 9–13. The materiality of the mirror is of course a concession to the limitations of human perception and understanding; see 1 Corinthians 13:12.

81 See Wisdom 7:26.

82 Augustine's *De Genesi ad litteram* is fundamental to a medieval epistemology that emphasizes human involvement in both the corporeal and the intellectual (and the mediation of body and idea by imaginative or spiritual vision).

83 Many late-antique and medieval writers – from pseudo-Dionysius to the Victorines to Thomas Aquinas, Bartholomaeus Anglicus, and Pierre Bersuire – define a similar epistemology of ascent. See Minnis, "Langland's Ymaginatif," and Wittig, "'Piers Plowman' B," on how the tradition manifests itself in several of these writers.

84 On the connections between self-knowledge and a knowledge of divinity, see Courcelle, *Connais-toi*, and Leisegang, "La Connaissance de Dieu."

85 Julian of Norwich, *A Book of Showings to the Anchoress Julian of Norwich*, part 2, Long Text, Edmund Colledge and James Walsh (eds.), Studies and Texts, 35, part 2 (Toronto: Pontifical Institute of Mediaeval Studies, 1978), chapter 68 (revelation 16), pp. 639–40. Compare the Short Text, in part 1 of the Pontifical Institute edition, chapter 22, p. 268.

86 Julian of Norwich, *Book of Showings*, Long Text, chapter 68 (revelation 16), pp. 642–43. In their notes, Colledge and Walsh here document Julian's indebtedness to Augustine's *Confessions*.

87 I cite Nicole Oresme, *Nicole Oresme and the Kinematics of Circular Motion: Tractatus de commensurabilitate vel incommensurabilitate motuum celi*, Edward Grant (ed. and trans.) (Madison: The University of Wisconsin Press, 1971), providing (parenthetically in my text) book and line numbers from Grant's Latin edition and page numbers from his English translation. Oresme (born *c.* 1320–25, died 1382), was one of the fourteenth century's greatest scientists. For a biographical sketch, see Nicole Oresme, *De proportionibus proportionum and Ad pauca respicientes*, Edward Grant (ed. and trans.) (Madison: The University of Wisconsin Press, 1966), pp. 3–10. The *Tractatus* cannot be precisely dated, but it was probably written between 1351 and 1362; see Grant (ed. and trans.), *Kinematics*, pp. 4–5.

88 For a basic discussion of the terms *commensurabile* and *incommensurabile*, see Nicole Oresme, *Quaestiones super geometriam Euclidis*, H.L.L. Busard (ed.), *Janus*, Suppléments, 3 (Leiden: E.J. Brill, 1961), esp. *quaestio* 7. For discussions of (in)commensurability more directly pertinent to Oresme's *Tractatus*, see both the *De proportionibus*

proportionum, esp. chapter 3, proposition X (pp. 246–55), and the *Ad pauca respicientes*. See also Oresme, *Nicole Oresme and the Astrologers: A Study of his Livre de divinacions*, G.W. Coopland (ed. and trans.) (Cambridge, Mass.: Harvard University Press, 1952), pp. 54–55; and Oresme, "Maistre Nicole Oresme, Le livre du ciel et du monde: Text and Commentary," Albert D. Menut and Alexander J. Denomy (eds.), *Mediaeval Studies* 3 (1941), 252–55. Grant (ed. and trans.), *De proportionibus proportionum*, pp. 74–80, argues that the *Tractatus* is a reworking and expansion of the *Ad pauca respicientes*.

89 On the (ultimately Platonic) idea of a Great Year, see Grant (ed. and trans.), *Kinematics*, pp. 103–24.

90 Chaucer, *Parliament of Fowls*, lines 67–69, *Riverside Chaucer*.

91 My addition.

92 The Latin here reads, "Tunc ego, bone pater mi, intelligo." I would translate somewhat differently than does Grant: "Then I [say]: 'my dear father, I understand.'"

93 See Wesley Trimpi, *Muses of One Mind: The Literary Analysis of Experience and its Continuity* (Princeton, N.J.: Princeton University Press, 1983), pp. 287–95, on the philosophical and rhetorical traditions of the *disputatio in utramque partem* and the implications of such traditions for literary works.

94 See Grant (ed. and trans.), *Kinematics*, pp. 71–72, for further discussion of Oresme's reasons for "employ[ing] two separate orations set within a dream rather than . . . a continuous but imaginary dialogue" (p. 71).

95 I have included my own translation of the last clause. The Latin reads, "que solent uti solum demonstrationibus omnem aliam argumentationem aspernantes," and Grant translates: "seeing how contemptuous they are of every other kind of argument usually employed solely in demonstrations."

96 For a neat summary of the main points of the argument, see Grant (ed. and trans.), *Kinematics*, pp. 68–69.

97 I would translate here: "with stronger, if fewer, arguments." Geometry's oration is, in fact, much shorter than Arithmetic's.

98 Grant (ed. and trans.), *Kinematics*, pp. 72–76.

99 As Grant notes, *Kinematics*, p. 348, the two quotations that end this passage are from Ovid, *Metamorphoses*, book 1, lines 85-86, and Claudian, *De raptu Proserpinae*, book 3, lines 41–42. I have completed the translation of the passage from Claudian – "Quid mentem traxisse polo, quid profuit altum erexisse caput" – (which Grant only translates in part) using the translation of Maurice Platnauer, *De raptu Proserpinae*, Loeb Classical Library: Claudian, 2 (London: William Heinemann; and New York: G.P. Putnam's Sons, 1922).

100 Also compare III.25–28 with III.439.

101 With Geometry's epistemological conclusions, compare the remarks in Oresme's Prologue, pp. 173–75.

102 See Grant (ed. and trans.), *Kinematics*, p. 322, textual note to book 3, line 481.

7 DREAMS AND LIFE

1 Mary Douglas, *Purity and Danger: An Analysis of Concepts of Pollution and Taboo* (London: Routledge and Kegan Paul, 1966), esp. chapters 2 and 6. Also see Lynch's use of the work of Victor and Edith Turner in her discussion of the vision's "liminality" (*High Medieval Dream Vision*, pp. 46–52).

2 Compare Russell's suggestion that "the late medieval dream vision is a consciously

constructed anomaly which deconstructs the literary and scientific dream taxonomies by occupying the impossible space between the pathological and the divine, the somatic and the significant" (*English Dream Vision*, p. 81). I would suggest, however, that "the impossible [middle] space" is a concern not only of literary works, but of the dream taxonomies themselves.

3 Jean-Claude Schmitt, "Rêver au XIIe siècle," in Gregory (ed.), *I sogni nel medioevo*, pp. 291–316, discusses what autobiographical writings (specifically Guibert of Nogent's *De vita sua*) suggest about the nature of medieval dreaming. For a broad treatment of "real-life" accounts of visions and dreams in the Middle Ages, see Peter Dinzelbacher, *Vision und Visionsliteratur im Mittelalter* (Stuttgart: Anton Hiersemann, 1981).

4 The Latin text of Guibert's autobiography is available in the *Patrologia Latina*, *De vita sua sive monodiarum libri tres*, PL 156, cols. 837–962, and in Georges Bourgin (ed.), *Guibert de Nogent: Histoire de sa vie (1053–1124)* (Paris: Alphonse Picard, 1907). I have used Bourgin's edition. C.C. Swinton Bland's English translation is available, revised and edited by John F. Benton, as *Self and Society in Medieval France*. I quote from this translation and provide page numbers from Benton and from Bourgin parenthetically in my text, along with book and chapter citations. For discussions of Guibert's life and work, see Benton's introduction, *Self and Society*, pp. 7–33; Georg Misch, *Geschichte der Autobiographie* (Frankfurt: G. Schulte-Bulmke, 1955), III, part 1, pp. 108–62; and Bernard Monod, *Le Moine Guibert et son temps (1053–1124)* (Paris: Hachette, 1905). For an excellent treatment of Guibert's dreams, see Schmitt, "Rêver au XIIe siècle"; on one particular dream in the *De vita sua*, and its importance for the history of purgatory, see LeGoff, *Birth of Purgatory*, pp. 181–86.

5 The association between dreams and conversion experience is an ancient one. See, for instance, the connection made between dreaming and the emperor Constantine's conversion to Christianity as presented in Cynewulf's *Elene*, P.O.E. Gradon (ed.) (New York: Appleton–Century–Crofts, 1966 [1958]), lines 69–193. On the close relation between visionary experience and "Krisensituation," see Peter Dinzelbacher, "Körperliche und seelische Vorbedingungen religiöser Träume und Visionen," in Gregory (ed.), *I sogni nel medioevo*, pp. 57–86, esp. pp. 76–81. For the more specific connection between dreams and the choice of vocation, see Lucian's "Dream"; and for a dream involved with the decision to enter, or remain in, the monastic life, see Marvin L. Colker, "The Lure of Women, Hunting, Chess, and Tennis: A Vision," *Speculum* 59 (1984), 103–05.

6 We find teachers dreaming of their future students elsewhere in the literature of the Middle Ages, most notably in the widely-circulated account of a dream Socrates had in anticipation of Plato's arrival at the Academy. See Apuleius, *De Platone et eius dogmate*, Jean Beaujeu (ed. and trans.), *Opuscules philosophiques (Du Dieu de Socrate, Platon et sa doctrine, Du monde) et fragments* (Paris: Société d'Edition "Les Belles Lettres," 1973), book 1, section 1, pp. 60–61; Diogenes Laertius, *Lives of Eminent Philosophers*, R.D. Hicks (ed. and trans.), Loeb Classical Library (London: William Heinemann; and New York: G.P. Putnam's Sons, 1925), I, book 3, section 5, p. 281; John of Salisbury, *Policraticus*, book 2, chapter 16; Pack, "De pronosticatione sompniorum," p. 272; Walter Burley, *Liber de vita et moribus philosophorum*, Hermann Knust (ed.), Bibliothek des litterarischen Vereins, 177 (Tübingen, 1886), chapter 52, pp. 214–17 (Burley adopts John of Salisbury's account); and the French commentary on the *Echecs amoureux* attributed to Evrart de Conty, *L'Harmonie des sphères: Encyclopédie d'astronomie et de musique extraite du commentaire sur Les Echecs amoureux (XVe s.) attribué à Evrart de Conty*,

Reginald Hyatte and Maryse Ponchard-Hyatte (eds.) (New York: Peter Lang, 1985), chapter 16, section h, p. 36. For further references, see Knust's edition of Burley's *Liber*, pp. 216–17.

7 The connection between dreaming and literary conversion recalls St. Jerome's dream of the other world, Letter 22, to Eustachium, in Fremantle (trans.), *Principal Works of St. Jerome*, pp. 35–36.

8 Guibert de Nogent, *Tractatus de incarnatione contra Judaeos*, PL 156, cols. 489–528; the quotation is from col. 490. The translation is my own, but I have followed Benton's version of the *De vita sua* (*Self and Society*, p. 87) where it is directly echoed by the *Tractatus*.

9 I cite Pusey's translation of Augustine's *Confessions*, giving references parenthetically in my text.

10 I first became aware of Hermann's *Opusculum* through a lecture presented by Jeremy Cohen at Stanford University (February 5, 1985), now published as "The Mentality of the Medieval Jewish Apostate: Peter Alfonsi, Hermann of Cologne, and Pablo Christiani," in Todd M. Endelman (ed.), *Jewish Apostasy in the Modern World* (New York and London: Holmes and Meier, 1987), pp. 20–47. Professor Cohen later kindly provided me with bibliographical information that has proved essential to my work. Hermann of Cologne is also known, in the medieval sources and in modern scholarship, as "Hermannus Israelita," "Hermannus Judaeus," "Hermannus ex Judaeo Christianus," "Hermannus quondam Judaeus," and Hermann of Scheda (Cologne is the place of his birth, Scheda where he was Provost in 1170). Gerlinde Niemeyer has most recently edited the text of the *Opusculum*: Hermannus quondam Judaeus, *Opusculum de conversione sua*, Monumenta Germaniae Historica, Quellen zur Geistesgeschichte des Mittelalters, 4 (Weimar: Hermann Böhlaus Nachfolger, 1963). The text is also presented in the *Patrologia Latina*: Hermannus ex Judaeo Christianus, *De sua conversione opusculum*, PL 170, cols. 803–36. I cite Niemeyer's edition, giving chapter and page numbers parenthetically in my text. On Hermann's life, and on the *Opusculum*, see, in addition to Niemeyer's introduction (pp. 1–67) and Cohen's essay, J. Aronius, "Hermann der Prämonstratenser," *Zeitschrift für die Geschichte der Juden in Deutschland* 2 (1888), 217–31; Reinhold Seeberg, *Hermann von Scheda: Ein jüdischer Proselyt des zwölften Jahrhunderts*, Schriften des Institutum Judaicum in Leipzig, 30 (Leipzig: Akademische Buchhandlung [W. Faber], 1891); Misch, *Geschichte der Autobiographie*, III, part 1, pp. 505–22; Bernhard Blumenkranz, "Jüdische und christliche Konvertiten im jüdisch–christlichen Religionsgespräch des Mittelalters," in Paul Wilpert (ed.), *Judentum im Mittelalter: Beiträge zum christlich-jüdischen Gespräch* (Berlin: Walter de Gruyter, 1966), pp. 275–78; Arnaldo Momigliano, "A Medieval Jewish Autobiography," in Hugh Lloyd-Jones, Valerie Pearl, and Blair Warden (eds.), *History & Imagination: Essays in Honour of H.R. Trevor-Roper* (London: Duckworth, 1981), pp. 30–36; and Raoul Manselli, "Il sogno come premonizione, consiglio e predizione nella tradizione medioevale," in Gregory (ed.), *I sogni nel medioevo*, pp. 242–44.

11 Hermann lends a large sum of money to Bishop Ekbert of Münster, but, trusting the bishop's honesty, fails to obtain the customary security for the loan. His family and friends, disturbed by such unprofessional behavior, send him to the bishop's court to collect the money. It takes the bishop almost twenty weeks to repay the loan, during which time Hermann, with avid curiosity, begins to learn about the Christian religion and the life of Christians.

12 The Premonstratensian order of canons regular, following the rule of St. Augustine, was founded in 1120 by Norbert of Xanten at Prémontré. Hermann was associated with the houses at Cappenberg (founded 1122) and Scheda. For more on the Premonstratensians, see the *New Catholic Encyclopedia*, XI, pp. 737–39.

13 See, for instance, Misch's comments, *Geschichte der Autobiographie*, III, part 1, pp. 505–06.

14 For Hermann, the movement from Judaism to Christianity is largely a movement away from demonic temptation toward divine grace; his depiction of this movement owes a debt to hagiographic traditions. See Misch, *Geschichte der Autobiographie*, III, part 1, p. 506.

15 Compare especially Augustine's emphasis on learning to read allegorically: *Confessions* VI.3–4.3–6 and VI.11.18, Pusey (trans.), pp. 97–100 and 110–11.

16 On the Jews' blindness and deafness, see also chapter 10, p. 102, and chapter 16, p. 113.

17 Although Hermann here still wavers between Judaism and Christianity, and although he explicitly worries about his ability to read, his allegorical interpretation of the Old Testament (Exodus 34:33–35; see 2 Corinthians 3:13) bodes well for his conversion.

18 Rupert of Deutz himself is the author of a *Dialogus inter Christianum et Judaeum* (PL 170, cols. 559–610) in which the difference between Christian and Jewish ways of reading figures prominently. Apparently, public debates between Christians and Jews (and literary versions of such debates) were not uncommon in the Middle Ages. On real and literary Jewish–Christian debates of the thirteenth century, see Jeremy Cohen, *The Friars and the Jews: The Evolution of Medieval Anti-Judaism* (Ithaca and London: Cornell University Press, 1982), pp. 22–32, 65–85, and throughout. Especially interesting, in the debate literature, is Peter Abelard's *Dialogue of a Philosopher with a Jew, and a Christian*, which is framed as a dream vision. See also the dream in Judah ha-Levi's *Kitab al Khazari*, Hartwig Hirschfeld (trans.) (London: Routledge; and New York: E.P. Dutton, 1905); and see, on the relation between Abelard's work and ha-Levi's, Aryeh Grabois, "Un Chapitre de tolérance intellectuelle dans la société occidentale au XIIᵉ siècle: Le 'Dialogus' de Pierre Abélard et le 'Kuzari' d'Yehudah Halévi," in René Louis, Jean Jolivet, and Jean Châtillon (eds.), *Pierre Abélard, Pierre le Vénérable: Les Courants philosophiques, littéraires et artistiques en Occident au milieu du XIIᵉ siècle* (Paris: Editions du Centre National de la Recherche Scientifique, 1975), pp. 641–54.

19 A similar argument occurs in Rupert's *Dialogus*, PL 170, col. 602.

20 Compare Augustine's use of the metaphor of rumination: *Confessions* VI.3.3 and XI.2.3, Pusey (trans.), pp. 97–98 and 253–54.

21 Compare Augustine's account of learning to speak: *Confessions* I.8.13, Pusey (trans.), pp. 8–9.

22 See esp. chapter 12, p. 108. Cohen, "Mentality," pp. 33–35, argues that Hermann's conversion is largely one of emotional crisis; see also Momigliano, "Medieval Jewish Autobiography," pp. 31–33. Certainly, however, there is also a large intellectual component to Hermann's Christianization.

23 The way in which Hermann chooses to fast, combining the customs of the two religions, dramatizes his position *between* Judaism and Christianity (chapter 8, p. 94). On the connections between fasting and revelatory dreams, see Rudolph Arbesmann, "Fasting and Prophecy in Pagan and Christian Antiquity," *Traditio* 7 (1949–51), 1–71; and Trachtenberg, *Jewish Magic and Superstition*, p. 243.

24 Note Hermann's awareness of the imaginative status of even this clearly divine dream.

25 See Momigliano, "Medieval Jewish Autobiography," p. 33.

26 Momigliano discusses the possible connection between Hermann's early dream and the rite of Bar Mitzvah ("Medieval Jewish Autobiography," pp. 35–36). See also Cohen, "Mentality," p. 34.

27 The framing of Hermann's narrative by discussions of the same dream calls to mind similar uses of dreaming in Guibert and Augustine (see above). But in neither of these two authors – nor, indeed, in any medieval autobiographer of whom I am aware – does the dream provide a frame as striking and complete as in Hermann. The closest analogue to the frame-structure of Hermann's *Opusculum* that I have been able to find is in Boccaccio's *Life of Dante*; there, the dream Dante's mother has while pregnant (recounted in chapter 2) is fully interpreted only in the biography's final chapter. See Boccaccio, *Vita di Dante e difesa della poesia*, Carlo Muscetta (ed.) (Rome: Edizioni dell'Ateneo, 1963); and Boccaccio, *The Earliest Lives of Dante*, James Robinson Smith (trans.), Yale Studies in English, 10 (New York: Henry Holt, 1901).

28 The kind of interpretation offered here calls to mind the dream-equivalences of the *Somniale Danielis*. On medieval Jewish traditions of dream interpretation, see Tocci, "Teoria e interpretazione dei sogni," pp. 279–86; and Trachtenberg, *Jewish Magic and Superstition*, pp. 230–48. For a broad treatment of medieval Jewish philosophical discussions of dreaming and related visionary phenomena, see Sirat, *Les Théories des visions*.

29 John Freccero's discussion of Dante the pilgrim and narrator has influenced me here; see "Medusa: The Letter and the Spirit," *Yearbook of Italian Studies* 2 (1972), 1–18.

Bibliography

Abelard, Peter. *A Dialogue of a Philosopher with a Jew, and a Christian.* Pierre J. Payer (trans.). Toronto: Pontifical Institute of Mediaeval Studies, 1979.

Adam of Buckfield. *In De somno et vigilia. In De somniis. In De divinatione per somnum.* In Thomas Aquinas. *Opera omnia.* Roberto Busa (ed.). Stuttgart: Frommann-Holzboog, 1980. VII. Pp. 14–20.

Adelard of Bath. *De eodem et diverso.* H. Willner (ed.). *Beiträge zur Geschichte der Philosophie des Mittelalters* 4, no. 1 (1903).

Agostino de Ancona [Augustinus Triumphus]. *Tractatus contra divinatores et sompniatores.* See Scholz, Richard, *Unbekannte kirchenpolitische Streitschriften aus der Zeit Ludwigs des Bayern (1327–1354).*

Aiken, Pauline. "Vincent of Beauvais and Dame Pertelote's Knowledge of Medicine." *Speculum* 10 (1935), 281–87.

Ailred of Rievaulx. *De anima.* C.H. Talbot (ed.). *Mediaeval and Renaissance Studies* (The Warburg Institute, University of London), supplement 1 (1952).

Alain de Lille. *Liber sententiarum ac dictorum memorabilium. PL* 210, cols. 229–64.

"Omnis mundi creatura." *PL* 210, cols. 579–80.

Summa de arte praedicatoria. PL 210, cols. 109–98.

Anticlaudianus. Robert Bossuat (ed.). Paris: J. Vrin, 1955.

Anticlaudianus, or the Good and Perfect Man. James J. Sheridan (trans.). Toronto: Pontifical Institute of Mediaeval Studies, 1973.

The Plaint of Nature [*De planctu naturae*]. James J. Sheridan (trans.). Toronto: Pontifical Institute of Mediaeval Studies, 1980.

Albert of Orlamunde. *Philosophia pauperum, sive Isagoge in libros Aristotelis Physicorum, De caelo et mundo, De generatione et corruptione, Meteororum et De anima.* In Albertus Magnus. *Opera omnia.* August Borgnet (ed.). Paris: Apud Ludovicum Vivès, 1890–99. V. Pp. 445–553.

Albertus Magnus. *Opera omnia,* 38 vols. August Borgnet (ed.). Paris: Apud Ludovicum Vivès, 1890–99.

De fato. In Thomas Aquinas. *Opera omnia.* Roberto Busa (ed.). Stuttgart: Frommann-Holzboog, 1980. VII. Pp. 47–50.

Alcuin. *Commentariorum in Apocalypsin libri quinque. PL* 100, cols. 1085–156.

Alford, John A. "Richard Rolle and Related Works." In A.S.G. Edwards (ed.). *Middle English Prose: A Critical Guide to Major Authors.* New Brunswick, N.J.: Rutgers University Press, 1984. Pp. 35–60.

Algazel. *Algazel's Metaphysics: A Mediaeval Translation.* J.T. Muckle (ed.). Toronto: St. Michael's College, 1933.

Bibliography

al-Kindi. *Liber de somno et visione.* See Nagy, Albino, "Die philosophischen Abhandlungen des Ja'qub ben Ishaq al-Kindi."

Allen, Hope Emily. *The Writings Ascribed to Richard Rolle Hermit of Hampole and Materials for His Biography.* New York: D.C. Heath, 1927.

Allers, Rudolf. "Microcosmus from Anaximandros to Paracelsus." *Traditio* 2 (1944), 319–407.

Apuleius. *De Platone et eius dogmate.* Jean Beaujeu (ed. and trans.). *Opuscules philosophiques (Du Dieu de Socrate, Platon et sa doctrine, Du monde) et fragments.* Paris: Société d'Edition "Les Belles Lettres," 1973.

Aquinas, Thomas. *Truth,* 3 vols. Robert W. Mulligan, James V. McGlynn, and Robert W. Schmidt (trans.). Chicago: Henry Regnery, 1952–54.

Summa theologiae, 60 vols. Thomas Gilby (ed.). N.p.: Blackfriars; New York: McGraw Hill; and London: Eyre and Spottiswoode, 1964–76.

Opera omnia, 7 vols. Roberto Busa (ed.). Stuttgart: Frommann-Holzboog, 1980.

Pseudo-Aquinas. *De humanitate Jesu Christi Domini Nostri.* In Thomas Aquinas. *Opera omnia.* Roberto Busa (ed.). Stuttgart: Frommann-Holzboog, 1980. VII. Pp. 687–706.

Super Apocalypsim. In Thomas Aquinas. *Opera omnia.* Roberto Busa (ed.). Stuttgart: Frommann-Holzboog, 1980. VII. Pp. 720–804.

Arbesmann, Rudolph. "Fasting and Prophecy in Pagan and Christian Antiquity." *Traditio* 7 (1949–51), 1–71.

Aristotle. *Parva naturalia.* In W.D. Ross (ed.). J.I. Beare and G.R.T. Ross (trans.). *Works,* III. Oxford: Clarendon Press, 1931.

De somno et vigilia liber, adiectis veteribus translationibus et Theodori Metochitae commentario. H.J. Drossaart Lulofs (ed.). Leiden: Burgersdijk and Niermans – Templum Salamonis, 1943.

De insomniis et De divinatione per somnum: A New Edition of the Greek Text with the Latin Translations, 2 vols. H.J. Drossaart Lulofs (ed.). Leiden: E.J. Brill, 1947.

De anima, In the Version of William of Moerbeke and the Commentary of St. Thomas Aquinas. Kenelm Foster and Silvester Humphries (eds. and trans.). Ivo Thomas (intro.). New Haven: Yale University Press, 1954.

Armstrong, A.H. "St. Augustine and Christian Neoplatonism." In R.A. Markus (ed.). *Augustine: A Collection of Critical Essays.* Garden City, N.Y.: Anchor Books, Doubleday, 1972. Pp. 3–37.

Arnould, E.J. *Le Manuel des péchés: Etude de littérature religieuse anglo-normande (XIIIme siècle).* Paris: E. Droz, 1940.

Aronius, J. "Hermann der Prämonstratenser." *Zeitschrift für die Geschichte der Juden in Deutschland* 2 (1888), 217–31.

Artemidorus. *The Interpretation of Dreams: The Oneirocritica of Artemidorus.* Robert White (trans.). Noyes Classical Studies. Park Ridge, N.J.: Noyes Press, 1975.

Aubrun, Michel. "Caractères et portée religieuse et sociale des 'Visiones' en Occident du VIe au XIe siècle." *Cahiers de Civilisation Médiévale: X^e–XIIe Siècles* 23 (1980), 109–30.

Augustine. *De cura pro mortuis gerenda.* PL 40, cols. 591–610.

De divinatione daemonum liber unus. PL 40, cols. 581–92.

On Care to Be Had for the Dead [De cura pro mortuis gerenda]. H. Browne (trans.). A

Bibliography

Select Library of the Nicene and Post-Nicene Fathers of the Christian Church, 3. Buffalo: The Christian Literature Company, 1887. Pp. 537–51.

On the Holy Trinity [*De Trinitate*]. Arthur West Haddan (trans.). A Select Library of the Nicene and Post-Nicene Fathers of the Christian Church, 3. Buffalo: The Christian Literature Company, 1887. Pp. 1–228.

De Genesi ad litteram libri duodecim. Iosephus Zycha (ed.). Corpus Scriptorum Ecclesiasticorum Latinorum, XXVIII, section 3, part 1. Prague and Vienna: F. Temsky; and Leipzig: G. Freytag, 1894. Pp. 1–456.

Confessions. E.B. Pusey (trans.). London and Toronto: J.M. Dent; and New York: E.P. Dutton, 1907.

Letters [*Epistolae*]. Wilfrid Parsons (trans.). The Fathers of the Church: A New Translation, 12, 20. New York: Fathers of the Church, 1951.

On Christian Doctrine [*De doctrina christiana*]. D.W. Robertson (trans.). The Library of Liberal Arts. Indianapolis: Bobbs-Merrill, 1958.

De Trinitate libri xv. W.J. Mountain (ed.), with Fr. Glorie. Corpus Christianorum, series latina, 50, 50A. Turnholt: Typographi Brepols Editores Pontificii, 1968.

Concerning the City of God against the Pagans. Henry Bettenson (trans.). Harmondsworth: Penguin Books, 1972.

The Literal Meaning of Genesis [*De Genesi ad litteram*], 2 vols. John Hammond Taylor (trans.). Ancient Christian Writers: The Works of the Fathers in Translation, 42. New York and Ramsey, N.J.: Newman Press, 1982.

Pseudo-Augustine. *De spiritu et anima.* See *De spiritu et anima.*

Averroes. *Compendia librorum Aristotelis qui Parva naturalia vocantur.* Emily Ledyard Shields (ed.), with Harry Blumberg. Corpus Commentariorum Averrois in Aristotelem, versio latina, 7. Cambridge, Mass.: The Mediaeval Academy of America, 1949.

Epitome of Parva Naturalia. Harry Blumberg (trans.). Corpus Commentariorum Averrois in Aristotelem, versio anglica, 7. Cambridge, Mass.: The Mediaeval Academy of America, 1961.

Avicenna. *Liber canonis.* Venice, 1507. Reprinted Hildesheim: Georg Olms Verlagsbuchhandlung, 1964.

Avicenna latinus: Liber de anima seu Sextus de naturalibus, 2 vols. S. van Riet (ed.). G. Verbeke (intro.). Louvain: Editions Orientalistes; and Leiden: E.J. Brill, 1968. Louvain: E. Peeters; and Leiden: E.J. Brill, 1972.

Bacon, Roger. *Compendium studii theologiae.* H. Rashdall (ed.). British Society of Franciscan Studies, 3. Aberdeen: Typis Academicis, 1911.

Baluzius, Stephanus [Etienne Baluze] (ed.). *Capitularia regum francorum,* I. Paris: Ex Typis Francisci-Augustini Quillan, 1780. Reprinted in Joannes Dominicus Mansi (ed.). *Sacrorum conciliorum nova et amplissima collectio,* XVIIB. Paris: Hubert Welter, 1902. Reprinted Graz, Austria: Akademische Druck-u. Verlagsanstalt, 1960.

Bartholomaeus Anglicus. *Liber de proprietatibus rerum.* Strasbourg [Argentine], 1505.

On the Properties of Things: John Trevisa's Translation of Bartholomaeus Anglicus De proprietatibus rerum: A Critical Text. M.C. Seymour (ed.). Oxford: Clarendon Press, 1975.

Bibliography

Bate, Henri. *Speculum divinorum et quorundam naturalium (Etude critique et texte inédit)*. G. Wallerand (ed.). Les Philosophes Belges, textes et études, 11. Louvain: Institut Supérieur de Philosophie de l'Université, 1931.

Speculum divinorum et quorundam naturalium, Edition critique, 2 vols. E. van de Vyver (ed.). Philosophes Médiévaux. Louvain: Publications Universitaires; and Paris: Béatrice-Nauwelaerts, 1960–67.

Bede. *Super Acta apostolorum expositio*. PL 92, cols. 937–96.

Behr, C.A. *Aelius Aristides and the Sacred Tales*. Amsterdam: Adolf M. Hakkert, 1968.

Bennett, J.A.W. *Chaucer's Book of Fame: An Exposition of 'The House of Fame'*. Oxford: Clarendon Press, 1968.

Chaucer at Oxford and at Cambridge. Toronto: University of Toronto Press, 1974.

Benson, Robert L., and Giles Constable (eds.), with Carol D. Lanham. *Renaissance and Renewal in the Twelfth Century*. Cambridge, Mass.: Harvard University Press, 1982.

Pseudo-Bernard. *Liber de modo bene vivendi, ad sororem*. See Thomas of Froidmont, *Liber de modo bene vivendi*.

Bernardus Silvestris. *De mundi universitate, libri duo, sive Megacosmus et microcosmus*. Carl Sigmund Barach and Johann Wrobel (eds.). Bibliotheca Philosophorum Mediae Ætatis, 1. Innsbruck: Verlag der Wagner'schen Universitaets-Buchhandlung, 1876.

The Cosmographia of Bernardus Silvestris. Winthrop Wetherbee (trans.). Records of Civilization: Sources and Studies, 89. New York and London: Columbia University Press, 1973.

Cosmographia. Peter Dronke (ed.). Leiden: E.J. Brill, 1978.

Bersuire, Pierre [Petrus Berchorius]. *Dictionarium morale. Opera omnia*, III–VI. Cologne: Apud Petrum Pütz, 1731.

Reductorium morale, De proprietatibus rerum. Opera omnia, II. Cologne: Apud Petrum Pütz, 1731.

Bible. *The Holy Bible*, translated from the Latin Vulgate [Douay-Rheims version]. Baltimore, 1899. Reprinted Rockford, Ill.: Tan Books, 1971.

Biblia sacra iuxta Vulgatam versionem, revised edition, 2 vols. Robertus Weber (ed.). Stuttgart: Württembergische Bibelanstalt, 1975.

Bloch, Ralph Howard. "A Study of the Dream Motif in the Old French Narrative." Dissertation, Stanford University, 1970.

Bloomfield, Morton W. *The Seven Deadly Sins: An Introduction to the History of a Religious Concept, with Special Reference to Medieval English Literature*. East Lansing: Michigan State College Press, 1952.

Blum, Claes. *Studies in the Dream-Book of Artemidorus: Inaugural Dissertation*. Uppsala: Almquist and Wiksells, 1936.

Blumenkranz, Bernhard. "Jüdische und christliche Konvertiten im jüdisch–christlichen Religionsgespräch des Mittelalters." In Paul Wilpert (ed.). *Judentum im Mittelalter: Beiträge zum christlich–jüdischen Gespräch*. Miscellanea Mediaevalia, 4. Berlin: Walter de Gruyter, 1966. Pp. 264–82.

Boccaccio, Giovanni. *The Earliest Lives of Dante*. James Robinson Smith (trans.). Yale Studies in English, 10. New York: Henry Holt, 1901.

Bibliography

Boccaccio on Poetry. Charles G. Osgood (ed. and trans.). Indianapolis and New York: Bobbs-Merrill, 1956 [1930].

De casibus illustrium virorum. Paris, 1520. Louis Brewer Hall (ed.). Gainesville, Florida: Scholars' Facsimiles and Reprints, 1962.

Vita di Dante e difesa della poesia. Carlo Muscetta (ed.). Rome: Edizioni dell'Ateneo, 1963.

The Fates of Illustrious Men. Louis Brewer Hall (trans.). New York: Frederick Ungar, 1965.

The Corbaccio. Anthony K. Cassell (trans. and ed.). Urbana, Ill.: University of Illinois Press, 1975.

Genealogiae deorum gentilium. Venice, 1494. The Renaissance and the Gods, 2. Stephen Orgel (series ed.). New York and London: Garland Publishing, 1976.

Bodenham, C.H.L. "The Nature of the Dream in Late Medieval French Literature." *Medium Ævum* 54 (1985), 74–86.

Boethius. *The Consolation of Philosophy*. V.E. Watts (trans.). Harmondsworth: Penguin Books, 1969.

Boethius of Dacia. *De somniis*. In Nicolaus Georgius Green-Pedersen (ed.). *Opera*, VI, part 2. Corpus Philosophorum Danicorum Medii Aevi. Copenhagen: Gad, 1976.

On the Supreme Good. On the Eternity of the World. On Dreams. John F. Wippel (trans.). Toronto: Pontifical Institute of Mediaeval Studies, 1987.

Bolte, Johannes. "Anhang. Zur Geschichte der Losbücher." *Georg Wickrams Werke*, IV. Tübingen: Gedruckt für den litterarischen Verein in Stuttgart, 1903. Pp. 276–347.

Bonaventure. *Commentaria in quatuor libros Sententiarum magistri Petri Lombardi*. In *Opera omnia*. Quarrachi: Ex Typographia Collegii S. Bonaventurae, 1885.

Bono, James J. "Medical Spirits and the Medieval Language of Life." *Traditio* 40 (1984), 91–130.

Boucher, Holly Wallace. "Nominalism: The Difference for Chaucer and Boccaccio." *Chaucer Review* 20 (1985–86), 213–20.

Boutaric, E. "Vincent de Beauvais et la connaissance de l'antiquité classique au treizième siècle." *Revue des Questions Historiques* 17 (1875), 5–57.

Boyle, Leonard E. "The Curriculum of the Faculty of Canon Law at Oxford in the First Half of the Fourteenth Century." *Oxford Studies Presented to Daniel Callus*. Oxford: Oxford Historical Society, 1964. Pp. 135–62. Reprinted in Leonard Boyle. *Pastoral Care, Clerical Education and Canon Law, 1200–1400*. London: Variorum Reprints, 1981.

Bradley, Ritamary. "Backgrounds of the Title *Speculum* in Mediaeval Literature." *Speculum* 29 (1954), 100–15.

Bregman, Jay. *Synesius of Cyrene: Philosopher–Bishop*. Berkeley: University of California Press, 1982.

Brownlee, Kevin. "Dante and Narcissus (*Purg.* xxx, 76–99)." *Dante Studies* 96 (1978), 201–06.

Bühler, Curt F. "Two Middle English Texts of the *Somnia Danielis*." *Anglia* 80 (1962), 264–73.

Bibliography

Bundy, Murray Wright. *The Theory of Imagination in Classical and Mediaeval Thought.* University of Illinois Studies in Language and Literature, 12, nos. 2–3. Urbana, Ill.: The University of Illinois, 1927.

Burgh, Benet (trans.). *Parvus Cato, Magnus Cato.* Fumio Kuriyagawa (ed.). Tokyo: Seijo University, 1974.

Burke, Peter. "L'Histoire sociale des rêves." *Annales: Economies, Sociétés, Civilisations* 28 (1973), 329–42.

Burley, Walter. *Liber de vita et moribus philosophorum.* Hermann Knust (ed.). Bibliothek des litterarischen Vereins, 177. Tübingen, 1886.

Burnett, Charles (ed.). *Adelard of Bath: An English Scientist and Arabist of the Early Twelfth Century.* Warburg Institute Surveys and Texts, 14. London: The Warburg Institute, University of London, 1987.

Caesarius of Heisterbach. *The Dialogue on Miracles*, 2 vols. H. von E. Scott and C.C. Swinton Bland (trans.). London: Routledge, 1929.

Calcidius. *Platonis Timaeus interprete Chalcidio cum eiusdem commentario.* Ioh. Wrobel (ed.). Leipzig: B.G. Teubner, 1876.

Calcidius on Matter, His Doctrine and Sources: A Chapter in the History of Platonism. J.C.M. van Winden (trans.). Philosophia Antiqua, A Series of Monographs on Ancient Philosophy, 9. Leiden: E.J. Brill, 1959.

Timaeus a Calcidio translatus commentarioque instructus. J.H. Waszink (ed.). Corpus Platonicum Medii Aevi: Plato Latinus. R. Klibansky (series ed.). London: Warburg Institute; and Leiden: E.J. Brill, 1962.

Calcidius on Fate, His Doctrine and Sources. J. den Boeft (trans.). Philosophia Antiqua, A Series of Monographs on Ancient Philosophy, 18. Leiden: E.J. Brill, 1970.

Calcidius on Demons (Commentarius ch. 127–136).. J. den Boeft (trans.). Philosophia Antiqua, A Series of Monographs on Ancient Philosophy, 33. Leiden: E.J. Brill, 1977.

Camus, Jules. "Notices et extraits des manuscrits français de Modène." *Revue des Langues Romanes* 35 (1891), 169–262.

"Un Manuscrit namurois du XVe siècle." *Revue des Langues Romanes* 38 (1895), 29–44.

The Catholic Encyclopedia, 15 vols. New York: Robert Appleton, 1907–14.

Cayré. "Note complémentaire: 'Augustinisme.'" *Dictionnaire de théologie catholique, Tables générales*, I. Paris: Letouzey, 1951. Cols. 317–24.

The Chastising of God's Children and The Treatise of Perfection of the Sons of God. Joyce Bazire and Eric Colledge (eds.). Oxford: Basil Blackwell, 1957.

Châtillon, J. "Achard de Saint Victor et le 'De discretione animae, spiritus et mentis.'" *AHDLMA* 31 (1964), 7–35.

Chaucer, Geoffrey. *The Riverside Chaucer*, third edition. Larry D. Benson (general ed.). Based on F.N. Robinson (ed.), *The Works of Geoffrey Chaucer.* Boston: Houghton Mifflin, 1987.

Chenu, M.D. "Spiritus: Le Vocabulaire de l'âme au XIIe siècle." *Revue des Sciences Philosophiques et Théologiques* 41 (1957), 209–32.

Cicero. *De senectute, De amicitia, De divinatione.* William Armstead Falconer (ed. and trans.). Loeb Classical Library. London: William Heinemann; and New York: G.P. Putnam's Sons, 1923.

Bibliography

Clarenbaldus of Arras. *Tractatulus*. See Häring, Nikolaus M., "The Creation and Creator of the World according to Thierry of Chartres and Clarenbaldus of Arras."

Claudian. *De raptu Proserpinae*. Maurice Platnauer (ed. and trans.). Loeb Classical Library: Claudian, 2. London: William Heinemann; and New York: G.P. Putnam's Sons, 1922.

Clemen, Wolfgang. *Chaucer's Early Poetry*. C.A.M. Sym (trans.). London: Methuen, 1963; and New York: Barnes and Noble, 1964.

Cohen, Jeremy. *The Friars and the Jews: The Evolution of Medieval Anti-Judaism*. Ithaca and London: Cornell University Press, 1982.

"The Mentality of the Medieval Jewish Apostate: Peter Alfonsi, Hermann of Cologne, and Pablo Christiani." In Todd M. Endelman (ed.). *Jewish Apostasy in the Modern World*. New York and London: Holmes and Meier, 1987. Pp. 20–47.

Coleman, Janet. *Piers Plowman and the 'Moderni*. Rome: Edizioni di Storia e Letteratura, 1981.

Colish, Marcia L. *The Mirror of Language: A Study in the Medieval Theory of Knowledge*, revised edition. Lincoln and London: University of Nebraska Press, 1983.

Colker, Marvin L. "The Lure of Women, Hunting, Chess, and Tennis: A Vision." *Speculum* 59 (1984), 103–05.

Collin, Simone. "L'Emploi des clefs des songes dans la littérature médiévale." *Bulletin Philologique et Historique*, II (1967). Paris: Bibliothèque Nationale, 1969. Pp. 851–66.

Collin-Roset, Simone. "Le *Liber thesauri occulti* de Pascalis Romanus (un traité d'interprétation des songes du XIIᵉ siècle)." *AHDLMA* 30 (1963), 111–98.

Compendium philosophiae. See de Boüard, Michel, *Une Nouvelle Encyclopédie médiévale: Le Compendium philosophiae*.

Courcelle, Pierre. "La Postérité chrétienne du *Songe de Scipion*." *Revue des Etudes Latines* 36 (1958), 205–34.

Late Latin Writers and Their Greek Sources. Harry E. Wedeck (trans.). Cambridge, Mass.: Harvard University Press, 1969 [1948].

Connais-toi toi-même de Socrate à Saint Bernard, 2 vols. Paris: Etudes Augustiniennes, 1974–75.

Crick, Francis, and Graeme Mitchison. "The Function of Dream Sleep." *Nature* 304 (1983), 111–14.

Cron, B.S. *A Medieval Dreambook*. London: The Gogmagog Press, 1963.

Curry, Walter Clyde. *Chaucer and the Mediaeval Sciences*, revised edition. New York: Barnes and Noble, 1960.

Curtius, Ernst Robert. *European Literature and the Latin Middle Ages*. Willard R. Trask (trans.). Princeton, N.J.: Princeton University Press, 1973 [1953].

Cynewulf. *Elene*. P.O.E. Gradon (ed.). New York: Appleton–Century–Crofts, 1966 [1958].

Dagens, Claude. *Saint Grégoire le Grand: Culture et expérience chrétiennes*. Paris: Etudes Augustiniennes, 1977.

Dahlberg, Charles. "Macrobius and the Unity of the *Roman de la Rose*." *Studies in Philology* 58 (1961), 573–82.

d'Alverny, Marie-Thérèse. "Translations and Translators." In Robert L. Benson

Bibliography

and Giles Constable (eds.). *Renaissance and Renewal in the Twelfth Century.* Cambridge, Mass.: Harvard University Press, 1982. Pp. 421–62.

Damon, Phillip Whitcomb. "Twelfth Century Latin Vision Poetry." Dissertation, University of California, Berkeley, 1952.

Dane, Joseph A. *"Integumentum* as Interpretation: Note on William of Conches' Commentary on Macrobius (1, 2, 10–11)." *Classical Folia* 32 (1978), 201–15.

Dante. *The Divine Comedy,* 6 vols. Charles S. Singleton (ed. and trans.). Princeton, N.J.: Princeton University Press, 1970.

Davy, Adam. *Adam Davy's Five Dreams About Edward II.* F.J. Furnivall (ed.). EETS, OS 69. London: N. Trübner, 1878.

de Boüard, Michel. *Une Nouvelle Encyclopédie médiévale: Le Compendium philosophiae.* Paris: E. de Boccard, 1936.

de Bruyne, Edgar. *Etudes d'esthétique médiévale.* Rijksuniversiteit te Gent: Werken Uitgegeven door de Faculteit van de Wijsbegeerte en Letteren, 97–99. Brussels: "De Tempel," 1946.

Deguileville, Guillaume de. *Pelerinage de la vie humaine.* See Lydgate, John, *The Pilgrimage of the Life of Man;* and *The Pilgrimage of the Lyfe of the Manhode.*

Delany, Sheila. *Chaucer's House of Fame: The Poetics of Skeptical Fideism.* Chicago and London: The University of Chicago Press, 1972.

de Ley, Herman. *Macrobius and Numenius: A Study of Macrobius, In Somn., I, c. 12.* Collection Latomus, 125. Brussels: Latomus, Revue d'Etudes Latines, 1972.

De spiritu et anima. PL 40, cols. 779–832.

[*Treatise on the Spirit and the Soul*]. Erasmo Leiva and Benedicta Ward (trans.). In Bernard McGinn (ed.). *Three Treatises on Man: A Cistercian Anthropology.* Kalamazoo, Mich.: Cistercian Publications, 1977. Pp. 179–288.

de Stoop, E. "Onirocriticon du prophète Daniel dedié au roi Nabuchodonosor." *Revue de Philologie de Littérature et d'Histoire Anciennes* 33 (1909), 93–111.

Dictionnaire des auteurs cisterciens, 2 vols. Emile Brouette, Anselme Dimier, and Eugène Manning (eds.). La Documentation Cistercienne, 16. Rochefort: Abbaye Notre-Dame de St. Rémy, 1975–77.

Dictionnaire de spiritualité: Ascétique et mystique, doctrine et histoire, 13 vols. [incomplete]. Paris: Beauchesne, 1937-.

Diels, H. (ed.). *Die Fragmente der Vorsokratiker,* second edition. Berlin: Weidmannsche Buchhandlung, 1906. Vol. I.

Dinzelbacher, Peter. *Vision und Visionsliteratur im Mittelalter.* Monographien zur Geschichte des Mittelalters, 23. Stuttgart: Anton Hiersemann, 1981.

"Körperliche und seelische Vorbedingungen religiöser Träume und Visionen." In Tullio Gregory (ed.). *I sogni nel medioevo.* Seminario Internazionale, Rome, 2–4 October 1983. Rome: Edizioni dell'Ateneo, 1985. Pp. 57–86.

Diogenes Laertius. *Lives of Eminent Philosophers.* R.D. Hicks (ed. and trans.). Loeb Classical Library. London: William Heinemann; and New York: G.P. Putnam's Sons, 1925.

Pseudo-Dionysius the Areopagite. *La Hiérarchie céleste.* Günther Heil (ed.). Maurice de Gandillac (trans.). René Roques (intro.). Sources Chrétiennes, 58. Paris: Les Editions du Cerf, 1958.

Disticha Catonis. See Burgh, Benet (trans.), *Parvus Cato, Magnus Cato.*

Bibliography

Dod, Bernard G. "Aristoteles latinus." In Norman Kretzmann, Anthony Kenny, Jan Pinborg, and Eleonore Stump (eds.). *The Cambridge History of Later Medieval Philosophy: From the Rediscovery of Aristotle to the Disintegration of Scholasticism, 1100–1600*. Cambridge: Cambridge University Press, 1982. Pp. 45–76.

Dodds, E.R. *The Greeks and the Irrational*. Berkeley: University of California Press, 1951.

Dondaine, Antoine. "Hugues Ethérien et Léon Toscan." *AHDLMA* 19 (1952), 67–134.

Douglas, Mary. *Purity and Danger: An Analysis of Concepts of Pollution and Taboo*. London: Routledge and Kegan Paul, 1966.

Drew, Alison. "The *De eodem et diverso*." In Charles Burnett (ed.). *Adelard of Bath: An English Scientist and Arabist of the Early Twelfth Century*. Warburg Institute Surveys and Texts, 14. London: The Warburg Institute, University of London, 1987. Pp. 17–24.

Dufner, Georg. *Die Dialoge Gregors des Grossen im Wandel der Zeiten und Sprachen*. Padua: Antenore, 1968.

Duhem, Pierre. *Le Système du monde: Histoire des doctrines cosmologiques de Platon à Copernic*, 10 vols. Paris: Hermann, 1913–59.

Dulaey, Martine. *Le Rêve dans la vie et la pensée de Saint Augustin*. Paris: Etudes Augustiniennes, 1973.

Economou, George D. *The Goddess Natura in Medieval Literature*. Cambridge, Mass.: Harvard University Press, 1972.

Eldredge, Laurence. "Chaucer's *Hous of Fame* and the *Via Moderna*." *Neuphilologische Mitteilungen* 71 (1970), 105–19.

Elferink, M.A. *La Descente de l'âme d'après Macrobe*. Leiden: E.J. Brill, 1968.

Erickson, Carolly. *The Medieval Vision: Essays in History and Perception*. New York: Oxford University Press, 1976.

Evrart de Conty. *L'Harmonie des sphères: Encyclopédie d'astronomie et de musique extraite du commentaire sur Les Echecs amoureux (XVe s.) attribué à Evrart de Conty*. Reginald Hyatte and Maryse Ponchard-Hyatte (eds.). New York: Peter Lang, 1985.

Fattori, Marta. "Sogni e temperamenti." In Tullio Gregory (ed.). *I sogni nel medioevo*. Seminario Internazionale, Rome, 2–4 October 1983. Rome: Edizioni dell'Ateneo, 1985. Pp. 87–109.

Favonius Eulogius. *Disputatio de Somnio Scipionis*. Roger–E. van Weddingen (ed. and trans.). Collection Latomus, 27. Brussels: Latomus, Revue d'Etudes Latines, 1957.

Fioravanti, Gianfranco. "La 'scientia sompnialis' di Boezio di Dacia." *Atti della Accademia delle Scienze di Torino: II. Classe di scienze morali, storiche e filologiche* 101 (1966–67), 329–69.

Fischer, Steven R. *The Dream in the Middle High German Epic*. Australian and New Zealand Studies in German Language and Literature, 10. Bern: Peter Lang, 1978.

The Complete Medieval Dreambook: A Multilingual, Alphabetical Somnia Danielis Collation. Bern and Frankfurt: Peter Lang, 1982.

Bibliography

Flamant, Jacques. *Macrobe et le Néo-Platonisme latin, à la fin du IVe siècle*. Etudes Préliminaires aux Religions Orientales dans l'Empire Romain, 58. Leiden: E. J. Brill, 1977.

Förster, Max. "Die Kleinliteratur des Aberglaubens im Altenglischen." *Archiv für das Studium der neueren Sprachen und Litteraturen* 110 (1903), 346–58.

"Beiträge zur mittelalterlichen Volkskunde II." *Archiv für das Studium der neueren Sprachen und Literaturen* 120 (1908), 296–305.

"Beiträge zur mittelalterlichen Volkskunde III." *Archiv für das Studium der neueren Sprachen und Literaturen* 121 (1908), 30–46.

"Beiträge zur mittelalterlichen Volkskunde IV." *Archiv für das Studium der neueren Sprachen und Literaturen* 125 (1910), 39–70.

"Beiträge zur mittelalterlichen Volkskunde V." *Archiv für das Studium der neueren Sprachen und Literaturen* 127 (1911), 31–84.

"Beiträge zur mittelalterlichen Volkskunde IX." *Archiv für das Studium der neueren Sprachen und Literaturen* 134 (1916), 264–93.

"Das älteste kymrische Traumbuch (um 1350)." *Zeitschrift für celtische Philologie* 13 (1921), 55–92.

"Die altenglischen Traumlunare." *Englische Studien* 60 (1925–26), 58–93.

"Mittelalterliche Orakelalphabete für Psalterwahrsagung." *Forschungen und Fortschritte* 4 (1928), 204–06.

"Vom Fortleben antiker Sammellunare im Englischen und in anderen Volkssprachen." *Anglia* 67–68 (1944), 1–171.

Forstner, Karl. "Das Traumgedicht Baudris von Bourgeuil (Carmen 37)." *Mittellateinisches Jahrbuch* 6 (1970), 45–57.

Fosshage, James L., and Clemens A. Loew (eds.). *Dream Interpretation: A Comparative Study*, revised edition. New York: PMA, 1987.

Foucault, Michel. *The Care of the Self: The History of Sexuality*, III. Robert Hurley (trans.). New York: Vintage Books, Random House, 1986.

Freccero, John. "Medusa: The Letter and the Spirit." *Yearbook of Italian Studies* 2 (1972), 1–18.

Freeman, Ann. "Theodulf of Orleans and the *Libri Carolini*." *Speculum* 32 (1957), 663–705.

"Further Studies in the *Libri Carolini*." *Speculum* 40 (1965), 203–89.

Freud, Sigmund. *Die Traumdeutung*. Leipzig and Vienna: Franz Deuticke, 1900. Reprinted in *Gesammelte Werke*, II–III. London: Imago, 1942.

The Interpretation of Dreams. James Strachey (trans. and ed.). New York: Avon Books, 1965.

Gaha, Michael D. Mc. "The Influence of Macrobius on Cervantes." *Revue de Littérature Comparée* 53 (1979), 462–69.

Gennadius. *Liber de ecclesiasticis dogmatibus*. PL 58, cols. 979–1000.

Gersh, Stephen. "Platonism – Neoplatonism – Aristotelianism: A Twelfth-Century Metaphysical System and its Sources." In Robert L. Benson and Giles Constable (eds.). *Renaissance and Renewal in the Twelfth Century*. Cambridge, Mass.: Harvard University Press, 1982. Pp. 512–34.

Giaccherini, Enrico. "Una crux chauceriana: I sogni nella *House of Fame*." *Rivista di letterature moderne e comparate* 27 (1974), 165–76.

Gibson, Margaret. "Adelard of Bath." In Charles Burnett (ed.). *Adelard of Bath:*

Bibliography

An English Scientist and Arabist of the Early Twelfth Century. Warburg Institute Surveys and Texts, 14. London: The Warburg Institute, University of London, 1987. Pp. 7–16.

Gilbert of Poitiers. *De discretione animae, spiritus et mentis*. See Häring, Nikolaus M., "Gilbert of Poitiers, Author of the 'De Discretione animae, spiritus et mentis.'"

Gilson, Etienne. *La Philosophie au Moyen Age: Des origines patristiques à la fin du XIVᵉ siècle*, second edition. Paris: Payot, 1944.

The Christian Philosophy of Saint Augustine. L.E.M. Lynch (trans.). New York: Random House, 1960.

Ginzburg, Carlo. *The Cheese and the Worms: The Cosmos of a Sixteenth-Century Miller*. John and Anne C. Tedeschi (trans.). Baltimore: Johns Hopkins University Press, 1980.

The Night Battles: Witchcraft and Agrarian Cults in the Sixteenth and Seventeenth Centuries. John and Anne C. Tedeschi (trans.). Baltimore: Johns Hopkins University Press, 1983.

Giraldus Cambrensis. *Itinerary Through Wales*. Richard Colt Hoare (trans.). W. Llewelyn Williams (ed.). London: J.M. Dent; and New York: E.P. Dutton, 1908.

Expugnatio Hibernica: The Conquest of Ireland. A.B. Scott and F.X. Martin (eds. and trans.). Dublin: Royal Irish Academy, 1978.

Gísla saga. The Saga of Gisli. George Johnston (trans.). Toronto: University of Toronto Press, 1963.

Glauche, Günter. *Schullektüre im Mittelalter*. Munich: Arbeo, 1970.

Glorieux, P. *Pour revaloriser Migne: Tables rectificatives*. Mélanges de Science Religieuse, 9, cahier supplémentaire. Lille: Facultés Catholiques, 1952.

Godefroy of St. Victor. *Microcosmus*. Philippe Delhaye (ed.). Lille: Facultés Catholiques; and Gembloux: J. Duculot, 1951.

Fons philosophiae. Pierre Michaud Quantin (ed.). Analecta Mediaevalia Namurcensia, 8. Namur: Godenne, 1956.

The Fountain of Philosophy. Edward A. Synan (trans.). Toronto: Pontifical Institute of Mediaeval Studies, 1972.

Goldin, Frederick. *The Mirror of Narcissus in the Courtly Love Lyric*. Ithaca, N.Y.: Cornell University Press, 1967.

Gower, John. *The English Works of John Gower*, 2 vols. G.C. Macaulay (ed.). EETS, ES 81, 82. London: Kegan Paul, Trench, Trübner and Co., 1900–01.

Grabes, Herbert. *The Mutable Glass: Mirror-Imagery in Titles and Texts of the Middle Ages and English Renaissance*. Gordon Collier (trans.). Cambridge: Cambridge University Press, 1982.

Grabmann, Martin. "Die Philosophia Pauperum und ihr Verfasser Albert von Orlamunde. Ein Beitrag zur Geschichte des philosophischen Unterrichtes an den deutschen Stadtschulen des ausgehenden Mittelalters." *Beiträge zur Geschichte der Philosophie des Mittelalters* 20, no. 2 (1918), 1–56.

"Die Werke des hl. Thomas von Aquin: Eine literarhistorische Untersuchung und Einführung," third edition. *Beiträge zur Geschichte der Philosophie und Theologie des Mittelalters* 22, nos. 1–2 (1949), 1–479.

Graboïs, Aryeh. "Un Chapitre de tolérance intellectuelle dans la société occiden-

Bibliography

tale au XIIe siècle: Le 'Dialogus' de Pierre Abélard et le 'Kuzari' d'Yehudah Halévi." In René Louis, Jean Jolivet, and Jean Châtillon (eds.). *Pierre Abélard, Pierre le Vénérable: Les Courants philosophiques, littéraires et artistiques en Occident au milieu du XIIe siècle*. Paris: Editions du Centre National de la Recherche Scientifique, 1975. Pp. 641–54.

Graffunder. "Daniels Traumdeutungen. Ein mittelalterliches Traumbuch in deutschen Versen." *Zeitschrift für deutsches Altertum und deutsche Litteratur* 48 (1907), 507–31.

Grandma's Lucky Number Dream Book. Baltimore: Grandma's Candle Shop, 1979.

Gratian. *Decretum*. Aemilius Ludovicus Richter (ed.). Revised by Aemilius Friedberg (ed.). *Corpus iuris canonici*, part 1. Leipzig: Ex Officina Bernhardi Tauchnitz, 1879.

Gregory the Great. *Morals on the Book of Job*, 3 vols. A Library of Fathers of the Holy Catholic Church. Translated by members of the English church. Oxford: John Henry Parker; and London: F. and J. Rivington, 1844–50.

Dialogues. Odo John Zimmerman (trans.). The Fathers of the Church: A New Translation, 39. New York: Fathers of the Church, 1959.

Dialogues [Dialogi]. Adalbert de Vogüé (ed.). Sources Chrétiennes, 251, 260, 265. Paris: Les Editions du Cerf, 1978–80.

Moralia in Iob. Marc Adriaen (ed.). Corpus Christianorum, series latina, 143, 143A, 143B. Turnholt: Typographi Brepols Editores Pontificii, 1979–85.

Gregory IX. *Decretales*. Aemilius Ludovicus Richter (ed.). Revised by Aemilius Friedberg (ed.). *Corpus iuris canonici*, part 2. Leipzig: Ex Officina Bernhardi Tauchnitz, 1881.

Gregory, Tullio. "I sogni e gli astri." In Tullio Gregory (ed.). *I sogni nel medioevo*. Seminario Internazionale, Rome, 2–4 October 1983. Rome: Edizioni dell'Ateneo, 1985. Pp. 111–48.

Gregory, Tullio (ed.). *I sogni nel medioevo*. Seminario Internazionale, Rome, 2–4 October 1983. Rome: Edizioni dell'Ateneo, 1985.

Grennen, Joseph E. "Chaucer and Chalcidius: The Platonic Origins of the *Hous of Fame*." *Viator* 15 (1984), 237–62.

Grub, Jutta. *Das lateinische Traumbuch im Codex Upsaliensis C664 (9. Jh.): Eine fruhmittelalterliche Fassung der lateinischen Somniale Danielis-Tradition*. Frankfurt: Peter Lang, 1984.

Guibert de Nogent. *De vita sua sive monodiarum libri tres*. PL 156, cols. 837–962.

Tractatus de incarnatione contra Judaeos. PL 156, cols. 489–528.

Guibert de Nogent: Histoire de sa vie (1053–1124). Georges Bourgin (ed.). Paris: Alphonse Picard, 1907.

Self and Society in Medieval France: The Memoirs of Abbot Guibert of Nogent (1064?–c. 1125). John F. Benton (ed.). C.C. Swinton Bland (trans.) [revised by Benton]. New York: Harper and Row, 1970.

Guido da Pisa. *Expositiones et glose super Comediam Dantis, or Commentary on Dante's Inferno*. Vincenzo Cioffari (ed.). Albany, N.Y.: State University of New York Press, 1974.

Guidorizzi, Giulio. "L'interpretazione dei sogni nel mondo tardoantico: oralità e scrittura." In Tullio Gregory (ed.). *I sogni nel medioevo*. Seminario Inter-

Bibliography

nazionale, Rome, 2–4 October 1983. Rome: Edizioni dell'Ateneo, 1985. Pp. 149–70.

Guillaume de Conches. *De philosophia mundi. PL* 172, cols. 39–102.

Dragmaticon. Stanford University Libraries, MS M412.

Glosae super Platonem. Edouard Jeauneau (ed.). Textes Philosophiques du Moyen Age, 13. Paris: Librairie Philosophique J. Vrin, 1965.

Guillaume de Lorris and Jean de Meun. *Le Roman de la rose.* Daniel Poirion (ed.). Paris: Garnier-Flammarion, 1974.

Gurevich, A.J. "Oral and Written Culture of the Middle Ages: Two 'Peasant Visions' of the Late Twelfth–Early Thirteenth Centuries." *New Literary History* 16 (1984), 51–66.

Categories of Medieval Culture. G.L. Campbell (trans.). London: Routledge and Kegan Paul, 1985.

Medieval Popular Culture: Problems of Belief and Perception. János M. Bak and Paul A. Hollingsworth (trans.). Cambridge Studies in Oral and Literate Culture, 14. Cambridge: Cambridge University Press; and Paris: Editions de la Maison des Sciences de l'Homme, 1988.

Guthlac A. See Krapp, George Philip, and Elliott Van Kirk Dobbie (eds.), *The Exeter Book.*

ha-Levi, Judah. *Kitab al Khazari.* Hartwig Hirschfeld (trans.). London: Routledge; and New York: E.P. Dutton, 1905.

"Die handschriftliche Überlieferung der Werke des heiligen Augustinus." See Oberleitner, Manfred, *et al.*, "Die handschriftliche Überlieferung."

Häring, Nikolaus M. "The Creation and Creator of the World according to Thierry of Chartres and Clarenbaldus of Arras." *AHDLMA* 22 (1955), 137–216.

"Gilbert of Poitiers, Author of the 'De Discretione animae, spiritus et mentis' Commonly Attributed to Achard of Saint Victor." *Mediaeval Studies* 22 (1960), 148–91.

"Commentary and Hermeneutics." In Robert L. Benson and Giles Constable (eds.). *Renaissance and Renewal in the Twelfth Century.* Cambridge, Mass.: Harvard University Press, 1982. Pp. 173–200.

Haskins, Charles H. "Leo Tuscus." *Byzantinische Zeitschrift* 24 (1923–24), 43–47.

Studies in the History of Mediaeval Science. New York: Frederick Ungar, 1960 [1924].

Havelok the Dane. In Walter Hoyt French and Charles Brockway Hale (eds.). *Middle English Metrical Romances.* New York: Prentice-Hall, 1930. Pp. 73–176.

Hazelton, Richard. "Chaucer and Cato." *Speculum* 35 (1960), 357–80.

Heinrich von Langenstein [Henry of Hesse]. *"Unterscheidung der Geister": Lateinisch und deutsch: Texte und Untersuchungen zu Übersetzungsliteratur der Wiener Schule* [*De discretione spirituum*]. Thomas Hohmann (ed.). Munich: Artemis, 1977.

Hélin, Maurice. *La Clef des songes: Fac-similés, notes et liste des éditions incunables.* Documents Scientifiques du XVᵉ Siècle, 2. Paris, 1925. Reprinted Geneva: Slatkine Reprints, 1977.

Henry, Avril. "þe Pilgrimage of þe Lyfe of þe Manhode: The Large Design, with Special Reference to Books 2–4." *Neuphilologische Mitteilungen* 87 (1986), 229–36.

Henry, Paul. *Plotin et l'Occident*. Spicilegium Sacrum Lovaniense: Etudes et Documents, 15. Louvain: Spicilegium Sacrum Lovaniense, 1934.

Henryson, Robert. *The Poems of Robert Henryson*. Denton Fox (ed.). Oxford: Clarendon Press, 1981.

Heraclitus. See Diels, H. (ed.), *Die Fragmente der Vorsokratiker*; and Marcovich, M. (ed.), *Heraclitus*.

Hermann of Carinthia. *De essentiis: A Critical Edition with Translation and Commentary*. Charles Burnett (ed.). Leiden and Cologne: E. J. Brill, 1982.

Hermann of Cologne. [Hermannus ex Judaeo Christianus]. *De sua conversione opusculum*. PL 170, cols. 803–36.

[Hermannus quondam Judaeus]. *Opusculum de conversione sua*. Gerlinde Niemeyer (ed.). Monumenta Germaniae Historica, Quellen zur Geistesgeschichte des Mittelalters, 4. Weimar: Hermann Böhlaus Nachfolger, 1963.

Hieatt, Constance B. *The Realism of Dream Visions: The Poetic Exploitation of the Dream-Experience in Chaucer and His Contemporaries*. De Proprietatibus Litterarum: series practica, 2. The Hague and Paris: Mouton, 1967.

Highbarger, Ernest Leslie. *The Gates of Dreams: An Archaeological Examination of Vergil, Aeneid VI, 893–899*. The Johns Hopkins University Studies in Archaeology, 30. Baltimore: The Johns Hopkins Press, 1940.

Hildegard of Bingen. *Causae et curae*. Paulus Kaiser (ed.). Leipzig: Teubner, 1903.

Hobson, J. Allan, and Robert W. McCarley. "The Brain as a Dream State Generator: An Activation-Synthesis Hypothesis of the Dream Process." *The American Journal of Psychiatry* 134 (1977), 1335–48.

Hoffmeister, Gerhart. "Rasis' Traumlehre: Traumbücher des Spätmittelalters." *Archiv für Kulturgeschichte* 51 (1969), 137–59.

Holkot, Robert. *Super librum Sapientie*. Venice, 1509.

In librum Sapientiae regis Salomonis praelectiones CCXIII. Basel: Jacobus Ryterus, 1586.

Honorius of Autun. *Elucidarium*. See Lefèvre, Yves, *L'Elucidarium et les lucidaires*.

Hugh of St. Cher (?). *Super Apocalypsim*. In Thomas Aquinas. *Opera omnia*. Roberto Busa (ed.). Stuttgart: Frommann-Holzboog, 1980. VII. Pp. 217–94.

Hugh of St. Victor. *Didascalicon: De studio legendi: A Critical Text*. Charles Henry Buttimer (ed.). The Catholic University of America Studies in Medieval and Renaissance Latin, 10. Washington, D.C.: The Catholic University Press, 1939.

The Didascalicon of Hugh of St. Victor: A Medieval Guide to the Arts. Jerome Taylor (trans.). Records of Civilization: Sources and Studies, 64. New York and London: Columbia University Press, 1961.

Iamblichus. *Iamblichus on the Mysteries of the Egyptians, Chaldeans, and Assyrians*, third edition. Thomas Taylor (trans.). London, 1821. Reprinted London: Stuart and Watkins, 1968.

Idley, Peter. *Instructions to His Son*. Charlotte d'Evelyn (ed.). Boston: D.C. Heath; and London: Oxford University Press, 1935.

Ijsewijn, Jozef, and Jacques Paquet (eds.). *The Universities in the Later Middle Ages*. Leuven: Leuven University Press, 1978.

Innocent III [Lothario dei Segni]. *On the Misery of the Human Condition* [*De miseria*

Bibliography

humane conditionis]. Donald R. Howard (ed.). Margaret Mary Dietz (trans.). The Library of Liberal Arts. Indianapolis and New York: Bobbs-Merrill, 1969.

Isaac of Stella. *Letter on the Soul.* Bernard McGinn (trans.). In Bernard McGinn (ed.). *Three Treatises on Man: A Cistercian Anthropology.* Kalamazoo, Mich.: Cistercian Publications, 1977. Pp. 153–77.

Isidore of Seville. *Etymologiarum libri XX. PL* 82, cols. 73–728.

Sententiarum libri tres. PL 83, cols. 537–738.

Pseudo-Isidore of Seville. *Sententiarum liber quartus. PL* 83, cols. 1153–200.

Isidoriana, sive in editionem operum S. Isidori Hispalensis prolegomena. PL 81, cols. 9–936.

Jean de la Rochelle [John of Rupella]. *Summa de anima.* Bibliothèque Nationale, MS Latin 6686.A, ff. 1–94ᵛ.

Tractatus de divisione multiplici potentiarum animae: Texte critique avec introduction notes et tables. Pierre Michaud-Quantin (ed.). Textes Philosophiques du Moyen Age, 11. Paris: Librairie Philosophique J. Vrin, 1964.

Jean de Meun. See Guillaume de Lorris and Jean de Meun, *Le Roman de la rose.*

Jeauneau, Edouard. *"Lectio philosophorum": Recherches sur l'école de Chartres.* Amsterdam: Adolf M. Hakkert, 1973.

Jerome. *Commentariorum in Isaiam prophetam libri duodeviginti. PL* 24, cols. 17–704.

Commentariorum in evangelium Matthaei ad Eusebium libri quatuor. PL 26, cols. 15–228.

The Principal Works of St. Jerome. W.H. Fremantle (trans.), assisted by G. Lewis and W.G. Martley. A Select Library of Nicene and Post-Nicene Fathers of the Catholic Church, second series, 6. New York: The Christian Literature Company; and Oxford and London: Parker, 1893.

Johannis Michaelis. *In Danielem.* In Thomas Aquinas. *Opera omnia.* Roberto Busa (ed.). Stuttgart: Frommann-Holzboog, 1980. VII. Pp. 306–31.

John of Salisbury. *Policratici sive de nugis curialium et vestigii philosophorum libri viii,* 2 vols. Clemens C.I. Webb (ed.). Oxford: Clarendon Press, 1909.

Frivolities of Courtiers and Footprints of Philosophers. Joseph B. Pike (trans.). Minneapolis: The University of Minnesota Press; and London: Oxford University Press, 1938.

Julian of Norwich. *A Book of Showings to the Anchoress Julian of Norwich,* 2 parts. Short and Long Texts. Edmund Colledge and James Walsh (eds.). Studies and Texts, 35, parts 1 and 2. Toronto: Pontifical Institute of Mediaeval Studies, 1978.

Jung, C.G. *Memories, Dreams, Reflections,* revised edition. Aniela Jaffé (recorder and ed.). Richard and Clara Winston (trans.). New York: Vintage Books, Random House, 1965.

Kålund, Kr. (ed.). *Alfraeði Islensk: Islandsk Encyklopaedisk Litteratur,* I. Copenhagen: S.L. Møllers, 1908.

Kaske, R.E. *"Piers Plowman* and Local Iconography." *Journal of the Warburg and Courtauld Institutes* 31 (1968), 159–69.

Kempe, Margery. *The Book of Margery Kempe.* Sanford Brown Meech and Hope Emily Allen (eds.). EETS, OS 212. London: Oxford University Press, 1940.

Bibliography

Ker, Neil R. "Oxford College Libraries before 1500." In Jozef Ijsewijn and Jacques Paquet (eds.). *The Universities in the Later Middle Ages.* Leuven: Leuven University Press, 1978. Pp. 293–311.

Kessels, A.H.M. "Ancient Systems of Dream-Classification." *Mnemosyne* series 4, 22 (1969), 389–424.

Kibre, Pearl. "The Intellectual Interests Reflected in Libraries of the Fourteenth and Fifteenth Centuries." *Journal of the History of Ideas* 7 (1946), 257–97.

Kolve, V.A. *Chaucer and the Imagery of Narrative: The First Five Canterbury Tales.* Stanford: Stanford University Press, 1984.

Koonce, B.G. *Chaucer and the Tradition of Fame: Symbolism in The House of Fame.* Princeton, N.J.: Princeton University Press, 1966.

Korger, Matthias E. "Grundprobleme der augustinischen Erkenntnislehre: Erläutert am Beispiel von *De Genesi ad litteram* XII." *Recherches Augustiniennes* 2 (1962), 33–57.

Krapp, George Philip, and Elliott Van Kirk Dobbie (eds.). *The Exeter Book.* The Anglo-Saxon Poetic Records, 3. New York: Columbia University Press, 1936.

Kruger, Steven F. "Mirrors and the Trajectory of Vision in *Piers Plowman*." *Speculum* 66 (1991), 74–95.

LaBerge, Stephen. *Lucid Dreaming.* New York: Ballantine Books, 1985.

Lacombrade, Christian. *Synésios de Cyrène: Hellène et Chrétien.* Paris: Société d'Edition "Les Belles Lettres," 1951.

Langland, William. *Piers Plowman: The A Version: Will's Visions of Piers Plowman and Do-Well.* George Kane (ed.). London: University of London, Athlone Press, 1960.

Piers Plowman: The B Version: Will's Visions of Piers Plowman, Do-Well, Do-Better and Do-Best. George Kane and E. Talbot Donaldson (eds.). London: University of London, Athlone Press, 1975.

Piers Plowman by William Langland: An Edition of the C-Text. Derek Pearsall (ed.). York Medieval Texts, second series. Berkeley and Los Angeles: University of California Press, 1979 [1978].

Piers Plowman: The Z Version. A.G. Rigg and Charlotte Brewer (eds.). Studies and Texts, 59. Toronto: Pontifical Institute of Mediaeval Studies, 1983.

Lavie, Peretz, and J. Allan Hobson. "Origin of Dreams: Anticipation of Modern Theories in the Philosophy and Physiology of the Eighteenth and Nineteenth Centuries." *Psychological Bulletin* 100 (1986), 229–40.

Lea, Charles Henry. *Materials Toward a History of Witchcraft,* 3 vols. Arthur C. Howland (ed.). Philadelphia: University of Pennsylvania Press, 1939.

Lefèvre, Yves. *L'Elucidarium et les lucidaires: Contribution, par l'histoire d'un texte, à l'histoire des croyances religieuses en France au Moyen Age.* Paris: E. de Boccard, 1954.

LeGoff, Jacques. "Dreams in the Culture and Collective Psychology of the Medieval West." *Time, Work, and Culture in the Middle Ages.* Arthur Goldhammer (trans.). Chicago and London: University of Chicago Press, 1980. Pp. 201–04.

The Birth of Purgatory. Arthur Goldhammer (trans.). Chicago: The University of Chicago Press, 1984.

Bibliography

"Le Christianisme et les rêves (IIᵉ–VIIᵉ siècles)." In Tullio Gregory (ed.). *I sogni nel medioevo*. Seminario Internazionale, Rome, 2–4 October 1983. Rome: Edizioni dell'Ateneo, 1985. Pp. 169–218.

L'Imaginaire médiéval: Essais. Paris: Gallimard, 1985.

Leisegang, Hans. "La Connaissance de Dieu au miroir de l'âme et de la nature." *Revue d'Histoire et de Philosophie Religieuses* 17 (1937), 145–71.

"Letters to the Editor." *The American Journal of Psychiatry* 135 (1978), 613–18.

Lewis, C.S. *The Discarded Image: An Introduction to Medieval and Renaissance Literature*. Cambridge: Cambridge University Press, 1964.

Libri Carolini. Monumenta Germaniae Historica, Concilia, supplement to vol. II. Hanover and Leipzig: Bibliopolii Hahniani, 1924.

Lieser, Ludwig. "Vinzenz von Beauvais als Kompilator und Philosoph: Text-kritische Untersuchung der Zitate aus der antiken und patristischen Literatur im Speculum naturale, Buch 23 bis 27 (Seelenlehre)." Inaugural-Dissertation, University of Cologne, 1927.

Ligota, C.R. "L'Influence de Macrobe pendant la Renaissance." in *Le Soleil à la Renaissance: Science et mythes*. Brussels: Presses Universitaires de Bruxelles; and Paris: Presses Universitaires de France, 1965. Pp. 463–82.

Lohr, C.H. "Medieval Latin Aristotle Commentaries." *Traditio* 23 (1967), 313–413; 24 (1968), 149–245; 26 (1970), 135–216; 27 (1971), 251–351; 28 (1972), 281–396; 29 (1973), 93–197; and 30 (1974), 119–44.

Lombard, Peter. *Sententiarum libri quatuor*. PL 192, cols. 519–962.

Lovejoy, A.O. *The Great Chain of Being: A Study of the History of an Idea*. Cambridge, Mass.: Harvard University Press, 1964 [1936].

Lucian. "The Dream, or Lucian's Career." A.M. Harmon (ed. and trans.). Loeb Classical Library: Lucian, 3. London: William Heinemann; and New York: G.P. Putnam's Sons, 1921.

Lucretius. *Of the Nature of Things* [*De rerum natura*]. William Ellery Leonard (trans.). New York: E.P. Dutton, 1957.

Lull, Ramon [Raymundus Lullus]. *Liber proverbiorum*. *Opera*, VI. Mainz, 1737. Reprinted Frankfurt: Minerva, 1965.

Lydgate, John. *The Pilgrimage of the Life of Man*. F.J. Furnivall (ed.). EETS, ES 77, 83. London: Kegan Paul, Trench, Trübner and Co., 1899, 1901.

Lynch, Kathryn L. *The High Medieval Dream Vision: Poetry, Philosophy, and Literary Form*. Stanford: Stanford University Press, 1988.

Macrobius. *Opera quae supersunt*, 2 vols. Ludwig von Jan (ed.). Quedlinburg and Leipzig: Typis et Sumptibus Godofredi Bassii, 1848–52.

Commentary on the Dream of Scipio. William Harris Stahl (trans.). Records of Civilization: Sources and Studies, 48. New York: Columbia University Press, 1952.

Commentarii in Somnium Scipionis. Iacobus Willis (ed.). Leipzig: B.G. Teubner, 1963.

Maimonides, Moses. *The Guide of the Perplexed*. Shlomo Pines (trans.). Chicago: University of Chicago Press, 1963.

Manitius, Max. *Geschichte der lateinischen Literatur des Mittelalters*, 3 vols. Handbuch der klassischen Altertums-Wissenschaft, 9, no. 2. Munich: C.H. Beck'sche Verlagsbuchhandlung, 1911–31.

Bibliography

Handschriften antiker Autoren in mittelalterlichen Bibliothekskatalogen. Karl Manitius (ed.). *Zentralblatt für Bibliothekswesen,* Beihefte, 67. Leipzig: Otto Harrassowitz, 1935. Reprinted Nendeln, Liechtenstein: Kraus Reprint; and Wiesbaden: Otto Harrassowitz, 1968.

Mannyng, Robert, of Brunne. *Robert of Brunne's "Handlyng Synne," A.D. 1303, With Those Parts of the Anglo–French Treatise on Which it was Founded, William of Wadington's "Manuel des Pechiez".* Frederick J. Furnivall (ed.). EETS, OS 119, 123. London: Kegan Paul, Trench, Trübner and Co., 1901, 1903.

Handlyng Synne. Idelle Sullens (ed.). Medieval and Renaissance Texts and Studies, 14. Binghamton, N.Y.: State University of New York at Binghamton, 1983.

Manselli, Raoul. "Il sogno come premonizione, consiglio e predizione nella tradizione medioevale." In Tullio Gregory (ed.). *I sogni nel medioevo.* Seminario Internazionale, Rome, 2–4 October 1983. Rome: Edizioni dell'Ateneo, 1985. Pp. 219–44.

Marchello-Nizia, Christiane. "La Rhétorique des songes et le songe comme rhétorique dans la littérature française médiévale." In Tullio Gregory (ed.). *I sogni nel medioevo.* Seminario Internazionale, Rome, 2–4 October 1983. Rome: Edizioni dell'Ateneo, 1985. Pp. 245–59.

Marcovich, M. (ed.). *Heraclitus: Greek Text with a Short Commentary.* Merida, Venezuela: The Los Andes University Press, 1967.

Markus, R.A. "Marius Victorinus and Augustine." In A.H. Armstrong (ed.). *Cambridge History of Later Greek and Early Medieval Philosophy.* Cambridge: Cambridge University Press, 1970. Pp. 327–419.

"The Eclipse of a Neo-Platonic Theme: Augustine and Gregory the Great on Visions and Prophecies." In H.J. Blumenthal and R.A. Markus (eds.). *Neoplatonism and Early Christian Thought: Essays in Honour of A.H. Armstrong.* London: Variorum Publications, 1981. Pp. 204–11.

Martène, Edmond, and Ursin Durand (eds.). *Thesaurus novus anecdotorum,* IV. Paris: Lutetiae Parisiorum, 1717. Reprinted New York: Burt Franklin, 1968.

Martin, Lawrence T. "The Earliest Versions of the Latin *Somniale Danielis.*" *Manuscripta* 23 (1979), 131–41.

Somniale Danielis: An Edition of a Medieval Latin Dream Interpretation Handbook. Lateinische Sprache und Literatur des Mittelalters, 10. Frankfurt: Peter Lang, 1981.

McCarley, Robert W., and J. Allan Hobson. "The Neurobiological Origins of Psychoanalytic Dream Theory." *The American Journal of Psychiatry* 134 (1977), 1211–21.

McDonald, Kim A. "Medical Researchers Investigate Dreams for Clues to Patients' Emotional and Physical Health." *The Chronicle of Higher Education* July 13, 1988, pp. A4–A6.

McGinn, Bernard (ed.). *Three Treatises on Man: A Cistercian Anthropology.* Kalamazoo, Mich.: Cistercian Publications, 1977.

Miller, Gustavus Hindman. *Ten Thousands Dreams Interpreted, or What's in a Dream: A Scientific and Practical Exposition.* Chicago: Rand McNally, 1980.

Minges, P. Parthenius. "Exzerpte aus Alexander von Hales bei Vinzenz von Beauvais." *Franziskanische Studien* 1 (1914), 52–65.

Bibliography

Minnis, A.J. "Langland's Ymaginatif and Late-Medieval Theories of Imagination." *Comparative Criticism: A Yearbook* 3 (1981), 71–103.

Misch, Georg. *Geschichte der Autobiographie*, 4 vols. Frankfurt: G. Schulte-Bulmke, 1955.

Momigliano, Arnaldo. "A Medieval Jewish Autobiography." In Hugh Lloyd-Jones, Valerie Pearl, and Blair Warden (eds.). *History & Imagination: Essays in Honour of H.R. Trevor-Roper*. London: Duckworth, 1981. Pp. 30–36.

Monod, Bernard. *Le Moine Guibert et son temps (1053–1124)*. Paris: Hachette, 1905.

Morse, Charlotte Nell Cook. "William Dunbar: His Vision Poetry and the Medieval Poetic Tradition." Dissertation, Stanford University, 1969.

Moser, Thomas C., Jr. "A Science for a King: William of Conches and the *Dragmaticon*." *The Imprint of the Stanford Libraries Associates* 10 (1984), 4–11.

Mras, Karl. "Macrobius' Kommentar zu Ciceros Somnium. Ein Beitrag zur Geistesgeschichte des 5. Jahrhunderts n. Chr." *Sitzungsberichte der preussischen Akademie der Wissenschaften: Philosophisch–historische Klasse* (1933), 232–86.

Muckle, J.T. "Greek Works Translated Into Latin Before 1350 (Continuation)." *Mediaeval Studies* 5 (1943), 102–14.

The Mystic Dream Book: 2500 Dreams Explained. New York: Arco, 1983 [1963].

Nagy, Albino. "Die philosophischen Abhandlungen des Ja'qub ben Ishaq al-Kindi." *Beiträge zur Geschichte der Philosophie des Mittelalters* 2, no. 5 (1897).

Nash, Ronald H. *The Light of the Mind: St. Augustine's Theory of Knowledge*. Lexington, Kentucky: The University Press of Kentucky, 1969.

Neckam, Alexander. *De naturis rerum libri duo*. Thomas Wright (ed.). Rerum Britannicarum Medii Ævi Scriptores, or Chronicles and Memorials of Great Britain and Ireland during the Middle Ages, 34. London: Longman, Green, Longman, Roberts, and Green, 1863.

Nemiah, John C. "Children of an Idle Brain?" *The American Journal of Psychiatry* 135 (1978), 1530.

New Catholic Encyclopedia, 16 vols. Catholic University of America. New York: McGraw-Hill, 1967.

Newman, Francis X. "Somnium: Medieval Theories of Dreaming and the Form of Vision Poetry." Dissertation, Princeton University, 1963.

"*Hous of Fame*, 7–12." *English Language Notes* 6 (1968), 5–12.

Nicolaus de Gorran. *In septem epistolas canonicas*. In Thomas Aquinas. *Opera omnia*. Roberto Busa (ed.). Stuttgart: Frommann-Holzboog, 1980. VII. Pp. 361–99.

Nolan, Edward Peter. *Now Through a Glass Darkly: Specular Images of Being and Knowing from Virgil to Chaucer*. Ann Arbor: The University of Michigan Press, 1990.

Oberleitner, Manfred, Franz Römer, Johannes Divjak, and Rainer Kurz. "Die handschriftliche Überlieferung der Werke des heiligen Augustinus." Österreichische Akademie der Wissenschaften. Philosophisch–historische Klasse. Sitzungsberichte (Vienna) 263 (1969); 281 (1972); 289 (1973); 292 (1974); and 306 (1976).

Ogilvy, J.D.A. *Books Known to the English, 596–1066*. Cambridge, Mass.: Mediaeval Academy of America, 1967.

Önnerfors, Alf. *Mediaevalia: Abhandlungen und Aufsätze*. Lateinische Sprache und Literatur des Mittelalters, 6. Frankfurt: Peter Lang, 1977.

Bibliography

Onulf. *Vita Popponis abbatis Stabulensis.* Georgius Heinricus Pertz (ed.). Monumenta Germaniae Historica, Scriptores, 11. Hanover: Impensis Bibliopolii Aulici Hahniani, 1854. Pp. 291–316.

Oppenheim, A. Leo. *The Interpretation of Dreams in the Ancient Near East, With a Translation of an Assyrian Dream-Book. Transactions of the American Philosophical Society* NS, 46, part 3 (1956), 179–373.

Oresme, Nicole. "Maistre Nicole Oresme, Le livre du ciel et du monde: Text and Commentary." Albert D. Menut and Alexander J. Denomy (eds.). *Mediaeval Studies* 3 (1941), 185–280.

Nicole Oresme and the Astrologers: A Study of his Livre de divinacions. G.W. Coopland (ed. and trans.). Cambridge, Mass.: Harvard University Press, 1952.

Quaestiones super geometriam Euclidis. H.L.L. Busard (ed.). *Janus,* Suppléments, 3. Leiden: E.J. Brill, 1961.

De proportionibus proportionum and Ad pauca respicientes. Edward Grant (ed. and trans.). Madison: The University of Wisconsin Press, 1966.

Nicole Oresme and the Kinematics of Circular Motion: Tractatus de commensurabilitate vel incommensurabilitate motuum celi. Edward Grant (ed. and trans.). Madison: The University of Wisconsin Press, 1971.

"Nicole Oresme: Quaestio contra divinatores horoscopios." S. Caroti (ed.). *AHDLMA* 43 (1976), 201–310.

Otloh of St. Emmeram. *Liber visionum tum suarum, tum aliorum.* PL 146, cols. 341–88.

Ovid. *Heroides and Amores.* Grant Showerman (ed. and trans.). Loeb Classical Library. Cambridge, Mass.: Harvard University Press; and London: William Heinemann, 1958.

Metamorphoses, 2 vols. Frank Justus Miller (ed. and trans.). Loeb Classical Library. Cambridge, Mass.: Harvard University Press; and London: William Heinemann, 1960.

Pack, Roger A. "De pronosticatione sompniorum libellus Guillelmo de Aragonia adscriptus." *AHDLMA* 33 (1966), 237–92.

"A Treatise on Prognostications by Venancius of Moerbeke." *AHDLMA* 43 (1976), 311–22.

Paradis, André. "Les Oniromanciens et leurs traités des rêves." In Guy-H. Allard (ed.). *Aspects de la marginalité du Moyen Age.* Montreal: Les Editions de l'Aurore, 1975. Pp. 118–27.

Pascalis Romanus. See Collin-Roset, Simone, "Le *Liber thesauri occulti* de Pascalis Romanus."

The Pearl Poems: An Omnibus Edition. I: *Pearl and Cleanness.* William Vantuono (ed. and trans.). The Renaissance Imagination, 5. Stephen Orgel (series ed.). New York and London: Garland, 1984.

Peck, Russell A. "Chaucer and the Nominalist Questions." *Speculum* 53 (1978), 745–60.

Peden, Alison M. "Science and Philosophy in Wales at the Time of the Norman Conquest: A Macrobius Manuscript from Llanbadern." *Cambridge Medieval Celtic Studies* 2 (1981), 21–45.

"Macrobius and Medieval Dream Literature." *Medium Ævum* 54 (1985), 59–73.

Bibliography

Pelton, Robert Wayne. *The Complete Book of Dream Interpretation*. New York: Arco, 1983.

Pépin, Jean. *"Ex Platonicorum persona": Etudes sur les lectures philosophiques de saint Augustin*. Amsterdam: Adolf M. Hakkert, 1977.

Petrarca, Francesco. *Le familiari*, 4 vols. Vittorio Rossi (ed.), Edizione nazionale delle opere di Francesco Petrarca. Florence: G.C. Sansoni, 1933–42.

Rerum memorandarum libri. Giuseppe Billanovich (ed.). Edizione nazionale delle opere di Francesco Petrarca. Florence: G.C. Sansoni, 1943.

"Coronation Oration." In Ernest Hatch Wilkins (trans.). *Studies in the Life and Works of Petrarch*. Cambridge, Mass.: The Mediaeval Academy of America, 1955. Pp. 300–13.

Rerum familiarium libri [*Letters on Familiar Matters*], 3 vols. Aldo S. Bernardo (trans.). Albany, N.Y.: State University of New York Press, 1975; Baltimore and London: The Johns Hopkins University Press, 1982, 1985.

Petrus Johannis Olivi. *Postilla in librum Geneseos*. In Thomas Aquinas. *Opera omnia*. Roberto Busa (ed.). Stuttgart: Frommann-Holzboog, 1980. VII. Pp. 486–540.

The Pilgrimage of the Lyfe of the Manhode. Avril Henry (ed.). EETS, OS 288. London: Oxford University Press, 1985.

Plato. *Charmides, Alcibiades I and II, Hipparchus, The Lovers, Theages, Minos, Epinomis*. W.R.M. Lamb (ed. and trans.). Loeb Classical Library: Plato, 8. London: William Heinemann; and New York: G.P. Putnam's Sons, 1927.

The Republic, 2 vols. Paul Shorey (ed. and trans.). Loeb Classical Library. Cambridge, Mass.: Harvard University Press; and London: William Heinemann, 1946, 1956.

Euthyphro, Apology, Crito, Phaedo, Phaedrus. Harold North Fowler (ed. and trans.). Loeb Classical Library: Plato, 1. London: William Heinemann; and Cambridge, Mass.: Harvard University Press, 1947.

Timaeus, Critias, Cleitophon, Menexenus, Epistles. R.G. Bury (ed. and trans.). Loeb Classical Library: Plato, 7. London: William Heinemann; and Cambridge, Mass.: Harvard University Press, 1952.

Pliny the Elder. *Natural History*, 10 vols. Harris Rackham, W.H.S. Jones, and D.E. Eichholz (eds. and trans.). Loeb Classical Library. Cambridge, Mass.: Harvard University Press; and London: William Heinemann, 1947–63.

Pratt, Robert A. "Some Latin Sources of the Nonnes Preest on Dreams." *Speculum* 52 (1977), 538–70.

Presson, Robert K. "Two Types of Dreams in the Elizabethan Drama, and their Heritage: *Somnium Animale* and the Prick-of-Conscience." *Studies in English Literature* 7 (1967), 239–56.

Priscianus Lydus. *Solutionum ad Chosroem liber*. I. Bywater (ed.). Supplementum Aristotelicum, I, part 2. Berlin: Typis et Impensis Georgii Reimer, 1886. Pp. 39–104.

Prudentius. *Liber Cathemerinon*. H.J. Thomson (ed. and trans.). Loeb Classical Library: Prudentius, 1. London: William Heinemann; and Cambridge, Mass.: Harvard University Press, 1949. Pp. 6–115.

Rabanus Maurus. *Commentariorum in Ecclesiasticum libri decem*. PL 109, cols. 763–1126.

Bibliography

Raby, F.J.E. *A History of Christian–Latin Poetry*. Oxford: Clarendon Press, 1927.

Raoul de Longchamps [Radulphus de Longo Campo]. *In Anticlaudianum Alani commentum*. Jan Sulowski (ed.). Polska Akademia Nauk Zakład Historii Nauki i Techniki. Zródta do Dziejów Naukii Techniki, 13. Wrocław: Zakład Naradowy Imienia Ossolińskich Wydawnicłwo Polskiej Akademii Nauk, 1972.

Reilly, George C. *The Psychology of Saint Albert the Great Compared with that of Saint Thomas*. Washington, D.C.: The Catholic University of America, 1934.

Richard of St. Victor. *Adnotatiunculae elucidatoriae in Joelem prophetam*. PL 175, cols. 321–75.

De eruditione hominis interioris libri tres. PL 196, cols. 1229–366.

In Apocalypsim Joannis libri septem. PL 196, cols. 683–888.

Selected Writings on Contemplation. Clare Kirchberger (trans.). New York: Harper and Brothers, 1955.

Rolle, Richard. *The Form of Living*. In C. Horstmann (ed.). *Yorkshire Writers: Richard Rolle of Hampole, an English Father of the Church, and his Followers*, I. London: Swan Sonnenschein; and New York: Macmillan, 1895. Pp. 3–49.

Rupert of Deutz. *Dialogus inter Christianum et Judaeum*. PL 170, cols. 559–610.

Russell, J. Stephen. *The English Dream Vision: Anatomy of a Form*. Columbus: Ohio State University Press, 1988.

Schedler, Phil. M. "Die Philosophie des Macrobius und ihr Einfluss auf die Wissenschaft des christlichen Mittelalters." *Beiträge zur Geschichte der Philosophie des Mittelalters* 13, no. 1 (1916), 1–159.

Schmitt, Jean-Claude. "Rêver au XIIe siècle." In Tullio Gregory (ed.). *I sogni nel medioevo*. Seminario Internazionale, Rome, 2–4 October 1983. Rome: Edizioni dell'Ateneo, 1985. Pp. 291–316.

Schmitt, Wolfram. "Ein deutsches Traumbüchlein aus dem späten Mittelalter." *Studia Neophilologica* 37 (1965), 96–99.

Schneider, Jean. "Communication: Recherches sur une encyclopédie du XIIIe siècle: Le *Speculum majus* de Vincent de Beauvais." *Académie des Inscriptions et Belles-Lettres – Comptes Rendus* (1976), 174–89.

"Vincent de Beauvais – Orientation bibliographique." *Spicae: Cahiers de l'Atelier Vincent de Beauvais*, I. Paris: Editions du Centre National de la Recherche Scientifique, 1978. Pp. 7–29.

Scholz, Richard. *Unbekannte kirchenpolitische Streitschriften aus der Zeit Ludwigs des Bayern (1327–1354)*, 2 vols. Bibliothek des königlichen preussischen historischen Instituts in Rom, 9–10. Rom: Verlag von Loescher, 1911, 1914.

Schönbach, Anton E. "Zu Zs. 17, 84." *Zeitschrift für deutsches Alterthum* 18 (1875), 81–82.

"Bedeutung der Buchstaben." *Zeitschrift für deutsches Alterthum* 34 (1890), 1–6.

Seeberg, Reinhold. *Hermann von Scheda: Ein jüdischer Proselyt des zwölften Jahrhunderts*. Schriften des Institutum Judaicum in Leipzig, 30. Leipzig: Akademische Buchhandlung [W. Faber], 1891.

Séjourné, Paul. *Le Dernier Père de l'Eglise: Saint Isidore de Séville: Son rôle dans l'histoire du droit canonique*. Paris: Gabriel Beauchesne, 1929.

Seneca. *Seneca's Tragedies*, I. Frank Justus Miller (ed. and trans.). Loeb Classical

Bibliography

Library. London: William Heinemann; and New York: G.P. Putnam's Sons, 1917.

Sievers, E. "Bedeutung der Buchstaben." *Zeitschrift für deutsches Alterthum* 18 (1875), 297.

"Bedeutung der Buchstaben." *Zeitschrift für deutsches Alterthum* 21 (1877), 189–90.

Silvestre, Hubert. "Une Adaptation du commentaire de Macrobe sur le Songe de Scipion dans un manuscrit de Bruxelles." *AHDLMA* 29 (1962), 93–101.

"Note sur la survie de Macrobe au Moyen Age." *Classica et Mediaevalia* 24 (1963), 170–80.

Sirat, Colette. *Les Théories des visions surnaturelles dans la pensée juive du Moyen-Age.* Etudes sur le Judaïsme Médiéval, 1. Leiden: E.J. Brill, 1969.

Spearing, A.C. *Medieval Dream-Poetry.* Cambridge: Cambridge University Press, 1976.

Speckenbach, Klaus. "Von den Troimen. Über den Traum in Theorie und Dichtung." In Helmut Rücker and Kurt Otto Seidel (eds.). *"Sagen mit Sinne":* Festschrift für Marie-Luise Dittrich zum 65. Geburtstag. Göppinger Arbeiten zur Germanistik, 180. Göppingen: Alfred Kümmerle, 1976. Pp. 169–204.

"Form, Funktion und Bedeutung der Träume im *Lancelot-Gral Zyklus.*" In Tullio Gregory (ed.). *I sogni nel medioevo.* Seminario Internazionale, Rome, 2–4 October 1983. Rome: Edizioni dell'Ateneo, 1985. Pp. 317–55.

Speroni, Charles. "Dante's Prophetic Morning-Dreams." *Studies in Philology* 45 (1948), 50–59.

Stahl, William H. "Dominant Traditions in Early Medieval Latin Science." *Isis* 50 (1959), 95–124.

Steinmeyer. "Bedeutung der Buchstaben." *Zeitschrift für deutsches Alterthum* 17 (1874), 84.

Stock, Brian. *Myth and Science in the Twelfth Century: A Study of Bernard Silvester.* Princeton, N.J.: Princeton University Press, 1972.

Strabo, Walahfrid. "De quodam somnio ad Erluinum," and "Ad eandem [Iudith imperatricem] de quodam somnio." Ernst Dümmler (ed.). Monumenta Germaniae Historica, Poetae Latini Aevi Carolini, 2. Berlin: Weidmann, 1884. Pp. 364–65 and 379–80.

Walahfrid Strabo's Visio Wettini: Text, Translation, and Commentary. David A. Traill (ed. and trans.). Lateinische Sprache und Literatur des Mittelalters, 2. Bern: Herbert Lang; and Frankfurt: Peter Lang, 1974.

Suchier, Walther. "Altfranzösische Traumbücher." *Zeitschrift für französische Sprache und Literatur* 65 (1943–44), 129–67.

Sulpitius Severus. *The Works of Sulpitius Severus.* Alexander Roberts (trans.). A Select Library of Nicene and Post-Nicene Fathers of the Christian Church, second series, 11. New York, 1894. Reprinted Grand Rapids, Mich.: Wm. B. Eerdmans, 1978.

Sumption, Jonathan. *Pilgrimage: An Image of Mediaeval Religion.* London: Faber and Faber, 1975.

Svenberg, Emanuel. *De Latinska Lunaria: Text och Studier.* Doktorsavhandlingar i Latinsk Filologi vid Göteborgs Högskola, 13. Göteborg: Elanders, 1936.

Bibliography

Lunaria et Zodiologia Latina. Studia Graeca et Latina Gothoburgensia, 16. Göteborg: Elanders, 1963.

Switalski, B.W. "Des Chalcidius Kommentar zu Plato's Timaeus: Eine historisch–kritische Untersuchung." *Beiträge zur Geschichte der Philosophie des Mittelalters* 3, no. 6 (1902), 1–113.

Synesius of Cyrene. *De insomniis. PG* 66, cols. 1281–320.

De insomniis. In Augustine Fitzgerald (trans.). *The Essays and Hymns of Synesius of Cyrene*, 2 vols. London: Oxford University Press, 1930. II. Pp. 326–59.

Tajo of Saragossa. *Sententiarum libri quinque. PL* 80, cols. 727–990.

Talmud. *The Babylonian Talmud*, 6 parts in 34 vols. I. Epstein (ed.). London: The Soncino Press, 1935–48.

Taylor, John H. "The Meaning of *Spiritus* in St. Augustine's *De Genesi*, XII." *The Modern Schoolman* 26 (1948–49), 211–18.

Tertullian. *On the Soul* [*De anima*]. In Edwin A. Quain (trans.). *Apologetical Works*. The Fathers of the Church: A New Translation, 10. Washington, D.C.: The Catholic University of America Press, 1950. Pp. 163–309.

Opera. Part 2: Opera Montanistica. J.H. Waszink (ed.). Corpus Christianorum, series latina, 2. Turnholt: Typographi Brepols Editores Pontificii, 1954.

TeSelle, Eugene. "Porphyry and Augustine." *Augustinian Studies* 5 (1974), 113–47.

Theiler, Willy. *Porphyrius und Augustin*. Halle (Saale): Max Niemeyer, 1933.

Thomas de Chobham. *Summa confessorum*. F. Broomfield (ed.). Louvain: Editions Nauwelaerts; and Paris: Béatrice-Nauwelaerts, 1968.

Thomas of Cantimpré. *Liber de natura rerum: Editio princeps secundum codices manuscriptos*. Part 1: Text. H. Boese (ed.). Berlin and New York: Walter de Gruyter, 1973.

Thomas of Froidmont [Thomas of Beverly]. *Liber de modo bene vivendi, ad sororem. PL* 184, cols. 1199–306.

Thorndike, Lynn. *A History of Magic and Experimental Science*, 8 vols. New York: Macmillan, 1923–58.

University Records and Life in the Middle Ages. Records of Civilization: Sources and Studies, 38. New York: Columbia University Press, 1944.

Michael Scot. London: Thomas Nelson, 1965.

Thorndike, Lynn, and Pearl Kibre. *A Catalogue of Incipits of Mediaeval Scientific Writings in Latin*. Mediaeval Academy of America, 29. Cambridge, Mass.: Mediaeval Academy of America, 1963.

Tocci, Franco Michelini. "Teoria e interpretazione dei sogni nella cultura ebraica medievale." In Tullio Gregory (ed.). *I sogni nel medioevo*. Seminario Internazionale, Rome, 2–4 October 1983. Rome: Edizioni dell'Ateneo, 1985. Pp. 261–90.

Trachtenberg, Joshua. *Jewish Magic and Superstition: A Study in Folk Religion*. New York: Atheneum, A Temple Book, 1970.

Trimpi, Wesley. *Muses of One Mind: The Literary Analysis of Experience and its Continuity*. Princeton, N.J.: Princeton University Press, 1983.

Turville-Petre, E.O.G. "An Icelandic Version of the *Somniale Danielis*." In Allan H. Orrick (ed.). *Nordica et Anglica: Studies in Honor of Stefán Einarsson*. The Hague and Paris: Mouton, 1968. Pp. 19–36.

Bibliography

Tuscus, Leo. See Dondaine, Antoine, "Hugues Ethérien et Léon Toscan"; and Haskins, Charles H., "Leo Tuscus."

Twycross, Meg. *The Medieval Anadyomene: A Study in Chaucer's Mythography*. Oxford: Basil Blackwell, Society for the Study of Mediaeval Languages and Literature, 1972.

Valentini, Roberto. "Vincenzo di Beauvais e la conoscenza della letteratura cristiana in Francia nella prima metà del secolo XIII." *"Didaskaleion": studi filologici di letteratura cristiana antica* 4 (1915), 109–67. Reprinted Amsterdam: John Benjamins, N.V., 1968.

Valerius Maximus. *Factorum et dictorum memorabilium libri I–IV*. I. Fabricius Serra (ed.). Pisa: Giardini, 1986.

van der Horst, P.W. "Macrobius and the New Testament: A Contribution to the Corpus Hellenisticum." *Novum Testamentum* 15 (1973), 220–32.

Viarre, S. "Le Commentaire ordonné du monde dans quelques sommes scientifiques des XIIe et XIIIe siècles." In R.R. Bolgar (ed.). *Classical Influences on European Culture: Proceedings of an International Conference Held at King's College, Cambridge, April 1974*. Cambridge and New York: Cambridge University Press, 1976. Pp. 203–15.

Vielliard, Jeanne. "Le Registre de prêt de la bibliothèque du collège de Sorbonne au XVe siècle." In Jozef Ijsewijn and Jacques Paquet (eds.). *The Universities in the Later Middle Ages*. Leuven: Leuven University Press, 1978. Pp. 276–92.

Vincent of Beauvais [Vincentius Bellovacensis]. *Speculum naturale*. Douai: Ex Officina Typographica et Sumptibus Balthazaris Belleri in Circino Aureo, 1624. Reprinted Graz, Austria: Akademische Druck-u. Verlagsanstalt, 1964.

Virgil. *Aeneid*, 2 vols. H. Rushton Fairclough (ed. and trans.). Loeb Classical Library. Cambridge, Mass.: Harvard University Press; and London: William Heinemann, 1934–35.

Wallach, Luitpold. *Alcuin and Charlemagne: Studies in Carolingian History and Literature*. Cornell Studies in Classical Philology, 32. Ithaca: Cornell University Press, 1959.

Walpole, A.S. (ed.). *Early Latin Hymns*. Cambridge: Cambridge University Press, 1922. Reprinted Hildesheim: Georg Olms Verlagsbuchhandlung, 1966.

Wasselynck, René. "Les Compilations des 'Moralia in Job' du VIIe au XIIe siècle." *RTAM* 29 (1962), 5–32.

"Les 'Moralia in Job' dans les ouvrages de morale du haut Moyen Age latin." *RTAM* 31 (1964), 5–31.

"Extraits du 'Remediarum Conversorum' du Pierre de Londres." *RTAM* 32 (1965), 121–32.

"L'Influence de l'exégèse de S. Grégoire le Grand sur les commentaires bibliques médiévaux (VIIe–XIIe s.)." *RTAM* 32 (1965), 157–204.

"La Présence des Moralia de S. Grégoire le Grand dans les ouvrages de morale du XIIe siècle." *RTAM* 35 (1968), 197–240.

Waszink, J.H. "Die sogenannte Fünfteilung der Träume bei Chalcidius und ihre Quellen." *Mnemosyne* third series, 9 (1940), 65–85.

"La Théorie du langage des dieux et des démons dans Calcidius." In Jacques Fontaine and Charles Kannengiesser (eds.). *Epektasis: Mélanges patristiques offerts au Cardinal Jean Daniélou*. Paris: Beauchesne, 1972. Pp. 237–44.

Bibliography

Werlin, Josef. "Das Traumbuch des Armen Nikolaus von Prag." *Stifter-Jahrbuch* 8 (1964), 195–208.

Wetherbee, Winthrop. *Platonism and Poetry in the Twelfth Century: The Literary Influence of the School of Chartres.* Princeton, N.J.: Princeton University Press, 1972.

William of Aragon. See Pack, Roger A., "De pronosticatione sompniorum libellus Guillelmo de Aragonia adscriptus."

William of St. Thierry. *The Nature of the Body and the Soul.* Benjamin Clark (trans.). In Bernard McGinn (ed.). *Three Treatises on Man: A Cistercian Anthropology.* Kalamazoo, Mich.: Cistercian Publications, 1977. Pp. 101–52.

William of Vaurouillon. "The *Liber de anima* of William of Vaurouillon O.F.M." Ignatius Brady (ed.). *Mediaeval Studies* 10 (1948), 224–97, and 11 (1949), 247–307.

William of Wadington. *Manuel des péchés.* See Mannyng, Robert, of Brunne, *Robert of Brunne's "Handlyng Synne"*, Frederick J. Furnivall (ed.).

Wingate, S.D. *The Mediaeval Latin Versions of the Aristotelian Scientific Corpus, with Special Reference to the Biological Works.* London: The Courier Press, 1931.

Winkler, John J. *The Constraints of Desire: The Anthropology of Sex and Gender in Ancient Greece.* New York and London: Routledge, 1990.

Wistrand, Erik. "Lunariastudien." *Göteborgs Högskolas Årsskrift* 48, no. 4 (1942), 1–41.

Wittig, Joseph S. "'Piers Plowman' B, Passus IX–XII: Elements in the Design of the Inward Journey." *Traditio* 28 (1972), 211–80.

Wright, Thomas, and James Orchard Halliwell (eds.). *Reliquiae Antiquae: Scraps from Ancient Manuscripts*, I. London: William Pickering, 1841. Reprinted New York: AMS Press, 1966.

Wünsch, Richard. "Volkskundliche aus alten Handschriften." *Hessische Blätter für Volkskunde* 2, no. 2 (1903), 89–95.

Wytzes, J. "Bemerkungen zu dem neuplatonischen Einfluss in Augustins 'De Genesi ad literam.'" *Zeitschrift für die neutestamentliche Wissenschaft und die Kunde der älteren Kirche* 39 (1940), 137–51.

Zolar. *Zolar's Encyclopedia and Dictionary of Dreams.* New York: Arco, 1963.

Index

Index

Index

Index